To

MITZI

CONTENTS

ACKNOWLEDGEMENTS

I WISH to thank the following authors (and publishers) for permission to quote from them: Louise Bogan and the Noonday Press (New York), for 'Several Voices out of a Cloud'; E. E. Cummings, *Collected Poems* (New York, Harcourt, Brace and Company); Eyre and Spottiswoode, *Selected Poems* of John Crowe Ransom and *Poems 1920–1945* of Allen Tate; Faber and Faber, *Collected Poems* of Marianne Moore and *Selected Poems* of Wallace Stevens; Princeton University Press, *The Poetical Works of Edward Taylor*, edited by Thomas H. Johnson, copyright 1939, Rocklands Editions, copyright 1943, Princeton U.P.; and William Carlos Williams and New Directions (Norfolk, Conn.), for 'The Red Wheelbarrow', etc.

NOTE ON THE
THIRD EDITION

THIS book has been reprinted several
times since it first appeared in 1954.
Each time I took the opportunity to
make minor changes and additions. I
have now attempted a more extensive revision, partly because I am less
ignorant of America than I once was
and partly because I have changed
my mind on certain authors, including Emerson. The final chapter is
almost entirely new. The main problem remains one of compression. It
would be easier, and more just to
many good writers, to produce a
book of twice the length.

Marcus Cunliffe
Brighton, England
June 1966

INTRODUCTION

As a small book on a large topic, this one has presented certain difficulties. There are scores of American writers who deserve at least a mention. But merely to list them all, with brief identifying comments, would be pointless: a good reference work like the *Oxford Companion to American Literature* does the job far more effectively. Instead, I have concentrated on a few authors, while uneasily aware that they are not the only pebbles on the beach. They have been chosen as the largest and/or most representative pebbles, with the result that others – Thomas Jefferson, Philip Freneau, William Cullen Bryant, Bayard Taylor, John G. Whittier, Upton Sinclair, Edna St Vincent Millay, Ellen Glasgow, and Conrad Aiken, to name only a few – are virtually or entirely ignored. However, my selection of authors has been fairly conventional, and so has the relative space allotted them, according to the current fashions in American literary history.

Here another difficulty arises. For though an American will recognize my arrangement and my remarks as orthodox, to the English reader they may seem a little odd, if he is not ready to accept my underlying assumptions. The first of these assumptions is that one can properly distinguish between English and American literature. Matthew Arnold thought otherwise:

I see advertised *The Primer of American Literature*. Imagine the face of Philip or Alexander at hearing of a Primer of Macedonian Literature! ... We are all contributors to one great literature – English literature.

But Arnold wrote eighty years ago, and even then his comparison was not very apt. In the widest sense, no doubt, there is only *literature*, a universal realm in which the writer struggles with his universally obstinate medium, language. But (as Arnold admits, in speaking of *English* literature) language is made up of languages; languages usually correspond to

national groups; and those national groups that have no language of their own invariably try to resurrect or to invent
one. Their attempt has nothing to do with pure literature, if
there is such a thing. It is often an ungainly, comic endeavour, as if one decided to abandon an old suitcase and, clutch-
ing its ignoble contents, walked through the streets in search
of a new one, after most of the shops were shut. More than
any other Europeans, the English, with their own ample and
well-sewn luggage, have been unsympathetic to the American language plight (though not to that of nations nearer at
hand; Arnold, for example, shows every sympathy for the
language problems of Burns, to whom dialect came more
easily than polite English). But to the Americans themselves
the need to find a suitable literary container for their own experiences has been a serious matter. It is impossible to understand American literature fully unless this is understood
to begin with. One reason why the Irish feel at home with
Americans (apart from the fact that half Ireland emigrated
to the United States) is that both nationalities have known
what it is like to be governed *culturally* as well as politically
from London.

The English reader may accept my assumption that there
is such a thing as American literature, and concede that
American writers, like the Irish, have managed surprisingly
well with their mixed-up heritage. Yet he may still be worried about pure literary values (or at any rate English ones),
and complain that in stressing the *American* qualities inherent in American literature there is a danger of cultural chauvinism. Americans, he might argue, harp on *American* humour, *American* democracy, and so on, as though they were
American discoveries, virtues peculiar to the United States.
They do the same, he may think, in respect to their vices: to
anti-intellectualism, commercialism, and the like, which are
characteristic of England also. Here I agree to some extent
with my imaginary English reader. American literary historians are perhaps prone to view their own national scene
too narrowly, mistaking prominence for uniqueness. They
do over-praise their own literature, or certainly its minor

figures (though their graduate-school system is partly to
blame. So voracious is its demand for raw materials that the
supply is not enough to go round: the most trifling of essayists and most unmemorable of poetasters are seized upon to
serve as subjects for doctoral dissertations, and be published
subsequently. It is like the siege of Paris in the Franco-
Prussian War, when even the mice and sparrows were taken
for food). And Americans do swing from aggressive over-
praise of their literature to an equally unfortunate, imitative
deference. But then, the English themselves are somewhat
insular in their literary appraisals. Moreover, in fields where
they are not pre-eminent – e.g., in painting and music – they
too alternate between boasting of native products and copy-
ing those of the Continent. How many English paintings try
to look as though they were done in Paris; how many times
have we read in articles that they really represent an 'English tradition' after all.

To speak of *American* literature, then, is not to assert that it
is completely unlike that of Europe. Broadly speaking,
America and Europe have kept step. At any given moment
the traveller could find examples in both of the same architecture, the same styles in dress, the same books on the
shelves. Ideas have crossed the Atlantic as freely as men and
merchandise, though sometimes more slowly. When I refer
to *American* habits, thoughts, etc., I intend some sort of quali-
fication to precede the word, for frequently the difference between America and Europe (especially England) will be one
of degree, sometimes only of a small degree. The amount of
divergence is a subtle affair, liable to perplex the Englishman
when he looks at America. He is looking at a country which
in important senses grew out of his own, which in several
ways still resembles his own – and which is yet a foreign
country. There are odd overlappings and abrupt unfamiliari-
ties; kinship yields to a sudden disjointure, as when we hail a
person across the street, only to discover from his blank response that we have mistaken a stranger for a friend.

The English reader, that is, needs to make a double approach to American literature. He should come off a certain

English high horse, and, putting aside what seems to me a hereditary disdain, should look for common elements in his and in the American experience. The task will be easier if (like me) he is a native of industrial England. For those who live under the northern soot-pall, in the wilderness of factories and housing estates; whose ancestors came from villages of which the family has preserved no memory; who will probably move in a few years to another home, another town; who know the atmosphere of those bleak English landscapes so well evoked by W. H. Auden, where mill and mine squat among the moors, neither urban nor rural, recent and yet of archaeological antiquity: for millions of such people the time-scale, the undercurrent (however faint) of alienation, the knowledge of ugliness, are closer to the American experience than is the England of our Christmas-card suppositions. Bearing these things in mind, the English reader who enjoys, say, Arnold Bennett, will enjoy a similar insight in the novels of Theodore Dreiser.

But he will not be completely at home with them; and if he realizes their foreignness, and accepts it as a valid quality, he will begin to share a deeper appreciation of American writing. The same applies to such writers as Henry James and T. S. Eliot, who are so much less 'American' than Dreiser that they can be studied with little reference to their homeland. In their case, and in some comparable ones, I have not been particularly concerned with nationality. My dividing line has been arbitrary: thus, Eliot has little space devoted to him because his work is already well known on this side of the Atlantic. I would only maintain, of American expatriate authors, that a consideration of their American origins is an additional help to understanding them individually, and that a study of them is a help toward a fuller grasp of American literature as a whole.

In other words, American literature is to our eyes a curious amalgam of familiar and strange. America is, of course, an extension of Europe in Europe's expansionist phase. It has been peopled mainly by Europeans. The 'involuntary immigrants' – Negro slaves – from Africa are an exception, and their presence has modified American society. But in general the United States was founded upon European, and especially British, precedents. Culturally speaking, America might be called a European colony. However, to say so is to draw attention to the complexity of the American scene. No other colony has been so heterogeneously populated, or so long politically independent of Europe. No other country whose origins lie in Europe has had so sharp an awareness of its cleavage from, and superiority to, the parent cultures. Running through American history, and therefore through American literature, is a double consciousness of Old World modes and New World possibilities. Yesterday has been dismissed and pined for: to-morrow has been invoked and dreaded. It has not been the most favourable of situations for the production of literature. As American, the writer has distrusted Europe; as writer, he has envied the riches available to his European counterpart. At any rate this was true of creative literature: the novel, the poem, and the play were for long inhibited in the United States. By and large, critical, historical, and polemical writing have flowed more easily from American pens.

Why this should have been so will perhaps emerge in the course of my account. The Calvinism of colonial New England has something to do with it. So, in a much wider context, has the whole process of settlement. Not all those who emigrated to America did so for exalted reasons. In colonial times some settlers were more attracted by trading prospects than by religion. In the nineteenth century some immigrants came in order to avoid military service in their homeland. But even so, the cumulative process had for most Americans a deep, almost mythological significance. Theodore Roosevelt said that whether those who came were called settlers or immigrants, they travelled steerage — the hard way. To transfer oneself and one's family across the ocean was a step not lightly taken. It was something of an act of faith, the beginning of a myth. In the mythology, Europe was associated with the past, with British redcoats at Concord, absentee landlords, dynastic pride: hunger, poverty, oppression.

America, by contrast, was the future: plenty, prosperity, freedom. Even to-day, the future is America's favourite tense; thus, a writer in the *New York Times Magazine* (27 July 1952) consoles his readers with the thought that 'in spite of everything, we still stand at the beginning of spring, and the point of dawn'. A European writer would not, I suspect, feel able to sound so auroral a note; in England the most we hope for is a 'new Elizabethan age' as good as the first one.

For much of its history America has been a busy, restless land, more interested in innovation than in conservation. Its people have been highly optimistic, setting great store by the ability of the individual to overcome obstacles.[1] The individual has had a *right* to expect success. Emerson, in a revealing phrase from his essay *Self-Reliance*, maintained that 'the nonchalance of boys who are sure of a dinner ... is the healthy attitude of human nature'. Or, as Melville said of the spoiled American overtaken by the Civil War, he thought himself 'Nature's Roman, never to be scourged'. Emerson's conviction has been widely shared in America, though Melville's disenchanted comment shows that it has never commanded total assent there. Various consequences of 'the healthy attitude' may be noted. When high expectations are thwarted, they are apt to throw the confident individual into the blackest pessimism. Optimism and pessimism mingle queerly in American writing: Mark Twain is a conspicuous example. Or, the individual tends to set himself up in a dramatic relationship to society – as anarchist, as nihilist, or even as a kind of Prometheus. One thinks here of Thoreau ('I am not the son of the engineer'); of the poet Robinson Jeffers ('Shine, Perishing Republic'); of Ernest Hemingway ('There was a war but we did not go to it any more'); and of Whitman, Thomas Wolfe, Henry Miller. One sees, too, the vulnerability of the American writer (despite his apparent detachment) to changes in the intellectual climate; in the

1. F. O. Matthiessen has pointed out (in *American Renaissance*, New York and Oxford, 1941, 5–6) that the first use of the word *individualism* occurs in the English translation of Alexis de Tocqueville's *Democracy in America*, where it was coined to describe a novel state of affairs.

last half-century he seems almost to have shed his mental skin every decade.

He has been able to stand outside society in this way partly because society itself was too fragmentary, too much in the flux of becoming, to lay close hold upon him. A general, abstract allegiance was expected; but more intimate ties were absent. For the novelist, as we see in the case of Hawthorne, the insubstantiality of society posed serious problems. The novelist, that is, lacked a structure of society about which to write, and (probably more important) the sense of an audience to whom he could address his work. It has been hard for American writers to get their national bearings. The great majority of them, whatever their reservations about America, genuinely believed (and still do) that it was a fairer, more virtuous place than any elsewhere. Its citizens had achieved a splendid equality; they all – except the Negro – walked upright. But how to combine social equality with the hierarchy of taste and patronage that the writer seems to need? The dilemma was, of course, not confined to America. Yet it was an acute one for certain American writers who cherished democracy but whose work lay exposed to popular derision. Herman Melville, in his novel *White-Jacket*, suggested a solution that cannot have satisfied him any more than it does the reader. Two seamen, plain Jack Chase and the poet Lemsford, are in conversation:

'Blast them, Jack, what they call the public is a monster, like the idol we saw in Owhyhee, with the head of a jackass, the body of a baboon, and the tail of a scorpion.'

'I don't like that,' said Jack; 'when I'm ashore. I myself am part of the public.'

'Your pardon, Jack; you are not. You are then a part of the people, just as you are aboard the frigate here. The public is one thing, Jack, and the people another.'

'You are right,' said Jack; '... The public and the people. Aye, Aye, my lads, let us hate the one and cleave to the other.'

It was not merely that men like Melville felt themselves vulnerable to the *public*; it was also that they acknowledged an emotional membership in the *people*. The nineteenth

century was a didactic era in Britain as well as in America;
not only in America was the novel liable to turn into the tract.
But there was an American didacticism that went beyond
condemning slavery or intemperance. Parallels between the
United States and Soviet Russia are much in vogue nowadays, and usually foolish. There is, however, a partial resemblance between the American situation of a century ago
and that of present-day Russia – or, better, of the Russia of
the 1920s. Both were new and radical experiments, considered by other countries subversive, or at least unpleasing
in their raw assertiveness. Both were somewhat hostile to
these other countries, whose principles they had come into
being to repudiate. Radical ideologies require to contrast to
their own goodness the wickedness of some other system. In the
case of Russia, capitalism was the villain. In the case of America, Europe had to be – and this has continued to be one of Europe's functions for America (though it is accompanied by
others which do much to cancel it out: a point to be developed in a moment). Again, both Russia and America looked
to the future to fulfil their millennial expectations. (This
helps to explain the appeal that communism held for some
American intellectuals in the 1920s and 1930s. Disappointed
in their own national vision of futurity, they sought another.
'I have seen the future,' said Lincoln Steffens, after a visit to
Russia, 'and it works'.) In both, the writer had a moral
obligation to hasten the triumph of the ideology, and not to
dwell upon such topics as the imperfection of human nature,
or of one's country, which implied that the millennium might
never arrive.

This was the particular American didacticism, then, as it
affected literature. What has been called the 'official' view
of the United States has weighed upon the writer, not as an
overt tyranny but as a subtle compulsion, a higher form of
the business-man's slogan: 'Don't knock, boost'. The word
American, with all its connotations, has got in the way, a
little as the word *Negro* gets in the way of the coloured writer.
America is something that has to be explained, not just to
uncomprehending Europeans but to other Americans, to

oneself. As a society founded with ideal aims, it finds that
the ideal is sometimes contradicted by the reality; and that
in any case the ideal and the real must always be referred
to one another. In literary terms, this American didacticism
has been an uneasy combination of *ought* and *is*. As a result,
even though the writer is often isolated, there is little in
American literature that could be described as mystical
(though no lack of spirituality; along with the American
myth, religion has been a most important influence). The
practical and pragmatic gainsay the utopian and transcendental. The would-be American mystic, like the American
President, is interrupted in his study to go and shake hands
with a deputation; the telephone is, so to speak, always ring-
ing. Occasionally the combination is expressed with a levity
that masks great earnestness. We can find it in Emily Dickinson, or in Thoreau:

> Great God, I ask thee for no meaner pelf
> Than that I may not disappoint myself ...
> And next in value, which thy kindness lends,
> That I may greatly disappoint my friends.

This is not a comic poem, in any ordinary sense : it is called *A
Prayer*, and Thoreau means what he says. But American humour, with all its shades, is in part a response to American
didacticism: a perception of the discrepancy between things
as they are and things as they are supposed to be. Every solemn,
'official' American utterance can be paired with another that
is sharply irreverent. If there is a *Congressional Record* with
its heavy rhetoric, there is a Mr Dooley or a Will Rogers to
poke fun at Congressmen and other spokesmen. Humour was
a means by which the American writer could win popular
acceptance, even in the act of abusing the public. It was, too,
a way of dealing with dialect and other raw materials of
literature which could not be treated with high seriousness.
Expressing a real informality in American behaviour, it has
led to the emergence of an American prose style of which
Mark Twain was the first master, and which has a supple
ease that few British writers can emulate. It is not only prose

style that has benefited; there is an American popular
poetry of song, owing a good deal to the Negro, that has a
wonderful vitality.

And then, of course, there has been the constant connexion
with Europe: Europe the bad place of ideology, and yet the
fountain-head – the inexhaustible source of inspiration.
Europe's influence, Europe's greater genius have been denied, admitted, agonized over. America's eventual supremacy has been predicted incessantly. Americans were urged
to forget Europe, to be native authors. But Europe has continued to haunt and heckle the American imagination. Some
Americans, indeed, have been better Europeans than any
European; from Benjamin Franklin and Count Rumford
down to T. S. Eliot and Ezra Pound, there have always been
Americans of a remarkable and cosmopolitan sort. The
English, with their proprietary feeling about the United
States, have not clearly realized how many links there have
been between America and that Continent which begins
across the Channel: how many Americans, for instance, used
to study at German universities.[1]

If Europe has had a complex mythological function for
America, America has also – less complicatedly – had its
function for Europe, as the land of newness, roughness,
wealth, violence, and improbability. Americans themselves
have been fascinated by this picture of their character. But
they have also been a little touchy about it. As many critics
have noted, there has been a split in American writing between a cultivated, Europeanized concept of literature, and
a notion of a native literature. One critic has christened the
two types of authors 'palefaces' and 'redskins', taking Henry
James and Walt Whitman as representative figures.[2] This is
one useful simplification for the English reader to bear in
mind. Another common and useful (though not identical)

1. Some of the first (including Everett, Ticknor, Bancroft, and Longfellow) are dealt with in Orie W. Long, *Literary Pioneers: Early American
Explorers of European Culture* (Cambridge, Mass., 1935).
2. Philip Rahv, 'Paleface and Redskin', reprinted in *Image and Idea*
(Norfolk, Connecticut, 1948).

division is between those authors like Emerson and Whitman who reveal the millennial optimism mentioned above, and those others – Hawthorne, Melville, Henry James – who are sceptical of their compatriots' confidence in moral progress. Both these distinctions are theoretical extremes: no one author in America has fully exemplified either of them.

Yet although American literature has revealed certain fairly permanent trends, it has not been a static affair. Its tone has changed from decade to decade; and there is an extraordinary alteration between that of the early nineteenth century and that of the century's end. The belief in futurity, though still strong, has received a series of violent shocks ; the 'official' view has been fiercely assailed; the *public* has been scorned by some (or ignored, notably by the modern American poets), and the *people* treated as a sentimental fiction. One feature of the changed mood has been the ripening of Southern literature. Challenging the general American mythology, the South had entangled itself in a severely conservative counter-mythology inimical to creative effort, and fully meriting the famous couplet of J. Gordon Coogler:

> Alas, poor South, her poets get fewer and fewer;
> She never was much given to literature.

But by the 1920s the Southern writer, while retaining with a good conscience some elements of his region's conservatism, was able to view its predicaments with reasonable detachment, and so make use of the marvellous material it offered. Here in America, certainly, there was no need to seek the past elsewhere, in Europe: it confronted the writer at every corner.

Such are some of the themes discussed in the chapters that follow. I hope the reader will share my conviction that they are relevant. I hope I can also convey something of my pleasure in American literature. It is easy to be flippant about American aspirations – this has been one of our national pastimes. It is easy, likewise, to portray the American writer as a tormented individual, as culturally displaced as the South African tribesman who works half the year in a European

compound. If I leave the reader with some such impression,
I did not mean to. Every nation has its literary problems;
not every writer is conscious of them; and for some they are
a help rather than a handicap, in defining for them the scope
of their activity. Each does what he can; and while there *are*
national literatures, there is also a writer's world outside
nationality, in which each may say, with Herman Melville:

> Gems and jewels let them heap –
> Wax sumptuous as the Sophi:
> For me, to grapple from Art's deep
> One dripping trophy!

CHAPTER ONE

COLONIAL AMERICA

ONE and three-quarter centuries in time, though only twenty miles in space, separated Jamestown and Yorktown. At Jamestown, in 1607, the English made their first successful settlement in North America. At Yorktown, just across the peninsula, in 1781, Cornwallis's encircled army marched out to surrender to General Washington, with the fife-music of 'The World Turned Upside Down' sounding in their ears. As we all know, it was not the end of British influence in America. Too much had been done that nothing could undo; in language, institutions, and ways of thought the thirteen English colonies along the Atlantic fringe of the continent were bound to exhibit some of the characteristics of what Nathaniel Hawthorne, seventy years after independence, still described as *Our Old Home*.

Nevertheless, the colonists shared experiences that set them apart from England and Europe. They had to adapt themselves to unfamiliar climates and crops; to deal with the Indians; to chart and survey, clear and plant, and build and improvise. By the end of the colonial period conditions were less strange and more comfortable. Some floors, figuratively and literally, were carpeted, where once the settlers had trodden on earth or clattered on bare boards. Yet, for the first years, when everything was uncertain, life was reduced to the starkest terms. William Bradford outlines the plight of the Pilgrim Fathers, landing at Plymouth Rock in 1620:

Being thus passed the vast ocean, and a sea of troubles before in their preparation ..., they had now no friends to welcome them, no inns to entertain or refresh their weatherbeaten bodies, no houses or much less towns to repair to, to seek for succour. ... Besides, what could they see but a hideous and desolate wilderness, full of wild beasts and wild men? and what multitudes there might be of them they knew not. Neither could they, as it were, go up to the top of

Pisgah, to view from this wilderness a more goodly country to feed
their hopes; for which way soever they turned their eyes (save upward to the heavens) they could have little solace or content in respect of any outward objects. For summer being done, all things
stand upon them with a weatherbeaten face. ...

In such circumstances, the early colonists could naturally
find little leisure for either the reading or the writing of
polite literature. William Penn's advice to prospective emi-
grants in 1685 was: 'Be moderate in Expectation, count on
Labour before a Crop, and Cost before Gain.' His words apply to most of the colonial period, as far as literature is concerned. America produced no writer who merits comparison
with Milton, Dryden, Pope, Swift, Sterne, Fielding – or with
Bunyan and Jeremy Taylor, if we are to name men whose
chief preoccupation was religion. Nor, in colonial times, did
America expect to.

> Here first the duties of to-day, the lessons of the concrete,
> Wealth, order, travel, shelter, products, plenty –

the lines are Whitman's, from his 'The United States to Old
World Critics'. But before the American Revolution there
were no strictures from Old World critics, and no United
States. There were only isolated colonies, on the edge of a
wilderness, busily consolidating and extending their gains.
They were not without cultivation, especially in New England, where what became Harvard College was founded as
early as 1636,[1] with a printing press set up nearby in 1639.[2]
But on the whole the New World was content to accept the
literary products of the Old, when it had time for them
and if they seemed suitable. Though books were among
the cargo of almost every ship from Europe, standards

1. Other foundation dates for American colleges are: *1693*, William and
Mary (Williamsburg, Virginia); *1701*, Yale (New Haven, Connecticut);
1746, Princeton (New Jersey); *1751*, Pennsylvania (Philadelphia); *1754*,
Columbia (New York) and Dartmouth (Hanover, New Hampshire);
1764, Brown (Providence, Rhode Island).

2. No further presses were established in the colonies until the 1690s,
when Philadelphia and New York had each acquired one. There were
five presses in Boston by 1715.

of taste were at first fairly austere in most colonial communities.

In the case of New England, the word 'Puritanism' has
been used to sum them up. It has been maintained on innumerable occasions that Puritan New England laid a
curse upon literature and the arts from which America is
still suffering. The Puritans, according to the familiar accusa-
tions of the 1920s, were joyless hypocrites. H. L. Mencken
and other critics [1] relished such jokes as:

When the Pilgrim Fathers landed, they fell upon their knees – and
then upon the aborigines.

They derived much amusement from the Puritans' scrutiny
of God's purposes: as, for example, the speculations of John
Winthrop (1588–1649) on the mice in his son's library, which
nibbled away the Anglican prayer-book but touched nothing else. They liked to jeer at colonial 'blue laws' (not noting
that these were in large part the fabrication of the hostile
Anglican minister Samuel Peters, in 1781). From the absence of the novel or the play in colonial New England,
and the virtual absence of Puritan poetry, they concluded
that American literature had been well-nigh throttled at
birth.

Since the 1920s there has been a closer, more sympathetic
examination of Puritan life and thought, led by the Harvard
scholars Samuel Eliot Morison, Perry Miller, and Kenneth
Murdock. It has been shown that, considering their difficult
origins, the New England settlements produced a surprising
quantity of literature (if – as we ought – we take literature to
embrace theology, history and chronicles, private journals,
and the like). Jonathan Edwards (1703–58) in particular has
been put forward as an author of great intellectual distinction. The anti-Puritan attack was recklessly over-stated.
There is now, however, a slight danger that scholarship may
err – though nothing like so far or so irresponsibly – in the

1. Writing in their magazine, the *American Mercury*, in 1925, Mencken
and his friend George Jean Nathan defined Puritanism as 'the haunting
fear that someone, somewhere, may be happy'.

opposite direction.[1] The earlier onslaught involved the 'debunking' of ancestors *as* ancestors. Yet is there not an element of ancestor-worship in the recent high praise meted out to colonial literature, especially that of New England? American literary historians, in quest of the 'usable past' of Van Wyck Brooks's well-known phrase, have naturally pushed the pedigree of their literature as far back as possible, and insisted on its integrity. They have also been concerned to establish the existence of a Puritan tradition. In many respects their reinterpretation of colonial writing has been necessary; and the best scholars in the field have been careful not to make exaggerated claims. Historically speaking, colonial writing is of absorbing value. The only point to be made is that its value *as literature* is less high. In saying this one is not denying the praiseworthy qualities of the Puritan mind (to leave out for the moment the colonies south of New England): its courage, its earnestness, its sense of purpose. Nor is one asserting that there is no Puritan tradition: New England had a distinctive moral and social order whose influence spread over much of the United States. But *for writers* the tradition, after the Revolution and until our own day, seems not to have been a strong *positive* force. Apart from Hawthorne, and to a lesser extent Harriet Beecher Stowe, J. G. Whittier, and perhaps J. R. Lowell, which of the chief authors of the nineteenth century was deeply stirred by it? When he was past sixty, Longfellow admitted that he had not read Jonathan Edwards, though he meant to; and Longfellow was a well-read man, if somewhat lazy-minded. At any rate, in common with most of his contemporaries, he was more drawn to the literature of bygone Europe than to that of his own region. Again, it is perhaps both a cause and an effect of the tradition's discontinuity that several pieces of colonial writing had to wait so long to be brought out in print. The elder John Winthrop's *Journal* was not published until 1790, and not in complete form (as *The History of New*

1. The debate is usefully summarized in George M. Waller (ed.), *Puritanism in Early America* (Boston, 1950), a volume in the admirable Amherst series, 'Problems in American Civilization'.

England) until 1825-6. The *History of Plymouth Plantation* by William Bradford (1590-1657), the manuscript of which disappeared during the Revolution – to reappear in the library of Fulham Palace – was not printed in full until 1856. The journal of Sarah Kemble Knight (1666-1727) did not reach the public until 1829, nor the diary of Samuel Sewall (1652-1730) until 1878-82. The poems of Edward Taylor (*c.* 1644-1729) remained in manuscript until a portion were printed in 1937.

As for the qualities of New England writing, it can be generally admitted that the Puritan atmosphere was discouraging to imaginative literature. The statement must not be made too strongly, for within a century of the first settlements the Puritan disciplines were a good deal relaxed. Moreover, in the colonies outside New England, where no strict theocracies had been set up, there was little evidence of a freer kind of literature – or indeed any kind of literature – until the end of the seventeenth century. But in New England itself, the first generations in the Calvinistic townships of Massachusetts and Connecticut wrote nothing for mere amusement. They regarded themselves as God's agents, sent under his 'wonder-working providence' to make homes for his chosen and to convert (or annihilate) the Indians – 'those miserable Salvages' whom, Cotton Mather (1663-1728) concluded, 'probably the Devil decoy'd ... hither, in hopes that the Gospel of the Lord Jesus Christ would never come here to destroy or disturb his Absolute Empire over them'. They took for guides the Bible and their own consciences.

The early literature that emerged from such a God-centred world was heavily weighted, in subject and style, by religious considerations. The best writing was held to be that which best brought home to the average church member a full awareness of his perilous, probationary status on earth. As the Puritans condemned the images and incense of the Roman Church, so in literature they distrusted the highly coloured. A plain style was commended, without unnecessary ornament and without allusions that might pass over the heads of the unlettered. New England authors did not

always confine themselves to their own rules. Look, for instance, at Nathaniel Ward's *The Simple Cobbler of Aggawam*
(1647). Here is an extract from the part of this lively pamphlet which is devoted to women's fashions:

But when I hear a nugiperous gentledame inquire what dress the
Queen is in this week, what the nudiustertian fashion of the court
... I look at her as the very gizzard of a trifle, the product of the
quarter of a cipher, the epitome of nothing, fitter to be kicked, if she
were of a kickable substance, than either honored or humored.

Or observe the endless classical references in *Magnalia Christi
Americana* (1702), the compendium of ecclesiastical history
written by Cotton Mather. Yet these are unusual cases.
Nathaniel Ward (*c.* 1578–1652) did not emigrate to Massachusetts until he was in his fifties. And while classical references were indulged in by some Puritan scholars (together
with such literary devices as the anagram),[1] Cotton Mather
– who confessed to his diary[2] that 'proud thoughts fly-blow
my best performances' – exhibits a quite special brand of
pedantry, unrivalled in the colonies even by his learned
father Increase Mather (1639–1723).

Otherwise, in general, New England writers relied upon
the Bible. Not only did they clinch their arguments with Biblical chapter and verse; they saw their whole situation in Biblical analogies, with themselves as the Jews and their enemies
as the enemies of the Jews:

Accordingly when the *Noble Design* of carrying a Colony of *Chosen
People* into an *American* Wilderness, was by *some* Eminent Persons
undertaken, *This* Eminent Person was, by the Consent of all, *Chosen*
for the *Moses*, who must be the Leader of so great an Undertaking ...

It seemed natural to Cotton Mather to refer thus to John
Winthrop. The Bible furnished him and his contemporaries
with images and illustrations to suit every occasion. It was
their source-book, as, in a minor degree, the catalogues of
Chippendale and his fellow-craftsmen in England provided

1. E.g.,   Thomas Dudley
                       ah! old, must dye –
an anagram of *c.* 1645 reprinted in H. S. Jantz (ed.), *The First Century of
New England Verse* (Worcester, Mass., 1944), 34.

2. Cotton Mather's *Diary* was first published in 1911–12.

designs for colonial cabinet-makers. In some ways it was an ennobling influence, that lent its great resonance to otherwise tame discourse. It has left its mark, for example, on the sturdy prose of William Bradford, whose *History* is one of the finest colonial works. But in other ways it limited Puritan writing, blurring and deadening the pages. Its superb phrases came too easily into the author's consciousness, and their formidable respectability ensured that they were used and used, until they had weakened into cliché.

Perhaps the dominance of the Bible also helped to widen the chronological gulf between colonial and English literature. In *Seventeenth-century English Literature*,[1] C. V. Wedgwood has suggested that the language of the Authorized Version was already a century out of date when this Bible was published in 1611. If so (and if it is true, too, that the Authorized Version soon supplanted the Geneva Bible, and that the Bible held an even greater sway than in England), then it may have contributed to the time-lag of colonial writing. New England authors, though often erudite men, were not always acquainted with the work of English contemporaries. Taste, and hence style, were archaic. Edward Taylor, the best poet of colonial America, wrote metaphysical verse after its vogue had passed in England. Milton and Marvell reached few New England readers in their own life-times. The poems of Edmund Waller were not introduced into America (by Dr Benjamin Colman of Boston) until 1699, when Waller had been dead for twelve years. Increase Mather, the president of Harvard, seems not to have known of Shakespeare and Ben Jonson, or – more surprisingly – of Bunyan.[2] Many years after their heyday at home, Addison and Steele were still carefully imitated in America; and, as Americans turned to political controversy in the second half of the eighteenth century, their reading of such seventeenth-

1. (Oxford, 1950), 16.
2. See Thomas J. Wertenbaker, *The First Americans, 1607–90* (New York, 1927), 240–1. But Benjamin Franklin (1706–90), who spent his boyhood in Boston, tells in the *Autobiography* of his early enthusiasm for Bunyan's works, which were available in small, inexpensive editions.

century thinkers as Locke may likewise have had its effect in
anachronizing style.

Another factor that affected and circumscribed Puritan
writing was the conviction that all events, however small, are
contrived by God, or else the Devil. Sometimes a moving
passage results, from the spectacle of strength in adversity, or
from the serenity of the righteous – as in this charming ex-
cerpt from a pamphlet by Samuel Sewall, in which he medi-
tates on the Book of Revelation, with special reference to
Newburyport:

As long as ... any Salmon, or Sturgeon shall swim in the streams
of Merrimack; ... as long as the Sea-Fowl shall know the time of
their coming, and not neglect seasonably to visit the places of their
acquaintance; as long as any Cattle shall be fed with the grass
growing in the meadows, which do humbly bow down themselves
before Turkey-Hill; ... as long as any free and harmless Dove
shall find a White Oak, or other tree within the Township, to perch,
or feed, or build a nest upon; ... as long as Nature shall not grow
old and dote; but shall constantly remember to give the rows of
Indian corn their education, by pairs: so long shall Christians be
born there; and being first made meet, shall from thence be Translated, to be made partakers of the Inheritance of the Saints in Light.

Sewall, whose *Diary* is one of the most fascinating pieces of
Puritan literature, here clearly shows his love of place and of
growing things; and the suggestion that Newburyport is only
a half-way stage seems a merely conventional one. But in
much other New England writing, especially of the seventeenth century, we are continually reminded of Winthrop's
mice; or of Cotton Mather's decision, on losing the manuscript of some lectures, that 'Spectres, or Agents in the invisible World, were the Robbers'. Human motive is rarely analysed, save in crude terms. Genuine emotion peeps through,
only to be squeezed back by some orthodox piety. Thus,
Anne Bradstreet (*c.* 1612–72), grieving for her dead child,
writes:

> By nature trees do rot when they are grown
> And plums and apples thoroughly ripe do fall,
> And corn and grass are in their season mown,
> And time brings down what is both strong and tall.

> But plants new set to be eradicate,
> And buds new blown, to have so short a date,
> Is by his hand alone that guides nature and fate.

The last line is intolerably lame, all the more so after the two deeply felt lines that precede it. Similarly, Urian Oakes (*c.* 1631–81) touches a nerve of agony in these lines of his laborious 'Elegy upon the Death of the Reverend Mr Thomas' (1677):

> My dearest, inmost, bosom-friend is gone!
> Gone is my sweet companion, soul's delight!
> Now in an huddling crowd I'm all alone,
> And almost could bid all the world goodnight –

only to flatten their appeal by adding:

> Blest be my rock! God lives: oh let Him be,
> As He is, so all in all to me.

Again, Mary Rowlandson (*c.* 1635–*c.* 1678), a minister's wife captured by Indians in 1676, describes her experiences with dignity and simplicity, but includes in her narrative a tortuous analysis of God's purpose in allowing the Indians to accomplish a massacre.

Even in the form of allegory, fiction had no place in New England. Except for hymnody and the ballad, poetry was of small account. Only three Puritan poets have much claim to notice: Anne Bradstreet and Edward Taylor, and Michael Wigglesworth (1631–1705). Wigglesworth gives a thorough demonstration of Calvinist doctrine in his lengthy *Day of Doom* (1662), but neither it nor his other theological verse-treatises rise far above doggerel. Perhaps the most notorious stanza of *The Day of Doom* is the one in which God settles the fate of those who, dying in infancy, 'never had good or bad effected pers'nally':

> A crime it is, therefore in bliss
>   you may not hope to dwell;
> But unto you I shall allow
>   the easiest room in Hell.
> The glorious King thus answering,
>   they cease, and plead no longer:
> Their Consciences must needs confess
>   his Reasons are the stronger.

Anne Bradstreet is more interesting, for her prose *Meditations* as well as for her poetry, which was published first in London (1650), as *The Tenth Muse Lately Sprung Up in America*. She thus anticipated the first English poetess, Kathleen Philips the 'Matchless Orinda', by a year. Her achievement, as the mother of a family in early colonial America, was possibly even more remarkable than Orinda's – especially if one remembers John Winthrop's story of the young wife of a Puritan dignitary who, in 1645,

was fallen into a sad infirmity, the loss of her understanding and reason, which had been growing upon her divers years, by occasion of her giving herself wholly to reading and writing, and had written many books ... For if she had attended her household affairs, and such things as belong to women ... she had kept her wits.

Anne Bradstreet, who had taken a good look at Du Bartas – 'a right *Du Bartas* Girle', Nathaniel Ward called her – as well as the Bible, is an attractive minor versifier. Yet she produced nothing to put beside the best lines of Edward Taylor. Taylor, who came to America in his twenties, served most of his life as minister to a Massachusetts frontier congregation. His poems, rescued so recently from obscurity, are reminiscent of Quarles and Crashaw in their elaborated metaphor:

> Thus in the usual coach of God's decree
> They bowl and swim
> To glory bright, if no hypocrisy
> Handed them in.

Now and then the reader perceives a likeness to Emily Dickinson, another solitary New Englander of a later time:

> Who would
> Wash with his blood my blots out? Crown his shelf
> Or dress his golden cupboard with such ware?

Somehow, Taylor is not cramped by his environment. Conceding that such things are mere 'wits wantonings', nevertheless he revels in a catalogue of marvels[1]:

1. From *Meditation Fifty-Six, Second Series* (1703).

The clock of Strasburg, Dresden's table-sight,
Regsamont's fly of steel about that flew,
Turrian's wooden sparrows in a flight,
And th'artificial man Aquinas slew,
Mark Scaliota's lock and key and chain
Drawn by a flea, in our Queen Betty's reign ...

This is awkward poetry, but it has passages of magnificent imagery:

Who laced and filleted the earth so fine
With rivers like green ribbons smaragdine?
Who made the seas its selvedge, and its locks
Like a quilt ball within a silver box?
Who spread its canopy? Or curtains spun?
Who in this bowling alley bowled the sun?[1]

No other Puritan writer in America displayed such verbal riches; Cotton Mather, who himself wrote verse on occasion, probably came nearest. But if the bulk of New England writing was ponderous, at least it was rarely trivial. Even where its authors are lost in the intricacies of a sermon or of a historical chronicle, they are never altogether lost. William Stoughton (1631–1701) of Massachusetts declared that 'God hath sifted a nation that he might send choice grain into this wilderness'. A like conviction pervades the writing of the seventeenth and early eighteenth centuries. In his *Phaenomena Quaedam Apocalyptica* (1697), Samuel Sewall predicts that New England will be the site of the New Jerusalem. The preacher grapples with his text, wasting no effort in wooing the audience; the chronicler sets down every detail, believing all to be of ultimate significance. This dramatic vigour is the chief strength of Puritan writing, and does much to redeem for the modern reader the long stretches of dull, crabbed or even absurd material in such works as Cotton Mather's *Magnalia*:

I write the wonders of the Christian religion, flying from the deprivations of Europe, to the American strand ...

A decisive battle is in progress; God watches for the outcome, and all posterity will speak of it. For as Mather (with a

1. From the preface to *God's Determinations Touching His Elect*.

welcome touch of humour) says of the struggle with the
Indians that went on from 1688 to 1698:

the author pretends that the famous history of the Trojan War itself comes behind our little history of the Indian War; for the best
antiquaries have now confuted Homer; the walls of Troy were, it
seems, all made of poet's paper; and the siege of the town, with the
tragedies of the wooden horse, were all but a piece of poetry. And if
a war between us and a handful of Indians do appear no more than
a *Batrachomyomachia* [1] to the world abroad, yet unto us at home it
hath been considerable enough to make an history.

Secularized, the Puritan attitude to the New World becomes
the belief in futurity which has already been mentioned. The
other side of Puritan thought – belief in what Thomas
Hooker of Connecticut (1586–1647) called 'the unconceav-
able hainousness of the hellish nature of sin' – has had a
weaker hold over the American mind, though its after-effects
are still apparent in Hawthorne.

Indeed, its hold was slackening in New England by the
early eighteenth century. The skull-and-crossbones crudely
carved on the first tombstones was replaced by a winged
cherub, and then even by attempts at portraiture. Jonathan
Edwards, who belonged to a younger generation than Cotton Mather, struggled tremendously with himself and with
his Northampton congregation to keep alive the grand, hope-
ful-hopeless tenor of ancestral thought. Yet the response he
evoked was a little more hectic and a little less profound. A
powerful revivalist, whose best-known work is a scarifying
sermon, 'Sinners in the Hands of an Angry God' (1741),
Edwards was also something of a philosopher on the eighteenth-century model, whose delight in nature has a pan-
theistic tinge:

God's excellency ... seemed to appear in every thing; in the sun,
moon and stars; in the clouds, and blue sky; in the grass, flowers,
trees; in the water, and all nature ... I often used to sit and view
the moon for continuance; and in the day, spent much time in
viewing the clouds and sky, to behold the sweet glory of God in
these things ... [2]

1. 'Battle of the Frogs and Mice': an early Greek burlesque of Homer.
2. *Personal Narrative* (c. 1740).

Though his *Freedom of Will*[1] (1754) might be regarded as a harsh document, the *Two Dissertations* (1765) of his last years breathe benevolence and gentleness.

Mather and Edwards were prolific authors, from their precocious childhoods to their last days. They led busy, public lives, but these were the outcome of intense private communings. Introspection, and with it the habit of keeping a diary, was a common Puritan trait. From John Winthrop's *Journal* (maintained from 1630 to 1649) to *The Education of Henry Adams* (1907, privately printed), such records have been impressive features of New England literature, whether or not intended for publication. Samuel Sewall's journal has been referred to. Different in tone, and highly diverting, is the brief journal of a trip made from Boston to New York and back, in 1704-5, by the forty-year-old widow Sarah Kemble Knight. To read her narrative is to pass into another world than that inhabited by the Winthrops and the Mathers:

Being at a merchant's house, in comes a tall country fellow...; he advanced to the middle of the room, makes an awkward nod, and spitting a large deal of aromatick tincture, he gave a scrape with his shovel-like shoe, leaving a small shovel full of dirt on the floor, made a full stop, hugging his pretty body with his hands under his arms, [and] stood staring round him, like a cat let out of a basket.

This is the tone of the eighteenth century in New England, relaxed and secular. We catch it again, more refinedly, in the cheerful accents of the Tory Minister Mather Byles (1707-88), Cotton Mather's nephew, whose lines[2] might serve as an epitaph of his uncle's régime:

> An hundred Journies now the Earth has run,
> In annual Circles, round the central Sun,
> Since the first ship the unpolish'd Letters bore
> Thro' the wide Ocean to the barb'rous Shore ...
> Solid, and grave, and plain the Country stood,
> Inelegant, and rigorously good.

1. This was the book that led Boswell to say, 'The only relief I had was to forget it' – and Dr Johnson to pronounce that 'All theory is against the freedom of the will, all experience for it'. See Paul E. More, *Selected Shelburne Essays* (Oxford, World's Classics, 1935), 250-1.
2. From 'To Pictorio, On the Sight of his Pictures' (1744).

Outside New England, a comparable urbanity could be found. In Pennsylvania, it is true, William Penn (1644–1718) wrote in the cool, charitable vein of the Quaker faith, while the colonies to the South were not without religious testimony. But by the mid eighteenth century the Quaker city of Philadelphia was beginning to represent commerce and the arts with some vigour; and, there or elsewhere, the New England combination of church, school, and town-meeting had never had an exact counterpart. In the Anglican colony of Virginia the secular tone is apparent in Robert Beverley's brisk, good-natured *History and Present State of Virginia* (1705), and – strikingly – in the pages of William Byrd of Westover (1674–1744). Byrd, a wealthy planter educated in England and resident there for long periods, had a home that by colonial standards was a mansion, with a library of 4,000 books (twice as many as Cotton Mather) and portraits of the English nobility hanging on his walls. He wrote various sprightly accounts of Virginia that remained in manuscript until published in 1841. He also kept a shorthand diary, which has been printed only recently and in part. Byrd has been described as an 'American Pepys' (nearly every American writer once had some such identification tag attached to him, often to his annoyance); and one thinks also of Boswell. The *Secret Diary* of Byrd, like Boswell's *London Journal*, reveals a man who is by turns shrewd and ingenuous. Certainly Byrd could not be taken for a Puritan; this is how he speaks of the first Virginia settlements, in his *History of the Dividing Line* (*c*. 1729):

From Kiquotan they extended themselves as far as James-Town, where like true Englishmen, they built a Church that cost no more than Fifty Pounds and a Tavern that cost Five Hundred.

And here is Byrd visiting some neighbours, in 1732:

I was carried into a room elegantly set off with pier glasses ... A brace of tame deer ran familiarly about the house, and one of them came to stare at me as a stranger. But unluckily spying his own figure in the glass, he made a spring over the tea table that stood under it and shattered the glass to pieces, and falling back upon the tea table, made a terrible fracas among the china. This exploit ...

surprised me, and perfectly frightened Mrs Spotswood.[1] But 'twas worth all the damage to show the moderation and good humour with which she bore this disaster.

By contrast, let us look at another domestic mishap that took place in Boston ninety years earlier, as described in John Winthrop's *Journal*:

A godly woman ..., dwelling sometime in London, brought with her a parcel of very fine linen of great value, which she set her heart too much upon, and had been at charge to have it all newly washed, and curiously folded and pressed, and so left it in press in her parlour over night. She had a negro maid went into the room very late, and let fall some snuff of the candle upon the linen, so as by the morning all the linen was burned to tinder. ... But it pleased God that the loss of this linen did her much good, both in taking her heart from worldly comforts, and in preparing her for a far greater affliction by the untimely death of her husband, who was slain not long after at Isle of Providence.

The difference is clear, and vast. In part it is the distance between Puritan Massachusetts and planter Virginia; but it is also the distance between one century and another. By the eve of the Revolution the colonies were established beyond possibility of failure. Daniel Boone had mounted the Pisgah of the Appalachians, and beheld thence the country of Kentucky. Samuel Mather, the last of the Mather dynasty, who died in 1785, was (to use a later idiom) a fourth-generation American. There were gentry and fine houses, though not many; there was litigation and slavery; there were several worthy colleges, and a quantity of schools. In Boston and Philadelphia, New York and Charleston (and in New Orleans, a French and now a Spanish city, not to join the United States until 1803), urban life brought urban refinements: newspapers and periodicals, libraries, clubs and societies, concerts, theatrical performances.[2] Colonial literature might henceforth develop in modest conjunction with that of the Mother Country: for there was little to distinguish it,

1. The wife of Alexander Spotswood, governor of Virginia (1710–22).
2. Though in Boston, even at the end of the eighteenth century, performances had to be disguised as 'moral lectures'.

seemingly, from that of England. It was clumsier; it lacked
the excitement of a great metropolis; a few of its words were
novel; some Indian names had crept incongruously among
the scriptural and classical references. But its models were
English – 'godlike Addison', 'thrice happy Dryden', and
(above all) 'heav'nly Pope'.[1] The colonial, one might say,
had become the provincial; in men like William Byrd and
Mather Byles there was evident the typical provincial yearning for London and all its glories. But since they were still
Englishmen, there was no need to apologize for their transatlantic enthusiasms – until the Revolution set them under
a new flag, making them Americans. They were, on the eve
of the Revolution, some way towards being a different
people. In the northern colonies, for example, the pro-
motional efforts of the Anglican church met with strenuous
resistance. Among the resisters in New York were William
Livingston and a couple of friends who in the 1750s made
their views felt through a polemical journal known as *The
Independent Reflector*. *The Reflector* was closely modelled on the
British *Independent Whig* of a generation earlier – in other
words, outspoken in a gentlemanly, Whiggish way. There
is a nice doubleness about the name of Livingston's venture.
One might argue that a 'reflector' cannot be 'independent'.
Such a quibble would not have troubled Livingston and his
friends. They were as yet far from revolutionary in spirit,
and one of the three did in fact remain loyal to the British
crown. The matter of deciding how to make a colonial
reflector independent of its original British image is discussed in the next chapter.

1. See Stanley T. Williams, *The Beginnings of American Poetry (1620–
1855)* (Uppsala, 1951), 43–4.

CHAPTER TWO

AMERICA AND EUROPE – THE PROBLEMS OF INDEPENDENCE

THE political events of the Revolution concern us only to the extent that the literature of the time was largely political. Some of it is too familiar to require discussion: no one should need to be told that the Declaration of Independence (1776) is a highly effective piece of prose. Not every writer could command the eloquence of Tom Paine –

Now is the seed-time of continental union, faith and honour. The least fracture now, will be like a name engraved with the point of a pin on the tender rind of a young oak; the wound will enlarge with the tree, and posterity read it in full grown characters –

But nearly everyone shared Paine's belief that the struggle was hugely important. Loyalist and American patriot alike set to work eagerly to expose folly and injustice and convert the reader. Whether the writer's immediate aim was to stir the emotions (as with Paine, or in some of the verse of Philip Freneau), to ridicule the enemy (as in John Trumbull's mock epic M'Fingal, 1782), or to convince by patient reasoning (as in the Federalist essays of Alexander Hamilton, James Madison, and John Jay), in all cases a certain urgency still communicates itself to the reader. Controversy does not on its own create good writing; yet it is usually a powerful aid.

For the infant nation, victory in the war and for the republican principle came as a heartening overture. The United States was brand new, or almost so; old errors and temptations had been eschewed, and the book of history lay open at a clean page. The former Puritan confidence in posterity had been retained, as we can see from Paine's words; but though Puritan optimism had not been rosy enough to embrace human nature, the emphasis in these glad deistic days now shifted from duties to rights, from innate depravity to innate virtue. The burden of wickedness was transferred to Europe; lighter reading, as the Bostonian Royall Tyler said, had replaced the study of 'some dreary somebody's day of doom'. America, it seemed, would rapidly arrive at a sublime maturity. Already there were American artists of the first rank: Benjamin West succeeded Reynolds as president of the Royal Academy, while John Singleton Copley and Gilbert Stuart were among the most popular of portrait-painters. In other branches of talent and learning American names began to count for something.

Foremost, perhaps, was that of Benjamin Franklin, of Boston, Philadelphia, London, and Paris. To D. H. Lawrence and some other critics he has seemed a sententious prig. His *Way to Wealth* (1758), and the aphorisms in general of his Poor Richard almanacs, have been classed with the rags-to-riches novelettes of Horatio Alger, and with the inspirational prose of Dale Carnegie's *How to Win Friends and Influence People*. Possibly Franklin's literary gifts have indeed been over-rated by some of his admirers. His maxims were as often as not – as he himself never denied – borrowed from other sources. The famous prose of his unfinished *Autobiography*,[1] while plain and effective, and at times engagingly humorous, is not quite as phenomenal as some Americans have urged. Swift had been as plain and as satirical, on occasion. Franklin, in fact, never posed as a man of letters; he was too busy with other things, and it is in the astonishing range of his activities that Franklin made so great a contribution to America's cultural prestige. Printer, editor, inventor, scientist, diplomatist: whatever the part, he seemed at ease in it. In Britain, where he spent some years as a colonial agent, Burke, Lord Kames, Hume, and Adam Smith had been among his friends. In Paris, where he was the first American minister, Franklin became enormously popular. Plainly garbed, genial, and unaffected, he was taken as the living embodiment of the idea of the natural man: the proof that the world's salvation might come from the backwoods (and this though Franklin spent nearly all his life in large towns).

1. Begun in 1771; not published as a complete work (in English) until 1867.

No doubt it amused him to conceal his 'deep worldly wisdom and polished Italian tact ... under an air of Arcadian unaffectedness' – as Melville wrote of him,[1] or rather of the likeness between him and the patriarch Jacob. In this respect Franklin can be regarded as an early example of the American humorist. For there is an American 'joke' (to which Henry James referred – see p. 48) that derives its wry flavour from the strange blend of sophistication and savagery in American life. The European is more fascinated by America's primitive aspects, and if the American mythology contains a good deal of toughness and roughness, it may well be argued that it was put there by Europeans.[2] The American joke is to play up to the European (and Eastern) legend of the West. So the frontiersman spoke of himself as 'this chile' in deference to Rousseau's vision of the child of nature; so Buffalo Bill wrote dime novels about his own adventures; so, probably, Chicago gangsters enjoyed gangster movies; and so, to return to Franklin, this 'didactically waggish' man blandly assured English readers that it was grand to see the whales leap like salmon up the falls of Niagara. Crèvecoeur's *Letters from an American Farmer* (1782), especially in its French version, further encouraged the illusion that the average American was an educated husbandman. Thomas Jefferson, when he appeared in Paris as Franklin's successor in 1784, reinforced the favourable impression made by Franklin.

The Philadelphia Quaker and botanist William Bartram

1. In *Israel Potter* (1855).
2. When her American friend Charles Eliot Norton sent some photographs of native scenery to the English novelist Mrs Gaskell, she told him disappointedly that she 'thought America would have been odder and more original; the underwood and tangle is just like England'. She had got a more satisfactory idea from a painting done by another Englishwoman, 'in some wild luxuriant terrific part of Virginia? in a gorge full of rich rank tropical vegetation, – her husband keeping watch over her with loaded pistols because of the alligators infesting the stream. – Well! that picture did look like my idea of America' (1860). *Letters of Mrs Gaskell and Charles Eliot Norton* (Oxford, 1932), 51–2. In France, the adoption of the word *Apache* (the name of an Indian tribe) to describe the hooligans of Paris is another example of the European version of America.

(1739–1823) likewise wrote of America as Europeans liked
to hear of it. 'Impelled by a restless spirit of curiosity, in pursuit of new productions of nature', and in order to look at
Indian customs, Bartram made a lengthy journey into the
South. His account was published in 1791, with the full title
of *Travels through North and South Carolina, Georgia, East and
West Florida, the Cherokee Country, the Extensive Territories of the
Muscogulges, or Creek Confederacy, and the Country of the Chac-
taws.* The book conjures up a strange remote world, lush in
vegetation and teeming with wild life. The human inhabitants of this world converse in the tones of Rousseau: one
settler

> who was reclining on a bear-skin, spread under the shade of a Live
> Oak, smoking his pipe, rose and saluted me: 'Welcome, stranger;
> *I am indulging in the rational dictates of nature,* taking a little rest, hav-
> ing just come in from the chace and fishing.' (Italics mine.)

Such passages alternate enchantingly with lists of plants and
precise descriptions of new species. Unlike many travellers,
Bartram makes light of personal discomforts; after a sleep-
less night spent alone in a swamp, surrounded by terrifying
reptiles and tormented by mosquitoes, he greets the dawn
with a brisk exclamation of relief, and pursues his investiga-
tions with the utmost good humour. How prosaic, and yet
how magical, are such paragraphs as this:

> ... we should be ready to conclude all to be a visionary scene, were
> it not for the sparkling ponds and lakes, which ... gleam through
> the open forests, before us and on every side ... And at last the
> imagination remains flattered and dubious, by their uniformity,
> being mostly circular or elliptical, and almost surrounded with ex-
> pansive green meadows; and always a picturesque dark grove of
> live oak, magnolia, gordonia, and the fragrant orange, encircling
> a rocky shaded grotto of transparent water, on some border of the
> pond or lake; which, without the aid of any poetic fable, one
> might naturally suppose to be the sacred abode or temporary resi-
> dence of the guardian spirit; but it is actually the possession and
> retreat of a thundering absolute crocodile.

The American poet Marianne Moore has written of the need
for poets to be 'literalists of the imagination' and 'to present

for inspection imaginary gardens with real toads in them'. These much-quoted words can apply also to the sonorous prose of Bartram. The poetry of the wilderness: here was a theme for the American writer, one might have thought. Certainly it captivated the European writer; Wordsworth, Coleridge, Southey, Campbell, and Chateaubriand all read and made use of Bartram's book. Campbell placed the characters of his poem *Gertrude of Wyoming* (1809) in an idyllic valley of Pennsylvania, Chateaubriand's three romances of America are situated farther south, one of them among the 'Muscogulges'; in both cases the wilderness has cast its spell.

Another view of the American frontier region was presented by Hugh Henry Brackenridge (1748–1816) in his lively novel *Modern Chivalry* (published serially, 1792–1815). There is little romance in Brackenridge; this is the frontier that William Byrd called Lubberland, in which the child of nature shows singularly little awareness of the charms of his existence, and reserves his enthusiasm for horse-trading and illicit whisky. Bartram's attitude emerges again in James Fenimore Cooper, Brackenridge's in Mark Twain. However, in the 1790s a patriotic American glancing at his country's literature could be content merely to note the variety of native authors. There was for example Charles Brockden Brown (1771–1810), with his brief spate of Gothic novels, each set in America. *Wieland* (1798), *Arthur Mervyn* and *Ormond* and *Edgar Huntly* (all published in 1799, when Brown was only twenty-eight), were good enough to impress Keats and other British writers. Brown avoided some of the absurdities of Gothic fantasy. He was more interested in states of mind than in 'puerile superstitions, Gothic castles, and chimeras'. One character is a ventriloquist, another a sleepwalker. Ormond believes himself licensed to act as he pleases, and attempts to rape the heroine. Though Brown was influenced by English fictional examples, his themes and settings were American. Though his stories were melodramatic and spasmodic, jerking from coincidence to coincidence, they were obviously the work of an original intelligence. As for the theatre, as early as 1787 Royall Tyler composed a comedy called *The Contrast*. 'Exult each patriot heart,' he cries in the prologue –

to-night is shown
A piece which we may fairly call our own.

He had reasonable cause for pride; despite its odour of Sheridan, the play is competent and amusing, and a present-day repertory company that is tired of Lady Teazle could do worse than stage *The Contrast* instead.

Such were some of the causes for congratulation that our patriotic American might recognize, at the close of the eighteenth century. But there were causes for alarm, or at any rate a certain disquiet, although these were not all immediately apparent. All branched from the central fact that political independence did not bring cultural independence, and that the former led to a clamour for the latter. There is a story that one of the more rabidly nationalistic of the delegates to the Continental Congress moved that henceforward the United States should cease to employ the English language; and that another delegate, Roger Sherman, proposed as an amendment that the United States should keep the English tongue, and force the English themselves to learn Greek. In the reaction that followed the American Revolution, the controversy between Federalists and Jeffersonians had its parallel in literature. And while politically the Jeffersonians won power, in letters the conservative Federalist viewpoint seemed far more ably presented. Tom Paine, once the hero of the colonies, was refused burial in consecrated ground when he died in America in 1809, after years of hostility or neglect. Radicalism, cultural or political, was repellent to Roger Sherman's fellow-citizens of Connecticut, the Hartford Wits. These – John Trumbull, Joel Barlow,[1] Timothy Dwight, and others – made the first protest of many in America against the swamping and debauching of standards by the freethinking, ignorant masses. Like the pro-

1. Though Barlow, after going to Europe in 1788, completely changed his political opinions.

testers of subsequent generations, they laid themselves open
to the charge of snobbery; the role of the conservative in the
United States has been an uneasy one, perhaps almost in-
trinsically untenable, however correct theoretically – like
that, so to speak, of a creditor in a mob of debtors. It is a
pity, because the intelligent conservative has had much to
offer America. However, the Hartford Wits were more self-
assured than their conservative successors; Timothy Dwight
(the grandson of Jonathan Edwards) did not consider himself un-American when he wrote in 1798 that

> Wherever wealth, politeness, talents, and office, lend their aid to
> the inherent efficacy of virtue, its influence is proportionately
> greater.

On the contrary, he was trying to save America's soul. Nor
did Joseph Dennie (1768–1812), editor of the Philadelphia
Port Folio (one of the best of America's early literary magazines), feel diffident when he accused Franklin of being

> the founder of that Grubstreet sect, who have professedly attempted
> to degrade literature to the level of vulgar capacities, and debase
> the polished and current language of books, by the vile alloy of pro-
> vincial idioms, and colloquial barbarism, the shame of grammar,
> and akin to any language, rather than English.

The laugh, one may think, is on Dennie. But not altogether.
At the time he wrote, the laugh was on the delegate who had
determined to abandon English. And it cannot be said, without falsifying history in the cause of clarity, that Franklin's
prose sustained, let alone created, an American style of plain
writing. Such a style did emerge, as we shall see; yet it has
never entirely ousted the polite style in America. If the latter
is less 'native' it surely cannot be denounced as 'alien'.

The problem of language was only part of the larger
American dilemma. The internal controversy between what
might be called stateroom and steerage styles could not be
carried on in isolation; as these categories imply, the dilemma was transatlantic in its wider terms. Dwight and Dennie
were quite as proud of America as were their opponents, but
the arguments of either side appeared to lead to equally gal-
ling conclusions. If America endeavoured to emulate British

and European patterns of literature, the results were inevitably provincial. If, on the other hand, she found and
followed a native line, the results were bound to be ungainly.
In general, the British (who naturally took a closer interest
than the Continental nations) were to prefer native American efforts; but in the early years of American independence
the British showered ridicule impartially on the majority of
American literary ventures. There was little consolation for
Americans in the assurance that British reviewers were notoriously savage to even their own authors: offence, when
proffered to the Americans, was taken and brooded over.
When an American wrote that

To study with a view to becoming an author by profession in America, is a prospect of no less flattering promise than to publish among
the Eskimos an essay on delicacy, or to found an academy of
sciences in Lapland,

his observation was accepted as that of a temporarily jaded
writer. It was another thing, however, when Sydney Smith
wrote (in the *Edinburgh Review*, December 1818):

Literature the Americans have none – no native literature, we
mean. It is all imported. They had a Franklin, indeed; and may
afford to live for half a century on his fame. There is, or was, a Mr
Dwight, who wrote some poems; and his baptismal name was Timothy. There is also a small account of Virginia by Jefferson; and
an epic by Joel Barlow[1] – and some pieces of pleasantry by Mr
Irving. But why should the Americans write books, when a six
weeks' passage brings them in our own tongue, our sense, science
and genius, in bales and hogsheads?

Such queries have echoed down the corridors, and if Sydney
Smith did not stay for an answer, each generation of American writers has felt impelled to give him one. Emerson's celebrated *American Scholar* address of 1837, in which he proclaimed that 'we have listened too long to the courtly muses
of Europe', was described by Oliver Wendell Holmes – in an
equally celebrated phrase – as America's Intellectual De-

1. *The Columbiad* (1807). Sydney Smith could have added that this epic
poem, though in heroic couplets, owes much to Milton; and that Barlow
got his facts from the *History of America* by the Scottish historian Robert-
son, who had never set foot in Barlow's country.

claration of Independence. It would be truer to say that
Emerson's was merely the most eloquent of a long line of
similar declarations. Thus, the talented Revolutionary poet
Philip Freneau had asked despairingly

> Can we never be thought
> To have learning or grace
> Unless it be brought
> From that damnable place?

Namely, Britain. In his 'Remarks on National Literature'
(1830), William Ellery Channing had maintained that 'it
were better to have no literature, than form ourselves unresist-
ingly on a foreign one'. And, a little later, Edgar Allan Poe
had announced that 'we have at length arrived at that epoch
when our literature may and must stand on its own merits or
fall through its own defects. We have snapped asunder the
leading-strings of our British Grandmamma.' These are only
a few samples of the genre; a dozen others, from a dozen
other authors before and after Emerson, could easily be
quoted.

Unfortunately, though – leaving aside patriotic sentiment
and British invective – American literature of the period was,
plainly, derivative and inferior. Noah Webster informed his
compatriots in 1789 that 'Great Britain ... should no longer
be *our* standard, for the taste of her writers is already corrupted and her language on the decline'. How simple it would
all have been if Webster had been right! But, a generation
later, there was no sign that European corruption had im-
paired European literature. Was it possible even that literature, like the pearl, was a secretion caused by impurities in
the body politic? If so, Whitman and others who considered
it brushed aside the query with the assertion that America
would create a new *kind* of literature. 'An American,' said
the *New Monthly Magazine* (London, 1821), unlike the rest of
mankind,

appeals to prophecy, and with Malthus in one hand and a map of
the back country in the other, he boldly defies us to a comparison
with America as she is to be, and chuckles in delight over the splendours the geometrical ratio is to shed over her story.

For the meantime, American writers had to face the facts of the present. They had to employ the English language in face of the jealous guardianship of Britain. ('To charge us with affecting a new language is a calumny', complained Edward Everett in the *North American Review*, in 1821.) They had to compete with English and Continental authors whose quality was as high as their reputation. Everett in the same article protested that

It is well known that our children's books are English; ... that our stage is supplied from England; that Byron, Campbell, Southey, Scott, are as familiar to us as to their own countrymen; that we receive the first sheets of the new novel before the last one is thrown off at Edinburgh; that we reprint every English work of merit before it is dry from the English; and that the English version of the Scriptures is the great source whence the majority of Americans imbibe their English language. How, then, is it possible that we should not speak good English?

There is something a trifle pathetic about his final query. But, not to debate the logic of his argument, his previous analysis was accurate enough. The native American author had little chance of selling as well as his English contemporaries. The disparity was made all the worse by the absence of an adequate international copyright. Until the Chace Act of 1891, the works of British and Continental authors could be ruthlessly pirated in America. The Philadelphia publisher Mathew Carey hired fast sailing-boats to meet incoming ships when new *Waverley* novels were expected, so that he could rush out an edition a few hours in advance of his rivals. Scott, and later Dickens, flooded the country in pirated editions – an iniquity against which Dickens thundered in vain, on his first visit (in 1842) to the United States. American authors were pirated in Europe to a lesser extent; in England, for example, they could secure copyright by residence and prior publication: an added inducement to Americans to cater for British tastes and British publishers. Their own publishers were naturally, if deplorably, reluctant to take their works and pay royalties when it was so easy to snatch up European products free from royalty.

Again, what were American authors to write *about*? Aiming despite themselves at Old World approval, they hesitated to handle native themes. Stephen Vincent Benét (1898–1943), speaking of the settlement of America, said:

> They tried to fit you with an English song
> And clip your speech into the English tale,
> But even from the first, the words went wrong,
> The catbird pecked away the nightingale.

True: yet it took a long time before the American poet could get away with a catbird instead of a nightingale, in serious verse. One of the first American poems to be widely praised in Europe, written by William Cullen Bryant (1794–1878) in 1815, was addressed to that unexceptionable and ubiquitous bird, the water-fowl. In another poem Benét wrote:

> I have fallen in love with American names,
> The sharp names that never get fat,
> The snakeskin titles of mining-claims,
> The plumed war-bonnet of Medicine Hat,
> Tucson and Deadwood and Lost Mule Flat.

We accept his statement; time has grown over even the clumsiest nomenclatures, and perhaps their very clumsiness adds an element of heartbreak to *Chancellorsville* or *Gettysburg*. But in 1800 ridicule overwhelmed the place-names of America –

> Ye plains where sweet Big-muddy rolls along,
> And Tea-pot, one day to be famed in song …

No wonder that run-of-the-mill American writing tended, like Bryant's, to be curiously placeless, faceless, and florid.

Should the American author accept his lot, as pictured by Scottish reviewers? Should he, like the American painter or sculptor, make his way to Europe? Was there really nothing to write about at home? Were there really no such things as 'native themes': was, for instance, the charm of the wilderness not an American theme but the projection of a European idea on to an American backcloth? *Blackwood's* roundly declared in 1819:

There is nothing to awaken fancy in that land of dull realities. No objects carry the mind back to contemplation of a remote antiquity. No mouldering ruins excite interest in the history of the past. No memorials commemorative of noble deeds arouse enthusiasm and reverence. No traditions, legends, fables, afford material for poetry and romance.

And this was a not uncommon opinion in America also. Hawthorne voiced it in the preface to his *Marble Faun*, and Henry James did the same in the well-known passage from his biography of Hawthorne (1879) that begins: 'one might enumerate the items of high civilization, as it exists in other countries, which are absent from the texture of American life, until it should become a wonder to know what was left.'[1] The passage ends:

The natural remark, in the almost lurid light of such an indictment, would be that if these things are left out, everything is left out. The American knows that a good deal remains; what it is that remains — that is his secret, his joke, as one may say.

Such were some of the perplexities of American literature in the first years of the new republic. Against them must be set the great American faith in betterment that warmed writer and land speculator alike. Give us time, pleaded the writer, a little disappointed that things were not going more smoothly, yet never doubting that time was on his side: not prevaricating, but rather prognosticating. As time went on, however, the situation was to get both better and worse. Better, in that American writing gained in volume and quality; worse, in that complete cultural independence still lay over the horizon. Walt Whitman inciting the American eagle to soar was participating in a national ritual of considerable importance to the native man of letters. As Henry James wrote in a young man's letter of 1872, 'it's a complex fate, being an American, and one of the responsibilities it entails is fighting against a superstitious valuation of Europe'. *Fighting* is a strong word; so is *responsibility*. The American eagle, bald-

1. In the celebrated letter 'What is an American?', Crèvecoeur, a century earlier, compiled a very similar list: 'Here are no aristocratical families, no courts, no kings, no bishops, no ecclesiastical dominion, no invisible power giving to a few a very visible one; no great manufacturers employing thousands, no great refinements of luxury.' But how different his conclusions, drawn in the halcyon days of 1782, are from those of James: 'We are the most perfect society now existing in the world'.

headed through too many platform appearances, or a superstitious valuation of Europe – which? The major American writers have been able to skirt the dilemma, yet none has been unaffected by it. And perhaps none has perceived as clearly as did the mature James that it is essentially a false dilemma: that America and Europe are wedded forever in a church that does not allow divorce. This was to be one of posterity's surprises that lay in store for the new-old country.

CHAPTER THREE

INDEPENDENCE – THE FIRST FRUITS

Irving, Cooper, Poe

WASHINGTON IRVING (1783–1859)

b. New York, youngest son of Presbyterian merchant. Studied law, but more attracted by literary interests of brothers William and Peter. Contributed 'Letters of Jonathan Oldstyle, Gent.' to newspaper edited by latter. Travelled in Europe for health, 1804–6. With brothers and brother-in-law J. K. Paulding brought out *Salmagundi* essays, Federalist in outlook. First important success, *History of New York* (1809), purporting to be the work of one Diedrich Knickerbocker. Went to Europe 1815, to assist in family hardware business at Liverpool. Remained in Europe seventeen years, travelling extensively. Gained recognition with *The Sketch Book of Geoffrey Crayon, Gent.* (1819–20), and further popularity with such works as *Bracebridge Hall* (1822); *Tales of a Traveller* (1824); biography of Columbus (1828); *A Chronicle of the Conquest of Granada* (1829); *The Alhambra* (1832). In the United States 1832–42; wrote on American topics, including *A Tour on the Prairie* (1832). In Europe again 1842–6, at first as minister to Spain. On return home, devoted remaining years to constant writing (lives of Goldsmith, Mahomet, etc.), culminating in massive biography of Washington.

JAMES FENIMORE COOPER (1789–1851)

Son of prosperous landholder who founded Cooperstown, on Lake Otsego in New York state. *ed.* Yale, but left without graduating. Went to sea, 1806–11; retired from navy on marriage into the distinguished De Lancey family, and lived as country gentleman. Began to write, with no serious professional intentions, at age of thirty: first novel, *Precaution* (1820), followed by many other novels, histories, etc. Lived in Europe 1826–33. Later, at Cooperstown, involved in numerous libel actions, almost all successful, against hostile Press. His popularity declined, partly as a result of notoriety thus gained, but continued to write until his death. Best-known works: *The Spy* (1821), *The Pioneers* (1823), *The Pilot* (1823), *The Last of the Mohicans* (1826), *The Prairie* (1827), *The Red Rover* (1827), *Gleanings in Europe* (1837–8), *Homeward Bound* and *Home as Found* (1838)—published in England as *Eve Effingham*, *The Pathfinder* (1840), *The Deerslayer* (1841), *Satanstoe* (1845).

EDGAR ALLAN POE (1809–49)

b. Boston, son of itinerant actors. Left an orphan, 1811; taken into home of well-to-do merchant, John Allan of Richmond, Virginia. Taken by Allans to England; attended school there 1815–20. Quarrelled with Allan after return to Richmond; never fully reconciled, and ignored in Allan's will when latter died (1834). Brief periods at University of Virginia, in U.S. Army (where rose to rank of sergeant-major), and as cadet at West Point. After deliberately incurring dismissal from West Point, supported himself as man of letters, in Baltimore, Richmond, New York, and Philadelphia. Connected with various periodicals, including the *Southern Literary Messenger*. 1836, married his thirteen-year-old cousin Virginia Clemm, who died of tuberculosis (1846). After her death, became more and more unbalanced. *d*. Baltimore, where found lying delirious in a gutter. Published three volumes of poetry: *Tamerlane* (1827), *Al Aaraaf* (1829), *Poems* (1831). Thereafter, most of his work – poems, stories, and critical articles – first appeared in periodicals. Stories first collected in *Tales of the Grotesque and Arabesque* (1840); others appeared in *Tales* (1845). Other writings included metaphysical study *Eureka: A Prose Poem* (1848), and *The Narrative of Arthur Gordon Pym* (1838).

INDEPENDENCE - THE FIRST FRUITS

—

WASHINGTON IRVING

WASHINGTON IRVING was – closely followed by James Fenimore Cooper – the first man of letters from the United States to win an international reputation. The reputation of the third author discussed in this chapter, Edgar Allan Poe, could likewise be described as international, though during his own life-time his fame was far surpassed by that of Irving and Cooper. The case of Poe is somewhat special, yet he, like the others, reveals some of the complexities of being an American.

As for Irving:

He is not a learned man, and can write but meagrely and at second-hand on learned subjects; but he has a quick convertible talent that seizes lightly on the points of knowledge necessary to the illustration of a theme ... his gifted pen transmutes every thing into gold, and his own genial nature reflects its sunshine through his pages.

This is Irving's appraisal of Oliver Goldsmith, but it could well have been written of Irving himself by his contemporaries, in Europe and at home, who so often called him the 'American Goldsmith' or spoke of him as a latter-day Addison or Steele. Most of those who met Irving liked him; Scott, Moore, and a score of others testified to his personal charm, and agreed that his literary style matched his personality. As with Charles Lamb, something of his appeal was bound to evaporate when he died. When he was alive, not everyone rated him highly. To one satirist he was 'Dame Irving'; another writer defined him as 'Addison and water'; Maria Edgeworth said of his *Bracebridge Hall* that 'the workmanship surpasses the work. There is too much care and cost bestowed on petty objects.' The present-day reader is more likely to agree with Irving's critics than with his admirers. But it is worth our while to examine why he had such stature in his own day.

Poe offers a clue, in observing that

Irving is much overrated, and a nice distinction might be drawn
between his just and his surreptitious and adventitious reputation –
between what is due to the pioneer solely, and what to the writer.

It is the word *pioneer* that arrests us. What has a man like
Irving, with 'his tame propriety and faultlessness of style'
(to quote Poe again), to do with pioneering? His prose, while
less archaic than some critics have maintained, has no new
note in it: though this statement will be qualified later. Why,
then, *pioneer*? We can begin to answer the question with a
sentence by Irving's biographer, Stanley T. Williams: 'Here
was an American with a feather in his hand instead of on his
head:'[1] a product of the New World who, emerging from a
family in trade and from the callow literary circles of New
York, managed to entertain the entire civilized world: an
author who could please both his own countrymen and the
English – both exacting in their different ways. How he did
so can be studied in the volume that brought him his re-
nown.

The Sketch Book of Geoffrey Crayon, Gent., including 'The
Author's Account of Himself' and 'L'Envoy', consists of
thirty-four sketches. The great majority depict English scenes:
'The Inn Kitchen', 'Westminster Abbey', and so on. Cott-
ages are thatched, churches ivied, forelocks tugged. Two
essays only might be thought 'controversial'. One was a
portrait of 'John Bull', the other about 'English Writers on
America'. John Bull has his weaknesses, says Irving: 'he will
contrive to argue every fault into a merit, and will frankly
convict himself of being the honestest fellow in existence'. But
Irving's amiable varnish shines over the subject; John Bull is,
after all, we learn, 'a sterling-hearted old blade'. As for the
English writers (and their reviewers) whose accounts of America had stirred up so much trouble, Irving managed to make
his reprimands acceptable by suggesting that instead of the
gentlemen of England, who are such fair-minded observers,
'it has been left to the broken-down tradesman, the scheming

1. *The Life of Washington Irving* (2 v., New York, 1935), i. 211.

adventurer, the wandering mechanic, the Manchester and Birmingham agent, to be her oracles respecting America'. It is not a very good essay, but it is a quite astonishingly tactful one.

Of the few pieces in the *Sketch Book* that deal with America, one on 'Traits of Indian Character' is a conventional glimpse of the noble savage, who after the day's hunting 'wraps himself in the spoils of the bear, the panther, and the buffalo, and sleeps among the thunders of the cataract'. Another piece, the most famous and enduring in the whole book, tells the tale of Rip Van Winkle, the Dutchman bewitched in the Catskill Mountains, who after a twenty-year sleep makes his way back to his native village: an old man whose former cronies are all dead. Thanks to Irving, the New World was now beginning to pass on its myths and legends to the Old. Or so his contemporaries believed. In fact, as Irving not too loudly hinted, he had borrowed the story from a German tale, translating some of its paragraphs so literally as to lay himself under the charge of plagiarism. And though he preserved the original, Spanish setting in some of his other and later stories, similar objections were made: he had, it was said, simply moved his material from one language to another, and added some incidental ornament.

But the charge did not much harm Irving's place in popular esteem. How did he win his place, and merit the description of *pioneer*? The first, and indispensable step, was to go to Europe. The second was to secure approval by European readers, without forfeiting his right to be considered an American. This was an extremely difficult problem, to which Irving came as near to a solution as was possible. He also indicated for subsequent Americans the necessary approaches to the problem. To begin with, style: it must be above all refined. For all practical purposes, Irving saw, America had no style of its own. British models must therefore be followed. Irving surpassed his models by evolving a fluent yet dignified prose that made a successful passage from the eighteenth to the nineteenth century. Next, subject: if he had merely given himself over to describing Europe, his countrymen would have rejected him. As it was, they reminded him continually during his seventeen-year absence of his obligation to come back home again. However, he did more than merely describe the contemporary scene. He dug into folklore. Others were at work in the same vein; Scott, his friend and hero, had put the balladry of the Border to good use, and Scott perhaps encouraged him to study German folk-literature. From German stories he passed to those of Spain. They were rich sources, and Irving explored them eagerly. His own land was deficient in such material; therefore he, like Ticknor and Everett and Longfellow, was driven to seek it in Europe. As later Americans searched diligently for old paintings and manuscripts, these pioneers hunted the neglected folk-past of the Old World.

Also, Irving lacked a creative gift; he needed plots ready-made. Temperamentally, like Hawthorne, he preferred a plot out of the past; though, more superficial than Hawthorne, he sought for something colourful, whimsical, a little melancholy: something that hinted, not too sternly, at change and alteration. If America was born in broad daylight, Irving brought it an imported twilight, to the best of his ability. In *Bracebridge Hall*, to take one example, he concocted an American version ('The Storm-Ship') of the *Flying Dutchman* legend. It would be wrong to imply that Irving had any clear notion of inventing, single-handed, a set of American traditions. Rather, he tried to please simultaneously audiences on either side of the Atlantic. He was born just early enough to escape the oppressive claims of nationality, and he was too equable to fret over the demands that were laid on him. When American material was of value, he used it. He journeyed out into the Indian country, and wrote *A Tour on the Prairie* about his trip; he became interested in the development of the American West, and compiled a competent account in *Astoria* (1836). But he was no frontiersman, and was too much the cosmopolitan to become one; while his enemies suggested that *Astoria* was proof of nothing but Irving's pleasure in the patronage of the millionaire fur-trader John Jacob Astor.

In fact, as Emerson saw, Irving and his American contemporaries were 'picturesque': a deeper power eluded them. His pioneering was a matter of setting the example for others to follow. He suggested lines of approach: he translated and adapted. He soothed native pride by becoming a great author. At the end, grinding out the enormous biography of George Washington, he was still a capable craftsman; however pedestrian the treatment, there was always the easy rhythm of the sentences, and the mild occasional relief of a pleasantry. Though his glory was beginning to tarnish, he had at any rate held out longer than most of his colleagues, men like Bryant and Fitz-Greene Halleck, who had either gone silent or turned into bores.

But did Irving set the wrong example? Yes, if one visualizes the relationship between America and Europe as a cops-and-robbers (or rather, snobs-and-patriots) melodrama, in which the hero (in terms of literature) is the man who stays at home and nurtures his American vocabulary, like a primeval Mencken, while the villain slips off to Europe to acquire an English accent and a mastery of French menus. We may allow that Irving was something of a snob: or, as he put it, a *Gent*. One of his favourite targets was the 'pale and bilious' taproom agitator, scheming to overturn John Bull's household, or Peter Stuyvesant's New York. Nor could he applaud the equivalent in literature. He confided to his diary in 1817:

There is an endeavour among some of the writers of the day (who fortunately have not any great weight) to introduce into poetry all the common colloquial phrases and vulgar idioms – In their rage for simplicity they would be coarse and commonplace. Now the Language of poetry cannot be too pure and choice.

Granted that he is speaking of poetry, not of prose, does not this exhibit place him among the villains?

Surely not, if we admit another and more substantial piece of contrary evidence, the *History of New York*, written eight years earlier. It is an uneven book, half fact, half fancy; yet it has a cocksure, irreverent quality that makes everything Irving wrote afterwards seem by comparison sadly

insipid. How was America peopled? Grotius, says Knicker-
bocker-Irving, supposed it was 'by a strolling company of
Norwegians', while 'Juffredus Petri' ascribed it 'to a skat-
ing party from Friesland'. The tone is that of Mark Twain;
and so is this:

And now the rosy blush of morn began to mantle in the east,
and soon the rising sun, emerging from amidst golden and purple
clouds, shed his blithesome rays on the tin weathercocks of Com-
munipaw.

True, there are only isolated paragraphs that have just the
Twain flavour; yet it is there, in 1809, sixty years before the
publication of *Innocents Abroad*, in which 'native' American
prose made a triumphant appearance. It is true also that
Knickerbocker's burlesque saga is a young man's squib. But
added years and personal worries are not enough to explain
why Irving abandoned Knickerbocker and Salmagundi for
Geoffrey Crayon, and in fresh editions of the *History* steadily
pruned away what he now held to be its vulgarities. Nor is
residence in Europe the explanation: that is to confuse cause
and effect. The reason is simple: 1809 was not 1869. American prose could not survive until conditions were more favourable. More recent writers than Irving have been unable
to accept the idea that a serious style could grow out of a
burlesque intention. Is Irving so much to blame in judging
his *History* a dead end, when it was only a false start?

JAMES FENIMORE COOPER

FOR Cooper, to be an American was indeed a complex fate.
Unlike Irving – for whom, incidentally, he had no great regard – Cooper was by birth and still more by marriage a
member of the American landed gentry. Staunchly patriotic,
proud of his three years as a midshipman in the United
States navy, he felt it to be his mission while in Europe to defend his countrymen from insult, and was hurt that they
seemed so ungrateful for such efforts on their behalf as *Notions of the Americans* (1828) and *Letter to General Lafayette*
(1831). Yet, while he condemned hereditary aristocracy,

much preferred republicanism to monarchy, and rejoiced in his nation's warlike prowess, he held firmly to his notion of gentlemanliness, based upon property, good birth, and upbringing, and paternal sway over the neighbouring community. Jefferson, an American 'gentleman' of the previous generation, had warned the young American against the lures of Europe:

If he goes to England, he learns drinking, horse racing, and boxing. These are the peculiarities of English education. The following circumstances are common to education in that, and the other countries of Europe. He acquires a fondness for European luxury and dissipation, and a contempt for the simplicity of his own country; he is fascinated with the privileges of the European aristocrats, and sees, with abhorrence, the lovely equality which the poor enjoy with the rich, in his own country; ... he recollects the voluptuary dress and arts of the European women, and pities and despises the chaste affections and simplicity of his own country. ... It appears to me, then, that an American, coming to Europe for education, loses in his knowledge, in his morals, in his health, in his habits, and in his happiness.[1]

Cooper had no hesitation in taking his children to France to be educated. But though he had remained, as he thought, sturdily American, he found it hard to conceal his distaste for American life when he returned. *Home as Found* is a caustic commentary on the failings of his native land: its mobrule, its abusive and irresponsible Press, its deference to Europe. Thus, a New York literary gathering lionizes a bluff seacaptain, under the mistaken impression that he is a famous British author:

'Ah! the English are truly a great nation! How delightfully he smokes!'

'I think he is much the most interesting man we have had out here,' observed Miss Annual, 'since the last bust of Scott!'

This observation had a particular edge for Cooper, who was so often told that he was the American Walter Scott. The compliment irritated him, for it assigned him a secondary status: no one would have dreamed, he knew, of speaking of

1. Letter to J. Bannister, Jr, 15 October 1785.

Scott as the English Cooper. Pulled between two worlds, how could he cut the English 'leading-strings' to which he once referred and emerge as America's first great novelist? How was he to create a world large and various enough to form a novelist's territory: how write of American society when there was none?

The answer must inevitably refer to Europe. Cooper's first book, *Precaution*, was a deliberate attempt to improve on an imported novel that he had been reading aloud to his wife, and its setting was in English society. For his second novel, *The Spy*, he prefaced chapters with quotations from Campbell's *Gertrude of Wyoming*. His third book, *The Pilot*, was meant to demonstrate that a better novel could be written about the sea than Scott's *The Pirate*; and in his introduction Cooper notes wryly that he has still other competition to face: the author 'will probably be told, that Smollett has done all this before him, and in a much better manner'.

Part of the solution to his problems lay in the American past. *The Spy* deals with the period of the American Revolution when the British occupied the port of New York, while Washington's men held the surrounding district. It is a satisfactory if not a great novel because it covers exciting events, and because it provides Cooper with a suitable social framework. In other words, most of the British and American characters are gentlefolk; indeed, they have mixed socially before the fighting began. Cooper is thus able to stand on neutral ground, though making it plain that his patriotic sympathies are with the Americans. Both sides have their heroes, or at any rate their gentlemen. The result pleased British readers; it also pleased Americans, who were prepared to accept in an historical novel social pretensions which, by the era of Andrew Jackson, had become theoretically obnoxious. For somewhat similar reasons Cooper scored another success with *The Pilot*, in which John Paul Jones fights a complicated little sea-and-land war along the Yorkshire coast. Here, again, are British as well as American worthies.

The Pilot offered another solution to Cooper. He had been

told, when venturing to criticize the evident lack of nautical experience revealed in Scott's *The Pirate*, that a novel which described life at sea in detail would bewilder the general reader. In disproving this contention he not only took for his own another field of adventure: he had a ready-made social order in miniature presented to him. For life on board ship, with all its customs and hierarchies, was a complete enough world, save that it lacked women. Though the details of seamanship might confuse the reader, shipboard life was in other respects sharply defined: as Melville was to insist, more forcibly than Cooper, it represented the whole human predicament:

Oh, shipmates and world-mates, all round! we the people suffer many abuses. Our gun-deck is full of complaints. In vain from Lieutenants do we appeal to the Captain; in vain – while on board our world-frigate – to the indefinite Navy Commissioners, so far out of sight aloft. Yet the worst of our evils we blindly inflict upon ourselves; our officers can not remove them, even if they would.[1]

If Cooper never reached this intensity of meaning, he, too, benefited as a novelist from the rigid differentiations of existence at sea. How blurred, by contrast, were the orders of society in Cooperstown; how unreal, in Melville's *Pierre*[2]. Cooper's sea-stories are sometimes weakened by the necessity for a heroine; for beautiful young heiresses, with names like Alinda de Barberie, are not often found on ships: they can be introduced on board only by dint of strenuous plot manipulation by the author. But if these improbable creatures appear in several of Cooper's sea-stories, they fail to spoil the storms and gunfights which he describes with a masterly relish.

With *The Pioneers*, published in the same year as *The Pilot*, Cooper found his other and better-known theme: the American wilderness. Within this, he had another social code, that of the Indians, to whom – despite their savagery – he attributes many of the traits of the white gentleman. He had no first-hand experience of Indian tribal life, though Otsego lake, where he lived and which he chose as the setting for *The Deerslayer*, had not long previously been Indian country. Some of his ideas about Indian behaviour (including his prejudice against the Iroquois) were adopted from the writings of the Moravian missionary Heckewelder. But his Indians, however idealized his account of them, were fascinating figures, to Europeans perhaps even more than to Americans. Equally fascinating was the landscape of the wilderness: the forests and lakes that were also to be the setting for Francis Parkman's great histories, and (in *The Prairie*) the open country across the Mississippi. The dynamic element was provided by the white man, intruding upon the Indian hunting-grounds, provoking wars, restless and even villainous, yet certain to conquer finally. Returning to Otsego after a long absence, Cooper noted in a letter that the encircling woods had been a good deal 'lacerated'. The word vividly expresses the process of white settlement. Even in the novels in which the Indians are holding their own, their future is heavy with foreboding. Sophistication wars with simplicity, with only one possible conclusion. Nor is it merely a clash between Indian and white man: in *The Pioneers* the parties to the struggle are society as represented by Judge Temple, and the wilderness as represented by the old white hunter, Natty Bumppo (or Leatherstocking).

This was the first of the Leatherstocking tales, five in all, which map out the life of the hunter. Natty, brave, kindly, and illiterate, hovers between the two worlds of Indian and white man. Endowed with all the forest skills of the Redskin, the bosom friend of the Mohican chief Chingachgook ('pronounced Chicago, I think', Mark Twain commented), gently tolerant of Indian beliefs, he nevertheless retains some white characteristics: he would not think of marrying a girl of another colour, nor will he take scalps, though he accompanies Chingachgook on the war-path. In *The Last of the Mohicans*, Natty – under the name of Hawkeye – is shown at a slightly earlier stage, travelling with Chingachgook and his son Uncas, who are the only survivors of their tribe. A year later, Cooper published *The Prairie*, in which

Natty, now an old man, has left his forests, driven out by the advance of civilization, and is living as a trapper on the Western plains. The novel closes, quietly and poignantly, with the death of Natty.

However, he was too good a character to lose. Cooper revived him in *The Pathfinder* and *The Deerslayer*. In the latter, Natty is a young man on his first war-path, and in *The Pathfinder* he and Chingachgook are still in their prime. But since the story has been told in reverse, we know that Natty is fated to wander the forests in isolation, until their laceration forces him to move westwards. At the end of *The Deerslayer*, fifteen years after the main events of the story, Natty revisits Glimmerglass (= Otsego). Here lived a girl who was in love with him; now the only reminder of her is a shred of faded ribbon, and her lake-cabin – a rotted ruin. The touch of the past stirs a strange anguish, in the reader as in Natty Bumppo.

Time's victory over the wilderness makes a large and vivid theme, and there is still strength in Cooper's writing. His defects have been mercilessly indicated by Mark Twain (in the essay entitled 'Fenimore Cooper's Literary Offences'). There are any number of improbabilities: for example, the fantastic punctuality of forest meetings between Natty and Chingachgook. Rescues are invariably delayed until the moment of extreme peril. Dialogue is often awkward; characters usually lack depth. Cooper's attempts at humour are somewhat lame, and he holds up the narrative with interminable stilted conversations, while the bushes fill up with hostile Indians. As Twain complained, there is little sensuous immediacy in Cooper; scene and characters are *imagined* rather than *visualized*. Where a passage calls for direct description, the novelist is apt to come between the reader and the situation. Thus Natty, spying on enemy Indians around a campfire,

saw at a glance that many of the warriors were absent ... Rivenoak, however, was present, being seated in the foreground of *a picture that Salvator Rosa would have delighted to draw*,[1] his swarthy features illuminated. ...

1. Italics mine.

We see what Cooper means by his allusion; but it makes us lose touch with Natty, who has certainly never heard of Salvator Rosa. Yet if Cooper's style cannot be called supple, it is serviceable; one might apply to it Cooper's own words on the gait of one of his characters: 'There was nothing elastic in his tread, but he glided over the ground with enormous strides, and a body bent forward, without appearing to use exertion or know weariness.' And it never seriously clogs the movement of his stories; they possess the elementary and yet fundamental virtue of activity. Their end is never really in doubt, but one wants to know what will happen next; fortunes change with dizzy abruptness, like a game of snakes-and-ladders, till the firm final throw.

Why, then, of his many writings are only the Leatherstocking tales at all popular, and why are these nowadays found on the juvenile shelf? It can be noted, first, that some of his plots seem off-centre. In them we are provided with conventional heroes and heroines, but also with other characters of far greater interest, who steal most of the action. In *The Spy*, for instance, Harvey Birch is never adequately linked with the other characters; and in *The Prairie*, the hero and heroine are almost redundant. We come back to the word 'society', with all its implications for Cooper as both American novelist and American gentleman. Cooper cannot bring himself to make an orthodox hero out of anyone who is of inferior social status. At times he resorts to grotesque expedients to prove that his chosen ones have the necessary social qualifications. In *The Pioneers*, Elizabeth Temple can have no truck with Oliver Edwards while he is thought to be a half-breed; but when he is found to be the grandson of old Major Effingham, and therefore 'a white man' in all senses of the term, the story proceeds to a fairy-tale finale in which Oliver wins Elizabeth and half her father's wilderness kingdom.[1]

1. The problem of how to make a white gentleman out of a coloured hero exercised a good many nineteenth-century purveyors of fiction. In *Across the Plains*, Robert Louis Stevenson speaks of a favourite work of his childhood 'which appeared in *Cassell's Family Paper*, and was read aloud

With Natty Bumppo the difficulty becomes crucial. So long as he is a free agent he can be admired, and serve as hero. But he does not belong to Indian society, and he can never be implicated in white society without too closely defining his status. He can, thus, never marry. Of the two chances given him, that in *The Deerslayer* is reasonably plausible; if Judith Hutter is in love with him, his refusals to consider matrimony are explained by the simple fact that he is not in love with Judith. But in *The Pathfinder* Natty is himself in love, with Mabel Dunham, the daughter of an army sergeant. She is offered as heroine, with all sorts of apologies and qualifications (as, that she is more refined than one might expect, because she has been in the care of an officer's widow). It is impossible, however, to trick Natty out in other colours than his familiar ones. He is illiterate; his origins are immitigably humble. So Natty must be rejected by Mabel.

Natty inhabits a kind of vacuum. His world is, on the whole, made wonderfully interesting. But it is insubstantial. The Cooper gentleman is a bore; the Cooper non-gentleman cannot be incorporated in a complete situation, since uncouth society in America could not, in Cooper's day and especially for someone of Cooper's temperament, be considered a proper subject for a novel. As a result, Natty's moves constitute an evasion of society, a series of renunciations. Compare the Leatherstocking tales, or Cooper's sea-stories, with the novels of his contemporary, Balzac. Balzac's is a dense and actual world; Cooper's, by contrast, is a mythological place, where in earlier times the knight-errant might have performed. It is the element of myth that makes the Bumppo stories more than mere adventure yarns. But in later times this element was to grow fainter and fainter; the adventure lost significance. In other words, the logical extension of

to me by my nurse. It narrated the doings of one Custaloga, the Indian brave, who, in the last chapter, very obligingly washed the paint off his face and became Sir Reginald Somebody-or-other; a trick I never forgave him. The idea of a man being an Indian brave, and then giving that up to be a baronet, was one which my mind rejected.'

Leatherstocking is the cowboy-hero: the simple, manly person whose feats are brave and chivalrous, but who, being a knight without title or crest, has no place in society, and so must – according to the genre – ride off into the sunset, without having laid a finger on the rancher's daughter, let alone married her. Cooper's achievement, though, is a remarkable one. It could be argued that his view of the American wilderness is essentially that of the cultivated European, as Bartram's had been, a generation previously. Whether or not that is so, he did succeed in casting an enduring literary spell. Very few to-day trouble to read Heckewelder, from whom Cooper drew his information, though his descriptions are no doubt more 'accurate'. It is the invented, mythological tincture that makes us still read Cooper, even if we usually leave his world behind with our childhoods. And though his novels of the sea have less of this capacity for magic, they, too, represent the power of Cooper to create fiction out of apparently unpromising material.

He is to be honoured also for an energy of invention almost as fierce if not as richly accomplished as that of Balzac. Certain of his later novels, while conventional in treatment and unresolved in attitude, shed considerable light on the social dilemmas of Jacksonian America. Cooper, like other contemporaries, found it easier to be a Democrat than a democrat. Though in less extreme form, he suffered some of the anguish of Crèvecoeur. Everyone knows the passages in Crèvecoeur's *Letters from an American Farmer* which praise the simplicity and harmony of American life at its best. Far less familiar are the passages from the *Letters* and from Crèvecoeur's *Sketches of Eighteenth-Century America* in which he bewails the upheavals of the American Revolution:

Ambition, we well know, an exorbitant love of power and thirst of riches, a certain impatience of government, by some people called liberty – all these motives, clad under the garb of patriotism and even of constitutional reason, have been the secret but true foundation of this, as well as of many other revolutions.

The final chapters of Crèvecoeur's *Sketches* take the form of dialogues between greedy, ignorant 'patriots' and dignified loyalists or would-be neutrals (of whom Crèvecoeur was one).

The events of the America of the 1840s led Cooper into a comparable fictionalized, frustrated discussion of the excesses of popular democracy. The immediate occasion was New York's Anti-Rent War. Some landlords still owned large estates, with titles going back as far as the seventeenth century. Most of them were good landlords who allowed their tenant farmers to pay small rents, or no rents at all in times of financial difficulty. The tenants began to object to even the mildest aspects of landlordism: they were determined to possess their farms outright. Cooper, himself a landlord of sorts, was convinced that a basic principle of property was at stake. In his *Littlepage Manuscripts* trilogy (1845–6) he traced the history, from colonial times to his own day, of lands acquired by the Littlepage family. The tone of the first novel in the trilogy, *Satanstoe*, is cheerfully anecdotal. In the second novel, *The Chainbearer*, it becomes more ironical. The Yankee tenants, who eventually change the name of the old 'Satanstoe' settlement to 'Dibbletonborough', find Mordaunt Littlepage's devotion to the patriot side almost a cause for complaint. If he had been a loyalist they would have been able to seize his lands for themselves, under confiscation. The third novel, *The Redskins, or Indian and Injin*, is a caustic account of the squatter mentality. There are good Indians in the trilogy, men of simple honour; and there are false 'Injins', white men in mobs who disguise themselves as burlesque redskins to terrorize their betters. Mordaunt Littlepage's grandson is engaged in the Anti-Rent War, though his defeat is inevitable.

Crèvecoeur had been over the same ground seventy years earlier. He thinks of retreating from the white men's corrupt democracy, to live with good Indians. His demagogues, who bear names like Aaron Blue-Skin, are as meanly truculent as Cooper's Anti-Renters. Cooper, in common with Crèvecoeur, does not know the answer. The settlement of the wilderness was a worthy endeavour. Honour is important, and courage and justice. Yet where does true justice lie? Who properly owns any of this land? The Indians perhaps, but they have been defeated and dispossessed. If they are made to yield by stronger force, what is to save the landlords from an equivalent fate? All that Cooper is sure of, in so equivocal a situation, is that things are deteriorating. The cycle obsesses him, as it was to obsess William Faulkner a century afterwards. Each is impelled to delve back into the past, in search of explanation and also of an elusive original perfection. Each is impelled to trace the story, whether of the Littlepage acres or those of Yoknapatawpha County, forward and downward to a present-day degradation. These transformations lie at the heart of much of American fiction, and these ambiguous grapplings with the notions of progress and democracy. They are the substance, for example, of Hawthorne's *House of the Seven Gables*.

One of Cooper's last words on the subject was his Utopian novel *The Crater* (1847). An idyllic society established by shipwrecked Americans on an island in the Pacific is ruined by enlargement, by litigation and religiosity and journalism and libertarianism. The island has come into existence through an earthquake. Cooper's revenge is to produce another earthquake which sinks the whole island and its squabbling cargo into the sea.

Edgar Allan Poe

WHATEVER might be said in disparagement of their work, it had to be admitted by their contemporaries that Irving and Cooper were eminent men of letters. Poe, however, never during his short life reached their level of eminence. 'Essentially a Magazinist', as he called himself, he struggled among the ruck of writers in the immature literary circles of America. He jostled in the crush of minor celebrities, amid all those authors of 'genius', so overpraised (by Poe himself, on occasion): the Mrs Sigourneys and Frances Sargent Osgoods, and N. P. Willises and Thomas Holley Chiverses. In a way, he was the 'Poor-Devil Author' of whom Washington Irving wrote a sympathetic sketch, the man who from vast dreams of literary fame descends to ignominious hackwork. Poverty dogged Poe also; his successes as an editor – and he seems to have been a very good one – were obliterated by unstable acts; and he, too, had his hackwork: the spate of scrappy reviews, the arrestingly bad humorous pieces, the textbook on conchology. Yet Poe never became abject; like Oscar Wilde with the customs inspector, he had his genius to declare. This word, so debased in the periodicals of the day, he cherished with a passion that must have appeared out of place in the shabby offices and lodgings he inhabited. But time, denying the description to the host of his contemporaries, and even to Irving and Cooper, has rewarded his tenacity and applied it to Poe.

It should be said that the verdict of posterity has not been unanimous. Until recently his own countrymen have tended to dismiss him as the 'jingle man' (Emerson's phrase), or else, while praising him, have said that he stands outside the main current (whatever that is) of American literature. Yet to many others there has been no question of his 'genius'. Tennyson conceded it; so did W. B. Yeats; and, above all, so have the French, from Baudelaire to Valéry. More than one American, involved in a literary conversation with a Frenchman, has heard the latter produce the word *Edgarpo*, as though it were both a talisman and a high compliment. In fact, *Edgarpo* is to the French almost another person than Edgar Allan Poe, as the English-speaking world knows him.

The casual reader, in Britain or America, thinks of Poe in connexion with certain gripping stories: who has not, at one time or another, read 'The Gold Bug' or 'The Pit and the Pendulum'? He may also remember details of a poem or two: Poe's 'Raven', croaking 'Nevermore', or his jangling 'Bells'. He will know of

> the glory that was Greece
> And the grandeur that was Rome

without necessarily being aware that they come from Poe's lines 'To Helen'. But if the reader refreshes his memory of

Poe's fifty poems and seventy stories, he may find himself
agreeing with Lowell's famous verdict that Poe is 'three-
fifths genius and two-fifths sheer fudge'. He will probably
agree with Whitman's opinion that Poe's verses 'belong
among the electric lights of imaginative literature, brilliant
and dazzling, but with no heat', and that they carry 'the
rhyming art to excess'. *Mechanical* is a word often applied to
Poe's poetry, and those who glance at his essays on prosody
will perhaps think it not inapt. These essays suggest that their
author, in his insistence upon the craft of poetry, allowed its
rules to triumph over him; that in eschewing 'truth' – 'the
heresy of "The Didactic"' – and seeking after 'beauty',
'purity', and 'melody', he, too, often lapses into doggerel.
Strict with others (see, for example, his close examination of
Elizabeth Barrett Browning), he is blind to faults in his own
work. Thus in 'Ulalume' he rhymes 'kissed her' with 'sister' and 'vista'; in 'For Annie', 'Annie' is paired with
'many'. In these and other poems all the stops of prosody
are pulled out, with shattering effect. 'Eulalie', for instance:

> I dwelt alone
> In a world of moan,
> And my soul was a stagnant tide,
> Till the fair and gentle Eulalie became my blushing bride –
> Till the yellow-haired young Eulalie became my smiling bride.

Mallarmé singled out the last line for especial praise; the
English reader may find it hard to take it or the others seriously. (To current taste, Poe's choice of names is singularly
unfortunate. *Eulalie* seems excessively melodious; while
Ligeia and *Porphyrogene* might be proprietary medicines.) The
opening lines of 'Lenore' are almost as bad as those from
'Eulalie':

> Ah, broken is the golden bowl! the spirit flown forever!
> Let the bell toll! – a saintly soul floats on the Stygian river;
> And, Guy de Vere, hast thou no tear? – weep now or nevermore!
> See! on yon dread and rigid bier low lies thy love Lenore!

If we are to be flippant about such resounding stanzas, we
may even catch premonitory likenesses. Is there not a hint
of Kipling's Suez in

Far down within the dim West
Where the good and the bad and the worst and the best
Have gone to their eternal rest –

or even of John Betjeman in this couplet from 'Al Aaraaf':

What guilty spirit, in what shrubbery dim,
Heard not the stirring summons of that hymn?

But this is, of course, unfair to Poe. Even in the bad poems
there are redeeming features. 'For Annie' has

Its old agitations
Of myrtles and roses.

'The City in the Sea' has a haunting weirdness:

Resignedly beneath the sky
The melancholy waters lie.
So blend the turrets and shadows there
That all seems pendulous in air,
While from a proud tower in the town
Death looks gigantically down.

And if it is hard to appreciate any part of 'The Bells', 'The
Raven', or the play-fragment 'Politian', there are shorter
poems of compelling beauty. In the 'Sonnet – to Science',
Poe laments the disappearance of magic:

Hast thou not torn the Naiad from her flood,
The Elfin from the green grass, and from me
The summer dream beneath the tamarind tree?

One may object to 'Elfin', but the cry of the poem is authentic. So is that of 'Romance', whose second stanza begins:

Of late, eternal Condor years
So shake the very Heaven on high
With tumult as they thunder by,
I have no time for idle cares
Through gazing on the unquiet sky –

though the poem continues with a regrettable poultry-
plucking image:

And when an hour with calmer wings
Its down upon my spirit flings ...

'Alone' and 'A Dream within a Dream' are excellent poems. But we must take into account the rest of his writing if we are to understand why he is thought a major figure.

Perhaps his stories form a more substantial claim to remembrance. If we leave out the comic ones, most of which are painful or even horrible (e.g., 'The Spectacles', in which a shortsighted man falls in love with a woman who proves to be his great-great-grandmother; or 'The Man Who Was Used Up', about a soldier so mutilated that he is like 'a large and exceedingly odd-looking bundle of something'),[1] they fall roughly into two kinds: those of horror and those of 'ratiocination'. Under the first head may be listed such stories as 'The Black Cat', 'The Cask of Amontillado', 'The Fall of the House of Usher', and 'Ligeia'; while the second group includes 'The Gold Bug', 'The Purloined Letter', and so on. The distinction is not a precise one; stories like 'The Murders in the Rue Morgue' combine the macabre with the methodical. And indeed all his stories have the special Poe flavour. Many of them are set in strange places – a ruined abbey, a castle on the Rhine – with elaborate and dimly or luridly lit *décors*. (His ideal room, as depicted in 'The Philosophy of Furniture', has window-panes of crimson-tinted glass.) Things usually happen at night, or in unlit interiors. The heroes and heroines are of ancient and aristocratic lineage (rarely are they American): they are erudite and accomplished – yet doomed. In such particulars Poe hardly differs from the mass of sensational writers who used the trappings of the Gothic Novel. The 'tale of effect' was by no means invented by Poe; he acknowledged the success of the examples that appeared in *Blackwood's Magazine*, and jibed at them in 'How to Write a Blackwood Article':

There was the 'Dead Alive', a capital thing! – the record of a gentleman's sensations when entombed before the breath was out of his body – full of taste, terror, sentiment, metaphysics, and erudition. You would have sworn that the writer had been born and brought up in a coffin.

1. For further comment on these, see pp. 172–4.

This quotation suggests in part what lifts Poe out of the ruck: namely, the quality of intelligence and self-awareness. His stories, as Baudelaire noted, show 'absurdity installing itself in the intellect, and governing it with a crushing logic'. Though the ghastliness is occasionally overdone,[1] it is made all the more nightmarish by the measured deliberation with which it is unfolded. Here we are reminded of Poe's own life – as when he could write (in a letter of 1848) of the visiting clergyman who 'stood smiling and bowing at the madman Poe!' It is this same terrible lucidity that makes his fiction better than melodrama. Calamity –

> the cloud that took the form
> (When the rest of heaven was blue)
> Of a demon in my view –

is inbred, not accidental: it cannot be averted. We may apply to Poe some lines of Baudelaire:

> Je suis les membres et la roue
> Et la victime et le bourreau.
> – – – –
> Je suis de mon cœur le vampire. ...

Je suis de mon cœur le vampire: the hero in Poe's tales destroys himself. Yet his destruction involves others, and in particular the heroine. In 'The Philosophy of Composition', in which Poe analyses the structure of 'The Raven' and implies that he wrote it according to formula, there occurs this much-quoted passage:

I asked myself – 'Of all melancholy topics, what, according to the universal understanding of mankind, is the *most* melancholy?' Death – was the obvious reply. 'And when,' I said, 'is this most melancholy of topics most poetical?' From what I have already explained ... the answer ... is obvious – 'When it most closely allies itself to *Beauty*': the death, then, of a beautiful woman is, unquestionably, the most poetical topic in the world – and equally is it beyond doubt that the lips best suited for such topic are those of a bereaved lover.

1. As in 'Ligeia', in which an artificially induced current of air keeps the draperies in constant motion. Theatrical devices such as this are discussed in Nathan B. Fagin, *The Histrionic Mr Poe* (Baltimore, 1949).

There is perhaps nothing in this statement to startle; love and death run close together in the world's literature, and the death of a beautiful woman is the theme of the unhysterical Henry James, in *The Wings of the Dove*.

But Poe's deaths are of a special order. It is the no man's land between death and life that obsesses him, and the strange, incestuous vampirism of the dead with the living. Ligeia and her husband; Roderick Usher and his twin sister Madeline; the painter and his wife in 'The Oval Portrait'; Berenice and her cousin; Morella and her nameless daughter – in all these cases the dead return from unquiet graves, as Poe's own cousin-wife seemed to slip from life to death and back again. Only in 'Eleonora' do the dead relinquish their hold upon the living; but even here there have been ties across limbo. This is the desperation of Poe's story-world: life ebbs away, swiftly and remorselessly, yet death does not bring peace. For him nothing is stable or sweet. Even his beautiful women are described as though they were corpses; they are like human beings with marble poured over them, smooth, white, monumental, and a little gruesome – like the academic sculpture of the period.

In common with such sculpture, some of Poe's stories leave us indifferent, or seem repellent. 'Ligeia', which Poe thought his best grotesque story, is now, for most readers, a jumble of morbid self-pity, diabolism, and gimcrack Gothicism. But other stories have retained their sinister spell; and these are the ones which avoid vampirism, and concentrate upon various forms of suffering. Poe's imagination is in many respects that of a brilliant and neurotic child. Like a child, he shows off, he dreams of power. But, like a child, he is vulnerable, not only to night-time fears (lamps blown out, waving curtains), but also to the physical pressure of a giant-adult world, whose doors are too heavy to open, and whose locks too stiff to turn. (Many of his plots are claustrophobic, vertiginous: victims are walled in, entombed alive, sucked down into whirlpools.) To these anxieties we still respond. Poe's *Narrative of Arthur Gordon Pym* is his most sustained piece of imaginative narrative. It was based on an account of an actual South Sea expedition. Such reports from the world's edges, with their evocation of the unknown, the marvellous and the ominous, exercised a powerful influence upon the sensibility of the age. In Poe's tale the matter-of-fact modulates into the sinister and supernatural. A young stowaway aboard a whaler becomes involved in a mutiny, then in a storm which claims the lives of almost the entire ship's company. At the end, the youngster and another survivor are borne in a canoe, through a dream landscape toward the South Pole, heading into a weird whiteness presided over by an immense white figure ... – here the narrative breaks off. And we still read with pleasure his pieces of 'ratiocination'; though he sometimes exhibits in them to a naïve degree his pride in logic and learning, they are admirably constructed; and his master-mind, Auguste Dupin, is one of the very first in literature's endless procession of omniscient criminologists.

A few poems, some stories: these are Poe's claim to fame as a creative writer. But in estimating his stature we must mention his critical essays. To compare them with the work of his master, Coleridge, is to realize Poe's limitations as a critic. He can be shrill and vindictive; too closely involved in the literary squabbles around him, he can castigate and praise for the wrong reasons. He smells out plagiarism with the fury of a witch-doctor. His insistence upon precision of language is apt to seem fussy; nor can one forget that he was capable of slack writing which he would not condone in others. His larger theories are – one may think – questionable, and the philosophizing in *Eureka* is mediocre. Nevertheless, he is full of perceptive comment (on Macaulay, for example: 'We assent to what he says, too often because we so very clearly understand what it is that he intends to say'). Above all, he takes his criticism seriously, pitching it on an ambitiously high level. Even if he is not always consistent, he provides theories for all that he has tried to write, theories that may serve others. Poetry should aim at beauty, but should be composed in obedience to rigorous technical standards. Like stories, poems achieve their maximum effect if they are fairly short; there is no place in Poe's system for the epic poem and not much for the three-decker novel. Perhaps his view that history's trend was toward 'the curt, the condensed, the pointed', was a rationalization of his own habit of writing for magazine publication; for the nineteenth century continued to absorb lengthy novels despite his prophecy. As far as America is concerned, the important facts are that Poe had ideas and standards; that he brought a welcome professionalism to American letters; and that though he now and then 'tomahawked' innocent victims, it was good for native authors to be warned that literature was an exacting trade.

But we have still not grasped his full significance, and cannot do so without considering *Edgarpo*: the man whom Baudelaire and Mallarmé acclaimed so fervently and translated with such rich sympathy. It might indeed be argued that they invented *Edgarpo*; that in their version the pinchbeck became gold, the flamboyant vocabulary was identified as 'poésie pure': the harried magazinist appeared (to paraphrase Baudelaire) as the tragic young aristocrat, alone in a barbarous, gaslit America. We must admit that this figure does not altogether correspond to Edgar Allan Poe. It does, however, correspond to Poe as he wished to present himself to the world, and to certain real aspects of his work that align him rather with the symbolists of a later generation than with the Gothic writers of a previous one. Where his English and American (especially Bostonian) contemporaries sought to 'inculcate a moral', he pleaded for the 'poem written solely for the poem's sake'. Yet though 'with me poetry has been not a purpose, but a passion', intellect came to the rescue of imagination. Underlying the extravagances and vulgarities of Poe's fantasy world are hints of subtle, hitherto-unanalysed correspondences and compulsions. We are accustomed by now in literature to the equation of one sense with another, or to be told that human behaviour is frequently cruel and irrational. To Baudelaire, on the other hand, it came with the excitement of a revelation to read, in Poe's *Marginalia*, that 'The orange ray of the spectrum and

the buzz of the gnat ... affect me with nearly similar sensations'; and to be asked, in 'The Black Cat', 'Who has not,
a hundred times, found himself committing a vile or a silly
action, for no other reason than because he knows he should
not?' For the French, such insights established Poe as one of
the great forerunners of modern literature, and they came
to venerate him as a symbolic figure as much as for his various discoveries. It has taken longer for the English-speaking
world to view him thus; the delay, it could be said, is explic-
able in terms of the time that it took English verse to respond
to the influences of the Continent. Baudelaire's *Fleurs du Mal*
was published in 1857; the only important volume of poetry
to come out that year in England was – *Aurora Leigh*. But
Whitman at any rate, though he disliked what Poe represented, was not blind to his inner meanings. In 1875, after
the ceremony at Poe's grave for which Mallarmé contributed
a famous sonnet, Whitman spoke of a dream he had had, in
which he saw

one of those superb little schooner yachts I had often seen lying
anchor'd, rocking so jauntily, in the waters around New York, or
up Long Island sound – now flying uncontroll'd with torn sails and
broken spars through the wild sleet and winds and waves of the
night. On the deck was a slender, slight, beautiful figure, a dim
man, apparently enjoying all the terror, the murk, and the dis-
location of which he was the centre and the victim. That figure
... might stand for Edgar Poe, his spirit, his fortunes, and his
poems. ...

His dream may recall to us Rimbaud's 'Le Bateau ivre',
which itself derived from Poe. Poe and *Edgarpo*, word and
echo, are in truth indistinguishable. One may feel that he is
more interesting to read *about* than to read; one may not
enjoy his work, but one cannot ignore it. It has become part
of us; we are his kin, and it is in this sense that the American
poet Allen Tate has spoken of him as 'Our Cousin, Mr
Poe'.[1]

1. An article reprinted in *The Forlorn Demon* (Chicago, 1953).

CHAPTER FOUR

NEW ENGLAND'S DAY

Emerson, Thoreau, Hawthorne

RALPH WALDO EMERSON (1803–82)

b. Boston, son and grandson of ministers. *ed.* Boston
Latin School and Harvard. Became pastor of Second
Church, Boston, 1829; *m.* Ellen Tucker, who *d.* 1831.
1832, resigned pastorate and made first of three visits to
Europe (other visits 1847, 1872). On return, settled at
Concord, Mass.; 1835, *m.* Lydia Jackson. Began career of
writing and lecturing, and gradually achieved fame. Continued to live in Concord, though frequently in Boston,
and absent on lecture tours. Kept himself as far as possible
remote from public affairs, though took his share of citizen
duties in Concord, and became heatedly interested in
abolitionism during 1850s. Works included: *Nature* (1836);
'American Scholar' oration, Harvard (1837); *Divinity
School* address, Harvard (1838); *Essays* (two series, 1841,
1844); *Poems* (1847); *Representative Men* (1850); *English
Traits* (1856); *The Conduct of Life* (1860); *May Day* (verse,
1867); *Society and Solitude* (1870); *Letters and Social Aims*
(1876).

HENRY DAVID THOREAU (1817–62)

b. Concord, Mass., son of unsuccessful storekeeper who
turned to the manufacture of pencils. *ed.* Harvard, where
he was undistinguished but read widely. After graduating,
had a brief skirmish with the teaching profession. Became
friendly with Emerson, and lived in latter's house 1841–3.
Spent a few months on Staten Island as tutor to Emerson's
nephew. Became acquainted with New York writers and
editors and placed one or two reviews, but was unhappy
and ill-at-ease ('They say there is a "*Ladies' Companion*"

that pays – but I would not write anything companion-
able'). Spent rest of his life (unmarried) in vicinity of
Concord. 1845–47, built himself a hut by Walden Pond and
lived there alone, reading, and writing in his journal.
Returning to Concord, divided his time between his
journal, lectures, walks in the country, and surveying.
1849, published *A Week on the Concord and Merrimack
Rivers*; also essay *Civil Disobedience* (originally called *Resistance to Civil Government*). Other main work *Walden* (1854);
sundry essays and poems.

NATHANIEL HAWTHORNE (1804–64)

b. Salem, Mass., son of sea-captain who *d.* 1808. *ed.*
Bowdoin College, Maine, where acquainted with Longfellow and with Franklin Pierce (later President of the
U.S.). On graduation, lived in seclusion at Salem, where
he wrote a novel (*Fanshawe*, published anonymously, 1828)
and short stories, sketches, etc. (collected for book-publi-
cation as *Twice-Told Tales*, 1837, 1842). Left Salem 1836
to work in Boston, as hack-writer and at Boston Custom
House. 1841, joined Brook Farm community; 1842, *m.*
Sophia Peabody, who was something of a transcendentalist ('Mr Emerson is Pure Tone'), and moved to the Old
Manse at Concord. Further tales and sketches in *Mosses
from an Old Manse* (1846). 1846–9, worked as port surveyor at Salem; afterwards lived in the Berkshires (where
friendly with Herman Melville); in Liverpool, as American consul, 1853–7; then in Italy; and back to Concord,
1860. First great success, *The Scarlet Letter* (1850), followed
by his other novels, *The House of the Seven Gables* (1851),
The Blithedale Romance (1852), and *The Marble Faun* (1860).
Other work includes *The Snow Image* (short stories, 1851);
books for children (*Tanglewood Tales*, etc.); *Our Old
Home* (1863), essays on England; and posthumous fragments.

NEW ENGLAND'S DAY

—

NEITHER Irving, Cooper, nor Poe liked New England. In his *History of New York*, Irving pictured it as a region of unscrupulous Yankee traders with names like Preserved Fish. Cooper objected to its solemnity and self-righteousness. Poe's opinions were still more decided. Boston he referred to as 'Frogpondium': never was a man less proud of his birthplace. Frogpondium was the home of 'that ineffable buzzard', the *North American Review*, which since its foundation in 1815 had steadily grown in influence and assurance. This periodical, he thought, abetted New England writers in maintaining a mutual admiration society. In a review of J. R. Lowell's *Fable for Critics* he burst out:

It is a fashion among Mr Lowell's set to affect a belief that there is no such thing as Southern literature. Northerners ... are cited by the dozen ..., while Legaré, Simms, Longstreet, and others of equal note, are passed by in contemptuous silence. Mr L. cannot carry his frail honesty of opinion even so far South as New York. All whom he praises are Bostonians; other writers are barbarians ...

Regional pride apart, Poe had serious reasons for disliking the products of Frogpondium. He insisted that the writer was an artist, and emphatically not a preacher; the literature of Boston and the New England hinterland was, however, packed with moral sentiment, even that of Longfellow, whose work he in general admired. As for Emerson and the others whom Poe thought of as 'transcendentalists', they offended against every article of his creed. Contrast his observations on the nature of poetry with Emerson's journal entry of 1838, that 'the high poetry of the world from the beginning has been ethical, and it is the tendency of the ripe modern mind to produce it'. Or set against Poe's

'Philosophy of Composition', Emerson's instruction to the bard (in 'Merlin') that

> He shall not his brain encumber
> With the coil of rhythm and number.

'Mr Ralph Waldo Emerson,' said Poe in his *Chapter on Autography*, 'belongs to a class of gentlemen with whom we have no patience whatsoever – the mystics for mysticism's sake ...' Elsewhere, giving sarcastic advice on how to imitate the 'tone transcendental', he said that its

merit consists in seeing into the nature of affairs a very great deal farther than anybody else. This second sight is very efficient when properly managed. ... Put in something about the Supernal Oneness. Don't say a syllable about the Infernal Twoness. Above all, study innuendo. Hint everything – assert nothing.

Poe's remarks form a good introduction to the New England writers, for he was right in detecting a special Boston tone. New England's history made for earnestness. The extremer Puritan mood had gone; around Boston itself Unitarianism – that 'feather-bed to catch a falling Christian' – had gained some hold; the wealthy merchant and shipowner were more interested in the solvency than in the religious zeal of their clients. Yet the 'didactic heresy' still hovered over the scene. New England's culture was still religious; its men of letters were, in one sense, men of God, even if they preferred to speak of the deity as Nature, and if – like Hawthorne – they belonged to no church. Transcendentalism, as Perry Miller has said in his anthology of the movement 'is most accurately to be defined as a religious demonstration'.[1] Interest in religion was not confined to New England; the nineteenth century saw religious controversy everywhere in the Western world, and the clash of dogma and secularism, the individual hesitations over unsatisfying alternatives, the succession of hard-fought rearguard actions: all these were staged in Europe with far more brilliance and intellectual weight. In New England it was rather a broadening of faith than a loss of faith that exercised the religiously minded; a

1. *The Transcendentalists* (Cambridge, Mass., 1950), 8.

search for limits, and – as always in American experience – an attempt to arrive at an attitude suitable to the American scene, with all its growth and confusion.

Towards the middle of the century Boston became, if not the hub of the universe (as Oliver Wendell Holmes genially described it), at any rate the cultural centre of the United States. Other cities – New York, New Orleans, Philadelphia – were larger; others again – Charleston, for example – had developed fairly elegant forms of society. But Boston took the lead, buttressed by nearby Harvard and nourished by the wealth its ships brought in. Private income matched public occasion; club, library, periodical, publishing house ran together. Much was still lacking; Henry James, in his admirable little biography of Hawthorne, points out the pathetic hungering for culture that beset the parlours of Boston, where a volume of Flaxman's weak engravings from Dante provided a whole evening's entertainment. It was, as he stresses, a provincial place. But it had metropolitan tinges, and the 'proper Bostonians' of the Boston–Cambridge axis, who will be discussed in Chapter Six, should not be too quickly dismissed.

Here, however, we are concerned with some New Englanders who were not strictly speaking Bostonians: who, indeed, resisted urban influences while undoubtedly drawing advantages from these in their rural homes. Hawthorne, visiting a family on a secluded New Hampshire island in 1852, saw on the parlour table a copy of Ruskin's *Pre-Raphaelitism* (published in England only the previous year), together with a tract on spiritualism. Many another New England home could have offered a similar choice of -isms. The young Harvard graduate, fresh from the Divinity School, carried his books and ideas to some quiet white township, and from his pulpit intimated truths that his predecessors would have at once condemned. If he wished to write, no grave financial difficulties stood in his way. The region around Boston, or behind any of New England's ports, was still simple, unspoiled countryside, in which the aspiring writer could live for next to nothing, growing his own food (as Emerson,

Thoreau, and Hawthorne all did), and making now and then a journey to Boston to borrow books or meet an editor. An occasional article or lecture appearance would bring him in a useful few dollars and keep his name before the public, such as it was.

In this world of literate, closely-knit communities, on the periphery of Boston, appeared the phenomenon of transcendentalism. It is an imprecise term, and hard to pin on to any of the major figures of the time. Emerson, reminiscing on the wrongness of the notion that a doctrinaire set was attempting 'to establish certain opinions and inaugurate some movement in literature, philosophy, and religion', contended that there were

only here and there two or three men or women who read and wrote, each alone, with unusual vivacity. Perhaps they only agreed in having fallen upon Coleridge and Wordsworth and Goethe, then on Carlyle, with pleasure and sympathy. Otherwise, their education and reading were not marked, but had the American superficialness, and their studies were solitary.

Emerson did well to emphasize the isolation of these people, to whom no collective noun – 'group' or 'movement' – seems quite to apply. Loneliness and apartness have characterized the American author, from Poe's day onward. Even the exuberant Americans – Whitman, for instance – have had surprisingly few friends with whom to associate, so to speak, professionally. In New England, if we except a circle of Bostonians, this has been especially true. It is easy to write of the literary activity of the time – the *Flowering of New England* of Van Wyck Brooks' title – as though its authors formed one big family. In a way, they did: Emerson, Thoreau, and Hawthorne lived for a while in the same village, Concord; and they and other personages pop continually in and out of one another's diaries and letters. Yet it would be less accurate to say that they knew one another than that they knew *of* one another. Each stood somewhat aside, a little critical of his companions, a little derisive, reluctant to commit himself. 'But how insular and pathetically solitary', Emerson confided to his journal, 'are all the people

we know!' In the same source he notes that the happy author
is the one who, ignoring public opinion, 'writes always to
the unknown friend'. Of the known, he remarks that 'my
friends and I are fishes in our habit. As for taking Thoreau's
arm, I should as soon take the arm of an elm tree.' After
Hawthorne's death, he reflects sadly that he has waited too
long in the hope that he 'might one day conquer a friendship'.

They were prepared to agree, as Emerson observed, on
very little. Something emanating from certain German
authors, and filtering through into England, attracted them
and provided them with a loose philosophical structure.
Transcendentalism suggested to them that theirs was a benevolent universe, which exhibited – or could exhibit – a steady
movement towards perfection. In Tennyson's words:

> Yet I doubt not through the ages one increasing purpose runs,
> And the thoughts of men are widened with the process of the suns.

So much was European, and part of the great humanitarian
surge of the century, with its concomitant interest in education, in temperance, in abolitionism, in women's rights, in
emigration to new countries. What was American about the
movement, as expounded by Emerson, Thoreau, Theodore
Parker, Margaret Fuller, George Ripley, several of the Channing family, and others (including Whitman), was the conviction that their country offered opportunities of a unique
order. As the Mormons located Zion 'on this continent', so
the transcendentalists were sure that only in America could
the 'private man' expand to his full stature.

Transcendentalism has its comic aspects. Its wilder followers had little but good-heartedness and enthusiasm to
commend them. One man who attended a transcendentalist
meeting said, according to Emerson, that 'it seemed to him
like going to heaven in a swing'. And 'at a knotty point in
the discourse, a sympathetic Englishman with a squeaking
voice interrupted with the question, "Mr Alcott, a lady near
me desires to inquire whether omnipotence abnegates attribute?"' This was Amos Bronson Alcott, the father of Louisa

May, who herself wrote an amusing account of 'Transcendental Wild Oats'. Alcott had a collection of 'orphic sayings', of which one on *Temptation* is a fair sample:

Greater is he, who is above temptation, than he, who, having been tempted, overcomes. The latter but regains the state from which the former has not fallen. He who is tempted has sinned; temptation is impossible to the holy.

There is a quite staggering innocence in such a belief, as there was in the Utopian communities which the transcendentalists briefly established at Brook Farm and Fruitlands. This is not the place, however, in which to examine such matters; they should, rather, be borne in mind as a backcloth to the New England scene, and to the work of Emerson, Thoreau, and Hawthorne, the three New Englanders implicated in transcendentalism who have any decisive claim to be read for their literary quality.

RALPH WALDO EMERSON

'MYSTICISM for mysticism's sake': these words of Poe were casually uttered. Like many others, he took Emerson for a type of the transcendentalists: the arch-villain because the reputed leader. Certainly Emerson stated the transcendentalist outlook more fully than any of his fellows. His main beliefs were indicated fairly early in life, in three works: *Nature*, a small book of which only 500 copies were sold in twelve years; the 'American Scholar' lecture; and the Harvard *Divinity School* address. In these he asserted that man and his world formed a perfect harmony, whose proofs were evident in every fact of nature and of human experience; that the voices of orthodoxy, of tradition, of the past were to be ignored in favour of one's own intuitive searchings. 'Books', therefore, 'are for the scholar's idle times'; 'only so much do I know, as I have lived.' Man's only duty was to be true to himself; and all his introspection, far from isolating him, would bring him out into the great arena of a common truth:

the deeper he dives into his privatest, secretest presentiment, to his wonder he finds this is the most acceptable, most public, and universally true. The people delight in it; the better part of every man feels, This is my music; this is myself.

Each Divinity School student was 'a newborn bard of the Holy Ghost', whom Emerson exhorted to 'cast behind you all conformity, and acquaint men at first hand with Deity'. The advice was considered shocking by the elders who heard his address; Deity had lost its definite article, and the place allotted it seemed too extra-curricular even for Unitarians, who were said only to require acceptance of 'the fatherhood of God, the brotherhood of Man, and the neighbourhood of Boston'. Life, it appeared, was a treasure hunt, with abundant clues, and prizes for everybody. The chief prizes went to the most active and observant; power, activity, genius were all near-synonyms. The only disabilities – it would be too harsh to call them sins – were torpor, incuriosity, or some excess of temperament, such as sensuality.

These were the themes of the lifelong secular sermon that Emerson went on preaching after he himself had left his Unitarian ministry. There were, he said, happy correspondences to be found throughout existence. His journal for March 1852 has the entry:

Beauty. Little things are often filled with great beauty. The cigar makes visible the respiration of the body, an universal fact, of which the ebb and flow of the sea-tide is only one example.

Nature was the great source of inspiration, for him as for Wordsworth. Hawthorne, walking near Concord one summer afternoon, saw a figure among the trees,

and, behold! it was Mr Emerson. He appeared to have had a pleasant time; for he said there were Muses in the woods to-day, and whispers to be heard in the breezes.

Out of such excursions Emerson derived material for his crowded journals: out of these and out of reading, for though he cautioned himself and others against books, he also told himself (in October 1842):

Thou shalt read Homer, Aeschylus, Sophocles, Euripides, Aristophanes, Plato, Proclus, Plotinus, Jamblichus, Porphyry, Aristotle,

Virgil, Plutarch, Apuleius, Chaucer, Dante, Rabelais, Montaigne,
Cervantes, Shakespeare, Jonson, Ford, Chapman, Beaumont and
Fletcher, Bacon, Marvell, More, Milton, Molière, Swedenborg,
Goethe.

And he did read them, as well as works by Coleridge, Wordsworth, Carlyle, and by oriental philosophers. Homer, Plato,
Dante, Rabelais, Montaigne, and Shakespeare particularly
impressed him, to judge from his journal.

Emerson's journal, indeed, was his life's task. For over fifty
years he set down in it his reflections, without any attempt at
regularity, but giving great care to indexing the volumes
(ten of them, produced in printed form). They were the raw
material of his writing; as he explained the process in a letter
to Frederic Hedge,

The notes I collect in the course of a year, are so miscellaneous that
when our people grow rabid for lectures, as they do periodically
about December, I huddle all my old almanacks together & look
in the encyclopaedia for the amplest cloak of a name whose folds
will reach unto & cover extreme & fantastic things. Staid men &
good scholars at first expressed mirth & then indignation at the
audacity that baptised this gay rag bag English Literature, then
Philosophy of History, then Human Culture, but now to effrontery
so bottomless they even leave the path open.

Out of the journal came the lecture, out of the lecture series
the volume of essays. His poems originated similarly, many
of them attached to his essays as preliminary chants. Thus,
the entry for 24 May 1847:

The days come and go like muffled and veiled figures sent from a distant friendly party, but they say nothing, and if we do not use the
gifts they bring, they carry them as silently away –

becomes the poem 'Days', which is one of his best:

> Daughters of time, the hypocritic Days,
> Muffled and dumb like barefoot dervishes,
> And marching single in an endless file,
> Bring diadems and fagots in their hands.
> To each they offer gifts after his will,
> Bread, kingdoms, stars, and sky that holds them all.

I, in my pleachèd garden, watched the pomp,
Forgot my morning wishes, hastily
Took a few herbs and apples, and the Day
Turned and departed silent. I, too late,
Under her solemn fillet saw the scorn.

Any number of other instances could be cited, most of
them representing less development of a germinal idea than
is here apparent. But whether in essay or in poem, it was the
central theme, 'the infinitude of the private man', that he
sought to explore. Given a constant theme, any amount of
variation seemed to him possible, without serious inconsistency or danger to consecutive reasoning. At twenty-one he
wrote in his journal of those rare books – 'the Proverbs of
Solomon, the Essays of Montaigne, and eminently the Essays of Bacon' – which 'collect and embody the wisdom of
their times, and so mark the stages of human improvement'.
He would like, he said, to add another volume to the series.

In his own terms, he succeeded. Like his models, he wrote
in aphorism, achieving a quality as personal as, though very
different from, that of Florio's *Montaigne* (of which he was
happy to think that Shakespeare and Ben Jonson possessed
copies). His journal entries were sometimes anecdotes, sometimes references to nature ('When Edward and I struggled
in vain to drag our big calf into the barn, the Irish girl put
her finger into the calf's mouth, and led her in directly'),
sometimes oblique and gnomic comments (like the note on
'the days'). His lectures were an assembly of aphorisms,
often admirably terse and unpompous, though not exactly
in 'the language of the street' which he found so much more
'vascular and alive' than a page of the *North American Review*.
Oratory dazzled him: he paid tribute to Edward Everett,
the great formal orator of Emerson's day. But he also noted
that official utterances put the audience to sleep ('every man
thinking more of his inconveniences than of the objects
of the occasion'), while concrete fact and allusion woke them
up. Fascinated by the organic properties of language ('the
word made one with the thing'), he said that he would like
to have been offered the professorship of rhetoric at some

country college. The statement is an interesting clue to both his temperament and his literary method.

The lecture platform was the nearest that he, a shy man lacking in 'animal spirits', could come to his fellows. The contact with the crowd exalted him; the rostrum separated him from too-close identification. As a sea of upturned faces, they were Melville's *people*, good, generous, and free. When he mingled with them they turned into Melville's *public*, vulgar, property engrossed, unreal. As he put it, 'I love man, not men.' 'Look into the stage-coach and see the faces!' he cried, in lines that recall T. S. Eliot's 'I had not thought death had undone so many':

Stand in State Street [Boston] and see the heads and the gait and gesture of the men; they are doomed ghosts going under Judgement all day long.

Busy with his journal, however, or addressing a lyceum, he was untroubled. Certainly the audiences of his day responded to him. J. R. Lowell wrote to a friend in 1867 that

Emerson's oration was more disjointed than usual, even with *him*. It began nowhere and ended everywhere, and yet ... it was all such stuff as stars are made of, and you couldn't help feeling that, if you waited awhile, all that was nebulous would be whirled into planets, and would assume the mathematical gravity of system. All through it, I felt something in me that cried, 'Ha, ha, to the sound of the trumpets!'

For us the rapture has gone; we are more likely to be arrested by, say, the suggestion of Henry James, that whereas other writers 'give one a sense of having found their form' (Wordsworth for example), 'with Emerson we never lose the sense that he is still seeking it'. His journal is only literature in embryo, his finished work stillborn. Though his sentences, Carlyle observed, were 'strong and simple', the Emersonian paragraph was 'a beautiful square *bag of duck-shot* held together by canvas'. When the theme is circumscribed, as in his delightful sketches of George Ripley and Thoreau, or in his perceptive *English Traits*, the product is far more satisfactory than in the unconfined essay. His poems, with their awkward, unusual little lines,[1] are also defective. They are never ornately platitudinous, like the verse of most of his contemporaries. At times they are brilliantly new:

> Things are in the saddle
> And ride mankind.

Too often, however, they are brittle and unmusical, or excessively didactic.

But the want of form is symptomatic of a larger deficiency in Emerson's thought. Its elements are as disparate as his sentences. Contradiction faces him at every turn. How to reconcile good with evil, the individual with society, the rival claims of nonconformity and neighbourliness, scholarship with intuition, the need to be up and doing with the equally imperative need to sit down and think? The charge against him is not that he sought to resolve these problems, but that he missed their serious implications by erecting contradiction into a system. Noting that such problems were stated in opposites, he concluded that they were like cosmic see-saws; each opposite cancelled out the other. The notion of polarity seduced him. So, in 'Uriel' (Emerson's mild revenge on the Harvard Divinity School), we are told:

> Line in nature is not found;
> Unit and universe are round;
> In vain produced, all rays return;
> Evil will bless, and ice will burn.

Evil will bless, eventually. Or rather, as Mary Baker Eddy might almost have said, 'Evil is merely privative, not absolute: it is like cold, which is the privation of heat.' In the 'Ode Inscribed to W. H. Channing', after some sharp words on slavery, he finds the consolation that

> Foolish hands may mix and mar;
> Wise and sure the issues are.
> Round they roll till dark is light.

1. Like that later American verbal pioneer, Gertrude Stein, he has a theory that phrase-rhythms should be determined by breathing. In his case, however, the theory may arise from the practice of oratory: in hers, she claims to have learned from the water-drinking of her white poodle, Basket.

Is Congress corrupt? Corruption is a proof of energy, inseparable from it. Fate is merely 'unpenetrated causes'; 'no
statement of the Universe can have any soundness which
does not admit of its ascending effort'. Poe's worm is the
Conqueror that at the last devours us; in Emerson's verse,

> striving to be man, the worm
> Mounts through all the spires of form.

For Emerson there is no cruel war of irreconcilable extremes;
extremes nuzzle one another in their eagerness to come
together. Mankind divides into pusher and pushed; but
those who go under do so willingly, recognizing the superiority of the leader who has the *plus* of energy which they lack.
We are not far here from the doctrine of the Superman,
though it would have horrified Emerson.

The case against Emerson may seem overwhelming. Again
and again passages in his essays exasperate or bewilder.
They suggest to us a person whose refinement, like that of
certain other Americans, was excessive. Very few authors
came up to his standard. Hawthorne and Tennyson fell
short; Shelley he dismissed in 1841, as 'wholly unaffecting to
me'. Shelley thought of the poet as the supreme type of man,
who must express a passionate awareness of the common
human fate: 'the pains and pleasures of his species must become his own'. The thinly fastidious Emerson of our
imagining, while he would have agreed in theory, stood
apart in practice, separated from his fellow-beings by the
walls of his reserve. 'Give all to Love', he advised in the
peculiarly unattractive poem of that title – only, do not give
all: be ready to relinquish the beloved. Marriage he ob-
liquely commended (in 'Illusions') by arguing that even the
worst marriages have compensations. Slavery moved him,
yet as a somewhat abstract cause.

Shelley was a rebel whose anarchism exiled him from his
own country, and who yet had a clear sense of his purpose as
a poet, and of the techniques of poetry. Emerson's rebellion
might appear relatively painless. His American Scholar is a
blurred figure, prophet (though not messiah) rather than

poet. His chief equipment seems to be disinterestedness. He moves in a void, without audience ('the literary man in this country', Emerson said in 1836, 'has no critic') and without literary antecedents, and yet not urgently desiring them, since he believes the performances of the artist, like the testimony of the inspired preacher, should be extempore.

The consequences of this belief have been unfortunate. If Emerson actually held it, one might trace a line from him down to the sloppy *bonhomie* of such a work as William Saroyan's *The Time of Your Life*. Or a connexion might be seen with the extraordinarily inward and extempore performances of abstract expressionism ('action painting') in the America of the 1950s. In Emerson's day, on the eve of the Industrial Revolution, the blend of oriental detachment and buoyant individualism seemed acceptable, as Lowell's remarks show; for as Lowell wrote on another occasion, 'perhaps some of us hear more than the mere words, are moved by something deeper than the thoughts'. Later formulations, in the shape of determinism and nihilism, jar us. If, bearing these in mind, we turn back to Emerson, there are some strange correspondences. Thus the tough-guy morality of a famous statement by Hemingway seems foreshadowed by the gentle Emerson, for whom the name *Concord* might have served as a motto:

Good and bad are but names readily transferable to that or this; the only right is what is after my constitution, the only wrong, what is against it.

No wonder that to the critic Yvor Winters, a man of stern lucidity, Emerson's central doctrine – that of 'submission to emotion' – is inadmissible: 'it eliminates at a stroke both choice and the values that serve as a basis for choice'.

The case for Emerson is less easy to state.

One aspect of his enduring strength can be described, simply, as honesty. This is the aspect that endeared him to Carlyle. There was a shrewd Yankee in Emerson, a blunt fellow who could strip an occasion to its essence. His version of the Norman Conquest was: 'Twenty thousand thieves landed at Hastings'. Though his thoughts seemed to dodge about, his life was an unremitting effort to find the truth by being true to himself. He was a New England seer and seeker, both an accepter and a renouncer, a quiet man and a busy man, who liked 'dry light, and hard clouds, hard expressions, and hard manners'. He was a modest man of boundless ambition. 'Genius', he sighed, weary of a pursuit he could not abandon, 'is sacrificed to talent every day.' Again, 'Miscellany is as bad as drunkenness.'

A more difficult aspect for us to grasp is Emerson's deliberate repudiation of the 'power of blackness'. Newton Arvin has pointed out[1] that Emerson had to struggle toward serenity. The cheerfulness he preached was always qualified by an awareness of the real world's iniquity. It was a non-tragic philosophy which though perilously near to inanity was by no means superficial. On the contrary, it was derived from a close study of Platonic and neo-Platonic ideas, and from long meditation. He did not say that men were good and wise. He demanded that they be better – more candid, more equable, more capable of *seeing*. John Jay Chapman has said that 'Emerson represents a protest against the tyranny of democracy ... If a soul be taken and crushed by democracy till it utter a cry, that cry will be Emerson.' Though the remark tells us more about the perversely courageous Chapman than it does about Emerson, it contains an important clue. Emerson *was* religiously committed to democracy. 'The grey past, the white future': he *must* believe that men might achieve liberation from their false selves. They must be reborn into wholeness. If this faith proved empty, all was empty. But nothing in the pilgrimage was simple. Good and bad were impossible to separate. Money was a curse, but also the expression of improvement. Change was unsettling, but also imperative. American expansionism was a greedy phenomenon but had a kind of

1. 'The House of Pain', reprinted in Milton Konvitz and Stephen Whicher, eds., *Emerson: A Collection of Critical Essays* (Englewood Cliffs, N.J., 1962).

rightness. Jacksonian Democracy, in some ways con-temptible, was nevertheless a generous faith. Where was the room in this for an absolute or a conventional morality? James Fenimore Cooper, wrestling with these problems, confessed to an angry defeat. Emerson's Scottish friend Carlyle, once gaily radical, turned sour: the extension of political democracy was like tumbling over Niagara in a barrel. Emerson at the extreme end of his life turned soft. It was a preferable development. He had won through to a genuine serenity. He no longer stirs us as Lowell was stirred. But we cannot understand the America of the nineteenth century without coming to terms with Ralph Waldo Emerson.

Henry David Thoreau

At first glance, no two authors seem closer than Emerson and Thoreau. Both lived in Concord, stirred by the same impulses. Like Emerson, the younger man – deeply struck by a reading of *Nature* – began to keep a journal, from which he culled items for publication. Like Emerson, he preached the gospel of independence and the great outdoors. He was, likewise, affected by only one 'cause' – that of anti-slavery. The two men even looked alike. It was natural, then, that Thoreau should be widely regarded as a disciple. Emerson himself, though he sought no relation as self-conscious as that of master-follower, felt that Thoreau's ideas were extensions of his own. J. R. Lowell, one of Thoreau's severest critics, spoke of him as picking up windfalls in Emerson's orchard.

In fact, the two men had different personalities, and some-what different aspirations. What they had in common, it might be said, kept them apart. As the years passed, contact became increasingly difficult. In May 1853 Thoreau wrote in his journal that he had 'talked, or tried to talk', with Emerson:

Lost my time – nay, almost my identity. He, assuming a false op-position where there was no difference of opinion, talked to the wind – told me what I knew – and I lost my time trying to imagine myself somebody else to oppose him.

At about the same time, Emerson was complaining to *his* journal that

as Webster could never speak without an antagonist, so Henry [Thoreau] does not feel himself except in opposition. He wants a fallacy to expose, a blunder to pillory, requires a little sense of victory, a roll of the drums, to call his powers into full exercise.

How revealing these two entries are: what wary, stiff-necked, no-surrender pride between the two nay-sayers! No wonder that neither liked novels, or that both wrote of friendship as something idealistic – and self-centred. How could the upright man be anything *but* self-centred?

Yet Thoreau has something to communicate that we miss in Emerson's writings. If he is even more wayward, he is also more robust. Emerson admired the ordinary skills of the world, the work done by hands, but a little wistfully; Thoreau had them at his finger-tips, and could act as surveyor, farmer, or carpenter as well as any man in Concord. Emerson's feeling for nature was real enough; but in comparison with that of Thoreau it was limited and 'literary'. 'It seems', Emerson noted in 1851, 'as if all the young gentlemen and gentlewomen of America spent several years in lying on the grass and watching "the grand movements of the clouds in the summer sky" during this century'. The remark charmingly sums up the behaviour of an age of nature-lovers, and it might apply in part to Thoreau. He, however, went farther into the secrets of nature, not as a professional naturalist – it has been alleged that, for all his minute observation, he added nothing to existing knowledge of local flora and fauna – but as one entering a world denied to most men, merging into the scene like the faun of classical mythology,[1] or like a sophisticated Bumppo.

1. A faun with – it must be said – his appetites well in check: see his fastidious chapter in *Walden*, 'Higher Laws', in which though he says 'I love the wild not less than the good', he also declares: 'He is blessed who is assured that the animal is dying out in him day by day, and the divine being established.'

The sophistication involved him in difficulties. He was an educated man, who contributed to the transcendentalist *Dial*, and participated in – or at any rate attended – transcendentalist 'conversations'. His problem was that of the complicated man seeking simplicity. He had to make a living, but one that would leave him free; he had to communicate his thoughts, yet be sure the act led to no entanglements. Like Emerson, he was concerned with the individual in relation to society, but in a special way. It was not a question of how the individual was to enter into a harsh, exclusive society, but how he was to ward off an all-too-friendly and intrusive one. 'Wherever a man goes', he said in *Walden*, 'men will pursue and paw him with their dirty institutions, and, if they can, constrain him to belong to their desperate odd-fellow society.'

His answers to his various dilemmas were uncompromising. Never married, he had no commitment to provide for others. Firmly part of a homogeneous community, he felt no need to seek a place in it. His place was understood, despite himself: he was Henry, the son of John Thoreau, who had not shown a disposition to settle down. Though neighbours disapproved of his vagaries, they did not treat him with hostility, as they might have done a stranger. Indeed, in few other communities could he have so organized affairs to suit himself. He could live in a civilized village, with men like Emerson, Hawthorne, and Alcott to talk to, and still find his beloved wilderness at the end of the street. Walden Pond, where he built his hut, was only a mile and a half from Concord. He said in a sympathetic review that Carlyle

speaks of Nature with a certain unconscious pathos. ... As we read his books here in New England, where there are potatoes enough, and every man can get his living peacefully and sportively as the birds and bees ... it seems to us as if by the world he often meant London ... the sorest place on the face of the earth. ... Possibly a South African village might have furnished a more hopeful, and more exacting audience, or in the silence of ... the desert, he might have addressed himself more entirely to his true audience, posterity.

In his own case, Concord served for London or for the desert, according to which way he set his steps; and posterity was the audience he aimed at.

Such was Thoreau's situation. It called for resistance to various pressures, but none was heavy enough to cause serious discomfort. Those who dislike Thoreau have, one feels, been irritated by the unfair ease of his solution. Like R. L. Stevenson, or J. R. Lowell, they have called him 'skulker', and told him that he ought to have lived like the rest of his countrymen instead of withdrawing to a vantage-point that was half-hermitage, half-ambush. They have objected that it cost him little to be gaoled in Concord for refusing to pay poll-tax to a government he considered unjust, since a friend paid the tax on his behalf and had him promptly released – so that he could at once go off and gather huckleberries. They have argued that there was nothing very extreme in living in his Walden hut for a couple of years, almost within smell of his mother's cooking. They have been repelled by the apparent sophistry of parts of his essay on 'Civil Disobedience', as when he announces:

I quietly declare war with the State, after my fashion, though I will still make use and get what advantage of her I can, as is usual in such cases.

Thoreau knew his position was open to criticism. 'I know of no redeeming qualities in me,' he confessed at twenty-four, 'but a sincere love for some things. ...' These are things in nature. He loves them completely, absorbedly, and without sentiment. He sits by a woodchuck for half an hour, talking to it:

He had a rather mild look. I spoke kindly to him. I reached checkerberry leaves to his mouth. I stretched my hands over him, though he turned up his head and still gritted a little. ... If I had had some food, I should have ended with stroking him at my leisure. ... A large, clumsy, burrowing squirrel. *Arctomys*, bear-mouse. I respect him as one of the natives. ... His ancestors have lived here longer than mine.

He has the same feeling about two moose, surprised in the Maine Woods: they are the rightful owners of the wilderness.

In a fine passage later in this narrative, he regrets the wanton destruction of game and of timber:

> Every creature is better alive than dead, men and moose and pine-trees. ... It is the living spirit of the tree, not its spirit of turpentine, with which I sympathize, and which heals my cuts. It is as immortal as I am, and perchance will go to as high a heaven, there to tower above me still.

J. R. Lowell, who accepted this piece for the *Atlantic Monthly*, enraged Thoreau by printing it with the last sentence omitted, as being too extravagant or too unorthodox for his readers. It was Thoreau's version of transcendentalism; and if he had too little contact with humanity to be a great imaginative writer, at least his close union with nature preserved him from most of the faults of transcendental literature. Work written deliberately for posterity tends to be ignored by posterity as well as by its own generation. The writer who is too much the seer becomes fatally oracular and tries too hard – as Emerson did – to load each symbol-sentence with meaning. The *sententia* is apt to sound sententious. Thoreau usually saved himself by writing of what he knew: namely, nature and his own character. Nature's innate rhythms gave shape to his writing, and allowed it to flow by like the seasons, instead of coagulating around a series of 'thoughts'. In particular they gave shape to *Walden*, the work by which he is best known. The day-to-day account of how he lived – the food he cooked, the few people with whom he talked, the details of the Pond and its wild-life: all these provide a firm base for his assaults upon conventional man: assaults delivered in a prose which is alert and trenchant like the best of Emerson:

> Let us settle ourselves, and work and wedge our feet downward through the mud and slush of opinion ... through Paris and London, through New York and Boston and Concord, through Church and State, through poetry and philosophy and religion, till we come to a hard bottom and rocks in place, which we can call *reality*, and say This is, and no mistake. ...
>
> Some circumstantial evidence is very strong, as when you find a trout in the milk.

Making the earth say beans instead of grass – this was my daily work.

Sometimes his writing has a metaphorical richness that reminds us of the debt Thoreau owes to such authors as Sir Thomas Browne:

Self-emancipation even in the West Indian provinces of the fancy and imagination – what Wilberforce is there to bring that about?

It has been said that – with the exception of passages like this one – Thoreau's style is conversational. Like Emerson's, though, it is not vernacular. It takes note of common speech, but not to reproduce it as Mark Twain does. Rather, it has its own special sound. This is in part contemporary: Thoreau says of Carlyle's books that 'they are ... works of art only as the plough, and corn-mill, and steam-engine – not as pictures and statues'; and one feels that he would like the statement to apply to his own pages. In part, too, his writing is reminiscent of the pamphleteering prose of a bygone England, as one may see in the hammer-blow sentences of his 'Slavery in Massachusetts', or in 'A Plea for Captain John Brown', who 'died lately in the time of Cromwell, but he reappeared here'.

As for his few poems, they are as unsatisfactory as Emerson's. Their lines have not fully made the transition from the prose of the journal to the form of verse. They rhyme too determinedly, ungainly as pairs tied together in a three-legged race. Like all the work that Thoreau managed to write during his fairly short life, they are on the *qui vive*. But their inadequacy brings us back to the general inadequacy of the literary world of Concord. Like Emerson, who said of Thoreau's poems that 'the thyme and marjoram are not yet honey', the younger man is a cleric without a pulpit, a scholar who condemns scholarship, a person with a rigorous conscience who recommends a kind of carefree anarchism. He is a Huckleberry Finn who has been to Harvard. The two sides of him are not fully united: we sympathize with his desire to live his life as well as utter it, but we suspect him of a typically transcendental determination to eat his cake and have it too. As Emerson wishes to combine 'acquiescence and optimism', to be passive and dynamic by turns, so Thoreau shifts his ground, until we echo Lowell's criticism (of *A Week on the Concord and Merrimack*) that 'we were bid to a river-party – not to be preached at'. But what preaching, and what a party! Thoreau's is magnificent literature almost in spite of itself. *Walden*, and his other writings, are a memorable vision of a period and a place in America when men – some men – thought it possible to find the godhead in the nearby woods: or, with a pride that seems to us the more inordinate for its modesty, to be like Adam before the Fall. It is a vision that has never ceased to tease the American imagination: and in noting its absurdity – which places it on a level with perpetual motion, or the philosopher's stone (confusing a carminative with carmot) – we would be wrong to miss the enduring element of human aspiration which it shares with those other searches.

NATHANIEL HAWTHORNE

ONE afternoon in 1842, shortly after Hawthorne had moved to Concord, he went on the river with Thoreau, to practise the management of a boat he had bought from the latter. He found himself quite unable to steer it, though

Mr Thoreau had assured me that it was only necessary to will the boat to go in any particular direction, and she would immediately take that course, as if imbued with the spirit of the steersman. It may be so with him, but it is certainly not so with me. The boat seemed to be bewitched, and turned its head to every point of the compass except the right one.

The anecdote affords a characteristic picture of both men: Thoreau, the resolute and capable, who had made the boat with his own hands; Hawthorne, half-amused, half-rueful, all too conscious of the perversities of existence.

The differences between him and Thoreau or Emerson are well known. For them, nature was man's true home; to him, nature was beautiful enough, but unconcerned with man. For them, the age-old torment over sin, predestination and damnation was needless; these, as Emerson wrote in 'Spiritual Laws', 'never darken-across any man's road who did not go out of his way to seek them. These are the soul's mumps and measles'. For Hawthorne, once they entered a man's life – as they were more than likely to do – there was no road by which they could be avoided.

Why he differed thus it is pointless to speculate. Emerson had only to open his window to hear the shrieks of a mad-woman confined nearby; his young wife died, and his son. Yet he discerned harmony wherever he looked. Hawthorne's own life was free enough from tragedy; yet he saw destiny's sombre operation all about him. The trite explanation is that Emerson was a transcendentalist, while Hawthorne, unable to accept transcendentalism's offers of emancipation, harked back to an earlier, grimmer New England. This explanation is of course too simple. Hawthorne did at least spend some months at Brook Farm, though he criticized its aims in *The Blithedale Romance*, and the larger implications of transcendentalism in 'The Celestial Railroad'. Nor was his gloom unrelieved: if he was haunted by his witch-hunting ancestor John Hathorne of Salem, he also delighted in the solid world of Trollope's novels. Moreover, his thought had something in common with that of Emerson and other transcendentalists. Like them, he sought the big in the little; as Emerson watching cigar-smoke thought of sea-tides, so Hawthorne was forever speculating on the larger significance of some material fact or phenomenon:

Meditations about the main gas-pipe of a great city, – if the supply were to be stopped, what would happen? ... It might be made emblematical of something.

Emblem, symbol, moral, analogy, type, image: these are favourite words of Hawthorne, and he would surely have agreed with Emerson's statement that 'every natural fact is a symbol of some spiritual fact'.

But despite these resemblances, Emerson and Hawthorne are at variance in several important respects. First, Haw-

thorne's observations are usually of man in society, not of
man in nature; and this though his theme is usually of a man
in some way set apart: there is always a crowd in the offing.
Second, while it is possibly unfair to set Hawthorne's notebooks against Emerson's more highly-wrought journal, they
are strikingly less certain in emphasis. Hawthorne asks questions but rarely answers them: he gropes, with no confidence
in the outcome. Third, as has been noted, he is concerned
with blacker and bleaker problems than Emerson ever acknowledged. And fourth, he is a writer of fiction, far more
occupied than Emerson with the technical questions of
authorship. As such, and for temperamental reasons, he is a
tentative writer, who speaks of his story-ideas as *hints*.

Could he have been more self-assured? This is the question
that Henry James poses, in his biography of Hawthorne.
Could a New Englander – or any American, at that time –
write satisfactory fiction in and about a land that had so
little experience of the art? No doubt Hawthorne's task was
difficult: was it impossible? Cooper and Irving before him
had to some extent succeeded, with the American as well as
with the European scene; and in his own lifetime Poe built
up imaginary worlds that were compelling, if unreal. Perhaps Henry James over-stressed the lack of subject-matter,
in his famous enumeration of the missing items in Hawthorne's America. For, as his notebooks show, Hawthorne had
plenty of themes to think about. If society in New England
was thin, it was more substantial than that of Mark Twain's
Missouri. Hawthorne's diffidence arises from a total uncertainty. Cooper and Irving were not novelists from whom
he could learn much; nor was Charles Brockden Brown.
In fact, though the sermon, the poem, or the private diary
were all familiar releases to the New Englander anxious
to express himself, the novel was a suspect form. In the
well-known words (from the preface to *The Scarlet Letter*) that
Hawthorne attributes to his ancestors:

'What is he?' murmurs one gray shadow of my forefathers to the
other. 'A writer of story books! What kind of a business in life, –
what mode of glorifying God, or being serviceable to mankind in

his day and generation, – may that be? Why the degenerate fellow might as well have been a fiddler!'

In Missouri, a fiddler was a useful acquisition to society, and a newspaper humorist like Mark Twain was a welcome, even an honoured figure in a Western community. But Hawthorne, by comparison, worked in the dark. New England was accustomed to didacticism in its literature, and unmitigated didacticism blights the novel. Yet Hawthorne brought himself up on two of the worst possible models for the would-be novelist (as the nineteenth century understood the word): Bunyan and Spenser. Half of him entered the world of allegory, and could never get out of it.

The other half remained in 'the ordinary world' (as he so often calls it), closely interested in the gestures and motives of his fellow-men, and in the look of their New England world. This half of Hawthorne is somewhat unimaginative; the character-sketches in his notebooks are a little prosaic. The people whose behaviour he jots down are not fully realized; he assembles them as a casting bureau collects actors, and they stand around as if waiting for some lines to say.

Hawthorne's problem was to bring the two parts together, to contrive 'a neutral ground where the Actual and the Imaginary might meet'. It was complicated by his reluctance to bring them together in a gloomy place. He believed in the virtues of America, its cheerfulness and newness (in this aspect, curiously, he was much more patriotic than Emerson or Thoreau). His publishers and many of his readers urged him to step out into the sunlight. But he did not know how, when nearly all his symbols derived their force – in the words of Melville's review of *Mosses from an Old Manse* – from 'that Calvinistic sense of Innate Depravity and Original Sin, from whose visitations, ... no deeply thinking mind is always and wholly free'. In *The Marble Faun* Hawthorne said of a building in Rome that

The prison-like, iron-barred windows, and the wide-arched, dismal entrance, ... might impress [the artist] as far better worth his pencil than the newly painted pine boxes, in which – if he be an American – his countrymen live and thrive. But there is reason to suspect that a people are waning to decay and ruin the moment that their life becomes fascinating either in the poet's imagination or the painter's eye.

He could not admit that his own land had reached such a stage of corruption. It was a country, he said in the preface to *The Marble Faun*, 'where there is no shadow, no antiquity, no mystery ... nor anything but a commonplace prosperity, in broad and simple daylight'. He did his best, therefore, to achieve 'a mood half sportive and half thoughtful', so as to square Calvin with the cheerfulness of contemporary America. In 1850, for example, he noted down an idea for an article on cemeteries, with various mottoes, 'facetious or serious'. And, in fact, some of his work – some stories and sketches, interludes in *The Blithedale Romance* and *The House of the Seven Gables*, the gloriously funny account of English-women in *Our Old Home*, his books for children, and so on – attains the lightness of heart and touch that he wished for. But he could not be facetious *and* serious, and where it was necessary to choose, the choice determined itself. It nearly always plunged him into the shadow and antiquity whose existence in 'my dear native land' he had denied.

The Actual and the Imaginary alternate in the 'hints for stories' that are scattered through his notebooks. At the one extreme there is the sort of situation that interested Henry James:

A virtuous but giddy girl to attempt to play a trick on a man. He sees what she is about, and contrives matters so that she throws herself completely into his power, and is ruined, – all in jest.

At the other extreme are such notes as:

A person to catch fire-flies, and to try to kindle his household fire with them. It would be symbolical of something.

or:

To personify winds of various characters.

Here we are back in the Imaginary with a vengeance. Other suggestions are: an insane reformer – a hero who never falls in love – a ghost by moonlight – thronged solitude – a body possessed by two spirits – return of images in a mirror – ice in the blood – a secret thing in public – a bloody footprint – an eating-house with poisoned dishes. Some of them seem the stock-in-trade of horror-romance; and indeed Hawthorne was always in danger of tumbling, as he knew, over 'the utmost verge of a precipitous absurdity'.

Year after year of his young manhood went by quietly and drably in Salem while, without much faith in his own talent, or much idea of where his notions might lead him, he turned out stories and sketches to exemplify the generalized jottings of his notebook. Sometimes he would destroy what he had written; if printed, it would often appear anonymously. Withdrawn, uneasy, commenting with a hurt humour on his lack of popularity with the public, he nevertheless began to make a reputation. Poe congratulated Hawthorne in one of his best reviews, that in which he outlined his belief in the short story as a literary medium. As Poe realized, and as *Twice-Told Tales* and *Mosses from an Old Manse* made apparent to others, this 'harmless Hawthorne' (of Melville's phrase) was producing some work of a quite special weight. There were conventional essays ('Fire Worship', 'Buds and Bird Voices'); satirical excursions ('The Celestial Railroad'); and every kind of tale, from fantasy to tableaux of New England history. Among them all, certain stories stand out as remarkably powerful, their effect heightened perhaps by the gentle, decorous prose in which they are narrated. In 'The Gentle Boy', for example, a Quaker child in an inimical New England settlement is stoned by the other children, and betrayed by one of them whom he had befriended. In 'Egotism; or, The Bosom Serpent', a man estranged from his wife is convinced that he has a live serpent inside him which perpetually gnaws at him. It leaves him only when he is able to meet his wife again and forget for a moment his obsession with his own ills. And in 'Young Goodman Brown', the finest of all his tales, Hawthorne tells of an early New England in which his hero attends a witches' sabbath, to discover that the company includes not only all the prominent people of his township, but even his wife Faith. Pride, envy, remorse nag his characters; and the unthinking community shuts out the unusual individual. Yet there are virtuous people, and only one sin is unpardonable: that of wilful estrangement from the rest of humanity. This results in the suicide of Ethan Brand; causes Rappaccini to lose his daughter; and leads Reuben unwittingly to kill his son, as expiation for having long ago left Roger Malvin to die. Let Hawthorne but find a usable symbol, and he would erect it into a story.

One such symbol took firm hold of him. As early as 1837, in 'Endicott and the Red Cross', he mentioned, as one of a crowd in seventeenth-century Salem,

a young woman, with no mean share of beauty, whose doom it was to wear the letter A on the breast of her gown ... Sporting with her infamy, the lost and desperate creature had embroidered the fatal token in scarlet cloth, with golden thread and the nicest art of needlework; so that the capital A might have been thought to mean Admirable, or anything rather than Adulteress.

He reverted to the same symbol in a notebook entry seven years later, and in 1847 began work on what was to be his greatest achievement, *The Scarlet Letter*. Such letters were actually worn in colonial New England; instances have been recorded of a D for Drunkard, and even of an I, signifying Incest. They furnished Hawthorne with just the combination of 'moral and material' that he could handle: here was a 'type' bodied forth: here also was 'a secret thing in public'. However, despite its near-perfect construction, few great books have been more hesitantly produced. Worries over money prevented him from giving his whole mind to the story. He was troubled by its 'hell-fired' quality, and tried to make the book more attractive by supplying a lengthy preamble on the Salem Custom House. Moreover, apart from his immature *Fanshawe*, Hawthorne had not written anything longer than magazine-stories. If his publisher had not badgered him, it is possible that *The Scarlet Letter* would never have been completed as a novel.

Yet the finished work was a masterpiece. Instead of seeming

like an over-expanded sketch, as *The Marble Faun* does, it reads as a brilliantly economical novel. There are only three chief characters – or four if we include the child Pearl. The three are Pearl's mother, Hester Prynne the adulteress; her implacable old husband Roger; and Arthur Dimmesdale, the pious young minister who has fathered her child, and who in failing to confess his sin endures agonies of guilt. The voluptuous and maternal Hester, expiating her offence, survives to a tranquil old age; but the two men are tortured and distorted, the one by conscience, the other by the luxury of revenge. In this one taut, subtle novel Hawthorne solves almost all his problems. Avoiding the *a priori* Americanism which is so crudely contrasted with European depravity in *The Marble Faun*, he sets his trio in colonial Boston. He is able to make the past more real than his American present; when he deals with the latter the 'broad and simple daylight' seems to defeat him: it is the sense of the past that redeems *The House of the Seven Gables*. In it, and in *The Blithedale Romance*, he dodges all around the question of contemporariness, insisting that they are 'romances', in which reality is to be done by mirrors.

Superb though *The Scarlet Letter* is, it does have certain minor defects, concerned with his use of symbols. Poe, and Henry James after him (not to mention Hawthorne himself), have pointed out this inveterate weakness of dressing up characters to exemplify a theme that is often quite incompatible with 'actuality'. Emerson put the matter a little differently when he complained that 'Hawthorne invites his readers too much into his study, opens the process before them. As if the confectioner should say to his customers, "Now, let us make the cake".' It is what he does in the preface to *The Scarlet Letter*; and in the book itself he searches too indefatigably for emblems. The central symbol of the letter worn on Hester's bosom is splendid. But Hawthorne cannot resist having a large A in the night sky, or on Dimmesdale's flesh. All too rarely does he trust himself to convey an idea: he must underline and make heavily explicit. Thus, in 'The Gentle Boy':

The two females, as they held each a hand of Ibrahim, formed a practical allegory; it was rational piety and unbridled fanaticism contending for the empire of a young heart.

Suddenly, a moving story has lapsed into public-monument cliché. At worst, the fault destroys his fiction. 'The Birthmark' is ruined by a mixture of fact and fancy that becomes preposterous; so is 'Drowne's Wooden Image'. In *The Marble Faun* Donatello, with his problematical furry ears, is acceptable neither as a person nor as a symbol. Though *The Blithedale Romance* is a much better book, it, too, is marred by tiresome symbols. Zenobia's exotic flower and Westervelt's false teeth, like other obvious motifs of Hawthorne, may remind the reader of the alarm-clock crocodile in *Peter Pan*. *The Seven Gables* comes next in stature to *The Scarlet Letter*; here Hawthorne deals with the crumbling old house and the malignant Pyncheons as novelist rather than allegorist. He is no more able than Cooper, or William Faulkner in a later generation, to answer finally whether Americans make too much of the past or too little of it. But he handles his pathetic characters with an acute sympathy, and his obnoxious ones with acute distaste. Victims and bullies are the types which he excels in drawing. The very limitations of Judge Pyncheon, his conceit, his thick-hided selfishness, made him the least symbolical and so the most solidly real of all of Hawthorne's characters. (This is not to say that reality was his only salvation; when he trusted himself wholeheartedly to fantasy, as in 'The Snow Image', he was sometimes highly successful.)

One other important fault, from which *The Scarlet Letter* is free, has to do with Hawthorne's view of 'ordinary people'. Ordinariness is his norm; what is extraordinary tends to be suspect. Human beings, he feels, should not tamper with one another – Chillingworth's sin, like Ethan Brand's, is to have 'violated, in cold blood, the sanctity of a human heart'. Any very strong interest or emotion, for Hawthorne, is next door to mania; the reforming zeal of Hollingsworth is only one step short of the madness of Rappaccini. Yet what is the novelist or artist but an extraordinary person who pries into the affairs of others? Hawthorne seems to deny his own vocation; and his position is the more ambiguous in that he does not like 'ordinary people'. If he fears the intellectual, he despises the boor. Try as he will, he cannot prevent the reader from preferring Ethan Brand to the cloddish villagers of the tale.

But these shortcomings should be seen as natural consequences of Hawthorne's struggle to find his way in fiction without a guide. As honest as Emerson or Thoreau – which is to say a great deal – he has a profounder knowledge than they of man's fate, and a correspondingly harder task as writer. Their lack of form, it might be argued, represents the weakening of an older line of didactic communication; his lack of certainty represents the beginning of a new line of communication. Paradoxically, he made use of the past in proportion as they rejected it. For him, even in his (theoretically) sunlit America, there was no new start. As Chillingworth tells Hester, .

My old faith ... comes back to me, and explains all that we do, and all we suffer. By thy first step awry thou didst plant the germ of evil; but since that moment, it has all been a dark necessity.

CHAPTER FIVE

MELVILLE AND WHITMAN

HERMAN MELVILLE (1819–91)

b. New York City, the son of a prosperous importer who went bankrupt and *d.* 1832, leaving his widow and children (who moved to Albany, N.Y.) to struggle along with the aid of relatives. Melville worked in a bank, taught school, and sailed as ship's boy to Liverpool and back before going to sea, 1841, in the whaler *Acushnet*, bound for the South Seas. 1842, deserted his ship in the Marquesas, encountered a cannibal tribe, and left the islands in an Australian whaler. After further adventures at Tahiti and Honululu, returned home 1844 aboard the frigate *United States*. Began to write, using his sea experiences as basis: *Typee* (1846), *Omoo* (1847, in which year he also married), both well received; *Mardi, Redburn* (1849), *White-Jacket* (1850), *Moby Dick* (1851), *Pierre* (1852). Of these, *Mardi* bewildered the public, *Moby Dick* met with a disappointing reception, and *Pierre* was a complete failure. Thereafter, gradually abandoned effort to support himself by writing, though not until he had produced a number of stories, six of which appeared as *Piazza Tales* (1856), and two more novels, *Israel Potter* (1855) and *The Confidence-Man* (1857). Turned to verse, most of it – including the long poem *Clarel* (1876) – privately printed. Worked in New York as customs inspector, 1866–85; then lived quietly in retirement, occupying his last months with *Billy Budd* (not published until 1924).

WALT WHITMAN (1819–92)

b. Long Island, of mixed Dutch and Yankee stock. Father a carpenter-builder. 1823, family moved to rapidly growing town of Brooklyn, across the East River from Manhattan. Left school 1830, to work as printer; 1838–9, schoolteaching on Long Island; 1841–5, journalist; 1846–7, editor of *Brooklyn Daily Eagle*. Disagreed with Democratic party over political opinions; also regarded as a somewhat lazy editor. Out of a job in consequence, made brief trip, 1848, to New Orleans. 1851–4, worked as carpenter in Brooklyn, while keeping a notebook from which grew poems published as *Leaves of Grass* (1855). These praised by Emerson and a few others, denounced by some reviewers, but in general aroused little attention. 2nd edition of *L of G*, 1856; 1860, 3rd edition. 1863–5, worked as clerk and hospital-nurse in Washington, tending Civil War wounded. 1865, *Drum Taps*. Further editions of *L of G* 1867, 1871, 1872, 1876, 1881, 1889, 1892. Continued to work in Washington until 1873, when he suffered paralytic stroke which left him semi-invalid for the rest of his life. 1871, *Democratic Vistas* (prose). 1879, made journey through West and Middle West. *Specimen Days and Collect* (autobiographical notes, 1882). In later years surrounded by disciples, and well known to men of letters, though still not to the general public. 1888, *November Boughs* (prose and verse). *d.* Camden, New Jersey, unmarried.

MELVILLE AND WHITMAN

—

HERMAN MELVILLE

THOUGH Emerson and Hawthorne travelled to Europe, they, like Thoreau, found literary sustenance in what lay under their noses. For all its inadequacies, New England nourished them, and like other New Englanders they extracted a kind of genius from provincialism. Years at sea, however, took Herman Melville far out of the familiar world of New York and Albany. Melville was not the only writer of the time who found the sea a rich source of metaphor. His contemporary, Flaubert, said in 1846 that 'the three finest things in creation are the sea, *Hamlet*, and Mozart's *Don Giovanni*'.[1] Perhaps Hawthorne would have benefited as a writer if he had accepted an offer once made to him to join in a voyage to the South Seas. At any rate, Melville, unlike these, actually made the voyage, and was thus able to bolster his romantic flights with personal knowledge. If the sea was a metaphor, it was also a real highway, along which real men earned their living. Indeed, in Melville's first books it is the reality – though a somewhat romantic one – that engages him. *Typee* pleased a public that was growing tired of travel narratives and sea-yarns by presenting them with a fresh and exciting situation, couched as autobiography. And in fact, though some of the material was the product of Melville's imagination, he does not seem to regard the book as a novel. In his preface he claims an 'anxious desire to

1. One may compare Melville's observation (in a letter, 3 March 1849) that 'I love all men that *dive* ... the whole corps of intellectual thought-divers that have been diving & coming up again with bloodshot eyes since the world began', with Flaubert's 'I am the obscure and patient pearl-fisher, who returns from his dive empty-handed and blue in the face. Some fatal attraction draws me down into the depths of thought, down into those innermost recesses which never lose their fascination for the strong of heart.' (Letter to Louise Colet, 7 October 1846.)

speak the unvarnished truth'. He equips the story with a map, and adds documentary chapters. (The title of the book as published in England – *Narrative of a Four Months' Residence Among the Natives of a Valley of the Marquesas Islands; or, A Peep at Polynesian Life* – was guaranteed to exclude it from the fiction-shelves). The style, as a whole, is that of the traveller on his best literary behaviour:

Those who for the first time visit the South Seas, generally are surprised at the appearance of the islands when beheld from the sea. From the vague accounts we have of their beauty, many people are apt to picture to themselves enamelled and softly swelling plains, shaded over with delicious groves, and watered by purling brooks ...

Typee is an account, told in the first person, of the adventures of a young American who with a companion (Toby) jumps ship. Making their way over a mountain range into an inland valley, the two find themselves among the cannibal Typees. Toby is able to leave them, but the narrator is compelled to remain with the tribe, who to his surprise and relief treat him kindly. The story ends with his escape from the Typees, who pursue him into the sea when he is picked up by a ship's boat. The point of this simple account lies in the contrast between the vices of civilization and the virtues of the supposedly barbarous natives, who are a beautiful and carefree group, with one of whom the young American conducts an idyllic though not very vivid love affair. But though the book has little creative interest, it exhibits in rudimentary form nearly all the themes that Melville developed in his more ambitious writing. In *Typee* he deals with a voyage and a journey; he castigates white civilization (conventionally enough, with a reference to Rousseau) and its clutter of moral codes; he suggests that the wandering narrator can find satisfaction neither among his own people nor among the savages. And, although Toby's cheerful, extravert character belies the description, Melville speaks of him as 'one of that class of rovers you sometimes meet at sea, who never reveal their origin, never allude to home, and go rambling over the world as if pursued by some mysterious

.fate they cannot possibly elude'. Here is sketched out the
idea he returns to in *Moby Dick*, in the briefly glimpsed yet
unforgettable figure of Bulkington.

In *Omoo*, Melville takes up the narrative where he left it
in *Typee* – with the escape of his hero. He establishes a more
ominous atmosphere; for the young American is now in an
ancient, condemned whaler, with a mutinous crew and a
weak captain. After a death, one of the sailors prophesies
that three weeks hence not one quarter of the men will be
left aboard. The ship is apparently doomed. But the tension
is dissipated, and a mutiny becomes a comic-opera situation,
in which the only serious stress is laid upon the degradation
of Tahiti. The islanders, their bodies ravaged by the white
man's diseases and their culture destroyed by well-meaning
missionaries, await extinction, chanting an old prediction:

> The palm-tree shall grow,
> The coral shall spread,
> But man shall cease.

Again, however, cheerfulness breaks in, as the narrator
(with his grotesque crony Dr Long Ghost) knocks about
the islands as a beachcomber, until a convenient end can be
made, out of his decision to leave Tahiti in an American
whaler.

Omoo reinforced the public's view of Melville as a writer
of jocular and lively reminiscence. But *Mardi*, which followed hard on its heels, was another matter. *Mardi* begins
straightforwardly, though the prose is markedly richer:

We are off! The courses and topsails are set; the coral-hung anchor
swings from the bow: and together the three royals are given to
the breeze, that follows us out to sea like the baying of a hound.
Out spreads the canvas – alow, aloft – boom stretched, on both
sides, with many a stun'sail; till like a hawk, with pinions poised, we
shadow the sea with our sails, and reelingly cleeve the brine.

Two similes and one adverbial coinage in a short passage:
these suggest the later Melville. But the tone is breezy, and
though the narrator complains of boredom on this particular whaling voyage, there is no suggestion that he is

anything other than an energetic, irresponsible young man, better educated than his shipmates but in no way alien to them. Soon, the narrator – Taji, as he is called for the greater part of the book – decides to desert, and accomplishes this in a whaleboat, taking with him an old sailor. They head westward for a chain of islands in the Pacific; their various adventures are exciting, but perfectly plausible.

Then comes the change. As Taji sees land on the horizon, he also sights a native boat, manned by young warriors who prove to be the children of an old priest. He sits guarding a lovely white girl, Yillah, who is to be offered up as a sacrifice. Determined to rescue her, Taji kills the priest in doing so. Melville has abruptly and entirely altered his story; his prose becomes lushly melodramatic.

But he changes course again, as the voyagers reach the archipelago of Mardi, where Taji is welcomed as a demigod and lives in bliss with Yillah, until she disappears. Determined to search the archipelago for her, he sets off on his quest in company with four Mardians, including the philosopher Babbalanja. The journey of these with Taji occupies the greater part of the book, and for most of their journey Yillah is only an excuse for travel: the interest is concentrated on what they see. True, there are reminders of Yillah; Taji is shadowed by three sons of the priest, who kill off a couple of characters whom the author seems to have found superfluous. But these and other intimations are submerged in the flow of satire and speculation on the Mardian universe. The satire is uneven, and functions on different levels: some islands represent human follies (religious dogmatism, pride of birth), others represent actual countries ('Dominora' is England, while 'Vivenza' is the United States). The speculation likewise fluctuates from serious to facetious. Taji merges with the author as narrator, and for long periods is passed over, while Babbalanja and the rest wrangle over the meanings of existence. Occasionally Melville-Taji speculates on his own account, or sets down strange lyrical fantasies:

Dreams! dreams! golden dreams: endless and golden, as the flowery prairies, that stretch away from the Rio Sacramento ...; prairies

like rounded eternities: jonquil leaves beaten out; and my dreams
herd like buffaloes, browsing on to the horizon, and browsing on
round the world; and among them, I dash with my lance, to
spear one ere they all flee.

He writes, as he says in the same chapter, as one possessed,
intent – as he makes Babbalanja declare:

upon the essence of things; the mystery that lieth beyond; the elements of the tear which much laughter provoketh; that which is
beneath the seeming; the precious pearl within the shaggy oyster.

As the book draws to an end, the voyagers have found the
island of Serenia, where is true love and peace. They call upon Taji to renounce his futile quest for Yillah; but he, discovering that she has been drowned in the whirlpool for
which the priest intended her, sails out from the calm la-
goon into the rough ocean, alone, still pursued by the priest's
sons. What began like a sea-chanty has become a cry of anguish. From the reasonable world of Marryat or Cooper we
have passed to one reminiscent of Poe's *Narrative of Arthur
Gordon Pym* (which also begins reasonably, but ends in a
weird commitment to disaster). Hawthorne attempts to dis-
sociate himself from the headlong calamity which he, too,
records, but in Melville as in Poe there is a sort of hectic excess: the high spirits in the one, and the intellectuality in the
other, engender hysteria. *Mardi* is an hysterical, over-
strained book, hopelessly confused in aim. Yet it is a good
bad book, and extraordinarily interesting to study as a preliminary to the wonderful *Moby Dick*.

After *Mardi*, Melville continued to write, almost without
pause. This time, however, aware perhaps that he had over-
reached himself as well as the public, he returned to some
extent to the tone of *Typee* or *Omoo*. In *White-Jacket* he wrote
what purported to be an account of his experiences aboard
the American warship *United States*. And in *Redburn* he enlarged upon his first voyage, from New York to Liverpool
and back. Again he presented himself as the bluff narrator
of actual events, as though he could not trust himself with
outright fiction. His prose, too, was simplified, though it

had become more supple than that of *Typee*. Here is his child's-eye view of an oil-painting, from *Redburn*:

[It] represented a fat-looking, smoky fishing-boat, with three whiskerandoes in red caps, and their trousers legs rolled up, hauling in a seine. There was high French-like land in one corner, and a tumble-down grey lighthouse surmounting it. The waves were toasted brown, and the whole picture looked mellow and old. I used to think a piece of it might taste good.

Save for the word 'whiskerandoes', there is little to connect this admirably direct description with his Mardian flourishes.

Within a few years Melville had thus written five books, none of which could be easily classified as a novel. The first three had dealt with the South Seas; but though there was plenty of shipboard incident in them, it was the islands that seemed chiefly to fascinate Melville – or rather, the whole tropical ambience of the area. His next two books, *White-Jacket* and *Redburn*, moved out of the tropics, and though there is a long interlude ashore in *Redburn*, the two works show a considerable interest in the crews as social microcosms, and in the voyage (rather than the landfall) as an extended metaphor of man's destiny. He was reading widely and intensely during the first years of authorship. There are traces of Dickens in his work, perhaps most noticeably in such later writing as 'Bartleby the Scrivener', in which the dull impersonality of the world of law and lawyers seems to echo the mood of *Bleak House*. One wonders too whether Melville may have read a jaunty, bawdy pamphlet written by an Englishman, Ned Ward, and first printed in 1760. Its title is *The Wooden World Dissected; in the Character of A Ship of War*. The sketch of a ship's captain begins:

He is a Leviathan, or rather a kind of sea-god, whom the poor tars worship as the Indians do the devil, more through fear than affection; nay, some will have it, that he is more a devil than the devil himself.

Leaving aside such possible sources, it is clear that Melville gained most from Shakespeare, though Sir Thomas Browne among others also delighted him.

Moreover, he threw himself into an important friendship, at a time when he had probably written one draft of his sixth book, on whaling. There are many indications in his previous work that, not content with conventional narrative, he wished his adventure tales to carry a greater load of significance. Until he read Hawthorne's stories, however, and made Hawthorne's acquaintance, there was no one to encourage him in what he called 'ontological heroics'. But in Hawthorne he discovered another fellow-American concerned with 'that which is beneath the seeming', and using fiction as his medium. Though the friendship dwindled away, much to Melville's regret, it was a vital tonic to him while he was engaged on *Moby Dick*. It may even have led him to rewrite the book, on a deliberately higher plane of meaning.

For *Moby Dick* he chose a South Sea voyage in a whaler. In so doing, and in sticking to the ship instead of roaming off among real or imagined islands, he provided himself with a firm social and occupational framework. Thus anchored to actuality, he could let his imagination run free. Metaphysical inquiry came out of physical fact (and not vice versa, as too often in Hawthorne). In the first draft it seems likely that the story was heavily documentary in approach – as it still is, in certain chapters – and owed its origin to such narratives as that of Owen Chase. But in final form the hunt for whales focused on one in particular, the White Whale, Moby (*Mocha*) Dick; and on the obsessive hatred of Moby Dick felt by the whaleship's captain, Ahab. The novel has tremendous power. It moves grandly through alternations of excitement and ease to the almost intolerable tension of the three-day chase of the White Whale, and the eventual, inevitable disaster when the whale kills Ahab, then smashes the *Pequod* as Owen Chase's *Essex* was smashed. The action-writing is unsurpassable; for once Melville's energy seems suited to the job in hand. His voyage, his seamen, their ship, their captain, the whale itself, are all tangible: they possess weight, dimension, colour. What is added is a genuine overplus, not an erratic moralizing and groping

after significances, as in *Mardi*. There is, for example, nothing false in the fact that Ishmael, Ahab, Elijah, Gabriel,
and others in the novel have Scriptural names: such names
were natural in their New England context (as it was natural for the wife of Goodman Brown to be known as Faith),
and Melville is thus legitimately able to suggest Biblical
analogies.

Ahab is in some ways a Hawthorne 'type'. In Hawthorne's
tale, 'The Great Carbuncle', we meet an 'aged Seeker' who,
roaming the mountains in search of the precious object, has
no hope of

enjoyment from it; that folly has passed long ago! I keep up the
search for this accursed stone because the vain ambition of my
youth has become a fate upon me in old age. The pursuit alone is
my strength, – the energy of my soul, – the warmth of my blood, –
and the pith and marrow of my bones!... Yet not to have my wasted lifetime back again would I give up my hopes of the Great Carbuncle! Having found it, I shall bear it to a certain cavern ... and
there, grasping it in my arms, lie down and die, and keep it buried
with me forever.

This is the apart man, the demoniac dreamer – Dr Heidegger
or Ethan Brand – doomed for his arrogant isolation. Since
Hawthorne treats them as examples of error, their diabolism
is often unconvincing; nor is it possible to take very seriously
such objectives as a Great Carbuncle. But we are soon engrossed in the character and problems of Ahab, the 'grand,
ungodly, godlike man' who, 'stricken, blasted, if he be',
still 'has his humanities', and whose objective is a credible
one. Ahab, like the Jonah of Father Mapple's magnificent
sermon, sins through wilfulness, for 'if we obey God, we must
disobey ourselves'. Yet courage and pride are – we learn in
the same sermon – fine qualities: 'Delight is to him ... who
against the proud gods and commodores of this earth, ever
stands forth his own inexorable self.' Hawthorne feels that
all excess is to be deplored; Melville, with a more generous
sense of human potentiality, insists that virtues and vices
alike depend upon a certain excess. Ahab, then, is both hero
and villain, dooming others where Taji dooms only himself.

Moby Dick is one of the world's great novels, whose richness increases with each new reading. But certain minor flaws link it with the other work of Melville's creative prime. In *Mardi*, though Taji is supposed to be the narrator, we lose our sense of who is telling the tale. In *Moby Dick* the same confusion is apparent. The first sentence – 'Call me Ishmael' – has a premonitory rumble. However, Ishmael adopts a rollicking air, devil-may-care rather than bedevilled; he seems to be the same person as the author-narrator of Melville's previous books. 'God keep me from ever completing anything,' he exclaims in Chapter 32. 'This whole book is but a draught – nay, but the draught of a draught. Oh Time, Strength, Cash, and Patience.' This is surely an author's aside. Befriended by the native harpooner Queequeg, Ishmael does hint at a complexity more in keeping with his name when he says, 'No more my splintered heart and maddened hand were turned against the wolfish world'; but nothing else in the novel bears out this picture of the young man. In general, he is like the narrator of *Typee*, and his friendship with Queequeg seems a similar vindication of primitive values. But this theme is discarded. It is as though Melville finds Ishmael a nuisance. For twenty-eight chapters he relates the story. Then for three chapters (beginning with 'Enter Ahab; to Him, Stubb') it is clearly not Ishmael's story – he cannot be aware of the soliloquies of others – and though the novel reverts to Ishmael's narration, it frequently dispenses with him. Melville, it would appear, is undecided who is – so to speak – in charge of the book, or what kind of book it is to be. His efforts at Shakespearean soliloquy can be construed as a somewhat awkward attempt to enlarge its scope, and rescue it from Ishmael's necessarily limited approach. Certainly *Moby Dick*, as it progresses, rapidly improves; one might say that Taji has been separated into his component parts, Ishmael and Ahab – though Ishmael and Melville still contend for the honours of narration.

There are, it must be repeated, minor flaws. They have nevertheless their interest when taken in relation to Melville's

next novel, *Pierre; or, the Ambiguities*, which he wrote so soon
afterwards that he must have had it in mind when completing *Moby Dick*. Like *Mardi*, *Pierre* is resoundingly unsuccessful, and curiously memorable. In it, for the first time,
Melville leaves the sea and far-off places to write – in the
third person – of contemporary America. Pierre is a young
man whom fortune has endowed with looks, family, talent –
even a beautiful fiancée. Then another girl comes into his
life, a strange creature who persuades him that she is the
illegitimate daughter of his dead, revered father. Strongly
drawn to her, Pierre is certain that his mother would never
accept the girl, or the idea of her husband's guilt. In Hamlet-
like torment – *Hamlet* is one of the books Pierre has been reading – and actuated by an insane high-mindedness, he takes
his half-sister to New York, allowing everyone to believe that
he has married her as the result of a sudden infatuation. The
shock of this behaviour kills his mother and prostrates his
fiancée. Penniless, installing his half-sister with him in
shabby lodgings, he begins to write a book that is to earn
them a living. But he writes in despair, and the result is a
demented book that no publisher will handle. The story
ends in a welter of gore, with the death of all the chief characters. Much of *Pierre* is melodramatic claptrap, interrupted
by bouts of harshly facetious satire upon the literary and reforming circles of the day. Like many of Poe's protagonists,
Pierre is a projection of the author, who likewise reveals the
extent of the author's alienation from America. Formerly,
Melville had been an ardent democrat; he objected, for example, as Whitman does, to what he thought was a toadying
to aristocracy in Shakespeare. Gradually, however, his
democratic faith became more qualified, as the inanities of
the public (partly in regard to his own work) and the revelation of human wickedness quenched his optimism. He makes
Pierre an aristocrat of the type of 1800, agonized and helpless in the America of 1850. Where he had previously tried to
distinguish between the *people* and the *public*, he could now
only offer to Pierre the consolation of a pamphlet by one
'Plotinus Plinlimmon'. This recommends virtuous ex-

pediency as the highest attainable goal of the average man,
and for the exceptional man a goodness that is not much
more rigorous: the whole tempered by a certain detachment.
Nor is the pamphlet of any use to Pierre, since he mislays it,
and since in any case he is no more rational than Taji or
Ahab. What a collapse is evident in the Melville who only
three years before could say in *Redburn* that

The other world beyond this, which was longed for by the devout
before Columbus' time, was found in the New; and the deep-sea-
lead, that first struck these soundings, brought up the soil of Earth's
Paradise.

After *Pierre* Melville slowly relinquished his effort to live
by the pen. For some years he continued to write prose, including a painfully desolate historical novel, *Israel Potter*,
whose American narrator spends forty years of unmerited
exile in London;[1] and *The Confidence-Man*, in which the Melvillian voyage is made in that relatively humdrum craft, a
Mississippi paddle-steamer. Melville's friend Hawthorne
said of him, at about this period: 'He can neither believe,
nor be comfortable in his unbelief; and he is too honest and
courageous not to try to do one or the other.' *The Confidence-
Man* reveals this total perplexity. Everything in it is possibly
something else, a masquerade, a paradox. The Melvillian
voyage in this instance is made on All Fools' Day, in a
Mississippi paddle-steamer sardonically named the *Fidele*. A
whole succession of tricksters or confidence-men appear on
the ship – seemingly the same man in various guises. The
readiness of Americans to deceive and be deceived was a
richly promising theme, as Mark Twain was to show with
his pair of travelling rogues in *Huckleberry Finn*. But Melville
was not content with mere comedy, even of the most mock-
ing sort. Preoccupied with truth and illusion, he leaves the
reader in as much uncertainty as the *Fidele's* passengers. Is
confidence wisdom or folly? What are we to take on trust –

1. For the story of the original Israel Potter, whose autobiography was
published in 1824, see Richard M. Dorson (ed.), *America Rebels: Narratives of the Patriots* (New York, Pantheon, 1953).

everything, nothing? If self-deception is a precondition of happiness, are swindlers necessary and even indispensable? Do drunkards blur reality, or come closer to it? The novel's message, like that of *Israel Potter* and of some of the short stories Melville wrote during the 1850s, seems to be a variant on Plotinus Plinlimmon. Secession was in the air; as Thoreau had declared his independence of society, and as the abolitionist Garrison had publicly burned the American Constitution, so Melville implied that, if lucky, one might survive by becoming a spectator. Secession was not always possible, and never as smoothly accomplished as by Thoreau: 'Benito Cereno', caught in a web of evil, is so dominated by the sinister Negro slave Babo that he can only 'follow his leader' and die likewise. Or, having escaped, one may die, like 'Bartleby the Scrivener'. This is not to say that Melville had written himself out, or that his short stories of this period were all despairing. One indeed, 'The Apple Tree Table', employs the hopeful image of the 'strong and beautiful bug' (eating its way out of wood that has been made into furniture) with which Thoreau ends *Walden*. But fine though some of them are, they are the work of a man who no longer wishes to grapple furiously with his universe.

A few years before the Civil War broke out in 1861, Melville turned from prose to poetry. Before his death he had written enough to fill a plump volume; and this excluding his long *Clarel*, which describes a symbolic, as well as actual, round trip to the Holy Land. One might apply to Melville's verse the observation made by Emerson on Thoreau's: namely, that his genius was better than his talent. Technically it is maladroit; perhaps only a dozen poems (and fragments of *Clarel*) are thoroughly satisfying, and not all of these few are metrically impeccable. Some of the best are about the Civil War. To Melville, as to Whitman, it was a deeply tragic affair. In a way, it proved him to have been right:

> Nature's dark side is heeded now
> (Ah! optimist-cheer disheartened flown)

But a residual faith in America, which he has never altogether lost, makes him sadly conjecture that even with victory, it will be like 'man's latter fall':

> the Founders' dream shall flee.
> Age after age shall be
> As age after age has been.

Still, the conflict restores his sense of human grandeur. After
it is all over, in the seventies and eighties, Melville's verse is
mainly a counsel of acceptance. Sometimes, as in 'The
Berg' or 'The Maldive Shark', it has a leaden melancholy;
sometimes it rises to the gentle, elegiac note of

> Where is the world we roved, Ned Bunn?

Last of all came *Billy Budd*, the long short story which
seems a coda to Melville's life. In it he returns to the setting
of a ship, with its rigid hierarchical discipline and its poetic
overtones. He returns, too, to a favourite early conception, of
the Iago-figure, the malign individual (Bland in *White-
Jacket*, Jackson in *Redburn*) who acts from a pure sense of evil,
and is therefore not the orthodox villain of fiction, but someone more to be pitied than hated. Claggart, the master-
at-arms who falsely accuses the pure young Billy Budd of
inciting mutiny, is struck dead by Billy, and thereby pairs
Billy with him in retributive death. Claggart is evil, but his
hatred for Billy is a subtly stated ambivalence. Perhaps too
much has been made of the Christ-like nature of Billy, and of
the Father-attributes of Captain Vere, in order to prove
(according to one interpretation) that Melville had finally
reached a Christian haven. Certainly Billy is supposed to be
innocent, and Vere just. But Billy is a little too elementary a
character to bear all the burdens that commentators have
recently put upon him; perhaps Melville, his taste for excess
gone, prefers to express the predicament of innocence in a
historical parable of the imposition of order after egalitarian
excesses. Order is unfair, but it is comforting to the tired
man. And surely *Billy Budd* has a passive, almost maso-
chistic tone? Defeat, Melville seems to say, is inevitable for
all: then why struggle, as did Taji, Ahab, Pierre? Rather,

with Billy, summoning up a mournful, uncomprehending dignity like that of the Tahitians of *Omŏo*,

> Just ease these darbies at the wrist,
> And roll me over fair.
> I am sleepy, and the oozy weeds about me twist.

WALT WHITMAN

MELVILLE's contemporary, Walt Whitman, was also a native of New York State. The two men have some qualities in common: a combination of exuberance and withdrawnness, of masculine energy and feminine (or homosexual) quiescence. Whitman's 'Mannahatta' –

> City of hurried and sparkling waters! city of spires and masts!
> City nested in bays! my city! –

sounds like the 'insular city of the Manhattoes, belted round by wharves', of the first chapter of *Moby Dick*. In the same book Melville speaks as glowingly as Whitman of the democratic dignity 'in the arm that wields a pick or drives a spike'. Both men find endless interest in the sea: to Whitman it is a great rhythmic pulse, with a loose surge to which he compares the movement of his own poetry. And there are transcendental affirmations in Melville as in Whitman: 'O Nature, and O soul of man!' exclaims Ahab – 'how far beyond all utterance are your linked analogies! not the smallest atom stirs or lives on matter, but has its cunning duplicate in mind.'

But of course Melville and Whitman (who seem never to have met, and to have been indifferent to one another's work) are dissimilar in other ways. Though Melville, like Whitman, has a fullness and vigour that appear foreign to the New England temperament, he seems nevertheless much closer intellectually to his friend Hawthorne than to Whitman; beneath the sunlit surface of the waves are monsters, and the threat of shipwreck. We do not find this sense of hidden calamity in Whitman: he, by contrast, is closer to Emerson, whose writings meant more to him during his formative

years than he later acknowledged. Two quotations, in each
case from their notebooks, will suggest their affinity. First,
Emerson:

I have been writing and speaking what were once called novelties,
for twenty-five or thirty years, and have not now one disciple. ... I
delight in driving them from me. What could I do, if they came to
me? – they would interrupt and encumber me. This is my boast
that I have no school follower. I should account it a measure of the
impurity of insight, if it did not create independence.

And here is Whitman:

I will not be a great philosopher, and found any school. ... But I
will take each man and woman of you to the window ... and my
left arm shall hook you round the waist, and my right shall point
you to the endless and beginningless road. ... Not I – not God – can
travel this road for you. ...

These are by no means identical utterances; but there is a
marked resemblance. Indeed, for some time now it has been
usual for critics to praise Hawthorne and Melville for their
'awareness of evil' and point contemptuously to the lack of
awareness displayed by the transcendentalists; and by Emerson in particular. One may well agree with this rolling-out-
of-the-red-carpet for the Awares: but must we simultaneously thrust the Unawares out at the back entrance? Perhaps
criticism is perpetually a matter of being unfair to some and
too fair to others. But it seems a pity that a recent able book[1]
should, in lauding Hawthorne, lambaste Whitman as Hawthorne's opposite 'in every respect', who 'did as much to
ruin American poetry and prose as any single influence in
America'. Whitman, like any other great writer, is unique:
he is nobody's opposite, except in an approximate way.
However, his work *is* extremely uneven; and it is in general
vulnerable to attack at the same points where New England
transcendentalism is vulnerable. 'Transcendentalism means,
says our accomplished Mrs B., with a wave of her hand, *a
little beyond*.' We can pair this note, from Emerson's journal

1. Marius Bewley, *The Complex Fate: Hawthorne, Henry James and Some
Other American Writers* (London, 1952).

of 1836, with Whitman's explanation (in an anonymous review of his own poetry!) that the lines never seem 'finished and fixed', but are 'always suggesting something beyond'. Like Emerson, he is accused of being indiscriminately optimistic and formless. His purpose, in his own well-known words, was 'mainly ... to put *a Person*, a human being (myself, in the latter half of the Nineteenth Century, in America,) freely, fully and truly on record.' He was to be 'the bard of personality', speaking for all Americans (and for all mankind), since he knew all other human beings were essentially the same as himself. Santayana objected that the doctrine was too elementary, and that there was no 'inside' to Whitman's perceptions. D. H. Lawrence, while praising much in Whitman, condemns his transcendental pretensions, making him say (in words that recall Poe's 'Supernal Oneness'): 'I am everything and everything is me and so we're all One in One Identity, like the Mundane Egg, which has been addled quite a while.'

Others have disliked aspects of Whitman which one does not find in Emerson: his flamboyant patriotism, for instance (which may have been a family matter, since his father christened three of his brothers George Washington, Thomas Jefferson, and Andrew Jackson: a not uncommon American habit), and his equating of quantity with quality. The Southern poet Sidney Lanier said Whitman's argument seemed to be that 'because a prairie is wide, therefore debauchery is admirable, and because the Mississippi is long, therefore every American is God.' Lanier presumably had in mind such statements as this, from the 1855 preface to *Leaves of Grass*:

Here is not merely a nation but a teeming nation of nations. Here is action untied from strings necessarily blind to particulars and details magnificently moving in great masses.

Or this, from Whitman's 1856 'Letter to Emerson':

Of the twenty-four modern mammoth two-double, three-double, and four-double cylinder presses in the world, printing by steam, twenty-one of them are in the United States.

Such declarations remind us of Samuel Butler's comment that America should not have been discovered all at once, but in pieces, each about as big as France or Germany; and of Emerson's reflection that 'I expected [Whitman] to make the songs of the nation but he seems content to make the inventories'.

These inventories have been ridiculed and parodied over and over again. So has his vocabulary, which Emerson described as 'a remarkable mixture of the *Bhagavat-Geeta* and the *New York Herald*'. He overworked some words like *copious, orbic*; he made howlers (using *semitic* where he meant *seminal*). He invented strange terminations: *promulge, philosophs, literats*. He borrowed from other languages, especially French: *formules, delicatesse, trottoir, embouchure, Americano, cantabile*. He took words from phrenology: *amative, adhesive*. The results are often ludicrous:

The freshness and candour of their physiognomy, the copiousness and decision of their phrenology. ...

In thy resplendent coming literati, thy full-lung'd orators, thy sacerdotal bards, kosmic savans, ...

The same doubtful enthusiasm that led him to admire a large painting of Custer's Last Stand permitted him to include lovely and laughable epithets within the same line, and prevented him from pruning them in subsequent editions. He revised constantly, but not always for the better.

In fact, Whitman at his worst is unbelievably bad. He flaunts his queer style as a savage might flaunt a top-hat retrieved from somebody's dustbin. Surrounded in later life by disciples only less odd than he, poseur, puffer, bearded ex-carpenter Christ-figure: this is the Whitman who sticks in so many gullets. But those who trouble to seek his closer acquaintance realize that his failings throw his achievement into greater relief. Somehow this mediocre journalist, the writer of pieces on Manifest Destiny and Decent Homes for Working-Men, conceived his scheme of celebrating man and America in what he decided was to be a thoroughly new and

appropriate form. All his miscellaneous tastes and experiences
went into its development: the Quakerism of his mother's
family; Shakespeare, and the opera – the excitement of the
sung or spoken word, communicated in a public place;
phrenology, which reassured him as to his own disposition;
the more permanently respectable sciences, in which he –
somewhat like Emerson – discovered cosmic patterns; the
trundling verse of Martin Farquhar Tupper; George Sand's
Consuelo, and its sequel, *The Countess of Rudolstadt*, which may
have helped him to visualize his role of spokesman for mankind; Poe, who pointed out for him the impossibility of the
long poem; the crowds on Broadway, or on the Brooklyn
Ferry; the tides washing in from the Atlantic; the sweet mo-
dulation of the seasons in the countryside; the feel of the
great continent, rolling interminably westward from the sea-
board where he lived: all these and many other ingredients
went into the first edition of *Leaves of Grass*, which appeared
in New York in July 1855, when he was thirty-six. It
contained twelve poems, of which the most considerable was
'Song of Myself'. Preface and poems alike (Whitman's prose
is very close to his verse) insisted on truths similar to those
propounded by Emerson: the divineness of ordinary men
and women, and their share in the miraculous cyclical patterns of life. Otherwise, their flavour was not Emersonian.
Nor was that of all the subsequent, modified, and expanded
editions of the book. True, they sometimes reveal the Emersonian complacence, especially in the early editions. But it
is expressed differently: sometimes more stridently, sometimes with a joviality that repels us almost as much as
Emerson's wintry summons, but almost always with a
sensuous warmth to which one cannot remain indifferent.
And at their best, they are incomparably more radiant:
there is a morning gladness about some of Whitman's
lines that Emerson hardly ever manages to infuse into his
work:

To behold the day-break!
The little light fades the immense and diaphanous shadows,
The air tastes good to my palate. ...

I hear bravuras of birds, bustle of growing wheat, gossip of flames,
clack of sticks cooking my meals. ...

The glories strung like beads on my smallest sights and hearings, on
the walk in the street and the passage over the river –

Who can resist lines like these, or cares to quibble whether
they can be defined as verse? This, we feel with Whitman,
'is the meal equally set, this the meat for natural hunger'.

Even if we were to agree that its message is less profound
than that of Hawthorne (though it is not), such poetry is only
one aspect of Whitman. The comic Whitman of Max Beer-
bohm's cartoon altered, and grew more subtle. Yet even in
his first editions Whitman is far less noisy than his critics
have pretended. He is a little detached, 'both in and out of
the game'. He is curiously secretive for one who, according
to some of his contemporary reviewers, liked to wash his
dirty linen in public. 'Suggestiveness', he says, is the word
that expresses the mood of his poems, in which 'every sentence and every passage tells of an interior not always seen.'
Possibly an instinctive desire to camouflage his homosexual
tendencies accounts in part for the obscurity of some of these
passages; at any rate they have nothing to do with the ex-
traverted Whitman of legend. These strange and lovely lines,
for instance:

Ever the hard unsunk ground,
Ever the eaters and drinkers, ever the upward and downward sun,
      ever the air and the ceaseless tides,
Ever myself and my neighbours, refreshing, wicked, real,
Ever the old inexplicable query, ever that thorn'd thumb, that
      breath of itches and thirsts,
Ever the vexer's hoot! hoot! till we find where the sly one hides and
      bring him forth,
Ever love, ever the sobbing liquid of life,
Ever the bandage under the chin, ever the trestles of death.

One could quote fifty passages as richly perplexing as this
from 'Song of Myself'. Nor is he maintaining in it, or in his
work as a whole, that there is no iniquity or pain in our
world. 'Agonies', he says, 'are one of my changes of gar-
ments.' He is capable, too, of castigating his own country:

Let there be no suggestion above the suggestion of drudgery!
Let none be pointed toward his destination!

— — — —

Let the sun and moon go! let scenery take the applause of the
    audience! let there be apathy under the stars!

'Respondez!', in which these lines occur, was left out of
later editions; but its anger and dismay can be found in
other poems, as well as in *Democratic Vistas*.

Dismay is not, however, a characteristic mood with him.
Balancing his joy in the 'refreshing, wicked, real' properties
of existence is his notion of immortality in death:

The smallest sprout shows there is really no death,
And if ever there was it led forward life, and does not wait at the
    end to arrest it,
And ceas'd the moment life appear'd.

— — — —

All goes onward and outward, nothing collapses,
And to die is different from what any one supposed, and luckier.

As Whitman grew older, death occupied his thoughts increasingly – but only as an interlude between one life and another.
For him, death has no sting; and indeed, he began to make
his *adieux* to life at a remarkably early age. In 'The Wound-
Dresser', written in his forties, he says:

An old man bending I come among new faces.

Perhaps the hospitals of the Civil War hastened the process;
for, as a Greek historian wrote, in time of peace the sons bury
the fathers: in time of war the fathers bury the sons. With
Melville, Whitman is almost alone among American authors
of the time in grasping the tragic significance of the war. He
felt himself a father, and as he saw all America stretched beneath the surgeon's knife, after enduring the torment of the
battlefields, he recorded his emotion in elegiac lines of magnificent dignity:

Word over all, beautiful as the sky,
Beautiful that war and all its deeds of carnage must in time be
    utterly lost,
That the hands of the sisters Death and Night incessantly softly
    wash again, and ever again, this soil'd world.

The same tranquil maturity is revealed in his great poem on the dead Lincoln, 'When lilacs last in the dooryard bloom'd'.

In his 1855 preface to *Leaves of Grass*, Whitman declares that 'of all mankind the great poet is the equable man'. The same phrase recurs in 'By Blue Ontario's Shore'; and it is the word *equable* that best sums up the peculiar temper of Whitman. Pride, he thinks, can and should be accompanied by humility. Democracy, that proud estate, is symbolized by the humblest of natural growths – the grass; his new man will speak in 'words simple as grass'. To him, the idea that life has the precise structure of classical architecture is a fiction; it is, rather, like an object in nature, with an organic form that is nevertheless unexpected, asymmetrical, even wilful. In his lecture on 'The Death of Abraham Lincoln' – a dramatic account – he says:

The main thing, the actual murder, transpired with the quiet and simplicity of any commonest occurrence – the bursting of a bud or pod in the growth of vegetation, for instance.

Far from ranting here – and how many would have resisted the opportunity? – he explains the event as he does his own poems, in which things happen 'with what appear to be the same disregard of parts, and the same absence of special purpose, as in nature'. The poet, he said elsewhere, speaking of himself, conceals 'his rhythm and uniformity ... in the roots of his verses, not to be seen of themselves, but to break forth loosely as lilacs on a bush, and take shapes compact, as the shapes of melons, or chestnuts, or pears.' Regretting the lack of spontaneity and real sensuousness in other contemporary poets, he deplores in Tennyson

The odor of English social life ... pervading the pages like an invisible scent; the idleness, the traditions, the mannerisms, the stately *ennui*; the yearning of love, like a spinal marrow, inside of all; ... the old houses and furniture ... the moldy secrets everywhere; the verdure, the ivy on the walls, the moat, the English landscape outside, the buzzing fly in the sun inside the window pane.

Against this brilliant evocation of airlessness we may put Whitman's view of the poet as one who 'judges not as the judge judges but as the sun falling around a helpless thing'.

Like any poet's theory of the poet's function, this is a personal testament. But it is more diffuse than most, and we can agree with Whitman's critics that it is a dangerous counsel to follow, if it encourages the would-be American poet to rely too exclusively on a rapt and bardic intuition. Certainly Whitman is least acceptable where most the Bard: as when he offers an antithesis between the Old and New Worlds, and glorifies the American pioneer, or supposes that ordinary Americans will rise to greet their 'full-lung'd orators'. His America of mates and camerados can be a little embarrassing; and there is a certain irony in the fact that his one thoroughly conventional poem ('O Captain! My Captain!') is the only one known to the general public to-day. But if his most 'public' poetry is his weakest, there is something characteristically American, and not at all silly, in his having made the effort to appeal to the multitude. Nor did his failure in this respect embitter him. If the poet cannot speak *to* mankind, he can (if he is good enough) speak *for* mankind; and this is what Whitman does, at his splendid best.

CHAPTER SIX

MORE NEW ENGLANDERS

The Brahmin Poets and Historians

═══════════

HENRY WADSWORTH LONGFELLOW (1807–82)

b. Portland, Maine. *ed.* Bowdoin College, where a classmate of Hawthorne. Travelled 1826–9 in France, Spain, Italy, and Germany, and on returning was appointed professor of modern languages at Bowdoin (1829–35). After a further European visit in 1835, became professor of French and Spanish at Harvard, in succession to Ticknor, and occupied the chair, though with growing reluctance, until 1854, when he resigned to devote himself entirely to literature. By then he was internationally known for such works in prose and verse as *Hyperion* (1839), *Voices of the Night* (1839), *The Spanish Student* (1843), and *Evangeline* (1847). His reputation grew steadily with the publication of *Hiawatha* (1855), *The Courtship of Miles Standish* (1858) and various later works. He was twice married, both wives dying in sad circumstances.

JAMES RUSSELL LOWELL (1819–91)

b. Cambridge, Mass. *ed.* Harvard. In 1844 he *m.* the ardent reformer Maria White, under whose influence he wrote various anti-slavery pieces. He won early recognition with *A Fable for Critics* and the first series of *Biglow Papers* (both 1848). Maria Lowell, *d.* 1853; after her death his interest in reform waned. In 1855 he succeeded Longfellow at Harvard, and after an interval of some years began to pour out poems and essays. The first editor of the *Atlantic Monthly*, Lowell was also associated with the *North American Review*. He was minister to Spain (1877–80) and to England (1880–5).

OLIVER WENDELL HOLMES (1809–94)

b. Cambridge, Mass. *ed.* Harvard, where, after medical study in France and teaching at Dartmouth, he became professor of anatomy and physiology (1847–82). Prominent in most of the cultural and convivial activities of Boston and Cambridge; his local fame as *raconteur* and versifier spread abroad with the publication of *The Autocrat of the Breakfast-Table* (1858), *The Professor at the Breakfast-Table* (1860), *The Poet at the Breakfast-Table* (1872) and other works, including three novels, and several volumes of verse. His son and namesake, O. W. Holmes, Jr (1841–1935), was a no less distinguished Harvard figure.

WILLIAM HICKLING PRESCOTT (1796–1859)

b. Salem, Mass., *ed.* Harvard. Travelling in Europe (1815–17), he began to apply himself to historical research. After the success of his painstaking *History of Ferdinand and Isabella* (3 v., 1838) – Longfellow described him as 'a striking example of what perseverance and concentration of one's powers will accomplish' – he embarked on his *History of the Conquest of Mexico* (3 v., 1843), and followed it with his *Conquest of Peru* (2 v., 1847). He had published 3 v. of a history of Philip II when he died.

JOHN LOTHROP MOTLEY (1814–77)

b. Boston, *ed.* Harvard. After two years of study in Germany, he worked at law in Boston, wrote two novels, *Morton's Hope* (1839) and *Merry Mount* (1849), and began to devote himself to the history of the Netherlands. His researches led to the publication of *The Rise of the Dutch Republic* (3 v., 1856), *History of the United Netherlands* (4 v., 1860, 1867), and *Life and Death of John of Barneveld* (2 v., 1874). Minister to Austria (1861–7) and to Britain (1869–70), he was recalled from the latter post through no fault of his own.

FRANCIS PARKMAN (1823–93)

b. Boston, he was *ed.* at Harvard, travelled in Europe (1843–4) and (1846) to the American West, where his strenuous life ruined his health, though providing material for his *Oregon Trail* (1849). Despite wretched health, he applied himself to his great series on the French and English struggles in colonial America. His *History of the Conspiracy of Pontiac* (1851) was followed after an interval by *Pioneers of France in the New World* (1865), and by six subsequent volumes, culminating in *A Half-Century of Conflict* (1892). He also wrote one novel, *Vassall Morton* (1856), and a book on horticulture – a subject in which he held a Harvard professorship.

MORE NEW ENGLANDERS

—

IN the years after the Civil War very few would have mentioned Melville and Whitman, if asked to list the chief living American authors. They would certainly have named Emerson, and perhaps the Quaker poet, John G. Whittier, both Massachusetts men. But pride of place would be given to the writers cited above: men associated not merely with Massachusetts in general, but with Boston (and Harvard, at nearby Cambridge) in particular. Their reputations, in their own day, were prodigious: a poem like Longfellow's 'Psalm of Life' was familiar equally to Baudelaire (as his sonnet 'Le Guignon' shows), and to a British soldier in the Crimea, heard to repeat one of its lines as he lay dying before Sebastopol.

To-day, it is otherwise. If the historians are still treated with respect, they are (with the possible exception of Parkman) no longer widely read. The poets, once so praised, are lumped unceremoniously together in our textbooks, in one curt chapter. Poets and historians alike are put on the defensive, to be contrasted unfavourably with both Awares and Unawares. Did not Emerson remark in his journal (October 1841) that 'the view taken of Transcendentalism in State Street is that it will invalidate contracts'? Did he not confide to the same source, a few years later:

If Socrates were here, we could go and talk with him; but Longfellow, we cannot go and talk with; there is a palace, and servants, and a row of bottles of different coloured wines, and wine glasses, and fine coats.

And did not Longfellow write (December 1840) that 'there is in all Cambridge but one Transcendentalist, – and he a tutor! In the Theological School there is none of it; the infected class is gone'? Instead of the simple world of Concord, we have thus a picture not altogether unlike the one of Tennyson's England conjured up by Whitman. It is a Boston peopled either by businessmen or by *Brahmins* (the word was adopted by one of them, Oliver Wendell Holmes). These Brahmins were born with silver spoons protruding from infant mouths, went to Harvard (or taught at it, usually both), had a distaste for democracy and the frontier, and for contemporary problems; they turned to Europe and the past for comfort, and failed to understand their own age or their own country; they were too refined.

So the charge runs, as levelled at the Brahmins by Vernon L. Parrington.[1] Parrington's 'Jeffersonian' bias is well known, but it is shared by so many other American scholars that to pot-the-Brahmins seems almost a national sport nowadays. Yet there is not very much sport in the game: so over-rated formerly, they are sitting targets. We must seek other explanations for the continued popularity of the pastime. The very idea of Brahminism – the very idea! – has something to do with it. As we have seen, America has lacked a self-assured conservative tradition; the word *gentleman* has tended to be a term of abuse, first cousin to *snob*. To non-Bostonian Americans, the Brahmins have seemed both snobbish and parochial, too pleased with themselves and too eager to minister metaphorically (as Lowell and Motley did literally) to the Court of St James. F. L. Pattee, a professor in Pennsylvania, said with some justice that Barrett Wendell's *Literary History of America* (1900) should be renamed *A Literary History of Harvard University, with Incidental Glimpses of the Minor Writers of America*. By 1900, works with this sort of emphasis were just beginning to appear a little absurd; but they were irritating to non-Bostonians not so much for their absurdity as for the large element of truth they contained. Boston, for much of the nineteenth century, was the intellectual capital of the United States. The best literary talent was drawn to it, or to New England within reach of it. It had good publishing houses, and distinguished periodicals – the *North American Review* was founded in 1815, the *Atlantic Monthly* in 1857. Boston–Cambridge was the only centre in America remotely equivalent to the English Oxford or Cambridge as a nucleus

1. See pp. 338, 348.

of culture; only in Boston could you point to a group of families (Nortons, Lowells, Adamses, Holmeses, Lodges) worthy to be mentioned with, say, the Trevelyans, Huxleys,
Wedgwoods, and Stephens of Victorian England. A high
proportion of the contributions to the *Atlantic Monthly* were
by Bostonians: Emerson tells a story in 1868 of 'a meeting of
the Atlantic Club, when the copies of the new number of the
Atlantic being brought in, every one rose eagerly to get a copy,
and then each sat down, and *read his own article*'. Here, we
may think, is the typical Boston inwardness. But where else
could the editor look for contributions? The *Atlantic* published W. D. Howells's first venture, a poem; it took a story
from Sarah Orne Jewett when she was only nineteen; it opened its pages to the young Henry James, and to Mark
Twain. If it neglected Melville and Whitman, so did nearly
every other American periodical. Otherwise, it took what
was available – and not much of merit was available, from
American authors, in the years following the Civil War. Boston, in fact, was an exasperating target. The nearest thing
to an American *Academy*, it was also much less reactionary
and impervious than that word connotes. Many of the attacks against it, including Parrington's, have been unfair,
and rather erratic; thus Parrington, while insisting on the
shortcomings of Oliver Wendell Holmes, makes him out to
be a charming and interesting figure.

One difficulty for the anti-Bostonians is that their enemies
have a knack of anticipating criticism, and disarming it. The
Bostonians were only too well aware of their defects. Henry
Adams, who belonged to a later generation but who spoke
for the writers of 1820–70, said:

God knows that we knew our want of knowledge! the self-distrust
became introspection – nervous self-consciousness – irritable dislike of America, and antipathy to Boston. ... Improvised Europeans
we were, and – Lord God – how thin! [1]

How can one label an opponent as 'smug', after he has made
such a confession? Again, though the Brahmins were on the

1. Or, as another Bostonian put it, 'The bother of the Yankee is that he
rubs badly at the junction of soul and body.'

whole well-to-do, they were not (in intention) frivolous. As Parrington admits, they were remarkably, even precociously diligent. Though Longfellow was lucky in securing a professorship of modern languages at Harvard, he qualified himself carefully for the appointment. If not a great scholar, he was a cultivated man, widely read in several languages, and capable of considerable application. Lowell, who succeeded him in the chair, also merited the appointment. Holmes was an able medical man, who held a professorship of anatomy at Harvard Medical School for thirty-five years. Prescott, Motley, and Parkman, the historians, conceived vast schemes, and carried them out to the limit of their powers. The Brahmins, in fact, resisted the temptation to indolence as manfully as their ancestors warded off the snares of the Devil. Prescott and Parkman were severely handicapped by weak eyesight; yet, like the others, they lived up to the resolute sentiment of Longfellow's 'Psalm of Life':

> Let us, then, be up and doing,
> With a heart for any fate;
> Still achieving, still pursuing,
> Learn to labor and to wait.

Nor is the charge of over-refinement altogether applicable to the Brahmins. Critics like to dwell on their expensive dinners and their cosy approval of one another, and to contrast to their delicate literary stomachs the gusty appetites of Twain or Whitman. Much has been made of Twain's icy reception at a Boston dinner when he attempted to poke good-natured fun at Longfellow, Emerson, and Whittier. But the contrast, though in some respects genuine, should not be exaggerated. Lowell, a thorough Brahmin, produced in his dialect *Biglow Papers* an important example of 'native' American literature. It was he who encouraged the Indiana novelist Edward Eggleston to write about the uncouth backwoods settlements. Longfellow could be robust at times, as in this account (from his novel *Kavanagh*) of the visit to a New England village of

Mr Wilmerdings the butcher, standing beside his cart, and surrounded by five cats. ... Mr Wilmerdings not only supplied the village with fresh provisions daily, but he likewise weighed all the babies. There was hardly a child that had not hung beneath his steelyards, tied in a silk handkerchief. ... He had lately married a milliner, who sold 'Dunstable and eleven-braid, openwork and coloured straws', and their bridal tour had been to a neighbouring town to see a man hanged for murdering his wife. A pair of huge ox-horns branched from the gable of his slaughter-house, and near it stood the great pits of the tannery, which all the schoolboys thought were filled with blood!

Or, if we are to mention Mark Twain, he can be set against Oliver Wendell Holmes, who in 1861 published a novel, *Elsie Venner*. In this, a savage dog, kicked by the hero in self-defence,

went bundling out of the open schoolhouse door with a most pitiable yelp, and his stump of a tail shut down as close as his owner ever shut the short, stubbed blade of his jack-knife.

In Twain's *Tom Sawyer* (1876), a poodle sits down on a pinch-bug during a church-service and goes 'sailing up the aisle'. This, originally, continued 'with his tail shut down like a hasp'; but of this latter phrase Twain's friend and adviser W. D. Howells wrote in the margin of the manuscript, 'Awfully good but a little dirty'. The offending phrase was removed; and if Howells had not objected, it is quite likely that Twain would have cut it out himself, being much more anxious than the Brahmins to achieve 'good taste'.

In short, the Parrington version of the fastidious and un-American Brahmins is a distorted one. Even if we were to accept some of Parrington's criteria, it would be hard to condemn the Brahmins without also condemning a great many other Americans. If none was an out-and-out abolitionist, they were still closely concerned with the outcome of the struggle. Longfellow praised the outrageous John Brown in his diary, and both he and Holmes had sons wounded in the war. As for 'native' literature, even Parkman, despite his dislike of the masses, praised the *national* quality of books like *The Life of David Crockett* and *The Big Bear of Arkansas*, 'which emanate from, or are adapted to, the unschooled classes of the people'; whereas, 'in the politer walks of literature, we find much grace of style, but very little originality of thought – productions which might as readily be taken for the work of an Englishman as of an American'.

In extenuating the Brahmins, there is a danger of erring in the opposite direction from Parrington. Certainly, where the poet-Brahmins are concerned, little of their work has retained its spell. We must beware, however, of attributing this thinness exclusively to Boston. Is there not, rather, a displacement of the poet which is almost as evident in nineteenth-century England as in America? Longfellow, Lowell, and Holmes were popular with the English public not because they deliberately aimed at it in an un-American fashion, but because their view of poetry closely corresponded to that approved in English (and American) parlours. The displacement in somebody like Tennyson reveals itself in the gulf between his verse and his private conduct: the one so graceful, the other so gruffly compounded of tobacco, beer, and slang. This is not to say that either Tennyson or the Brahmins were seriously worried by the fact that they did not write as they spoke – what writers ever *have*, exactly? But in the case of the Brahmins there were the American complications outlined in Chapter 2: that neither the polite nor the popular idiom quite suited them. This was, so to speak, an all-American problem: the special Bostonian difficulty was, perhaps, that its New England heritage of unsensuous integrity made it a little politer than it need have been. In this sense we can agree with Parrington that the total impression left by the Brahmins is of undue refinement: the Anglo-American vice of the period, with extra Bostonian nuances that account for the Brahmin-poets' vast success in their own day, and failure to communicate to ours.

What has Longfellow, the most successful of them all, to offer us? In prose, flimsy novels like *Hyperion* and *Kavanagh*: priggish in sum, though with interludes of pleasant commonsense. In verse, a great quantity, from little ditties to the ambitious long poems: *Evangeline*, *Hiawatha*, the translation of

Dante. As Poe[1] and Whitman both testified (with reservations), Longfellow had abundant talent; there is no strain in his verse, for the meaning carried in it is always amply contained by the vocabulary and the metre. By contrast, technically, Melville is the clumsiest of amateur poets, though of course the load of meaning is greater. Nor was Longfellow without originality, of a limited order. He rummaged busily in the attics of European literature, bringing to light much of interest. Like Irving, he did his best to supply America with its own folklore. In January 1840 he wrote that he had

broken ground in a new field; namely, ballads; beginning with the 'Wreck of the Schooner Hesperus', on the reef of Norman's Woe, in the great storm of a fortnight ago. ... I think I shall write more. The *national ballad* is a virgin soil here in New England; and there are great materials.

He did write more, with gratifying results: few American schoolboys have escaped acquaintance with 'Paul Revere's Ride', to choose one example. But the *national* ballad, as such, made no real appeal to him; he was amused and sceptical at the endless argument on the need for a *national* literature. The juxtaposition was not America–Europe, but 'my ideal home-world of Poetry, and the outer, tangible Prose world'. That the latter sometimes attracted him is shown by the quotation from *Kavanagh*. But the world of poesy was more his home, and whether he wrote of Europe or America, he did so without much desire for actuality. He never visited the American West, and saw no need to do so (nor, in his own terms, can one blame him). When he wished to describe the Mississippi, in *Evangeline*, he was satisfied to go and look at Banvard's canvas Panorama of the river, which happened to be touring the neighbourhood. His material for *Hiawatha* came out of Schoolcraft and others, the metre for the poem – a metre he clung to in face of unfavourable comment – came from Finland. When he wrote of his boyhood, in 'My Lost Youth', his memory of Portland, Maine, was prompted by

1. Longfellow noted in his *Journal* (24 February 1847):

> In Hexameter sings serenely a Harvard Professor;
> In Pentameter him damns censorious Poe.

lines from Dante. 'Siede la terra dove nato fui/Sulla marina', became 'Often I think of the beautiful town/That is seated by the sea'. And the chorus –

> A boy's will is the wind's will,
> And the thoughts of youth are long, long thoughts –

came from Herder's translation into German of a Lapland song:

> Knabenwille ist Windeswille
> Jünglings Gedanken lange Gedanken.

There is nothing wrong with such adaptations, which have been a godsend to some modern poets. But whereas with Ezra Pound and T. S. Eliot the adaptation (or direct quotation) is used purposely for its associative effect, with Longfellow it seems merely part of a miscellaneous literary stockpile. The reader is usually unaware that there has been something borrowed; even so, there is a slight odour of potpourri emanating from Longfellow. In *Hiawatha*, for instance, his Indians are not unreal because he failed to go and look at some actual redskins, but because they are the product of a romantic rather than a creative imagination. Hence, they have 'dated' in a slightly ridiculous way, like bygone fashion-drawings. Parody overwhelms them, as it fails to overwhelm a poet of Whitman's stature:

> He killed the noble Mudjokivis.
> Of the skin he made him mittens,
> Made them with the fur side inside
> Put the inside skinside outside.

Time has been unkind to Longfellow; not his Brahminism, but an inability to transcend the requirements of his generation which he so admirably met. For, as Emerson said with his polite acuity of *Hiawatha*, ' I have always one foremost satisfaction in reading your books – that I am safe. I am in variously skilful hands, but first of all they are safe hands.'

Lowell also has faded. Not all of his writing, though, has lost its colour. *The Fable for Critics* (1848) has witty and perceptive things to say about contemporary American writers, Whittier for instance –

A fervor of mind which knows no separation
'Twixt simple excitement and pure inspiration –

(and about Lowell himself, for in characteristic New England manner he is his own best critic). Some of the *Biglow Papers* have remained alive, with their quick, angry, or humorous comment on humankind. A few of his literary essays are good – those on Chaucer and Emerson, for instance – and most of them are readable. His work is fluent and rather felicitous. Poems and essays alike abound in neat turns of phrase, and epigrams that are immediately pleasing –

[Wordsworth] was the historian of Wordsworthshire

[Thoreau] watched Nature like a detective who is to go upon the stand –

though they will usually not bear a closer scrutiny. For the last few years of his life he was America's most distinguished man of letters, to whom Oxford proffered a chair, and who was godfather to Adeline Stephen (better known, later, as Virginia Woolf).

To-day he is mainly interesting – and indeed, extremely interesting – as one whose career illustrated all the main aspects of American literature. As a young man he believed ardently in democracy and the anti-slavery cause. In his prime he was a Harvard professor, who also helped to edit the *Atlantic Monthly* and the *North American Review*. As an elderly figure he seemed conservative: a Brahmin who could write to Henry James that 'the best society I ever saw was in Cambridge, Mass., take it by and large'; who saw nothing in Whitman, and who regretted that Wordsworth 'did not earlier give himself to "the trade of classic niceties". It was this precisely which gives to the blank verse of Landor the severe dignity and reserved force ... to which Wordsworth never attained.' As a cultivated gentleman, Lowell liked to feel cosmopolitan; European literature was an area in which he knew the best authors as he knew the best hotels and regional dishes, and his pages are crowded with literary allusions. The idea of a national American literature seemed to him as foolish as it did to Longfellow; as he said in an

ironical review of a minor American poet, James Gates
Percival,

If that little dribble of an Avon had succeeded in engendering
Shakespeare what a giant might we not look for from the mighty
womb of Mississippi! Physical geography for the first time took her
rightful place as the tenth and most inspiring Muse.

But as an American, Lowell never doubted that his country
could give points to others. In the second series of the *Biglow
Papers*, written during the Civil War, he addresses John Bull
in accents that are far from anglophile:

> Why talk so dreffle big, John,
> Of honor when it meant
> You didn't care a fig, John,
> But jest for *ten per cent*?

And in his essay 'On a Certain Condescension in Foreigners',
he makes it plain that he is an American – though with all
the appropriate quotations from European literature at his
elbow. In fact, like some of the other Brahmins (and like
Cooper before him), he was impelled to defend gentility to
his own countrymen, and the ruggeder virtues of his native
land to Europeans. As he mellowed, he joined Holmes and
the others under the Brahmin umbrella, in the belief that
Boston–Cambridge offered the best of both worlds. Yet as
a writer he never fully occupied either, and so never found
the perfect mode of expression. Thus, in 'Mason and Slidell:
A Yankee Idyll' are these lines:

> O strange New World, thet yit wast never young,
> Whose youth from thee by gripin' need was wrung,
> Brown foundlin' o' the woods, whose baby-bed
> Was prowled roun' by the Injun's cracklin' tread …

They are modified from lines in an earlier poem, 'The
Power of Sound: A Rhymed Lecture':

> O strange New World that yet wast never young,
> Whose youth from thee by tyrannous need was wrung,
> Brown foundling of the forest, with gaunt eyes,
> Orphan and heir of all the centuries. …

It may be debated which is the better version. The one in dialect is a little more informal: *griping* is a stronger word than *tyrannous*: yet the dialect does not sit very comfortably on the lines. *The Injun's cracklin' tread* is an unfortunate substitution; and indeed the dialect as a whole has a stagey sound. The speaker drops it a little later, when he refers genteelly to the 'vassal ocean's mane', only to recollect himself hastily. Both versions are dexterous, but neither is powerful. There is a similar though less conspicuous duality in other Brahmins: in Prescott the historian, to choose one. Three generations of William Prescotts before him had occupied his room at Harvard; there was a coat-of-arms on the family plate; his style was indistinguishable from that of an Englishman; and yet he was not an Englishman – he was a Brahmin, whom the English landscape made homesick for a 'ragged fence, or an old stump ... to show that man's hand had not been combing Nature's head so vigorously. I felt I was not in my own dear, wild America.'

Given a larger talent, Lowell might have overcome whatever handicap Brahminism imposed. As it was – and as perhaps the lines above suggest – versemaking came too easily to him. Stanza succeeds stanza, and still his nimble mind is not done with the theme. His much-praised 'Harvard Commemoration Ode' is too graceful, too felicitous through too many lines. It is in perfect taste; but the agony and the triumph are too readily explained. Lowell knew his fault; nearly twenty years before, he had written to Longfellow that when the *Fable for Critics* was finished he would abandon poetry for a while, since he could not 'write slowly enough'.

The same can be said, in general, of Lowell's friend Oliver Wendell Holmes; he, too, could versify without effort, was keenly interested in problems of language and dialect, adored puns and epigrams, and thought himself a gentleman. In addition, he was a man of science: and, as befitted one who had produced an important treatise on puerperal fever, he was a little scornful of romantic notions. His favourite poets were Pope, Goldsmith, and Campbell; both the bluffness and the elegance of their age appealed to him. 'Mysticism' he used as a term of reproach. 'The imaginative writer', he declared, 'is after effects, the scientific man is after truth.' He did not mean that there was no room for imagination, but that it should be a whimsical subordinate to science. 'Life', his Autocrat said, 'is maintained by the respiration of oxygen and sentiments'; and his work is just such a medley. At one extreme comes his occasional verse, devised for dinner-tables and college reunions, and his light conversation ('the whole art of love may be read in any Encyclopaedia under the title *Fortification*'); at the other, his interest in the application of scientific discovery to human behaviour. Thus, in his novels *Elsie Venner*, *The Guardian Angel*, and *A Mortal Antipathy* he mingles light-hearted local colour with themes that could be of great significance: all of them concerned with the extent to which men are free moral agents. Elsie Venner is an evil person, but the evil is inherited (grotesquely, as in a Hawthorne tale, from the rattlesnake-venom that entered her mother's blood), and so she is 'not to blame'. The conduct of the principal characters in the other two novels is similarly predetermined. Are we, then, responsible for our own actions? Should society punish us? Such doubts, when coupled with the conviction that society was a sham, racked the great naturalist writers of the century's end. But for Holmes, society was Boston, the city of which he was poet-laureate. Private jokes, the ritualizing of talk and gustation, a hint of self-satisfaction, even a tiny tinge of inbred (and of course *wellbred*) malice: these are not entirely unknown in Oxford and Cambridge. Perhaps they are concomitants of intellectual communities. At any rate it seems a little hard to blame Holmes and his Boston, especially as he loved the place, when we are told that American writers too often emulate Whitman, in embracing the whole continent instead of an area of manageable size. Alas, though, exonerate Holmes as we may, we cannot make a great writer out of him. His work is ephemeral. Even the best of his poems, 'The Deacon's Masterpiece; or, The Wonderful "One-Hoss Shay",' is not much more than vivacious light verse; while the other poem by which he is chiefly known, 'The

Chambered Nautilus', is – like Longfellow's 'Psalm of Life'
– hortatory, melodious – and flat. The novels of Holmes are
not sufficiently concentrated; they show an inquisitive mind
casting about in a variety of directions. The *Breakfast Table*
volumes have the same defect; after a few chapters one begins to fidget, and wonder why they are not as good as Pea-
cock or *Tristram Shandy*. They seem on a level with W.H.
Mallock's *New Republic*, but without the fun of guessing
whom the characters represent. In the *Breakfast Table* books
the characters are Holmes and his sparring partners: and he
floors them too infallibly, like an expert on a quiz programme.

Longfellow, Lowell, Holmes: all three, great men to their
own age, have dwindled subsequently. There is no weight to
their work. For this quality we must turn to the Brahmin
historians Prescott, Motley, and Parkman. With no financial
need to engage in arduous work, they seem nevertheless to
have yielded to the pressure of a New England atmosphere
that compelled industry. (A Boston hostess is said to have replied to a visiting Englishman who complained to her that
America had no leisure class, 'Oh yes we have, but *we* call
them tramps'). The same atmosphere may have directed
them into historical study. Motley would have preferred to
be a novelist, but after two unsuccessful attempts, and some
less unsuccessful efforts at literary criticism, he concluded
that history (which called for 'sappers and miners') rather
than the novel (a task for 'lancers') should be his field. Parkman also tried his hand at a novel (*Vassall Morton*, 1856), but
the stiffly autobiographical result made it clear that his talent lay elsewhere. Whatever was missing in New England
that inhibited creative writing can almost be said to have encouraged the scholar and the critic. Taking American literature as a whole, almost the most impressive part is that which
cannot be called 'creative'. Travel, political controversy,
biography, reminiscence, history: each has produced its
masterpieces.

This trio of historians arrived at a suitable moment. The
New World needed chroniclers. Historians like Jared Sparks

and George Bancroft were celebrating the growth of American democracy. As Brahmins, however, Prescott, Motley, and Parkman had little wish to engage in the political history of the United States; in doing so they might appear no better than party hacks. Casting about for a theme, the first two were drawn to Spanish history, an area of study that Irving and Ticknor had helped to popularize. Ticknor directed Prescott's early studies, Irving relinquished to him the theme of the conquest of Mexico by Cortés; and Prescott in turn assisted Motley in preparing his *Rise of the Dutch Republic*, though he was himself at work on a history of the reign of Philip II, and was hence allowing 'the cream of my subject' to be skimmed off. Parkman chose differently. As an undergraduate with a strong taste for the outdoors, he had determined to write the story of early French activity in Canada. Then gradually, as his interest developed, he

enlarged the plan to include the whole course of the American conflict between France and England, or, in other words, the history of the *American forest*; for this was the light in which I regarded it. My theme fascinated me, and I was haunted with wilderness images night and day.

So the three chose their subjects and set patiently to work. To all three, history was a branch of literature. It was the drama of their themes – the expansion of Spain in the sixteenth century, the clash between democracy and tyranny in the Netherlands, 'the history of the American forest' – that enticed them. All, in fact, used the word *drama* to describe their aim. Though they set themselves high standards of accuracy and took great pains to accumulate material, they arranged their work so as to tell a story, hoping to make it as readable as the novels of Scott. They included chapters of social history, but wherever possible related their narrative to some outstanding figure: Cortés, William the Silent, Pontiac. Prescott, in his best book, *The Conquest of Mexico*, discusses in the preface whether he may not, in prolonging the drama past the fall of Mexico to the death of Cortés, have fallen into the error of 'a premature *dénouement*'; and trusts that he has preserved 'the *unity of interest*'.

In all three cases the combination of scholarship and dramatic interest is successful. Some reservations may be made. As Protestants, the three are apt – Parkman less than the others – to deal ungently with the Catholic Church. Prescott's style, though in his diary he wrote 'bother euphony', is euphonious; bosoms swell with indignation, characters partake of bountiful collations, the 'polished nations' are contrasted to the 'barbarous' ones. Motley, for his part, makes his villains excessively villainous and his heroes wearisomely heroic. He (and Prescott to a lesser extent) are sometimes slipshod in handling their sources. Parkman occasionally allows a supercilious tone to creep into his writing. But these faults are far outweighed by the excitement of the themes and the narrative skill with which they are developed.

Parkman is the greatest of the three. He first attracted attention with his *Oregon Trail*, to give the book the title by which it is now known. In it he describes his experiences as a young Harvard graduate, among the Plains Indians, whom he visited at a time (1846) when they were still powerful, though in contact with white hunters and emigrant trains. He also unwittingly reveals his own temperament. He shows himself to be confident, addicted (almost compulsively) to hardship, somewhat contemptuous of the Indians, and considerably more so of the unkempt and uneducated white men whose wagons passed westward along the trails. The noble savage for him is at least half a myth, though none the less interesting for that. What may be called gentlemanly traits arouse Parkman's admiration; he likes his wilderness to be peopled by men of breeding. But they must be strong men: one of his favourite words is *manly*.

These predilections appear, though less obviously, in Parkman's major historical works, which run (chronologically) from *Pioneers of France in the New World* to *Montcalm and Wolfe*; *The Conspiracy of Pontiac* is not formally part of his great series. Reverencing veracity no less than virility, he criticizes Longfellow for sentimentalizing the Acadians (in *Evangeline*) and the Indians (in *Hiawatha*), and jeers at Cooper's improbabilities of plot. He avoids such pitfalls in his own writing.

Knowing the ground of which he writes – one reason why, he believes, historians should write about their own countries – and ransacking the archives for documentary evidence, he erects his narrative on a firm basis of fact. As a result, his enthusiasm for his principals – La Salle, Frontenac, Montcalm, and the rest – does not seem misplaced or melodramatic. His prejudices, such as they are, do not run away with him. Parts of *Montcalm and Wolfe* come a little too near to set-piece splendours. Otherwise his pages, though never drab, are free from purple passages. They march on, direct, competent, and masterful. Before we dismiss the Brahmins as sweet and thin, we must reckon with Francis Parkman, who converted his wilderness dream into hard, solid, satisfying history.

AMERICAN HUMOUR AND THE RISE OF THE WEST

Mark Twain

———

SAMUEL LANGHORNE CLEMENS ['MARK TWAIN'] (1835–1910)

b. Missouri, son of John Marshall Clemens, a restless and unsuccessful lawyer–land speculator, who settled (1839) at Hannibal, Missouri, on the Mississippi. Left school 1847, on father's death, to work as apprentice-printer. Followed printer's trade in Eastern and Middle-Western cities, 1853–4; journeyed down to New Orleans, 1856, intending to make his fortune in Brazil, but abandoned scheme and became Mississippi river-pilot instead. This first part of his life furnished basis of his best books, *The Adventures of Tom Sawyer* (1876), *Life on the Mississippi* (1883), and *The Adventures of Huckleberry Finn* (1884). After a short period as Confederate volunteer, he spent remainder of Civil War years in Nevada and San Francisco, writing humorous newspaper items under pseudonym of 'Mark Twain', and establishing himself as popular lecturer. Scored great success with *The Innocents Abroad* (1869), a travelogue. 1870, *m.* Olivia Langdon, and soon settled with her at Hartford, Connecticut. Wrote many books, nearly all well-received, including *Roughing It* (1872); *The Gilded Age* (1873, in collaboration with Hartford neighbour, C. D. Warner); *A Tramp Abroad* (1880); *The Prince and the Pauper* (1882); *A Connecticut Yankee in King Arthur's Court* (1889); *The Tragedy of Pudd'nhead Wilson* (1894), and *Personal Recollections of Joan of Arc* (1896), as well as many stories, sketches, and articles.

AMERICAN HUMOUR AND THE RISE OF THE WEST

—

THE Brahmins, in writing and in person, upheld a polite America to Europeans. Europeans, for their part, responded; the London *Times*, as Whitman quoted it in 'The Poet and his Program' (1881), said that the well-known American poets had 'caught the English tone and air and mood only too faithfully, and are accepted by the superficially cultivated English intelligence as readily as if they were English born'. They were read with enjoyment; yet their work was 'afflicted from first to last with a fatal want of raciness'. J.R. Lowell, for instance, 'can overflow with American humour when politics inspire his muse; but in the realm of pure poetry he is no more American than a Newdigate prizeman'. Here *The Times* is discussing the need for a native American literature much as the Americans themselves discussed it, and with something of the same inconsistency. For Longfellow and Lowell were New English (and so American) rather than English, and no more capable of writing like ruffians (except occasionally, as in the *Biglow Papers*) than Leslie Stephen or Matthew Arnold. When an American ruffian appeared, the English greeted him with delight, but regarded him (insultingly, to American eyes) as being thoroughly typical where Lowell and Longfellow were somehow slightly fraudulent. Thus, Motley was succeeded as minister to Great Britain, in 1870, by a General Schenck. Motley, as a scholar and a gentleman, had been an acceptable minister; Schenck, however, became the hit of the London season by introducing draw poker, a game which he played with a consummate nerve born of long practice. Unfortunately, though, the General became involved in a dubious mining venture in which several British acquaintances lost heavily. He was recalled; and went to join the long list of English proofs that the Americans, if quaint, were uncivilized.

Nevertheless, the British were rather more eager than the majority of Americans to welcome signs of a really indigenous American literature (even if only, in some cases, to feed their own preconceptions of life in the United States). Whitman, under the sponsorship of W.M.Rossetti, had been somewhat more generally admired in England than at home. And in the years of the Civil War and after, the English appetite for authentic Americanism was fed. The lectures and *Punch* contributions of Artemus Ward; the personality of Joaquin (né Cincinnatus) Miller, 'the Byron of Oregon'; the mining-frontier poems and stories of Bret Harte; the aphorisms of Josh Billings, and the writings of Mark Twain: these burst upon the London scene with an explosive vitality comparable to that of the American musical comedies of recent years. As with *Oklahoma* and *Annie Get Your Gun*, they were not everybody's dish; in his *American Literature* (1885) the Scottish critic John Nichol deprecated the 'degenerate style' of some American humour, and singled out Mark Twain as one 'who has done perhaps more than any other living writer to lower the literary tone of English speaking people'. On the whole, though, British critics were kinder to the new 'Western' humour than were their colleagues in the eastern United States, since, as Howells explained,

The West, when it began to put itself into literature, could do so without the sense ... of any older or politer world outside of it; whereas the East was always looking fearfully over its shoulder at Europe, and anxious to account for itself as well as represent itself.

'Western' or 'frontier' humour was not in fact confined to the West. Some of its characteristics were shared with New England or 'Down East' humour: the habit of hyperbole, for example (evident in Lowell's description of a wooden shingle 'painted so like marble that it sank in the water'), had been acquired by Easterners before it spread West. Artemus Ward and several other humorists came from the East. Bret Harte was brought up in Brooklyn and New York; he was a dandy who had little, if any, first-hand experience of the mining camps he wrote about. Joaquin Miller, as *The Times* noticed, was nowhere near as rugged as his clothing and his demeanour indicated: his 'verse has fluency and movement and harmony, but as for the thought, his songs of the sierras might as well have been written in Holland'. East and West were as much states of mind as actual regions; and in this respect the East was inclined to repudiate its Western behaviour. John Hay came East from Indiana (as did many another Westerner), and it is difficult to reconcile the suave elder Hay with the young man who endeared himself to the American and British publics with his *Pike County Ballads* (1871). The New York writer E. C. Stedman told a friend in 1873 that 'the whole country ... is flooded, deluged, swamped, beneath a muddy tide of slang, vulgarity ... impertinence, and buffoonery that is not wit': several critics had been no kinder to Hay's *Pike County* humour. Three years later an Eastern reviewer described a book by an Indiana author as the work of 'the invading Goths from over the mountains'.

It is a revealing phrase – though the reviewer probably did not mean to imply that his quasi-Roman civilization was doomed. It is worth looking at this Gothland in order to understand the Chief Goth, Mark Twain. The American Gothland included several widely dissimilar areas: the Old South-west, the mining frontier, and the Pacific coast, to name only three that Twain knew. But we may speak loosely of the whole area as West or Frontier, to define parts of America still in process of settlement. Much of it was wilderness, thinly populated by Indians and white hunters and trappers, until the first settlers came. Life was hard; they survived by developing self-reliance to an extraordinary degree, and in so doing developed a contempt for niceties of law, speech, or social observance. Charles Dickens, touring America in 1842, met his first Westerner on a canal-boat making for Pittsburgh: a strange, scornful man who told the other passengers:

I'm from the brown forests of Mississippi, *I* am, and when the sun shines on me, it does shine – a little ... I'm a brown forester, I am ... There are no smooth skins where I live. We're rough men there.

Such men assembled a new vocabulary abounding in words like *absquatulate*, *flabbergast*, *rampageous*; and in vague, compendious terms like *fixings*, *notions*, *doings*, which covered a multitude of situations.

Frontier life could be lonely and empty. The solitude bred melancholy. John Nichol suggested that 'transatlantic humour ... is the rare efflorescence of a people habitually grave, whose insight is more clear than deep; it relies mainly on exaggeration, and a blending of jest and earnest, which has the effect, as in their Negro melodies, of singing comic words to a sad tune'. In other words, the optimism of the West, though often merely the product of breezy well-being, became at times obligatory, almost to the verge of despair. Failure, because possible, was unthinkable. How could a straggling frontier village maintain its existence (as Lincoln's New Salem failed to do) unless you pretended that it was already a city?

Constance Rourke, in her *American Humour* (1931), says that 'the backwoodsman conquered the Indian, but the Indian also conquered him', by turning him into a somewhat similar savage, a taker of scalps and a prey to superstitious fears. True; yet the line of settlement moved fast: seventeen miles a year on average, according to Tocqueville. The steamboat and the railroad cut deep into the wilderness. What had lately been a frontier community swiftly acquired a newspaper (there were seven in Mark Twain's Hannibal), a school, a church, a law-office. Emerson thought it was religion that brought 'the piano ... so quickly into the shanty': Bret Harte assured him that, on the contrary, it was vice: 'It is the gamblers who bring in the music to California. It is the prostitute who brings in the New York fashions of dress there, and so throughout.'[1] Both no doubt had their effect; certainly the American woman was ready to play her part, and the man to let her. Dickens, though affronted by American manners, had to admit that in all his travels he never saw 'a woman exposed to the slightest act of rudeness, incivility, or even inattention'. If the West gloried in being wild

1. A conversation with Harte noted in Emerson's journal, 18 October 1872.

and woolly, it was also eager to be tame and cultivated. Dickens met a Choctaw chieftain who greatly admired *The Lady of the Lake* and *Marmion*. Squalid mining towns put up opera-houses, and paid to hear Oscar Wilde lecture on tastefulness. Tom Sawyer's robber gang finds itself raiding – a Sunday-school picnic: and this on a Saturday, since the gang-members' parents would not let them play on the Sabbath.

Constance Rourke's statement needs to be complemented with that of Tocqueville, who said of the backwoodsman that 'everything about him is wild, but he himself is the result of the labour and experience of eighteen centuries'. His frontier passed; forests were cleared and game slaughtered in a frenzy of waste. Everything changed; and in the midst of the hurrying, exuberant process there came moments of intense sadness. For a short while, flat-boats and horse-drawn barges were supreme on the inland waterways. Then the steamboats supplanted them. The 'old way' disappeared, leaving behind little more than the legend of Mike Fink, king of the flatboatmen, and his cry: 'What's the use of improvements? Where's the fun, the frolicking, the fighting? Gone! all gone!' Artemus Ward caught the same mood in the 'jernal of a vyge' undertaken 'when I was a young man (in the Brite Lexington of yooth, when thar ain't no sich word as fale) on the Wabash Canawl'. He ends his account: 'This was in the days of Old Long Sign, be4 steembotes was goin round bustin their bilers & sendin people higher nor a kite. Them was happy days …' And the steamboats, though their reign was longer, were ephemeral craft. 'Pasteboard', as Thackeray called them, they consisted of 'an engine and $10,000 worth of fretwork', not built to last, since they were apt to reach a sudden end on a sandbar.

The Westerner's reaction to his environment was natural enough. If the factitious and the shortlived could hardly be lamented in formal terms, it only remained to laugh at them. Though the frontier lacked a mythology, it was easy to invent one. These folk-heroes were supermen, but there was nothing portentous about them: they were comic figures, like Mike Fink, who could eat more, drink deeper, fight harder, and shoot straighter than any mortal. Davy Crockett, the hero of the South-west, had similar attributes: he was 'the darling branch of old Kentucky that can eat up a painter, hold a buffalo out to drink, and put a rifle-ball through the moon'. The growth of the Crockett legend shows well how the self-conscious, even spurious aspects of the frontier could achieve a certain authenticity. For in life Davy Crockett was a backwoods mediocrity, who had a spell in Congress and then took a dislike to his party's President, Andrew Jackson. The rival, Whig party, anxious to capture the backwoods vote, seized upon Crockett, wrote his memoirs for him, and – embodying in them all kinds of existing swagger and tall tales – blew him up to monstrous proportions, as the 'half-hoss, half-alligator', that backwoodsmen had been calling themselves for a generation. Fortunately for his myth, he died nobly at the Alamo, fighting for Texan independence, and thus secured immortality. Manufactured though his story was, it served a real need, in contriving a figure around whom legend might grow. Davy Crockett can scarcely be blamed for allowing himself to become a god: others, like Buffalo Bill and Wild Bill Hickok, did the same. The honorary title – Judge, Major, Colonel, or even General – was a useful adjunct in myth-making. Sometimes the titles were genuine: true and false were intertwined, as when Kit Carson found among the wreckage of a wagon pillaged by Indians a dime-novel relating the exploits of the Indian scout, Kit Carson.

The element of fraud, indeed, permeated American life and was a conspicuous element in American humour, from the Yankee pedlar with his wooden nutmegs to Bret Harte's poem of the Heathen Chinee who had twenty-four jacks stuffed in his sleeves. Life was competitive and offered endless opportunities for swindling. Dickens said that 'smartness' was extolled at the expense of honesty. Trollope found the same. 'You see,' he was told, 'on the frontier a man is bound to be smart. If he ain't smart he'd better go back East; – perhaps as far as Europe. He'll do there.'[1] The ugliness of

1. Anthony Trollope, *North America* (London, 1862), i. 188.

fraud was made into a joke, and then even into a delight in
deception. Humour softened a swindle as moonlight beauti-
fied the shapeless streets of the Western town. If everyone
was something of a showman, nobody ultimately was victi-
mized. You could not fool all of the people all of the time, because they were busy fooling one another. This was the
theory, and it seems to have worked. P. T. Barnum's successive hoaxes only brought him greater popularity, so long as
he altered them often enough. Joaquin Miller claimed to
have been wounded by an Indian arrow; if he sometimes
limped with the wrong leg, as Ambrose Bierce alleged, it
simply showed that his role needed more rehearsal. Certainly
Miller worked hard at his part; later in life he toured a vaudeville circuit dressed in a Klondike outfit – a fur suit, with
buttons made of gold nuggets. Probably none of his audience
knew that he had once studied Latin and Greek. Or if they
did, this was one more of the hilarious incongruities of America. Who could help but laugh at them: at the non-existent
towns, for instance, advertised with pictures that portrayed
them as long-established communities? Laurence Oliphant
visited one in Wisconsin:

Having inspected the plan of the city in the land-office ..., we sal-
lied forth to choose some lots ...; and having been particularly fascinated by the eligible position of some, situated within two doors
of the bank, just round the corner of the grand hotel, opposite the
wharf, fronting the principal square, and running back to Thomp-
son Street – in fact, in the very thick of the business part of the
town – we commenced cutting our way with billhooks through the
dense forest ... called Third Avenue ..., until we got to the bed of a
rivulet, down which we turned through tangled underwood (by
name West Street), until it lost itself in a bog, which was the principal square, upon the other side of which, covered with almost
impenetrable bush, was the site of our lots.[1]

Or who could resist the comedy of American names (except
Matthew Arnold, whom they offended)? Abraham Lincoln,
for instance, when on his way to the Black Hawk War (which

1. Laurence Oliphant, *Minnesota and the Far West* (Edinburgh, 1855),
159–60.

he burlesqued in Congress) paddled in a canoe from Pekin to Havana – and all in the state of Illinois.

Western humour was bound to reflect these incongruities. The tall tale, which had been popular in America since Colonial days (there were twenty-four American editions of Baron Munchausen by 1835), spread West to reach inspired heights of mendacity: as in the story of the hunter who, charged by a bear and a moose at once, from opposite directions, fired at the sharp edge of a rock; the bullet split in two, killing both animals, while rock-splinters brought down a squirrel in a nearby tree. The recoil of his gun knocked the hunter into the river at whose edge he stood; climbing out of the water, he found his clothes full of fish.

The essence of the tall tale was that it was *told*. It required a narrator and an audience – fittingly, among a people who liked nothing better than to be lectured at, whether by hucksters, showmen, humorists, clergymen, Congressmen, or authors. The English theatre-agent Edward Hingston, to whom the subject was of obvious interest, said that

America is a lecture-hall on a very extensive scale. The rostrum extends in a straight line from Boston, through New York and Philadelphia, to Washington. There are raised seats on the first tier in the Alleghanies, and gallery accommodation on the top of the Rocky Mountains.

There may be some truth in the hyperbole of the morning drum-beat of the British army unceasingly encircling the globe; but yet more true is it that the voice of the lecturer is never silent in the United States.

And Artemus Ward relates how

There was an execution in Ohio one day, and the Sheriff, before placing the rope round the murderer's neck, asked him if he had any remarks to make. 'If he hasn't,' said a well-known local orator, pushing his way rapidly through the dense crowd to the gallows – 'if our ill-starred fellow-citizen don't feel inclined to make a speech, and is in no hurry, I should like to avail myself of the present occasion to make some remarks on the necessity of a new protective tariff.'

Political oratory, especially of the spread-eagle sort with its gorgeous metaphors, became in its burlesque moments a variant of the tall tale. A great deal of frontier humour was oral. Ward, Twain, and others were highly successful lecturers (or at any rate performers), and a large proportion of the comic ballads and stories of their genre are, apparently, monologues set down on paper.

These monologues were usually in dialect; or, if the piece in question was not a transcription of talk, it was often deliberately misspelt. The humorist posed as a plain uneducated man. He would make a shot at a Latin tag, but mangle it; he would quote Shakespeare, with equally disastrous results. Since the joke depended on the reader's knowledge of the correct form of the quotation, the humour was less artless than it seemed. Even so, it was free from the class-consciousness implicit in British humour of the same sort. Not much of it had lasting merit. Puns exasperate after a while, tall tales have a certain sameness, misspelling is a strain to read. To-day, Bret Harte is best remembered for a few poems and stories that he himself thought trivial: Ward, Josh Billings, and a host of others have survived only in scattered shards of humour. John Nichol said of America that

the anxiety to be national has led many of her minor authors to make themselves ridiculous. To avoid walking like Englishmen they have gone on all fours: ... tabooing the speech of Addison and Steele, they have delighted themselves with a jargon of strange tongues.

Though he is wrong in suggesting that the humorists purposely avoided writing like Englishmen, there is some truth in his stricture. Now and then, however, the strange tongues spoke in a kindred idiom to Lear, Carroll, and Joyce: they broke through into the same nonsense world, as in these reflections by B. P. Shillaber's Mrs Partington ('the American Mrs Malaprop'):

When I was young, if a girl only understood the rules of distraction, provision, multiplying, replenishing, and the common denunciator, and knew all about rivers and obituaries, the convents and dormitories, the provinces and the umpires, they had eddication enough. But now they have to study bottomy, algebery, and have to demonstrate supposition about the sycophants of circuses, tangents, and Diogenese of parallelogromy, to say nothing about the oxhides, corostics, and the abstruse triangles.

Punning, facetious, irreverent, the American funny man filled the newspapers and lighter periodicals with his material. Like his British contemporary – Thackeray, one recalls, wrote once as 'Michaelangelo Titmarsh' – he chose a preposterous pen-name. David Ross Locke masqueraded as 'Petroleum V. Nasby', Robert Henry Newell turned into 'Orpheus C. Kerr' (an atrocious pun on the 'office-seeker' who plagued American presidents). Each had his particular patter – his 'fort' as Artemus Ward called it – but collectively they produced the humour known as Western. In them the ordinary sensual American had his say, shrewd, cynical, and sometimes refreshingly vulgar in a country 'now wholly given over to a d—d mob of scribbling women', as Hawthorne wrote disgustedly in 1855.

And they prepared the way for Mark Twain: he came up through their ranks. The elements of his humour were all familiar to America before he began to write. But for the spelling, these observations by Artemus Ward on the imminent Civil War might be Twain's:

I said the crisis had not only cum itself, but it had brought all its relations. It has cum ... with a evident intention of makin us a good long visit. It's goin to take off its things and stop with us.

It was Twain who said:

Let us be thankful for the fools. But for them the rest of us could not succeed.

But Josh Billings had already had the same thought:

God save the phools! and dont let them run out, for if it want for them wise men couldn't get a livin.

Plagiarism? The question has little meaning. Through the exchange system, newspapers printed whatever pleased them from newspapers elsewhere. An amusing bit of copy would circulate until no one could be sure of its origin. It could easily pass into speech and back again into print in a modified form. In old age Mark Twain related what he thought was an incident of his own boyhood, but which had actually come from the 'autobiography' of Davy Crockett, and had no doubt been borrowed there from somewhere else. What was undeniable was the wide appeal of this popular humour, to which Abraham Lincoln was notoriously addicted. Both friends and enemies were fond of quoting what was supposed to be his invariable conversational gambit: 'that puts me in mind of a little joke ...' Perhaps he felt, more deeply than those who ridiculed him, the unifying force of folk-humour in a country so huge and heterogeneous.

A good deal of the humour of Twain differs from that of Ward and the rest only in being funnier. As a newspaper-man out in Nevada and California, when he had recently adopted his pen-name (from the Mississippi leadsman's cry for *two fathoms*' draught), he assiduously followed the techniques of the others. It was thanks indirectly to Artemus Ward that he scored his first important success with his story of Jim Smiley and his celebrated jumping frog of Calaveras County. He tried lecturing in California, again with great success, in the Artemus Ward style of zany inconsequence. Ward's lecture-posters had once read:

> Artemus Ward delivered lectures before
> ## ALL THE CROWNED HEADS OF EUROPE
> ever thought of delivering lectures

Twain's declared:

> Doors open at 7½. The trouble will begin at 8.

To his pleasure and relief, the lectures went down equally well with New York audiences. Next, he acted as correspondent on a chartered Mediterranean tour. The letters he sent back were made into a book, *Innocents Abroad*: it was an immediate hit. Twain was not the first American to draw attention to the shortcomings of the Old World, but he was the first to face it with such bravado; to say that Lake Tahoe far exceeded Como in beauty, that the Arno would suffice as a river if only it had some water, that many of the Old Masters were over-rated and that 'their nauseous adulation of princely patrons' was undemocratic, that foreigners ought to learn to talk properly. Not all his ammunition was reserved for Europe; his fellow-countrymen came in for their share of derision. But the book voiced the thoughts of the thousands of Americans who with glazed eye and aching feet had followed the rule of their guide-book round Europe; it announced that America had something better than refinement, and was not impressed – or at least, not bowled over. *A Tramp Abroad*, written some years later, was less proudly philistine, but made similar kinds of jokes about Americans in Europe.

Some of this humour has not worn well. Nevertheless, it represented a sustained effort beyond the capabilities of the Nasbys and Billingses. Books and articles flowed from Twain, and each increased his reputation as America's greatest humorist. *Roughing It*, about his adventures in the Far West, contained some richly funny episodes. *The Gilded Age* was a novel satirizing the get-rich-quick years after the Civil War. The central character, 'Colonel' Beriah Sellers, is a visionary Micawber, forever dreaming up infallible projects to make himself and his friends millionaires. Twain is fierce enough with crooked Congressmen, but Sellers is too much a projection of the author (and the author's father) to engage his wrath, although Sellers is no more honest than the Senators and lobbyists in Washington. There is a certain insane charm about Sellers; the very vastness of his schemes redeems them: they are on the Western scale (and Dickens, it may be said in passing, was right to ship Micawber off to Australia: his optimism needed the room of a frontier in which to spread itself). But, apart from giving us Sellers, *The Gilded Age* is a confused book: its villains and its heroes are too easily interchangeable.

A Connecticut Yankee is similarly uneven, though for farcical invention it would be hard to beat the episodes in which the young man from contemporary Connecticut, equipped with such modern appliances as the bicycle, the telegraph, and the Colt revolver, comes to grips with a feudal never-never-land. Twain intended to draw a contrast between American-ism (democracy, open-mindedness, energy) and the cruelty, stupidity, and superstition of the Old World. He meant to ridicule the England of his own day, and in particular the kind of English condescension represented by Matthew Arnold. He meant to show the liberating magic of industrial technology. And of course he meant to be funny. Twain's countrymen thought he had succeeded in each of these aims. Some, including his illustrator Dan Beard, in addition re-garded *A Connecticut Yankee* as an indirect attack upon such latter-day robber barons as the rascally Jay Gould. British critics were less enthusiastic; their national pride was hurt, but they could more easily discern the inconsistencies in Twain. The burlesque element weakens the serious portions of the book. Like so many of his contemporaries, Twain was not whole-hearted in his praise of industrialism. At mo-ments, instead of indicting King Arthur's England, he speaks of it nostalgically in much the same terms as when he recalls the Missouri of his boyhood. They are simple and fragrant, green vivid worlds, lost paradises. Twain's hero Hank Morgan is heartbroken at the end because he cannot get back to his Arthurian sweetheart. At other times, per-haps unwittingly, he implies that the industrial order is crude, greedy, and destructive. Moreover, Morgan's growing contempt for mankind in the mass undermines the notion that there is any such thing as progress in world history.

If we are to deal purely with Twain the humorist, we have to fall back upon the details of his art. There are puns: he knows the newspaper business 'from Alpha to Omaha'. There are all kinds of straight-faced exaggeration, of repeti-tion, of anti-climax: as, of the man who 'had a wart on his nose and died in the hope of a glorious resurrection'. He is the master of all the tricks of travesty and invective.

Yet, having said this, we have said very little about Twain's humour: its motives, its range, and its curious fail-ures. One facet is his enormous pessimism. Humour is, of course, perfectly compatible with sadness – as John Nichol noted of the Negro songs (which Twain so much loved) – or with anger and disgust – as in the satire of Swift. The other American funny men were not all mere *farceurs*. American newspapermen have long been a special group, the licensed jesters and cynics at the court of public opinion; budding authors, budded authors, blown authors; consumers of late-night coffee, smokers of cigars, singers of ribald songs; lie- and cliché-detectors, disenchanted men; men somewhat detached from the world they watch. As writers, they cherish economy, and witty phrases; they are often bitter, like Ambrose Bierce and Ring Lardner, but their rage at human folly has to be disguised and made entertaining. In consequence, their work frequently reveals a strange unbalance; and the greater their talent, the greater the danger of disparity between motive and medium: between what they say and what they mean.

Though he spent only part of his life as a newspaper humorist, Mark Twain had the newspaperman's outlook, coupled with immensely more talent than most. Gregarious, impatient of humbug and pomposity, adoring gadgets and technological improvements, absorbedly interested in the writer's craft, he loved the *people* and hated the *public*. An author, but not an intellectual, he was irritated by writing he thought too cerebral. Henry James bored him; George Eliot and Hawthorne likewise, with their 'niggling analysis'. Jane Austen he would not read: he would read Poe only if somebody paid him.

Mark Twain and Poe: there is no need to enlarge on the gulf between them. There are, however, certain similarities – though the suggestion may at first sight seem absurd; and these help to clarify the nature of Twain's pessimism. As a 'magazinist', Poe lived in a neighbouring world to that of the newspaper. Much of his work was done in a hurry; and his humorous sketches in particular were calculated to catch the public fancy. In general, they are bad: it is the quality of their badness that is interesting. They are shrill, strained, grotesque, even macabre; they are facetious in a knowing way; and they reveal a special fondness for cryptograms and hoaxes (as in 'The Balloon Hoax', or in 'Diddling Considered as One of the Exact Sciences'). Underlying them is a contempt of the author for his audience. He is cleverer than they; he knows exactly what their response will be to any given stimulus; they are vicious and gullible. More than once in his tales Poe quotes Chamfort in support of his view: '*toute idée publique, toute convention reçue, est une sottise, car elle a convenue au plus grand nombre*'. And underlying this contempt again, there is a profound pessimism in Poe. People are not only unlovely: they are helpless. The universe, he maintains in *Eureka*, exhibits a perfect harmony; but, like that of his own story-plots, it is a hideous harmony. 'Cause and effect', says Emerson, '... seed and fruit, cannot be severed; for the effect already blooms in the cause, the end pre-exists in the means, the fruit in the seed.' Poe says: 'In the original unity of the first thing lies the secondary cause of all things, with the germ of their inevitable annihilation.' Here are completely different conclusions reached from similar premises. Men, says Poe, are the victims of a trap sprung long ago.

Twain comes far closer to Poe than to the cheerful Emerson. He, too, is often violent in his humour; he writes of bloodshed with an almost unholy glee, he makes ghastly fun out of the odour of corpses. There is, at times, an exaggeration in his work beyond what is called for in the scene in question: an exasperated rubbing of the reader's nose into unpleasantness. This cannot be explained away as a coarse Western deficiency; though his taste swung from joyous profanity to extremes of prudishness (as when he exclaims in horror at one of Titian's nudes, or at that 'dastardly seducer' Abelard), Twain was a highly sensitive man, who, like Poe, had a quite unusual responsiveness to sounds and colours. Again, like Poe he is given to hoaxes. He has a similar histrionic sense of manipulating situations. He admires the resourceful person who diddles others (often, as with Huckleberry Finn, by ingenious lying), or the strong man who stands off a mob ('no mob,' he writes in 'The United States of Lyncherdom', 'has any sand in the presence of a man known to be splendidly brave'). In either case, there is a latent scorn for mankind – 'this sackfull of small reptiles', as he describes humanity, as early in his career as 1871. And beneath this scorn there is a gloom that Twain cannot exorcise. It is a 'damned human race' in a not merely expletive sense. His short story, 'The Man that Corrupted Hadleyburg' (1900), tells of a practical joke of the grimmest kind, that proves the leading men of a whole town to be dishonest, and without defence except that 'it was ordered. *All* things are'. And in *The Mysterious Stranger* (1916, posthumously), Twain develops still further his long-held belief that free will is an illusion. His last message is not simply that the world has no virtue, but that it has no reality. Humanity is left 'wandering forlorn among the empty eternities'. The tall tale has here, one may think (as in the Nevada atom bomb), reached its ultimate.

Mark Twain was a determinist even before he wrote *Huckleberry Finn*. Yet he never ceased to scold the human race. Poe likewise, in his criticism, is forever nagging at other authors – a soured yet dedicated schoolmaster, who has learned from experience that his class are dolts (and worse), but who nevertheless strives to beat some rudiments of knowledge into them. Twain, too, is something of the cynical pedagogue: though one of his San Francisco nicknames was 'the Wild Humorist of the Plains', he was also known as 'the Moral Phenomenon', and he insists over and over that his task is not buffoonery, but *teaching* (or even *preaching*). The difference between the two men's creative methods is enormous, though both stress with professional pride the deliberation with which they arrive at their effects. Here, Poe eschews didacticism, and seeks an unreal beauty. Twain chooses burlesque: the public is to be coaxed and tickled into understanding.

It is no wonder that his work is so uneven. Part of him is coltish, part is saturnine. Part of him revels in the chaos of Western life; for, as Howells wrote,

He had the Southwestern, the Lincolnian, the Elizabethan breadth of parlance, and I was often hiding away ... the letters in which he had loosed his bold fancy to stoop on rank suggestion; I could not bear to burn them, and I could not, after the first reading, quite bear to look at them.

This is the free-thinking, free-spoken, democratic Twain who girds at slavery, aristocracy, and intolerance. But he has to come East to escape the last-named. Discussing Southern politics, he writes from Connecticut to a Missouri friend in 1876:

I think I comprehend their position there – perfect freedom to vote just as you choose, provided you choose to vote as *other people* think, social ostracism otherwise. ... Fortunately a good deal of experience of men enabled me to choose my residence wisely. I live in the freest corner of the country.

In other words, in the New England of Longfellow and Lowell. But the 'Eastern' Twain can be delicate to the point of prudery. And why campaign to overthrow aristocracy, if it is only to be replaced by mob-rule? And what is the use of campaigning, if we are all the victims of circumstance? It seems appropriate that his pen-name, *Twain* should suggest dualism; that he should be intrigued by the idea of twinship, and use twins and mixed identities as a plot device (in *The Prince and the Pauper* and *Pudd'nhead Wilson*); and that he should claim descent on his father's side from a regicide judge, and – on his mother's – from the earls of Durham.

Perhaps he sought to resolve his difficulties – to combine beauty with burlesque, to enjoy the pageantry of aristocracy while attacking its social iniquities – by writing of the past. He was encouraged to do so by his reviewers as well as by his Hartford neighbours, who convinced him that *Joan of Arc* was beautiful where *Tom Sawyer* and *Huckleberry Finn* were only comic. He was disposed to agree with them. But his settings, while as unreal as Poe's, lack Poe's concentrated atmosphere. They shift vagariously from farce to satire, and even to mawkishness. The product of a skilled and gifted humorist, they are often funny and almost always readable. But the humour becomes mechanical, the aim divided, as in Chaplin's later films. Sometimes we are chewing a sweet, sometimes a sugar-coated pill, and sometimes a pill with no coating at all.

The classic Twain, however, like the early Chaplin, is a great artist whose touch is sure. Posterity will remember him for the books in which neither farce nor bleakness has the upper hand, but in which affection and close knowledge are united. These are *Tom Sawyer, Life on the Mississippi*, and – above all – *Huckleberry Finn*. In them he wrote with warmth and accuracy of the life he most vividly knew, the life of his boyhood river town and of the river. To Dickens, the Mississippi was a foul ditch 'running liquid mud', with 'nothing pleasant in its aspect, but the harmless lightning which flickers every night upon the dark horizon'. To Mark Twain, as a youngster and through the eye of reminiscence, it was all existence. Treacherous to the unaware, yet safe and generous to those who (like Huck Finn) know it, the Mississippi becomes in Twain's pages the symbol of the human journey. *Tom Sawyer* is a little too much the 'story of a bad boy' (equipped with an adult's dexterity) to be entirely satifying, and *Life on the Mississippi* falls away in its final chapters, though the opening ones are magnificent. But *Huckleberry Finn*, apart from the Tom-Sawyerish rescue of Jim, is perfect, the unforgettable portrait of a frontier boy. Whether or not determinism is sound philosophy, it is a bad doctrine for the novelist, for he deals with ordinary people, and ordinary people do not *feel* that their lives are predetermined, whatever the novelist may have decided on their behalf. If he imposes his view too firmly, his characters become listless puppets. In *Huckleberry Finn*, however, the characters are (in Whitman's words) 'refreshing, wicked, real'. Some of them, it is true, are caught, in apathetic squalor, in small-town brutality, in meaningless blood-feuds, or (like Jim) in Negro slavery. But Huck himself is still free, the natural being not yet moulded and ruined by an environment that seeks to civilize him. He is able to free Jim from the immediate evil of slavery, though not from the disability of being black. But at the end Huck, like Natty Bumppo, must get away from civilization if he is to save himself. It is the American renuncia-

tion once more, though in Huck's case unaccompanied by
the asceticism of – say – Thoreau's choice. The New World
is still new so long as it is possible to slip away into the wilderness, to live by the senses as wild animals do. Otherwise,
there begins the sad, irrevocable tick-tock of destiny. Commerce comes; churches and moralities; the falsehoods of the
printed word and of the platform; humanity in herds, mobs,
armies ('a company of soldiers is an offensive spectacle', said
Emerson). Twain avoided some of these things: after a few
weeks' soldiering in the Civil War, he lit out west for the Nevada Territory – but to join others in making the desert
blossom, only to regret what he had done, in somehow des-
poiling the transcendental innocence, as all pioneers must.

Ernest Hemingway is another American writer who has
striven, at some cost, to preserve the truth of direct experience. He has rightly praised *Huckleberry Finn*, and Mark
Twain's great incidental achievement, in it and his other
work, of creating a prose-style suited to the American ethos.
Washington Irving had once tried; so had Lowell; so had
the newspaper humorists. The approach in all cases was
through humour; only in light, unaffected pieces could
Americans convey the ease and informality of their national
idiom, and avoid the heavy classicism in which it was usually
expressed. Noah Webster had asked for a genuine American
style; but not until Twain's day was there truth (mixed with
pardonable exaggeration) in his claim that

There is no such thing as 'the Queen's English'. The property has
gone into the hands of a joint stock company and we own the bulk
of the shares.

In his hands, comic jargon and dialect became a finished
literary weapon, unemphatic, visual, and deceptively simple,
sounding like speech and yet not quite the same. Howells
said that orthodox English, as written by the accepted masters, 'is scholarly and conscious; it knows who its grandfather
was'. With Mark Twain, *content* – like Western life – had a
mongrel incongruity; but *form* began the lineage that has led
to Hemingway.

CHAPTER EIGHT

MINOR KEY

Emily Dickinson and Others

SIDNEY LANIER (1842–81)

b. Macon, Georgia, and *ed.* at Oglethorpe University in the same state. Hopes of a musical career were shattered by the Civil War, in which he was taken prisoner, to the detriment of his already poor health. This experience furnished material for his novel *Tiger-Lilies* (1867). Hampered by illness and poverty, he devoted himself to poetry and to music, becoming a flautist in a Baltimore orchestra. His *Poems* appeared in 1877, and some lectures were printed as *The Science of English Verse* (1880).

GEORGE WASHINGTON CABLE (1844–1925)

b. New Orleans, he became a writer after Confederate service during the Civil War. His first sketches were printed in newspapers and periodicals; some were collected as *Old Creole Days* (1879). *The Grandissimes*, a novel, appeared in 1880, followed by many other stories of the South, though he lived in the North.

JOEL CHANDLER HARRIS (1848–1908)

b. in Georgia, he worked for various Southern newspapers before associating himself (1876–1900) with the *Atlanta Constitution*, where his first Uncle Remus story was printed (1879). Many other stories followed, as their popularity kept on increasing the demand for them; an Uncle Remus Memorial Association was founded at Harris's death. He also wrote stories and novels on other aspects of Southern life.

HARRIET BEECHER STOWE (1811–96)

b. in Connecticut, Harriet Beecher moved with her father to Cincinnati (1832), where she married C. E. Stowe (1836), a professor in her father's theological seminary, and became strongly opposed to slavery. Living in Maine, she wrote *Uncle Tom's Cabin* (1852), which was sensationally successful and led her to write many other works, including another anti-slavery novel, *Dred, A Tale of the Great Dismal Swamp* (1856). For some years she lived in Hartford, Connecticut, close to Mark Twain, though she became interested in Florida real-estate and spent some time in this Southern state.

SARAH ORNE JEWETT (1849–1909)

b. in South Berwick, Maine, she began to write in her teens. Her first sketches, published as *Deephaven* (1877), were well received; others followed, and some novels and poems, most of them concerned with Maine. *The Country of the Pointed Firs* (1896) has remained her best-known work.

EMILY DICKINSON (1830–86)

b. Amherst, Mass., where she spent nearly all her life, except for a year at Mount Holyoke Female Seminary. Gradually withdrawing into seclusion, she lived at home with her father, a well-to-do lawyer. Her few friends and correspondents included Thomas Wentworth Higginson, the Harvard man of letters, whose advice on her poetry she solicited and who edited her poems at her death.

MINOR KEY

—

THE Civil War produced little literature of merit, if we except the poems of Whitman and Melville, and such lesser works as John W. DeForest's *Miss Ravenel's Conversion from Secession to Loyalty* (1867) – a better book than the title might suggest. Very few important American authors were involved in the fighting. Ambrose Bierce was, and Sidney Lanier; but Twain, Howells, and Henry James were jeeringly described by H. L. Mencken as 'draft-dodgers'. In poetry, the war did call forth a crop of martial and commemorative pieces like Lowell's Harvard 'Ode' and the 'Ethnogenesis' of the young Southerner, Henry Timrod. But however moving these may be for American readers, they are not for export. As might have been expected, the war also brought a new clamour for native writers, to celebrate America's virtues in ink, when these had lately been attested in blood. Thus, Horace Bushnell (a prominent minister) delivered an oration at Yale in 1865 on 'Our Obligation to the Dead'. One obligation, he felt, was 'henceforth ... not ... to write English but American. We have gotten our position, we are now to have our own civilization, think our own thoughts, rhyme our own measures.'

A few years later Mark Twain was to 'write American'. But his example was not followed at once; indeed, some American writers never have followed it, refusing to admit that it is adequate for their purposes. In general, American literature of this time betrayed considerable anxiety. Younger writers sat under the shadow of the elders. Emerson and Longfellow lived until 1882; Lowell, Whittier, Holmes, and Parkman all survived into the 1890s, their reputations terrifyingly grand. In the uneasy years of Reconstruction, of the 'Gilded Age', a hostile critic might conclude that there was little sign of the civilization Horace Bushnell called for. A kindlier observer, however, might notice the work of such isolated figures as Sidney Lanier, and watch the growth (in the South and in New England as well as in the West) of literature pitched in a minor key, a literature of local colour based upon keen awareness of local scenery and speech.

The South, parochially entangled in the issues of slavery and State-rights, had before the war devoted its energies to polemicism. Apart from Poe, the occasional humorist and a few second-rate figures like William Gilmore Simms (who suffered the double provincial indignity of being described as 'the Southern Cooper' – after Cooper had already been once-qualified as 'the American Scott'), there was no Southern tradition of imaginative literature. The young poet-musician Lanier yearned for friendship and support; 'you have no idea,' he wrote to a Northern friend, 'how benighted we all are'. Though his poems began to win recognition, and to be published in the North, Lanier, like Poe before him, was prey to a terrible restlessness; there was no security of tenure in the life of either. Both dreamed extravagantly. Chivalry, pure and passionless women, unearthly beauty: some high Southern fantasy possessed them. Both developed doctrines of prosody. Lanier maintained in *The Science of English Verse* (1880) that music and verse are much the same, since the same laws govern them. Metre in poetry, he believed, obeyed the metronome: time and not accent was the essential feature. In an elaborate diction, he strove to create poetry that would sound as music does. The result, as in Poe, is frequently over-melodious:

Oh, what is abroad in the marsh and the terminal sea?
   Somehow my soul seems suddenly free
From the weighing of fate and the sad discussion of sin,
By the length and the breadth and the sweep of the marshes of Glynn.

Lanier wrote some lovely lines, but he is not quite a major poet; his seems to be the failure of a fine sensibility left too much to its own devices. Yet he and Poe helped to initiate a Southern literary attitude which, though marred now and then by Southern romanticism, has in our time produced excellent poetry.

Lacking the fanciful, erudite, gentlemanly quality of Lanier, other Southern writers nevertheless made successful efforts to catch the atmosphere of their section: its heat and luxuriance, its decaying social order – and its Negroes. Here was the other main line of Southern literary development: a line discernible in Twain (to the extent that he is a Southerner), perhaps in Poe's comic sketches, certainly in Augustus Longstreet's *Georgia Scenes* (1835), and in George Washington Cable and Joel Chandler Harris. (Present-day Southern writers – William Faulkner, Robert Penn Warren, Eudora Welty, Carson McCullers, Flannery O'Connor – have been able to fuse, or at any rate embody, both lines, the high rhetoric and the low life.) Cable, a Southerner with a Northern mother, had a remarkable understanding of the intricacies of Louisiana life. His *Old Creole Days* (1879) and *The Grandissimes* (1880) gave so accurate an account of old French families in New Orleans, and of partly coloured people with their complicated defensive attitudes, that these communities took offence at his stories. (There was another side to Cable. Though he served as a Confederate cavalryman, he became convinced after the war that slavery had been evil, and that the continued Southern mistreatment of the freed Negro was hardly less evil. He wrote some admirable essays on this momentous subject – and was assailed as a traitor to his section.[1]) Some of Cable's Louisiana fiction is a little slick, and the Creole dialect is a hindrance: one cannot always see the locality for the colour. Similar comments apply to a great deal of local-colour writing, North as well as South.

However, in the best work of Joel Chandler Harris the local becomes universal. Uncle Remus, the old Negro, explaining the world to the white boy, is an immortal character; and so are the irrepressible Brer Rabbit, the malign and frustrated Brer Fox, and the other creatures of his bestiary. Though Harris was persuaded to write too many Uncle Remus stories (there are ten volumes of them), and though he was emphatically a Southerner, he does not make Uncle

1. See George W. Cable, *The Negro Question: A Selection of Writings on Civil Rights in the South*, ed. Arlin Turner (Garden City, N.Y., 1958).

Remus a propaganda figure. Remembering the time 'befo' de war, endurin' de war, en atter de war', Remus might easily have been a mouthpiece for Southern self-pity, or a quaint old darky of the kind that Thomas Nelson Page loved to describe. Instead, he is a shrewd old man with a profound sense of the underdog, and a great delight in the methods by which the underdog scores off those who are more powerful. For as Harris wrote,

it needs no scientific investigation to show why [the Negro] selects as his hero the weakest and most harmless of all animals, and brings him out victorious in contests with the bear, the wolf, and the fox. It is not virtue that triumphs, but helplessness; it is not malice but mischievousness.

The fables of Uncle Remus, funny and touching in themselves, are dependent to some extent on the narrator's dialect. But it is his philosophy that makes them timeless: the philosophy of the gentle and the poor, which was that of his creator. Harris's favourite book was *The Vicar of Wakefield*. 'Its simplicity, its air of extreme wonderment,' he said, had moved him all his life. To Harris, literature came nearest to its true function when it dealt with common people; Henry James's remarks on the barrenness and tedium of life in Hawthorne's New England provoked him to furious denial. Certainly in his own region the presence of the Negro lent a special depth to life; he was among the first to make subtle use of this material.

With Uncle Remus, and Mark Twain's Jim, the best-known Negro in American fiction is the Uncle Tom of Harriet Beecher Stowe's spectacularly successful novel. He is, by contrast, a caricature, so pious and loyal that he is too good to be true. Indeed, one Southerner declared that *Uncle Tom's Cabin* contained no more insight into the Negro than *The Nautical Almanac*. More recently, the Negro writer James Baldwin has criticized it as 'Everybody's Protest Novel' – a basically prejudiced book calculated to make white liberals feel comfortably indignant. Harriet Beecher Stowe was not quite free from the covert prejudices of her age, and Baldwin is correct in arguing that the 'protest novel' is a peculiar American genre whose effect may be merely to reassure the reader that he is generously inclined even if others are not. But he is too hard on Mrs Stowe. Under slavery some Negroes were conditioned to behave like 'Uncle Toms': the type existed. Nor did she pretend that mistreatment and misunderstanding of the Negro was confined to Southerners. The villainous overseer, Legree, is a Vermonter (though he has a South Carolina name), and there is an acid portrait of Miss Ophelia, a squeamish New England spinster who does not like to have Negroes touch her. Mrs Stowe wrote a tract for the times, in the hope of arousing public sentiment. By all odds, her book should have been as bad as the innumerable other specimens of anti-slavery (or pro-slavery) fiction. It was immeasurably better, because its author, while caring passionately about her subject, brought to it an exceptional energy, curiosity, narrative power, and sense of standards. This was the book that Palmerston read three times, and that brought tears to Gladstone's eyes. A hundred years later, one's reaction is milder. Even so, it remains an effective novel. If Uncle Tom is endowed with too many virtues, the same can be said of a large number of Dickens's characters. And the other figures in the book – Topsy, St Clare, Shelby, even Simon Legree – all stick in one's mind, although the set-pieces that made the dramatized version so popular – Eliza's flight across the ice, the death of little Eva – belong with the taste of another age.

Mrs Stowe's 'sense of standards' is evident in some of her other, less famous novels, in which she draws upon her New England background, writing of small, tense communities where religious observance and debate furnish the main fabric of existence. The people in her books are serious, in that certain aspects of life seem serious to them. Their problems do not always arouse our sympathy; in *The Minister's Wooing* (1859), for instance, the heroine is anguished by the thought that her sweetheart, who is believed to have been drowned, died while not in a state of grace. Her villains – Aaron Burr in the same book, Ellery Davenport in *Oldtown Folks* (1869)

– are sinful and sophisticated to the point of being preposterous. Yet she is not devoid of humour and high spirits. Though Cotton Mather's *Magnalia Christi Americana*, which she read as a child, 'made me feel the very ground I trod on to be consecrated by some special dealing of God's providence', and though she was forbidden to read any novels save those of Scott, her clergyman-father could throw off his dignity when out with his family – even to the extent of shinning up a high chestnut-tree that grew out over a precipice, 'and then whirling himself over the abyss to beat down the chestnuts for the children below'. However, such incidents do not often occur in her novels; their tone is reserved, as in Hawthorne, whom she rivals in her knowledge of the Puritan heritage. Still, as evocations of the New England scene and of the Calvinist character, the books mentioned (together with *The Pearl of Orr's Island*, 1862, and *Poganuc People*, 1878) have a quality that is stronger than charm. Indeed, the closer they come to description and analysis, the better they are; weak as novels, they are strong as sketches of an environment she understood intimately – not vicariously, as with the South of *Uncle Tom's Cabin*.

This side of Mrs Stowe's work can be described as local colour; certainly it inspired New England's best writer in the genre, Sarah Orne Jewett. As a girl she read (and loved) *The Pearl of Orr's Island*, a novel about the coast of Maine, where Miss Jewett grew up, and which she soon began to depict – first in short stories, then in novels. The range of her work is restricted. In general, it deals with simple folk, on farms and in small towns which are never far from the sea. Most of her characters are women who have known one another all their lives; and while they would not agree with Emerson that people 'who know the same thing are not long the best company for each other', they can be so laconic as to seem brusque. This presents Miss Jewett with a problem in understatement. 'It is difficult,' she realizes, 'to report the great events of New England; expression is so slight, and those few words which escape us in moments of deep feeling look but meagre on the printed page.' Much of their life is retrospection; their settlements and harbours are, as a rule, declining, and there seem to be more deaths than births. (One whole island was in fact depopulated when its farmers and their families left for the Western goldfields.) Not an obviously rewarding situation for the novelist, it is one exactly suited to Miss Jewett's gentle, economical talent. Her best book, *The Country of the Pointed Firs* (1896), is a series of sketches about the imaginary Dunnet, a 'salt-aired, white-clap-boarded little town' seen through the eyes of a narrator who can be taken as Miss Jewett herself. Through Mrs Todd, the woman with whom she boards, the narrator enters unobtrusively into the lives of the townsfolk. Some of them have travelled far: Captain Littlepage has been to Hudson's Bay, and lived there with an insane old Scotsman who believes he has discovered an Arctic Purgatory; while Mrs Fosdick, as a child, has sailed in her father's ship: 'Ought to see them painted savages I've seen when I was young out in the South Sea Islands! That was the time for folks to travel, 'way back in the old whalin' days ... I used to return feelin' very slack an' behind the times, 'tis true, ... but 't was excitin', an' we always done extra well, and felt rich when we did get ashore.' But they are all elderly now; the world has drawn in upon them, and even the travelled ones are sure that no place can compare with their own corner of Maine.

Sarah Orne Jewett's writing is as neat and unaffected as the homes of her characters, though, like those homes, it reveals an occasional decorative flourish. It is reticent, yet not trivial; it balances between a mournful recognition of decay and a New England briskness which differentiates it sharply from the local-colour writing of that other decaying region, the South:

There was an old house on the height, facing southward, – a mere forsaken shell of an old house, with empty windows that looked like blind eyes. The frost-bitten grass grew close about it like brown fur, and there was a single crooked bough of lilac holding its green leaves close by the door.

'We'll just have a good piece of bread-an'-butter now,' said [Mrs

Todd], 'and then we'll hang up the basket on some peg inside the house out o' the way o' the sheep. ...'

Her stories are the work of a writer who for all her love of Maine was perfectly aware of the world outside – who, for instance, had read Balzac and Zola and Gustave Flaubert. Firm, feminine, amused, mature, her writing reminds the reader at once of Willa Cather (1876–1947), though she was to write of Nebraska and New Mexico, areas remote from Maine. Indeed, there is a succession here, from Harriet Beecher Stowe to Sarah Orne Jewett and thence to Willa Cather, who ranked *The Country of the Pointed Firs* with *The Scarlet Letter* and *Huckleberry Finn* as 'three American books which have the possibility of a long life'. And the succession prompts the suggestion that women writers have made a quite special contribution to American literature. In part, it has been of the pernicious sort that enraged Hawthorne: the sort typified by *The Wide, Wide World* (1851) and *Queechy* (1852), by Susan B. Warner, lachrymose romances contemporary with his best work but far outselling his. But at its best, as in Willa Cather and Ellen Glasgow (1874–1945), with its attachment to place, to heritage, and family ties, it has provided (like the piano in the shanty) a necessary counter-mood to the grandiose, outdoor, masculine tendencies of American prose.

One could name other women – Mary Wilkins Freeman (1852–1930), for example – who like Mrs Stowe and Miss Jewett illustrate the aura of New England. So too, perhaps, does America's greatest woman poet, Emily Dickinson, who lived in complete obscurity in the small Massachusetts town of Amherst. Nowhere but in a New England community could a woman be at once so unhappy, so alone, and yet so spry and so articulate: so aware of the contiguity and interrelatedness of this world and the next. Or, one might add, so uneven, so unfinished despite her genius. For here is the paradigm of 'local' colour – writing that has shrunk in scale to the boundary of a house, the garden surrounding it, and the view from the lawn or its windows. Here is a seclusion so complete as to seem wilful – that has on the one hand almost the agonized force of Calvinism, and on the other, the transcendental ecstasy derived from the communion of a human being with nature.

At her death Emily Dickinson left over a thousand unpublished poems. Only a few friends knew that she had written them. Many were mere ideas for poems jotted down on whatever scrap of paper lay to hand. Others had been revised with some care. All, however, were short poems, broken for the most part into four-line stanzas; and all have an unmistakable personal stamp. They are as compressed as a telegram. They are like oracular messages, but witty – jaunty at times – and sometimes trembling on the edge of whimsy. They have a scale all of their own; the far-away and enormous are seen in terms of the humble and familiar, or vice versa. In her miniature world crumbs serve for a banquet; small creatures – fly, spider, bee, robin, butterfly – can loom immensely against the eye. Thus:

> The cricket sang,
> And set the sun,
> And workmen finished, one by one,
> Their seam the day upon.
>
> The low grass loaded with the dew,
> The twilight stood as strangers do
> With hat in hand, polite and new,
> To stay as if, or go.
>
> A vastness, as a neighbour, came, –
> A wisdom without face or name,
> A peace, as hemispheres at home, –
> And so the night became.

This poem is not one of her finest, but can be looked at as fairly typical. The prosody is erratic; perhaps there are too many conflicting images; perhaps the end – with its characteristic squeezing of a transitive verb into an intransitive role – is too abrupt and anticlimactic. Even so, as this particular poem shows, her work is extraordinarily rich and alert. *Cricket, workman, stranger, neighbour*: with these homely and small figures she tackles the coming of night. Yet, in the final stanza, the small has become 'a vastness', something prodigious and mysterious – 'a wisdom without face or

name'. Notice also Emily Dickinson's acute susceptibility to
mood, especially as this is affected by the change of light. Light
reveals the subtle alteration of things, the sly or calamitous
impermanence of mortal life:

> Presentiment is that long shadow on the lawn
> Indicative that suns go down;
> The notice to the startled grass
> That darkness is about to pass.

These lines form a complete poem. Another, in four stanzas,
begins:

> There's a certain slant of light,
> On winter afternoons,
> That oppresses, like the weight
> Of cathedral tunes,

and ends:

> When it comes, the landscape listens,
> Shadows hold their breath;
> When it goes, 'tis like the distance
> On the look of death.

The look of death: she is preoccupied with death, as the gate-
way to the next existence. This is conceived of as a special
glory that has something, though not everything, in common with the conventional paradises offered in the hymns
and sermons of her day, or with the Book of Revelation that
was among her favourite reading. Death means leisure,
grandeur, recognition; it means being with the few, rare
people whom it was not possible to know fully upon earth.
The house is prelude to the tomb:

> We paused before a house that seemed
> A swelling of the ground;
> The roof was scarcely visible,
> The cornice but a mound.

Beyond the tomb, after the 'white election', God presides
over an opulent kingdom whose splendours she denotes in
words like *purple, royal, privilege, emerald, diadem, courtier, Po-
tosi, Himmaleh*. All help to reinforce her view of immortality.
Much of life is anguish endured in an anteroom to death;

'empress of Calvary', she might have said with Whitman
that

> To die is different from what any one supposed, and luckier.

The poet, in such a situation, is the keen observer who keeps
his life uncluttered as far as possible: who,

> spreading wide my narrow hands
> To gather Paradise,

catches whatever clues of Paradise are vouchsafed in the
external world. Nature supplies some hints, not of the
transcendental order but altogether more tantalising and
momentary:

> We spy the Forests and the Hills,
> The tents to Nature's Show,
> Mistake the outside for the in,
> And mention what we saw.

It is the 'in' she watches for, the instantaneous flash when
the mortal seems about to pierce the veil. It happens, almost,
when light changes, as at the approach of a storm; or when
seasons pass ('These behaviours of the year hurt almost like
music'); or – above all – when there is a death. At such times
she could feel that

> The only news I know
> Is bulletins all day
> From Immortality.

In the poem 'Just lost when I was saved', an illness from
which she has recovered appears as an unsuccessful explora-
tion:

> Therefore, as one returned, I feel,
> Odd secrets of the line to tell!
> Some sailor, skirting foreign shores,
> Some pale reporter from the awful doors
> Before the seal!

However, Emily Dickinson's vision of the next world is
tempered by her whimsical, domestic cast of mind; by what
has been well described as the 'rococo' (as distinct from the

'sublime')- element in her character.[1] Though she speaks again and again of isolation in this world, she is not a mystic like St Teresa of Avila, or a religious poet like St John of the Cross. Rather, she flirts with eternity, she is coquettish with God, forgiving him his 'duplicity', sometimes distressingly coy with him, as in this early poem:

> I hope the father in the skies
> Will lift this little girl, –
> Old-fashioned, naughty, everything, –
> Over the stile of pearl.

God is indeed a puzzling figure in her work. The Creator who does not perhaps know why he has created, He is 'burglar, banker, father', gentleman, duke, king: a being apparently personified at times as Death, at other times as a sort of lover. Perhaps these are all versions of the men with whom she may have been secretly in love, or of her own father. In correspondence with men, including her mentor Thomas Wentworth Higginson, there is a sort of display of plumage, the hint of a complexly momentary courtship. Sometimes one suspects an edge of New England humour, sometimes the recklessness evident in the behaviour of sensitive and unloved children. At any rate, she takes amazing liberties with sacred themes. No wonder that Christina Rossetti, after highly praising Emily Dickinson's poetry, went on to deplore 'some of the religious, or rather irreligious pieces'. Perhaps the defect is not so much a matter of irreligion as of immaturity; a concern with the small and the familiar can so easily approach garden-ornament whimsy – as when she signs her correspondence, 'Your Gnome'.

But the final impression of her work is of astonishing integrity and originality. Despite her interest in death, she exhibits a quick sensibility to the world around her, and to the materials of her craft. Technically a poor poet, she does most effective violence to vocabulary. Terms from many sources – law, geometry, engineering – are used to suit her purposes.

1. By Richard Chase, *Emily Dickinson* [*American Men of Letters*] (London, 1952).

Commonplace words come alive in new contexts, and she never hesitates to substitute parts of speech:

> Kingdoms like the orchard
> Flit russetly away.

Sometimes her economy is that of New England idiom:

> And 'twas like midnight, some, –

The laconic *some* could only have been used by an American poet.

Not without friends, she keeps them at arm's length, so that she may discuss her affairs with a poet's abstraction (like Thoreau, who closed a letter by saying, 'You will perceive that I am as often talking to myself, perhaps, as speaking to you'). And what letters result! 'The lawn is full of south and the odors tangle,' she tells one correspondent, 'and I hear to-day for the first the river in the tree.' Again, 'If I feel physically as if the top of my head were taken off, I know that is poetry.' One critic, comparing her with Whitman, has said that both 'wrote as though no one had written poetry before'.[1] The remark is both a fair criticism, and a great and merited compliment. In her finest lines she has all the magic of a major poet. The words

> Farther in summer than the birds,
> Pathetic from the grass,

to take one example from hundreds, wonderfully defy analysis. But the poem they introduce is disappointing. She has patches of genius, but not often whole poems. Hawthorne whispers at us, as if he were deaf; Melville shouts, as if he suspected his *audience* were deaf; and Emily Dickinson too is unsure how to pitch her work. But like these others, she draws strength from her disturbing loneliness.

1. A. C. Ward, *American Literature: 1880–1930* (London, 1932), 43.

REALISM IN AMERICAN PROSE

From Howells to Dreiser

─────────

WILLIAM DEAN HOWELLS (1837–1920)

b. Ohio, the son of a poor but well-educated printer. After several moves – one interlude of which is described in *A Boy's Town* (1890) – the family settled in Columbus. Here young Howells continued to educate himself, while writing for a newspaper. Appointed for services to the Republican party as consul to Venice (1861–5), he made the most of his opportunity to study Europe and its literature at first hand. Returning to America, he rapidly became one of its foremost novelists, essayists, and editors, working in Boston and later in New York.

HAMLIN GARLAND (1860–1940)

b. Wisconsin, and spent some of his early years also in Iowa and South Dakota. After a high-school education, he made his way to Boston, where he decided to write of the region he knew, according to the 'veritist' technique described in his *Crumbling Idols* (1894). Perhaps never entirely wholehearted in his realism, he abandoned it by stages, his last books dealing with spiritualism.

STEPHEN CRANE (1871–1900)

b. in New Jersey, and lived there and in New York State, achieving an erratic education combined with casual journalism. His first book *Maggie* (1893), was published at his own expense, and largely ignored until the success of *The Red Badge of Courage* (1895). The last years of his brief life were restless; his experiences included newspaper work in Mexico, a filibustering expedition to Cuba (1896), war-reporting in Greece and Cuba, a spell of hectic country life in England, and final death of tuberculosis in Germany.

FRANK NORRIS (1870–1902)

b. Chicago, Norris moved to San Francisco (1884) with his parents, who allowed him to study medieval art in Paris before he returned to attend the University of California. There he gradually forsook his early taste for romantic subjects and began to write realist fiction. In 1895–6 he acted as travel correspondent in South Africa; he reported the Spanish–American fighting in Cuba (1898); and became a publisher's reader in New York, producing a great deal of fiction before his sudden death.

JACK LONDON (1876–1916)

b. San Francisco, of uncertain parentage, and raised along the water-front, where he began at an early age to indulge his boundless appetite for adventure. Education was sandwiched in between journeys as a tramp and participation (1897) in the Klondike gold rush. His stories first appeared in book form with *The Son of the Wolf* (1900); thereafter, his many books reached an enormous public, whether his subject was socialism, or the great outdoors, or both.

THEODORE DREISER (1871–1945)

b. Indiana, the son of an impoverished German immigrant whose strong religious faith soon became repugnant to his son, and whose lack of financial acumen inspired in Dreiser an intense respect for wealth on the grand scale. Until middle age he worked for newspapers and periodicals, in several large cities of the U.S., his novels unregarded.

REALISM IN AMERICAN PROSE

—

IN his *Devil's Dictionary*, Ambrose Bierce – that cynical *Ur*-Mencken – defined READING as

> The general body of what one reads. In our country it consists, as a rule, of Indiana novels, short stories in 'dialect' and humor in slang.

Local-colour work, which he is in effect describing, aroused him only to facetiousness. REALISM, though, was another matter. It was, he said:

> The art of depicting nature as it is seen by toads. The charm suffusing a landscape painted by a mole, or a story written by a measuring-worm.

This is the vocabulary of abuse. In fact, it is typical of the abuse that greeted those who called themselves 'realists'. The 'realists', for their part, replied with manifestoes that usually included the words *reality* (as opposed to *idealism*, *romanticism*, *sentimentality*), *truth* (frequently *unvarnished*), *honesty*, *accuracy*. They claimed to represent *real life*, *life as it is*. Such statements are unsatisfactory as definitions, since they beg the question of what is meant by *life* or *reality*. A clearer idea of 'realism' can be arrived at in terms of the material held suitable for the novelist:

> So forgive me once more, patient reader, if I offer you no tragedy in high life, no sentimental history of fashion and wealth, but only a little story about a woman who could not be a heroine.

Perhaps the humility of this passage gives away its early date. It comes from a short story published in 1861, by the New England writer Rose Terry Cooke. A decade or two later similar statements of intention were offered much more often and much less apologetically. 'Realism', then, entailed writing about the environment one knew, with strict regard to its actual properties – speech, dress, scene, behaviour. It had

certain particularly American connotations. Henry James
agreed with Bierce as to the prevalence of dialect 'in the subject-matter of the American fictions of the day'. No such pre-
dominance, he thought, 'exists in English, in French, in German work of the same order'. It seemed to him, however,
part of 'the great general wave of curiosity on the subject of
the soul aboundingly not civilized that has lately begun to
well over the Anglo-Saxon globe and that has borne Mr
Rudyard Kipling, say, so supremely high on its crest'.

It would be easy to write of the development of American
realism as though it were a movement growing out of local
colour by virtue of its greater sophistication, and then yield-
ing in turn to the movement known as 'naturalism' – and all
the while doing battle with the fiction-writers grouped under
the banner of 'romanticism'. Romance confronting reality:
high life versus low, or at any rate middle, life: the exotic
versus the demotic: the daydream versus broad daylight:
sentimentality versus common sense. Easy, and not altogether wrong. For there were novelists of the time, like William Dean Howells, who avowed that they were 'realists',
who explained the articles of their creed in the face of their
opponents, who championed other writers whom they considered as allies, and who employed the metaphors of controversy – battles, skirmishes, camps, campaigns – as though
a clear-cut literary war were in progress. And there were
novelists like Francis Marion Crawford who, if they did not
call themselves 'romanticists', nevertheless disagreed expli-
citly with Howells and his protégés. There *was* a cleavage:
there is a wide difference of outlook and tone between Frances
Hodgson Burnett's *Little Lord Fauntleroy* and Howells's *Indian
Summer*, both published in 1886; or between Thomas Nelson
Page's *In Ole Virginia* and Joseph Kirkland's *Zury, the Mean-
est Man in Spring County*, which appeared in the following
year.

But on closer inspection the battle – to adopt the metaphor
popular with literary historians as well as with Howells –
seems to have been a confused affair, of civil strife, in which
not all the combatants wore uniform or were certain of their

war-aims. If we are to pick sides, to which does Ambrose
Bierce belong? Or Henry James, who with Howells had been
an early protagonist of 'realism' but who by 1886 was resident in England, and writing *The Princess Casamassima*? Can
we agree with one critic that Mark Twain (whose *Huckleberry Finn* had come out in 1884) 'took to dealings with the
romanticists...after his single effective blow for the realists
in *The Gilded Age* (1873)'?[1] What are we to make of Charles
Dudley Warner (Twain's collaborator in that work), whom
the same critic describes – justly enough – as a 'polite com-
mentator'? It seems laughable to compare him with John
Dos Passos; yet like Dos Passos he did write a trilogy about
ill-gotten wealth and its miserable consequences. Again, the
romanticists' leader, Marion Crawford, concocted thirty-
odd novels set in such *locales* as fifteenth-century Venice and
fourteenth-century Constantinople; but he also wrote seven
about the contemporary American scene, including one (*An
American Politician*, 1884) about the corruptions of the Gilded
Age; and, although he did not altogether live up to his own
advice, he told an interviewer in 1893 that the United States
offered the novelist the richest field in the entire world. And
if to write of past times and far-off places was to qualify as
a romanticist, must one therefore condemn R. L. Stevenson
and Rudyard Kipling, whose work Howells much admired?
Or, to take one more example, there is the case of 'Sidney
Luska', whom Howells described in 1888 as 'a most delightful fellow, and a most ardent convert to realism'. 'Luska'
was the pseudonym of the young author Henry Harland,
who wrote novels about Jewish immigrants in New York.
Only a couple of years later he suddenly abandoned his
pseudonym and went to live in Europe, where he edited *The
Yellow Book* and produced such elegant trifles as *Grey Roses*
(1895 – a title that perfectly epitomizes what one thinks of
as the decadent side of the nineties), *The Cardinal's Snuff-Box*
(1900), and *My Friend Prospero* (1903). What happened? Was

1. Grant C. Knight, *The Critical Period in American Literature: 1890–1900*
(Chapel Hill, N.C., 1951), 169. Professor Knight's book is, in the main,
an admirable study.

the conversion followed by apostasy? Did the recruit (to mix metaphors) go over to the other army?

Yes, to some extent. But we miss much of the nature of realism if we speak exaggeratedly of victories and betrayals. 'Realism' is a label we cannot do without: it helps to isolate certain features common to a great deal of fiction written in the last third of the nineteenth century. But like other labels it is apt to acquire a false and tyrannical plausibility. Reified, it leads us to search for lowest common denominators in literature, and to overlook or condemn more important factors. Perhaps this is why Howells praised Stephen Crane's *Maggie* (as an orthodox naturalistic novel which nobody read) and did not like Crane's *Red Badge of Courage* (a far better book, which could not be neatly labelled and which was popular with the general public). Perhaps, too, Howells was so grateful for allies that he did not look too closely into their war aims. If he had, he might not have been so sure of Harland, who wrote of the New York Jews not *primarily* as the downtrodden poor, but as an exotic race who would add to the American stock a much-needed element of colour and creative imagination.

In fact, realism and romanticism were both expressions of their time. In an article defending Frank Norris, Howells said that his novels were a response to the needs of his generation: 'It is not for nothing that any novelist is born in one age'. He went on to deny the same necessity to 'that aoristic freak, the historical novelist'; but he erred in doing so, as his followers indicated, either consciously or unconsciously, in their work. Norris himself argued that the true romance lay in realism, and he was not merely playing with words.

Howells's comment reveals a self-consciousness characteristic of the period, and even more apparent in America than in the rest of the western world, though Europe actually led the United States in artistic formulation of the fresh sensations and insights that are collectively referred to as 'the modern movement'. 1886, the year of *Little Lord Fauntleroy* and of Emily Dickinson's quiet death, was also the year of the Haymarket Massacre in Chicago; and, too, of the steel-magnate Andrew Carnegie's *Triumphant Democracy*, in which he declared that 'the old nations of the earth creep on at a snail's pace; the Republic thunders past with the rush of an express'.

He was right in that America was altering with staggering rapidity. Between 1860 and 1900 its population soared from thirty-one to seventy-six million, and the balance began to shift from rural to urban living. Towns appeared overnight, and grew to cities within a decade. Chicago, the most spectacular example, was in 1833 a village of 350 inhabitants. By 1870, the 350 had increased to over 300,000; by 1880, to 500,000; and by 1890, to over a million. The human scale seemed to vanish, as vast industrial enterprises reared themselves, only to be swallowed up by still vaster ones, knit together by complex financing from which the few enormously rich – Carnegie, Frick, Vanderbilt, Rockefeller, and their kind – apparently battened upon everyone else, intensifying what Henry George (in his *Progress and Poverty*, 1879) called 'the contrast between the House of Have and the House of Want'. A helpless immigrant proletariat was squeezing into the slums of New York, Pittsburgh, Chicago, Detroit, and a dozen other cities. Many of these immigrants were now coming, for the first time, from central and eastern Europe. Simple peasants from Italy, Jews from Polish ghettos, they were ill-equipped to face their new world. Emma Lazarus, in the sonnet carved on the pedestal of the Statue of Liberty, spoke a welcome for Europe's tired and poor, the 'huddled masses yearning to breathe free'. The concept of free immigration was magnificent, the reality inevitably less so. Nor did the native-born accept the fact with equanimity. How could a united nation emerge from such polyglot origins? Surely there must be a saturation point; had it not been reached? Henry James, visiting his homeland in 1904–5, after a long absence, was jolted to the depth of his being by Ellis Island, the immigrants' clearing-station, a 'visible act of ingurgitation on the part of our body politic and social'. 'This affirmed claim of the alien, however immeasurably alien, to share in one's supreme relation,' gave him an acute sense of 'dispossession', and he could not help sighing for 'the luxury of some such close and sweet and *whole* national consciousness as that of the Switzer and the Scot'.

A fastidious person like James might think that little was left of the older, finer America. The ideal of democracy was mocked when the *nouveau-riche* married his daughter into the aristocracy of Europe, and the bewildered immigrant placed his vote in the keeping of the ward-heeler. Nor was corruption confined to city politics: it thrived in state legislatures and in the Federal Government itself. As for rural America, the farmer was often as discontented as the urban poor whose ranks he swelled. Once the hero of Jefferson, the virtuous husbandman, he was now the *rube*, the *hick*, the *hayseed*. Agriculture over-extended itself as it reached into the rainshadow of the Rockies. Angry and disappointed homesteaders found themselves prey to natural scourges – droughts, locusts, prairie fires – and to man-made evils: exorbitant freight rates, low prices, tight credit. In the 1890s Americans were told, too, that the frontier, the open zone of unsettled land, no longer existed. Even when the Mississippi formed the western limit of the United States, Jefferson had congratulated his fellow-citizens on 'possessing a chosen country, with room enough for our descendants, to the hundredth and thousandth generation'. But after less than a century it might seem that there was no more room; at any rate the idea of illimitable westward territory was gone.

Puzzled by the rapidity of the changes overtaking their land, Americans groped for explanations and panaceas. Some were embodied in Utopian novels, of which Edward Bellamy's *Looking Backward: 2000–1887* is one of the few still remembered. Widely read and admired, by Mark Twain among others, *Looking Backward* puts its hero to sleep for a hundred and thirteen years. He wakes up in a Boston which has been cleansed of all its follies and miseries. Life is rational, benevolent, and staid. Yet the book in its day had the force of a vision, and some of its comments on the unregenerate society of 1887 stand out boldly in their bland context. Thus the old order is compared to travel in a coach:

the well-to-do are the passengers and the poor are the 'teams' which drag the coach along. In the Boston of A.D. 2000 when it rains the pavements are protected by water-proof awnings. The heroine says:

The private umbrella is Father's favourite figure to illustrate the old way when everybody lived for himself and his family. There is a nineteenth-century painting at the art gallery representing a crowd of people in the rain, each one holding his umbrella over himself and his wife, and giving his neighbors the drippings, which he claims must have been meant by the artist as a satire on his times.

Plunged back into a complacent dinner party in the Boston of 1887, and asked where he has been lately, the hero cries out:

I have been in Golgotha. I have seen Humanity hanging on a cross! Do none of you know what sights the sun and stars look down on in this city, that you can think and talk of anything else?[1]

A more plaintive uneasiness was voiced by J. R. Lowell, in the wistful jingle of his poem 'Credidimus Jovem Regnare', published in the same year (1888) as Bellamy's novel:

> Men feel old systems cracking under 'em;
> Life saddens to a mere conundrum
> Which once Religion solved, but she
> Has lost – has Science found? – the key.

Many thought that Science *had* found a key, in Darwin's theory of evolution. As expounded and popularized by Herbert Spencer, it made an extraordinary impression on the general public as well as on such young writers as Hamlin Garland, Jack London, and Theodore Dreiser. It was not a comforting revelation for all of them, but at least it seemed to fit the facts. In addition to providing a biological analogy for the struggle to survive that went on in the business world and in the teeming city streets, it lifted a load of guilt. Sins

1. This passage may have been appropriated by William Jennings Bryan for his impassioned 'Cross of Gold' speech at the Democratic party convention in 1896.

were no longer sins, if men's actions were determined by heredity and environment. Nor of course was it necessary to interpret Spencerian Darwinism as a pessimistic and passive doctrine. If progress was ensured, it did not matter that the method of improvement was predetermined; so long as the fittest *did* survive, and perfection came about after trial and error, it was possible to accept Darwinism as a scientific reinforcement of the poetic truth of Longfellow's 'Excelsior'.

And indeed, for the majority of Americans, whether or not they summoned Spencer to their aid, the era was one of great vitality. Grievances were aired, abuses bred reform. Those who were worst off – ruined farmer or under-paid artisan – were still no worse off than their European equivalents, and could look forward to a brighter future for their children. Yet the rate of change, though exhilarating, was disturbing. 'The Republic thunders past': it rushed past Americans, past the relatively tranquil country of their childhoods, depriving them of whatever had featured as their heritage, and revealing to them a tomorrow of further flux. For some, it merely heightened the pleasurable, nostalgic ache of reminiscence. This is evident in a good deal of local-colour writing; so is the determination to set down the scene before one's eyes before it has altered irrevocably. Heartache for the time *Befo' de War* (the title of one of Thomas Nelson Page's books) was almost a chronic Southern emotion; but the whole country responded to the Southern fable of bygone gracious living, and extracted an agreeable melancholy from the Negro's plight,

> Still longing for the old plantation
> And for the old folks at home.

The words are by Stephen Foster, a Northerner who paid only one brief visit to the South.[1] He makes the Negro serve as a surrogate for white emotion. There is no harshness, no acknowledgement of wrong. The Negro, for Foster, is an in-

---

1. Foster (1826–64) is the composer of dozens of Negro melodies, including *My Old Kentucky Home* and *Massa's in de Cold, Cold Ground*, as well as of *Jeannie with the Light Brown Hair*.

nocent, exiled from a forgotten Africa (as white Americans were exiles from a forgotten Europe, and from the America of their childhoods), and now doubly exiled as he is taken away from his Old Kentucky Home to some new corner barren of association. As the past receded like the view from the observation car of Carnegie's express, Americans hankered after it a little, liking modernity in the bathroom – and the old-world in the bookcase. Or, in terms of the United States, fascinated and rather envious of New England when they lived in regions farther west, complaining of its outmoded conservatism, but secretly proud that the United States, also, had its antiquities.

W. D. Howells, whose career illustrates all the phases in the growth of realism, made no secret of his early respect for New England. A bookish little boy in Ohio, he determined to be a poet. At twenty-three he was able to head eastward for Boston, where the *Atlantic Monthly* had recently accepted one of his poems. Its editor, Lowell, gave him a dinner, attended also by Oliver Wendell Holmes and the publisher J. T. Fields. They were pleased with the young man; the meal, he wrote ecstatically to his father,

lasted four hours, ... and involved an intoxication to me, as entire as that of Rhine wine. Lowell and Holmes both seemed to take me by the hand, and the Autocrat, about the time the coffee came in, began to talk about the apostolic succession. Tomorrow evening I am to take tea with him ...

After such encouragement it was natural for Howells to tell Fields, quite in the tone of his apostolic masters, that 'there is no place quite so good as Boston – God bless it!' By contrast, the more he saw of New York on this eastern pilgrimage, 'the more I did not like it'.

The Civil War found him in Italy, established as American consul in Venice (as the reward for a campaign biography he had done of Lincoln). But though the experience put him closely in touch with European contemporary letters (a knowledge he kept up-to-date for the rest of his life), Europe shocked him. His appreciation of Dickens, Heine, and other

Europeans was pushed firmly into a subordinate place in his
new perspective. He wrote from Venice in 1862:

You will read ... that life in Europe is more cheerful and social than
ours. Lies, I say – or stupidities, which are almost as bad. ... The
pleasure which we have innocently in America, from our unre-
strained and unconventional social intercourse, is guilty in Europe
– brilliant men and women know something of it; but they are also
guilty men and women ... I think these things over a great deal
... and the most earnest, earnest prayer that my heart can conceive
is that America may grow more and more unlike Europe every day.
I think when I return home I will go to Oregon – and live as far
as possible from the influence of European civilization.

When Howells sent this letter he was no doubt homesick: one
must make allowances for the fact that he was writing to his
sister; and it may be noted that on his return to America he
was soon installed not in Oregon but in Boston, as assistant
editor of the *Atlantic*. But it is a genuine expression of Howells's belief in America's moral virtues. **America's** highest
product, he thought, was the American girl, so gay and yet
full of sensibility.[1] There was a Miss Wing in Ohio, for example, who, when he was about to terminate a call:

said, 'Don't go, Mr Howells, I'm about to sing for you, though you
haven't asked me.' She is a glorious singer. I had heard her at Dr
Smith's, where she sang 'Excelsior' in a manner that made my
heart ache ... So she sat down, and sang ...[2]

It is tempting to ridicule such a scene; and indeed Howells
has been ridiculed for his famous statement that 'our novelists ... concern themselves with the more smiling aspects of
life, which are the more American. ... It is worth while, even
at the risk of being called commonplace, to be true to our
well-to-do actualities.' Mencken dismissed Howells as 'a
contriver of pretty things', 'an Agnes Repplier in panta-
loons'. Yet in the 1860s and 1870s, when Howells was

1. The Boston wit Tom Appleton (Longfellow's brother-in-law) wrote
in 1874 of 'that big exclamation mark behind her eyes which American
girls have'.
2. *Life in Letters of William Dean Howells* (2 v., London, 1929), i. 18.

evolving his creed, he was able to make such statements in complete sincerity: they were for him, quite simply, the truth.

Moreover, they enabled him to come to grips with realism, and to separate the disagreeable licence of contemporary European novelists from their underlying principles, of which he heartily approved. Realism in America, given the purer and more 'commonplace' nature of its society, meant writing about people of the kind to be met every day. These, the divine American average, were not murderers, seducers, burglars, prostitutes; nor princes in disguise, nor unwitting heirs to fortunes and estates. Coincidence operated only mildly in their lives, according to a sensible consideration of probability and not in obedience to the demands of romance. As young people, they fell in love, and often married. But there was no suggestion that two soul-mates had thus guaranteed one another unalloyed happiness. On the contrary, Howells was at pains to point out the limitations of his heroes and heroines – if one can call them that. If his characters fell in love, they might fall out of it (as in *A Chance Acquaintance*, 1873); or their marriage might end disastrously (as in *A Modern Instance*, 1881); or (as in *An Open-Eyed Conspiracy*, 1897) a successful match might be mildly exasperating to the friends of the couple. Apart from love and matrimony, the Americans whom Howells saw around him worried about their jobs, and about their position – for he never pretended that there was no class distinction in America: the plot of *A Chance Acquaintance* hinged upon the impossibility, for a young Bostonian, of moving out of his circle in order to marry a girl from what he regarded as a backwoods community. His Americans were confronted by moral decisions which were real to them, though of the domestic variety. Should a woman pursue a career? Apparently not, to judge from *Dr Breen's Practice* (1881), and *A Woman's Reason* (1883). Should a young girl (*Indian Summer*, 1886) marry a middle-aged man? She relinquishes him to a partner more appropriate.

Such was the world – largely a woman's world – that Howells set on paper, once he had decided that his principal

interest lay in the novel. He seemed to turn naturally to no-
vel-writing, as to most forms of literature in fact: for he never
ceased entirely to be a poet; he made plays; he read widely,
and wrote innumerable reviews and articles; and after a
mere five years of work on the *Atlantic*, he became its editor-
in-chief. His first two books were travel accounts of Italy;
his first novels were about travellers, or about Americans in
relation to Venetians. At this stage he was very close to Henry
James, with whom he maintained a lifelong friendship that
did not prevent the two from criticizing one another. In 1880
they were 'those badly assorted Siamese twins, J. and H.',
who 'treat intercontinental passion'.

But Howells soon began to concentrate upon the American scene, wrangling genially with James over the latter's
decision to make Europe his base. By the early 1880s Howells's brand of realism was in certain respects fixed. He was
prepared to support anyone calling himself a realist, but
though he 'read everything of Zola's that I can lay hands
on', he said in 1882 that while 'the new school' was 'largely
influenced by French fiction in form', ... 'it is the realism of
Daudet rather than the realism of Zola that prevails with it,
and it has a soul of its own which is above recording the
rather brutish pursuit of a woman by a man, which seems to
be the chief end of the French novelist.' Never wholly at ease
with literature that could not safely be read aloud within the
family circle, he saw little need to justify himself for not emu-
lating Zola: American life as well as American taste was more
refined than that of Paris. Choosing a few characters, rely-
ing not upon a formal plot but upon the presentation and
solution of a problem (since he firmly believed, as a tenet of
realism, that the novel's first object should be instruction
rather than amusement), presenting his theme neatly and
economically, in dialogue and not in the heavily intrusive
author-to-reader manner that irritated him in Thackeray,
reproducing the look and sound of his situations with painstaking accuracy: Howells was, despite his faintly old-maidish
quality, the most professional of writers, and the most
generously sympathetic of critics. Who else could have been

on terms of intimate friendship with two writers as immensely unlike as Mark Twain and Henry James? On such a man – so warmly intelligent, so anxious to acknowledge new talent, so concerned for the unique moral standing of his country – the America of strikes and slums was bound to make a profound impression.

His finest novel, *The Rise of Silas Lapham* (1885), shows him at the height of his powers, before the spectacle of industrialized America had deeply stirred him. Lapham is a self-made businessman living in Boston with his wife and two daughters, Penelope and Irene. The Laphams are emphatically not gentlefolk, though the daughters are more presentable than their parents. In contrast are the Coreys, an old Boston family in which the father is a witty dilettante and the mother a moderate snob. The son, Tom, is 'an energetic fellow ... with the smallest amount of inspiration that can save a man from being commonplace'. (Much of Howells is a skirmish around that word *commonplace*, which he uses as a measure rather than a criticism.) The Laphams and the Coreys are thrown together when Tom, going into business, establishes himself in Lapham's firm, and then falls in love with one of the Lapham girls. The difference between the two families is a perfect theme for Howells; he makes this juxtaposition of polish and social barbarism deliciously funny, yet very touching, notably at a dinner-party in which the Laphams are exposed to the Corey circle. Less successful is the situation that arises when Tom's attentions to the daughters are mistaken; Irene, believing him to be in love with her, falls in love with him, though in fact Tom is in love with her sister. Here Howells is something of the doctrinaire, in his own harmless version of realism: his point that no serious harm is done in such cases has led him to contrive a subplot that seems a little implausible. One's withers are wrung, gently enough, while Howells is insisting that none *should* be.

The other main theme of the novel, to which Howells intended the title to refer, is the struggle within Lapham's mind when he runs into financial difficulties. Should he, on the brink of ruin, save himself by selling a property to an interested group, when he knows – though they do not – that it will soon become worthless? Rising above temptation, he keeps clean hands – and becomes a bankrupt. Or rather, by so doing he cleans his hands of a piece of sharp practice of earlier days, of which his wife's reminders have always kept him ashamedly aware.

A bare recital of the novel's themes gives no idea of its skill. High-minded in the kindest sense of the word, within its compass it is masterly. It flows; it is full of slyly observant, affectionate comment. Holmes's benevolent reference to the apostolic succession turned out to have been a remarkably good guess. For in Howells, Boston reached its silver age. As much as this age would permit, Howells exhibited Boston's far from contemptible traits: its erudition (as a boy, he studied five languages at once, on top of a day's work), its commitment to the written word, its prim honesty, its good-humoured knowledge of its own limits.[1]

Yet Howells left Boston for New York in the 1880s – a move that Alfred Kazin has called 'the great symbolic episode in the early history of American realism',[2] since in making it Howells showed that Boston was no longer the literary headquarters of America. New York was now more *real*. The *North American Review* had transferred itself to New York in 1878;[3] periodicals and publishing houses were flourishing there; it had, Howells told a friend, 'lots of interesting young painting and writing fellows, and the place is lordly free'. Ensconced as an editor of *Harper's Magazine*, and as an eminent novelist, he could speak out as he pleased and be sure of an audience.

1. For a witty reminiscence of Boston, see M. A. DeWolfe Howe (ed.), *John Jay Chapman and His Letters* (Boston, 1937), 195.

2. *On Native Grounds* (New York, 1942), ix.

3. Longfellow wrote of this event (in a letter of 30 October 1877): 'Osgood has sold or given and conveyed the North American into the hands of the Appletons. Henceforth it will be edited, printed, and published in New York. Mr Clarke, at the printing-office, said: "It is like parting with the New England Blarney-Stone." He might have said, in more classic language: "Troy has lost her Palladium."' (Samuel Longfellow, ed., *Final Memorials of Henry Wadsworth Longfellow*, London, 1887, 267.)

He continued to speak out for realism, against romanticism, and against a new enemy – capitalism. It cost him nothing, emotionally, to attack romanticism, which was merely
the flimsy veil that hid the fine features of American life. But
could these features be fine, when capitalism was one of
them? The constitutional debates at Philadelphia had been
eloquent and profound; the debates over slavery had likewise
engaged all America in a sober consideration of moral and
social values. But with the end of the Civil War noble motives disappeared (Howells began to think); there was then
'no question but the minor question of civil-service reform to
engage the idealist's fancy or the moralist's conscience. After
the war we had, as no other people had in the world, the chance
of devoting ourselves strictly to business, of buying cheap
and selling dear.' Something had gone terribly wrong with
the pure, uncomplicated America whose image had inspired
his earlier realism; American life was now, he felt, 'a state
of warfare and a game of chance, in which each man fights
and bets against fearful odds'. The industrial brutality of the
era – shown in such affairs as the Homestead strike of 1892 –
sickened him; the execution of the Haymarket anarchists, on
dubious evidence, was 'an atrocious piece of frenzy and cruelty for which we must stand ashamed forever before history'.
He became a socialist, with Tolstoy as his master. In such
novels as the excellent *Hazard of New Fortunes* (1890), he described the moral decay of competitive society, and developed
his Tolstoyan notion of the 'complicity' of all in the human
predicament. The same truth was explored in *Annie Kilburn*
(1889), which he called 'a cry for justice', and in his Utopian
novel, *A Traveller from Altruria* (1894). In this he advocated
socialism; yet, as the name of his Utopia suggests, it was
rather altruism that he aimed at, something not to be realized
simply by espousing a political programme.

Howells never retracted his general attachment to socialism; he condemned the imperialism of the war with Spain in
1898, and as late as 1907 wrote another Utopian novel,
Through the Eye of the Needle. But he was not happy with the
ideas of the time, any more than with the social unrest that

bred them. He liked to argue, in Tolstoyan vein, that 'the author is, in the last analysis, merely a working-man'. An author's days are numbered when he begins to apologize for his *métier*; but Howells did not pursue his own work to the last analysis. As his comment reveals, he was worried about his responsibilities as America's most prominent realist. He postulated a divine average American. In the chaos of the 1890s, however, the average seemed to disappear; all that one could see, as literary fact, was the cleavage between the very rich and the very poor, the despoilers and the despoiled. He could not handle either group effectively; he was a cultivated man who could write of lack of cultivation in his characters, but as a *lack*, a deficiency, not as an absolute fact. Though the Darwinian metaphor appalled him, it did not spur him to write. He found it invigorating to speak of the struggle for realism, yet depressing to think of life itself as struggle.

Howells compromised by writing as he knew how – the majority of his novels published after his move to New York are not concerned with Darwinian strife – and encouraging younger men, gulping down their prescriptions even when the medicine tasted sour. It did not, always: the advent of realism was in many ways an exciting and stimulating matter for the young author. If in *social* terms the modern era contradicted the moral idea to which Americans were attached, in *literary* terms it upheld the moral idea. American writers, as we have seen, had long maintained that they should deal with their own country, in its own idiom. In practice, though, they had failed. The language was somehow wrong, the time seemed too ordinary: no one was quite ready to bell the cat. Local-colour writing had done much to remedy the situation. Even so, in one important respect the local-colour novel nearly always failed to do justice to the American ideal. It could not, try as it would, make its hero and heroine humble people of the kind Whitman pictured. The hero and heroine might be poor, but they must be educated and genteel; half a century after Cooper, the convention was still in force.

Realism broke it, partly by getting rid of the hampering

formal plot, with its formal 'hero' and formal 'heroine'. Indeed, realism/naturalism almost enjoined the study of the poor, the underdog, the obscure human particle in the social mass. Howells, on behalf of his protégés, delighted in the abundance of material that was at last within the provenance of the writer. The naturalist could tackle the city poor; he could handle the farmer; he could open up the great region of the West, which others had attempted to do, and then somehow abandoned. Now, however, discontent and a perhaps excessive dismay urged the writer on. He wrote unevenly, with anger and enthusiasm, not sure whether he was cheering on a revolution or mourning a collapse, undecided as to whether his theme was *the people*, or *the public*, or mankind in the grip of inexorable fate.

One such writer was Hamlin Garland ('the Ibsen of the West'), who came out of the prairie, a farmer's son. For the theme of his high-school graduation address, he chose Horace Greeley's injunction – 'Go West, Young Man'. As soon as he was able, however, he went East, to Boston, as Howells had done before him. After the raw life of his boyhood, New England struck him as wonderfully old and interesting. But as he educated himself in the East (largely, it would seem, by giving lectures, picking up the subject as he went along), it was not romance that appealed to him, but Spencer, Henry George, Whitman, Taine, Max Nordau: anyone whose work appeared alive. In his middle twenties he began to write articles and short stories, his head in a whirl with hopes, theories, denunciations. At this stage he considered Howells and James trivial, while he hated 'Lowell, Holmes, and the other fossil representatives of classicism'. At twenty-seven he planned to deify the common people in a great work on 'Literary Democracy'. By then he had revised his opinion of Howells, who befriended the rather bumptious young man and encouraged him to write of his own region as his radical inclinations prompted – of its resentment and envy of the city, its bleak poverty, its women old before their time. He was not quite the first American to view Western life with disenchantment. There had been

Edward Eggleston's *The Hoosier School-Master* (1871), which
had deeply impressed Garland when he read it as a boy.
And there was Edgar W. Howe's *The Story of a Country Town*
(1883). Howe, a Kansas newspaper-editor, published it at
the age of thirty; yet it reads like the work of an old man
whose hope is evaporated, leaving only a desire to get out of
his system all the joyless monotony of his existence. In this
awkward, bitter, compulsive novel Howe makes one of the
characters ask:

Haven't you noticed that when a Western man gets a considerable
sum of money together, he goes East to live? Well, what does it
mean except that the good sense which enabled him to make money
teaches him that the society there is preferable to ours? ... Men
who are prosperous ... do not come West, but it is the unfortunate,
the poor, the indigent, the sick – the lower classes, in short – who
came here to grow up with the country, having failed to grow up
with the country where they came from.

A few years later Garland told an interviewer that

There is a mystic quality connected with free land, and it has always allured men into the West. I wanted to show that it is a myth.

When he went back to his family for a visit in 1887, he saw
the Western farmer in one of the worst periods of his history.
Howe's farmers had been, at least, relatively prosperous:
Garland's were crushed with debt. He was a better writer
than Howe, and in his earlier work was able to disguise
his own limitations through the warmth of his pity for the
farmer's lot, which he had managed to escape, and also
through the excitement of applying the principles of realism.
His own brand of this he chose to call 'veritism', to indicate that he stood somewhere between the realism of Howells and the older generation, and the naturalism of Zola, by
which he was shocked. He wrote coarsely; his ear for dialogue, especially for polite discourse, was poor. But in the
six stories called *Main-Travelled Roads* (1891) he conveyed
with sincerity and dignity the atmosphere of heart-breaking
drabness that enveloped people like his parents. 'A man like
me', says one of his farmers, 'is helpless. Just like a fly in a

pan of molasses. ... The more he tears around the more liable he is to rip his legs off.'

In subsequent volumes Garland – a prolific writer – tended to spoil his stories by preaching Populism or the single tax remedies of Henry George. But gradually his interest in good causes ebbed away. His books had sold badly; much as he valued the opinion of Howells and other champions of realism, he craved success. Moreover, by 1900 he, like Howells, had grown accustomed (if not entirely reconciled) to the new America. The West now 'allured' him, not the flat land of Iowa or South Dakota, but the spectacular Rocky Mountain West. If it was a myth, he accepted it, and wrote copiously of it. He wrote too of his boyhood, each successive volume rosier and weaker than the previous one. Both he and Howells, perhaps, lived too long for their own good; tranquil old age, however well-earned, seemed not to accord with the vigour of their best work. The brief careers of some writers who followed them formed a hectic contrast. Stephen Crane died at twenty-nine, Frank Norris at thirty-two, Jack London at forty; while Harold Frederic (who on the strength of at least one of his novels, *The Damnation of Theron Ware*[1] (1896), can be included with these others) was dead at the age of forty-two.

In 1893 Crane published a sombre little novel whose very title – *Maggie, A Girl of the Streets* – invited the literary world to side with him, or against him. Howells and Garland, whom Crane once called his 'literary fathers', sided with him and gave him what support they could. Howells told Crane about the recently published poems of Emily Dickinson, and Crane produced some of his own, jerky, individual, full of unexpected images and epithets – as though Emily Dickinson had been jumbled together with the newspaper wit of Ambrose Bierce. Indeed, Crane was a newspaperman, and one of his poems discussed the matter:

> A newspaper is a court
> Where everyone is kindly and unfairly tried
> By a squalor of honest men.

1. Published in England as *Illumination*.

But these were side issues in the advancement of naturalism;
Howells, when Crane was dead, felt that *Maggie* was 'the
best thing he did'. *Maggie*, which Crane said 'tries to show
that environment is a tremendous thing in the world, and
frequently shapes lives regardless', is important chiefly as a
document in the history of naturalism.[1] It is dated and violent and absurd like a primitive film; and its most remarkable
feature – a descriptive vocabulary similar to that in Crane's
poems – has nothing to do with orthodox naturalism.

This feature Howells disliked in Crane's short stories, and
in the latter's Civil War masterpiece, *The Red Badge of Courage*. War as a theme had not hitherto been treated by the
American realists. Its horror, its enormity, its revelation of
the brutality that lay beneath the surface of human beings:
all these have made warfare one of the major topics for the
modern movement – together with the obvious fact that in
the twentieth century a great many men have had some experience of it. Crane had none when he wrote *The Red Badge*. The
Civil War, however, fascinated his generation, and subsequent generations of Americans. It was *their* war, something
that no European had known or could quite understand.
Moreover, it was a modern war, a war mainly of civilians,
not professionals; a war that was photographed, that depended on the factory and the railroad; a protracted, bloody,
clumsy war; a war without romance in which, as Melville
had perceived, 'a singe ran through lace and leather'.

Crane made his short amazing novel out of war, then, not
out of farmers' woes or the iniquities of the great city. His
dialogue is naturalistic ('We've helt 'em back; derned if we

1. Several writers have suggested that *Maggie* must have been influenced by Zola's *L'Assommoir*. Possibly: but one can point to material
nearer at hand: for example, to the sensationally popular sermons of the
Brooklyn minister, De Witt Talmage, which were reprinted in 1885 as
The Night Side of New York Life. In one of these sermons he asks his congregation to pity a poor prostitute (whom he calls 'Maggie'), for whom one
of the few ways of escape is 'the street that leads to East river, at midnight
the end of the city dock, the moon shining down on the water making,
it look so smooth she wonders if it is deep enough. It is. No boatman near
enough to hear the plunge...' This is how Crane's Maggie ends her life.

haven't'); the 'hero', Henry Fleming, is an ordinary youngster in the ranks, an uneducated farm-boy whose name is not
even introduced until half-way through the book. He and
his comrades are as helpless in other ways as Maggie was,
alone in New York. Nobody wins; all is confusion. Collective pride, animosity, berserk fury account for what 'heroism' is displayed. Yet to discuss the novel as an example of
naturalism is to miss its mood. Crane is preoccupied with the
personal reaction to fear: so while Fleming, judged by his
conversation, is loutish, his inward turmoil is that of the
sensitive man (a discrepancy less evident in the book as
printed than in the manuscript draft). Crane is also interested in the spectacle of war, which he describes with a painter's or poet's responsiveness to colour and the pathetic fallacy. A wound is a 'red badge'; fear is a 'red and green
monster'. Everything is sharp, nervous, oddly gorgeous:

He stared ... at the leaves overhead, moving in a heraldic wind of
the day ...

The bugles called to each other like brazen gamecocks. ...

Each distant thicket seemed a strange porcupine with quills of
flame. ...

The Red Badge ends on the somewhat unconvincing idea
that though war is dreadful, the young man has finally overcome his fears, for the rest of the war. However, the general
sense of this brilliant book is that the world is a chaos whose
only consolation lies in the tenuous fellowship between man
and man. The conclusion is reinforced in Crane's best short
story, 'The Open Boat', a rewritten account of a shipwreck
he himself experienced. Occasionally it is marred by a facetious phrase:

As soon as the correspondent touched the cold, comfortable sea-
water in the bottom of the boat ... he was deep in sleep, despite the
fact that his teeth played all the popular airs.

But it is a moving testimony to the tenderness of which men
are capable, isolated in their frail boat, drifting toward a
coastline where 'the furniture of the world' consisted of two

lights. 'Otherwise there was nothing but waves.' And to the indifferent cruelty of the sea, which drowns one of the men at the moment the others are saved.

These quotations show how much romanticism there was in Crane, mingled with the racy, hard-boiled cynicism of the journalist. The two sides are both expressed in his crowded months as a war correspondent in Cuba and Greece. And as the newspaperman's role is one of the typical aspects of the American writer, so in a special way is that of the correspondent, travelling in strange and dangerous corners, 'both in and out of the game', no more fully committed than Whitman or Thoreau, testing himself isolatedly in an unfamiliar context.

Frank Norris also acted as a war correspondent, in Cuba and South Africa; and he likewise cannot be pinned down as a realist/naturalist. The copy of *The Octopus* which he gave to his wife is inscribed from 'Mr Norris, Esq. (The Boy Zola)!'; yet he told a friend that the novel was 'the most romantic thing I've ever done'. His first published writing was an article on ancient armour; he would not at this stage have been amused by Bierce's definition of ARMOUR as 'the kind of clothing worn by a man whose tailor is a blacksmith'. But his first novels – *McTeague* (1899), *Vandover and the Brute* (1914, posthumously), and *Moran of the Lady Letty*[1] (1898) – bear many of the marks of naturalism. They abound in such adjectives as *vital, real, elemental, bestial*. Their characters are moulded by circumstance: creatures whose deepest instincts are animal, and who in moments of stress revert to brutishness.

The alternating optimism and pessimism of the Darwinian literary attitude, plus a certain exoticism that links Norris with such men as Henry Harland, are all to be seen in Norris's most ambitious effort, the uncompleted trilogy which he entitled *The Wheat*. The third part was never written; the second, a strong account of the Chicago wheat-market, was published posthumously in 1903 as *The Pit*. The first part, *The Octopus* (1901), deals with the growing of wheat

1. Published in England as *Shanghaied*.

in California, and with the struggle between the farmers and
the railroad, which strangles them (hence the title). It rules
their lives entirely, dispossessing and killing those who stand
in its way. The farmers band together to oppose it, but are
beaten and ruined by the heartless machine. At the close of
the book, a farmer's widow wanders the streets of San Francisco with her little daughter, penniless and starving, one
foggy evening. Her collapse and death are paired, in brief
scenes, with an elaborate dinner-party given in the same
city, on the same evening, by one of the heads of the railroad.

All this is fiery radical writing. But it is robbed of some of
its effect by a determinism especially noticeable in the later
stages of the book, as in a curious conversation between a
young poet and the president of the railroad, who easily con-
vinces him (and is meant to convince the reader) that

you are dealing with forces ... when you speak of Wheat and Railroads, not with men ... The Wheat is one force, the Railroad another, and there is the law that governs them – supply and demand.
Men have only little to do in the whole business.

However, Norris arrives at a benigner view, by celebrating
the force of *growth*. He does this in a sub-plot of a mystical
shepherd who, yearning for a lost love, discovers her again in
the person of her daughter. There is, the shepherd concludes,
no death; and, as on this human scale, so in a vaster way the
immense fields of wheat prove the matter:

Untouched, unassailable, undefiled, that mighty world-force, that
nourisher of nations, wrapped in a Nirvanic calm, indifferent to the
human swarm, gigantic, resistless, moved onward in its appointed
grooves. ...

Norris's rhetoric is not his strong suit, and to quote only from
the more inflated passages in *The Octopus* does little justice to
its narrative power. Though less gifted than Crane, he is still
worth reading despite his doctrinaire confusion; he has the
energy and zeal of a young man whom one likes almost because of his wrongheadedness.

Jack London, Norris's fellow-Californian, has even more energy and rather less sophistication. Nietzsche and Karl Marx clash in his many books, though this has not prevented Soviet readers from coupling him with Upton Sinclair as America's greatest novelists. Enterprises at sea (some of them illicit), socialist campaigning, the Klondike gold-rush, London slums, observing the Russo-Japanese War for the Hearst Press: these and many other experiences were wedged into his short life – and out again into his innumerable books. The Superman and the underdog, the class war and the law of the wolf-pack, the mission of the Nordic peoples and the doom of capitalism: he handles these seemingly ill-assorted themes with an irresistible bounce, like some dexterous and strident Barnum of the printed word. The hero of his socialist novel *The Iron Heel* (1907) is presented as 'a superman, a blond beast such as Nietzsche described, and in addition he was aflame with democracy'. This sounds ridiculous; yet the novel has a compelling though unsubtle eloquence. It shares with Ignatius Donnelly's *Caesar's Column* (1891), another prophetic novel, an apocalyptic and slightly sinister fascination with destruction on the grand scale. Both books were meant as warnings: society would go down in violent collapse if its abuses were not soon remedied. Jack London's is the better novel in being rather less lurid and rather more consistently grim. His hero is not so much a victor as a martyr in a protracted class-struggle. If London is a busker, he is a self-deluded one; the crudest of writers, for all his journalistic clichés and his talk of muscle and virility he is remarkably readable. And even in his most slap-dash performances, there are signs of a poetic flair that he never allowed himself leisure to cultivate. To take a random example from a Yukon pot-boiler (*A Daughter of the Snows*, 1902), what could be more unexpected than this, as a picture of a man trapped by a wall of ice borne down a flooded river?:

The rainbow-wall curled up like a scroll, and in the convolutions of the scroll, like a bee in the many folds of a magnificent orchid, Tommy disappeared.

True, Tommy is a miserable coward and deserves to die; but who would have anticipated such an exquisite end for him?

Howells had to work hard to convince himself and the public of the value of latter-day realism/naturalism. Perhaps Jack London's stress on red-blooded tribal instincts, or Norris's conscientious sexuality (e.g., in *McTeague*) were honest and American. But realism had gone a long way from Howells's modest spectrum of virtue. Indeed, it had largely replaced moral judgements. Instead of good and bad, there were the weak and the strong. A few exceptional men might rise above circumstance: the majority were its slaves, women even more completely than men. Still, Norris was redeemed for Howells by his eager, sunny acquiescence; and there were vestiges of a moral code in London, who at any rate heartily approved of his strong men and despised his weaklings. But Theodore Dreiser, whom Howells could not stomach, was another matter, as Norris enthusiastically recognized when he read Dreiser's first novel (*Sister Carrie*) for a publisher. The publisher changed his mind about it, and though the book came out in England in 1901, America had to wait another seven years to see it. Even then, Dreiser said, 'the outraged protests far outnumbered the plaudits'. Subsequent books were to meet with similar difficulties, so that Dreiser achieved no prominence as a novelist until the 1920s, by which time he was middle-aged. The question of his real ability was thus obscured, as in the case of James Branch Cabell's *Jurgen* (1919), by the question of his alleged obscenity; Mencken and his colleagues would defend the right of any book, however mediocre, to reach the public, and its unpopularity with their enemies became a criterion of its merit.

Sister Carrie was a naturalistic book in that it had the usual denominators. Carrie is a poor but pretty country girl who comes to Chicago, is tempted and seduced, first by a commercial traveller and then by a restaurant manager. The first chapter is called 'The Magnet Attracting: A Waif Amid Forces'. Carrie cannot help herself; nor can her lovers, the second of whom ruins himself by stealing money and taking her to New York. People are 'chemisms'; as Dreiser argues in *The Financier* (1912), 'We suffer for our temperaments, which we did not make, and for our weaknesses and lacks, which are no part of our willing or doing.' All of us crave affection and power; some men – notably the chief character in *The Financier* and *The Titan* (1914), its sequel – are innately powerful, but they are the exceptions: the vast majority are those who succumb to life's snares. This Dreiser demonstrates at length, and with his customary mass of detail, in *An American Tragedy* (1925). The central character, a poor boy on the fringes of opulence, hopes to gain entry into the magic circle by getting rid of a girl whom he has made pregnant and who stands in his way. He is executed for a murder that he committed and yet did not commit, since the girl's death was in part accidental.

There is no suggestion here that Clyde Griffiths, the executed man, should have been acquitted. Dreiser does not know what should be done with him; he can only explain the awful absence of absolutes. Everybody and nobody is to blame. One thing is certain, for Dreiser: the moral and social codes of his America misrepresent the truths of human nature, and so does conventional fiction. Carrie is not punished for her immorality, as the contemporary reading public would have had her; like Dreiser's own sister, she is well treated by the man whose mistress she becomes. *Jennie Gerhardt* (1911), another 'fallen woman', behaves better than anyone else in the book.

There is considerable disagreement about Dreiser's stature as a novelist. His critics have argued that he writes ponderously and pretentiously like the hack-journalist he was for a long period, that his philosophy is elementary (even if he meant it to be elemental), and that his books are shapeless grey affairs. Irving Babbitt, while admitting that *An American Tragedy* is a harrowing novel, denies that it is a tragedy: 'We are harrowed to no purpose'. Lionel Trilling, in an essay on 'Reality in America',[1] maintains that Parrington and others have praised Dreiser's serious weaknesses because they have

1. Reprinted in Lionel Trilling, *The Liberal Imagination* (London, 1951).

a false reverence for American authors who manage to seem not like men of letters. Dreiser's admirers, on the other hand, argue that his clumsiness is tolerable, or even an asset: in either event it reminds us that Dreiser (the first important American writer not to have an English-sounding name) was the first novelist to catch the full native flavour of the American of modern times (Europe hardly comes into his work), and to leaven his naturalistic sagas with a pity not to be found in any other writer of the type.

Perhaps we can agree that Dreiser has a particular significance for Americans, whether or not they like him. Europeans can read his novels with a close interest, but only Americans fully share his intimation that it is all, so to speak, in the family (as most that he wrote about *had* happened to his own family). He gives them a relief from rhetoric – the American rhetoric of the moral law that emerges from the pages of Howells, the Western he-man rhetoric proclaimed in Norris and Jack London. He gives them a relief from good manners, from the tiring awareness that Americans have, with European literature, of being among strangers: strangers who make them feel uncouth, who miss their jokes, who throw them back on to the defensive conviction that though their pattern of life may be indefensible, it is not to be laughed at. Dreiser knows the pattern: it is *there*, in his writing, actual, lived, working, complex: a maze of streets, buildings, fields, rivers, railroads, stores, hotels, tastes, temperatures, appointments, songs, accents, things understood. There is, E. M. Forster says, a truth of feeling as well as a truth of thought. Dreiser's is the truth of feeling, and of incident. His novels are often as formless as life itself, unfortunately; but they are not lifeless. They tell of an America that perhaps Howells unconsciously set out to discover, when he quitted Boston for New York. If he did not like it, no more did Dreiser – except that *he* knew it better.

CHAPTER TEN

THE EXPATRIATES

Henry James, Edith Wharton, Henry Adams, Gertrude Stein

=====

HENRY JAMES (1843–1916)

b. New York. *ed.* privately by tutors and in Europe (1855–8) as well as in the resort town of Newport, Rhode Island. Studied law at Harvard, but abandoned this project in order to write critical articles and pieces of fiction, travelling frequently between Europe and his home in Cambridge, Mass. From 1875 to the end of his life he lived in Europe, making two visits to the U.S. in the early 1880s and another – to furnish material for a commissioned travel book – in 1904–5. From 1889 to 1895 he was largely engrossed in the theatre; otherwise his energies were concentrated chiefly upon fiction, though of all his writing perhaps only *Daisy Miller* (1879) excited the general public. His last visit to America was made in 1910–11. At the outbreak of World War I, greatly stirred, he moved from his Sussex home to London, to assist in war work. He became a British citizen in 1915, and just before his death was awarded the Order of Merit.

EDITH WHARTON (1862–1937)

b. New York, into a socially distinguished family, she was *ed.* expensively at home and in Europe, before making an appropriate marriage. As she struggled to become a writer, her social situation grew increasingly irksome; and after 1907, divorced from her invalid husband, she lived chiefly in Europe, travelling widely and writing travel books as well as novels and short stories. During World War I she devoted herself whole-heartedly to relief work in France.

HENRY ADAMS (1838–1918)

Raised in the vicinity of Boston, Adams was *ed.* at Harvard and in Germany. During the Civil War he lived in England, where his father was American minister and employed Henry as secretary. After writing a number of careful articles, he abandoned his vague ambitions of a political career, and left Washington for Harvard (1870–7), where he was professor of history and edited the *North American Review*. He lived again in Washington, having *m.* Marian Hooper in 1872, but after her suicide in 1885 he became increasingly restless, and travelled all over the world, returning to Washington intermittently, and keeping in touch with his friends through a voluminous correspondence.

GERTRUDE STEIN (1874–1946)

b. Pittsburgh, of well-to-do German–Jewish stock, she was *ed.* in California, in Europe and at Radcliffe (next to Harvard), and at Johns Hopkins (Baltimore). Quitting her formal studies, she followed her brother Leo to Paris in 1902 and made it her permanent home, establishing a famous *salon* and writing steadily, though not always achieving publication. Her books include *Geography and Plays* (1922); *Lucy Church Amiably* (1930), a novel; *Four Saints in Three Acts* (1934), an opera-libretto for the music of Virgil Thomson; *Picasso* (1938); *Paris France* (1940); and *Wars I Have Seen* (1945).

THE EXPATRIATES

—

At a time when the realists were urging one another to regard America as the true prose-poem, a good many American writers were doing otherwise. The romantic impulse, it has been seen, exerted a contrary pull. Mark Twain liked to write of the past; the American West, as Bret Harte viewed it from London, or Joaquin Miller from his log cabin in Washington D.C., was a softer place than either of them had known it to be in practice. Or there were the American dandies (the figure of the dandy, that 'Hercule sans emploi' who intrigued Baudelaire, belongs to the modern movement equally with the Zolas and Jack Londons): men like Henry Harland, Edgar Saltus, and James G. Huneker with their now-dated extravaganzas. And there were other American writers who had little in common with the *Yellow Book* world of Harland, but who, like him, came over to Europe to live, or make protracted visits. For one reason or another Europe suited them better. They were the 'expatriates', and their apparent defection began seriously to worry their fellow-countrymen. By the 1920s, expatriation had become so characteristic a gesture for American writers that Matthew Josephson (who was himself an example of the phenomenon) asked:

Is the emigration of intelligence to become an issue as absorbing as the immigration of strong muscle? With a greater frequency than ever our *illuminati* buy tickets for a more possible world, for a more breathable air.[1]

It was not that Americans were strangers to Europe. The Old World had always been, and for the most obvious reasons, a place to see. But on the whole, until after the Civil War Americans had not wished to settle there permanently. Hawthorne had called England *Our Old Home*, but his book of

1. *Portrait of the Artist as American* (New York, 1930), 294.

that name displayed little of the emotional anglophilia of a later generation. 'Not an Englishman of them all,' Hawthorne had said in his preface, 'ever spared America for courtesy's sake ...; nor ... would it contribute in the least if we were to besmear each other all over with butter and honey.'

And even after the Civil War, a visit to Europe, for the vast majority, implied no 'disloyalty' to America. It was a matter of having enough money; travel was a function of national wealth; and the fact that 90,000 tourists returned through the New York customs in 1891 was – above all – proof that America was now a rich country. What could be more natural, then, that she should spread herself: that she should scoop in art treasures, titled husbands, grouse moors, Loire chateaux? That her artists – Sargent, Whistler, Mary Cassatt – should join the eastward throng? That some of her writers – Henry James, Edith Wharton, Henry Adams, Francis Marion Crawford, Howard Sturgis, Stuart Merrill, Gertrude Stein, Ezra Pound – should do the same? Especially as those who stayed permanently in Europe were unusually cosmopolitan in their origins. Harland, for instance, was born of American parents in St Petersburg, and lived in Rome and Paris before going to America. Henry James became acquainted with Europe as a child. Edith Wharton, Marion Crawford, Sturgis, and Merrill were all raised in Europe, to greater or less extents. Why, if Landor or the Brownings could settle themselves abroad without arousing indignation: why must Americans incur criticism for doing likewise?

In truth, such criticism was often silly, and the rebuttals made by Matthew Josephson and others were not always much better. The fact remained, however, that to elect to live in Europe was to associate oneself in the popular mind with class-distinction: to be considered a 'miserable little snob', as Theodore Roosevelt described James.[1] Crude though such verdicts were, they were accurate in the very

---

[1] James, for his part, defined Theodore Roosevelt as 'the mere monstrous embodiment of unprecedented resounding Noise'.

limited sense that the 'expatriates' did, in various ways, have
reservations about their own country. If no more alienated
from their culture than, say, Twain, Melville, or Emily
Dickinson, the quality of their aloofness was more apparent
– and therefore more resented.

Such remarks, though, hardly begin to explain that prodigiously gifted author Henry James. His brother William
wrote to their sister Alice in 1889 that Henry's 'anglicisms
are but "protective resemblances" – he's really, I won't say
a Yankee, but a member of the James family, and has no
other country'. Henry belonged to a uniquely articulate,
sensitive, and lively-minded family. Henry James Senior encouraged his children to be serious but not lugubrious, to be
ambitious but unworldly: to endeavour according to individual light, trimmed by the friendly yet ruthless advice of the
rest of the family. The result was wonderfully exhilarating,
even ennobling. It also imposed a pressure that partly revealed itself in the curious ailments that beset the children.
These ailments, certainly in the cases of William and Henry,
had something to do with their impulsion to excel, coupled
with a difficulty in determining the desirable field of activity.
Once they had chosen, family disposition bound them to unremitting effort.

In Henry's case the choice was for literature. To begin
with, he applied himself to the idea of realism; like his friend
Howells, who invited him into the pages of the *Atlantic*,
James thought of fiction as an art, with its own exacting
forms and standards, not merely as a piece of narrative, still
less as a disguised sermon. The line of the novel, as Howells
later said of James,[1] ran to him from Hawthorne and George
Eliot, not through the slack and untidy – though fascinating – work of Thackeray and Dickens. This was to be a literature that aimed at psychological truth, conveyed with economy and precision.

It was natural that he should go to Paris to study his art
in company with Turgenev (himself an example of the

1. And as F. R. Leavis has argued in *The Great Tradition* (London,
1948).

expatriate), Zola, Daudet, Flaubert, and the Goncourts. Des-spite their 'ferocious pessimism and their handling of un-clean things', he had the deepest regard for their 'truly infernal intelligence' and honesty. Yet Paris left him unsat-isfied: he sought for a form of society on which to focus his theories of fiction.

America would not do in this respect. He recognized that it might do for others: he admired Howells for making the most of the material to hand. But in his own view, Ameri-cans in America were not enough. Too much was missing, as he explained in his book on Hawthorne; defending the book to Howells, he accepted as a truism 'the idea that it takes an old civilization to set a novelist in motion'. 'It is,' he continued, 'on manners, customs, usages, habits, forms, up-on all these things matured and established, that a novelist lives – they are the very stuff his work is made of.' He did not mean (though many of his irritated compatriots judged otherwise) that without aristocratic institutions a country could have no culture. He did mean that, as far as he was concerned, his writings had to be anchored in Europe. It was a matter of preferring the larger to the lesser view. Though a European might ignore America, an American must take Europe into account. How could a man 'who has the passion of observation and whose business is the study of human life' fail to opt for Europe-and-America, and be content with the meagreness of America alone?

When he had made up his mind, with deliberation, he set-tled in England. London was 'the biggest aggregation of human life – the most complete compendium of the world'. Like the English social scene as a whole, it had perspectives that the Continent seemed to lack. This is not to say, of course, that he was blind to the defects of Europe, or to the virtues of his own land. Indeed, like Howells, he started with the notion, which he never entirely abandoned, that Ameri-ca was more innocent than Europe. If purity were the only thing at stake, America won hands down. As a novelist, how-ever, he had to show purity – which he valued very highly, in all its aspects – assailed and even overborne, by temptation, by greater sophistication, by cruelties and complexities of old-established social orders.

It is nevertheless the purity that he exalts and loves, even while he points to its downfall. His heroes and heroines seek perfection, as James sought it in his style, in his technique, and in the life about him. Like other Americans before and since, he conceived of an ideal and believed that it existed – or should exist. In America, he found ideal aims suspended in a void. In Paris he found artistic integrity, in Italy a wonderful outward beauty of building and landscape, in England a system of society defined with admirable firmness. But all of these were in some measure inadequate. The Continent was crumbling and corrupt; while much of English life was 'grossly materialistic', and 'the British country-house' had 'at moments, for a cosmopolitanised American, an insuperable flatness'.

Even so, in the conjunction of America and Europe James had a rewarding theme. *Roderick Hudson*, his earliest real novel (1876) deals with the disintegration of a young American sculptor in Italy – a subject that Hawthorne, his predecessor in several ways, had handled unsuccessfully in *The Marble Faun*. In *The American* (1877), a much finer study than *Roderick Hudson*, an American is confronted by Parisian society; Christopher Newman, a millionaire (and surely one of the most sympathetic pictures in literature of a *nouveau riche*), comes to Europe to seek its best, including a bride. He finds one, but loses her when her family decide that the connexion would be ignoble. Newman, with a purity as genuine as theirs is perverted, renounces a chance to revenge himself, and quits Europe. In *The Portrait of a Lady* (1881), one of James's greatest novels, he again explores the theme of an American's quest in Europe. Isabel Archer, a handsome and intelligent girl, comes to Europe as the ward of a rich aunt. An English suitor, Lord Warburton, proposes to her, but his advantages – name, appearance, kindness, a superb country house – are not enough: she is able to refuse him in the assurance that something hardly to be defined, but far, far better, awaits her. (It is the Emersonian attitude again: *the nonchalance of boys who are sure of a dinner.*) Thinking that she has found her perfect person in Osmond, a cultivated man of American origins, she marries him – only to learn by painful stages that he is a vicious and heartless snob who has taken her for her money. The only fine gesture possible is to accept her fate with dignity – which she does. The 'international theme' is handled here with the greatest subtlety. James hints that his heroine's demands on life are inordinate, and that she is somewhat to blame for her own misfortune. But the Europe–America antithesis still holds. Whatever the minor faults of Isabel, her friend Henrietta, her admirer Goodwood, or of the others who are wholly American, they are *good* people; and the Americans who are not good – Osmond, Madame Merle – have been contaminated by Europe. This not a question of chauvinism, but simply of a frame of reference that James is able to invest with vast significance. The fruit is eaten, the Eden so confidently glimpsed disappears among dark shadows. Virtue must be its own reward, for there is no other.

The international theme, though valuable to James, is not his only one. In the poignant novel *Washington Square* (1881) he is concerned with Americans in New York; the heroine rejects the chance of escape from an oppressive situation as dutifully as Isabel Archer, if with less initial sensibility. In *The Bostonians* (1886), where he is again dealing with his own country, he shows that his reservations about America enter the very region in which America seems to him so much finer than Europe: the realm, that is, of illimitable hopes, especially those cherished by women. Women are important for James, as for Howells and Henry Adams; to a great extent he shared the belief of certain contemporaries that the American woman was superior to the male, in courage as well as in refinement. Yet in *The Bostonians* he attacks the American woman *qua* reformer (in this instance as advocate of women's rights) because he dislikes the shallow perfectionism of such movements and – more seriously – because they threaten 'the masculine character, the ability to dare and endure, to know and yet not fear reality, to look the world in the face and take it for what it is – a very queer and partly very base mixture'. These words may be taken as representative of James himself, with his constant injunction to live to the utmost, though in the book they are spoken by Basil Ransom. Ransom is a Southerner, and James opposes his conservatism to the arid radicalism of Boston. However, Ransom's ideas are vitiated by the 'false pride', the 'thread of moral tinsel' that runs through the Southern fabric; and though the novel ends with Ransom winning a Boston girl, James will concede them little likelihood of happiness together: perhaps one is too innocent, and the other too jaded.

It can be debated whether this ending, in which James so typically resists the reader's expectations, is a sign of his genius or of an exasperating impalpability. There are indications in this novel, at any rate, that James was by now at one remove from American subjects. Its combination of light satire and sober criticism is not quite fused; he is remembering, improvising, theorizing. *The Princess Casamassima* (also 1886), a study of extreme European radicalism, is a richer and more deeply felt book. Europe seems to have more 'reality' for him, and in most of his subsequent works Europe is the stage. America remains a convenient point of reference, a place to which characters may depart (as do Peter and Biddy Sherringham in *The Tragic Muse*, 1890), or from which they may arrive (as do Milly Theale in *The Wings of the Dove*, 1902, and Maggie Verver in *The Golden Bowl*, 1904), bringing with them America's special ambience. But the *mise-en-scène* is Europe, and was to remain Europe – if we except James's travel book, *The American Scene* (1907) – until his death. It was once fashionable to explain James as a sad exile whose work lost its firmness in proportion as his memory of the homeland grew indistinct. It is true that his writing became increasingly complex, but there is no need to suppose that he had lost his way. Indeed, he is unique among American authors, and rare in any group of writers, for a brilliance sustained through half a century. Nor does his comment upon America suggest a hopeless hankering after an actual country. On the contrary: *The American Scene* is

clear evidence that he would not have known what to do
with America as fictional material; while his short story 'The
Jolly Corner' projects a horrifying vision of another James
who stayed behind, to become evil. Rather, he depended on
America for one element of his dialectic. It was the land of
miracle from which might emerge princesses like Milly
Theale, in the image of his own dead cousin, Minny Temple,
whom he had adored. In fact, James searched throughout his
life for a literary equivalent to the James Family: if he could
retrieve a simulacrum of family ties among European society, he had to present this society as more advanced than
he knew it to be; and he still had to bring to it from an *imagined* America the spirituality of Minny Temple, or for that
matter of his closer relatives.

As he grew older James had more and more, not less and
less, to say. He became lonelier not because he lost touch
with the United States, but because he lost touch with his
audience, never a large one and never predominantly an
American one. His attempts to find an audience through the
medium of the London theatre ended in severe disappointment; superb novels like *The Princess Casamassima* were badly
received; and though he never faltered in his attachment to
literature, he did reveal his perturbation in a number of
stories about the isolation of the artist that recall Hawthorne's
insights into the same theme. 'The Madonna of the Future'
(1879) relates the failure of an American painter in Rome,
who has dreamed so absorbedly of a masterpiece that he accomplishes nothing, and dies as obscurely as he lived. In
other stories James is concerned more directly with a writer
such as himself, mature, dedicated, and known only to a few
disciples amid the general indifference or hostility. This is
the fate of 'The Author of "Beltraffio" ' (1884), and of the
dying Dencombe in 'The Middle Years' (1895) – a title that
James took later for a fragment of autobiography – who declares:

We work in the dark – we do what we can – we give what we have.
Our doubt is our passion and our passion is our task. The rest is the
madness of art.

At the end, James left behind him a steadily amassed *œuvre* of short stories, *nouvelles*, articles, plays, travel books, and novels, that represent – in terms of effort alone – an achievement of the most solid order. The additions and prefaces of the Collected Edition are in themselves a considerable labour, and yet another proof of James's unsparing devotion to his art. From comparative neglect, his reputation has soared to the heights. Critics like Lionel Trilling and F.R.Leavis have ranked him with the greatest of the English novelists.

But in his lifetime many found him unreadable, and today his writing still presents difficulties which some commentators brush aside too lightly. The famous style of his latter years is perplexing not merely because it is the vehicle of intricate ideas and perceptions, but also as an arrangement of words. Often James's sentences are peculiarly opaque when there seems no reason why they should be. Here is one, from *The Wings of the Dove*:

It was wonderful for Milly how just to put it so made all its pieces fall at present quite properly into places.

A short sentence, with simple words. Yet the adverbial qualifications – *at present, quite properly* – clog it; and the unexpected *places*, instead of *place*, adds to one's faint bafflement. When thousands of such sentences are encountered, the effect is dazing: especially since James makes other, heavy demands upon the reader. His themes are important, and clear: H.G.Wells complained that they are too clear, and too obtrusive. But in James's later work they are developed to a formidable degree of virtuosity. It is as though the reader is being escorted through a long art-gallery by a companion whose interest in the exhibits is far more discriminating and enthusiastic, and whose scrutiny of each is therefore more prolonged and more exacting. Such companionship is improving; it is also tiring, and a little shaming. The reader has been drawn into a competition in sensibility, and tends either to proclaim a greater enjoyment and understanding than he has really felt, or else to withdraw in a huff, saying that it is all nonsense. Even the hypothetical honest reader who does neither, finds himself at times unable to stand the pace – or lack of pace: he longs for it to be quicker, even if more superficial.

Another way of putting this is to say that James is not a moralist or a thinker: he is a writer for whom the truth of art and the truth of life are the same thing. Hence, his characters' search for meanings in life is equated with the artist's creative processes. Both, for James, have their climax at fleeting, mysterious (though schemed-for) *moments* which constitute what he calls experience. His equation is of the greatest interest and validity to other professionals, since it resembles their own viewpoint. But to the general reader (the *mostpeople* of E. E. Cummings's rather truculent coinage) the Jamesian 'passion' seems precious. Just as he does not mean by passion what mostpeople mean, so his moments of 'experience' are often *not* experience as mostpeople think of it.

At any rate, in some of James's fiction motive seems to smother event, and the event when it does come – though sometimes in a magnificently explosive moment – is liable to disappoint because of its ambiguous indirectness. The characters reach out to one another with the most delicate of antennae: something passes between them, beyond the reach of words: the reader thinks he understands, but he would give anything to *know*. What was 'the figure in the carpet'? What *was* Milly Theale's ailment? James will not tell. His refusal is deliberate; his obscurity has nothing to do with incompetence. It is a matter of the very highest skill and can be convincingly defended (as F. O. Matthiessen has shown in *Henry James: the Major Phase*). Undoubtedly his ambiguity is superior to Hawthorne's. Hawthorne offers a supernatural phenomenon together with a possible material explanation, and thus frequently softens the blow too much. Where James is dealing with the supernatural – as in *The Turn of the Screw* (1898), or 'The Jolly Corner' – his ambiguity, offering the reader no vulgarly easy way out, has a tremendous impact. Where, however, it is an ambiguity of situation that leaves the reader to make his way through a maze of possibilities, the characters become impalpable, and the defatigable reader retires from the contest, unequal to the James Family as Henry abstracted it.

It should be stressed that these remarks do not apply to the bulk of James's writing, though the seeds of his final method lie in his early work. And such books as *The Wings of the Dove* and *The Ambassadors* (1903), if failures, are Jamesian failures, which are still a great deal better than most writers' successes. They are either preposterous, or perfect, or something of both. Whichever the reader decides, he can see that James is *sui generis*; and that every one of his works, from the smallest story to the longest and most involute of novels, shows a consistent, warm, but unwinking gaze upon a humanity capable of abysmal treachery and evil, capable of undying loyalty and goodness: these chronicled with a degree of perception that no other novelist has surpassed.

'Every great novel must first of all be based on a profound sense of moral values, and then constructed with a classical unity and economy of means.' The writer must 'bear in mind at each step that his business is not to ask what the situation would be likely to make of his characters, but what his characters, being what they are, would make of the situation'. These are, near enough, the views of Henry James. But the words are those of his close friend Edith Wharton. Like James, she felt out of touch with America ; after divorcing her husband she lived in France. Like James, she preferred on the whole (with the exceptions of *Ethan Frome*, 1911, and *Summer*, 1917) to write of people in polite society. Both deal with the tension between the individual and the social framework. Neither supposes that the social framework is ideal: James, as we have seen, imports his ideality from America, in the shape of the individual. Nevertheless, the rules of his society, no matter how arbitrary or unsatisfactory, are observed: there is no doubt that they operate. By contrast, society for Edith Wharton is a collapsing affair. Its pressure, though real, is vulgar and uneven; and her leading characters are people with grudges that they cannot resolve.

Edith Wharton never achieved the detachment of her friend. If he belonged to any society, it was that of the New York world of Washington Square; yet the James Family, as Henry represented it, belonged everywhere and nowhere. Edith Wharton, however, was by upbringing quite definitely a member of the older New York society. She was raised in it so as to become, after a season or two of dances and summers at Newport, one of its hostesses. As an exceptionally intelligent girl, loving literature, she found her society intolerably narrow and uncultivated. Its standards were negative, though snobbish, and as soon as a newer aristocracy of wealth appeared in New York, the world of Edith Wharton fell apart. An old name counted for something, but not very much; more important was the money that made it possible for the *parvenus* to raise their mansions along Fifth Avenue. Her feeling about the fashionable strata of New York might be summed up in words employed by someone in another context: 'it's not as good as it used to be, and what's more, it never was'. As a sensitive and isolated girl, she regretted the rigidity of her upbringing, with its indifference to the creative world she longed to explore. On the other hand, what succeeded it was even worse. In either case, the person such as herself was a misfit.

Given this somewhat unsatisfactory basis, Edith Wharton made fine fiction from her material. She has a sharp eye for social absurdities, and compassion for the victims of social change. In *Ethan Frome*, where her background is the barrenness not of New York society but of a New England farmstead, she draws an overpowering picture of human helplessness. The novels that deal with New York – *The House of Mirth* (1905), *The Custom of the Country* (1913), and *Hudson River Bracketed* (1928), to name only three – make convincing use of the author's special knowledge. Lily Bart (*The House of Mirth*) suffers because, despite her extravagance and frivolity, she is an honest person in a shoddy society. Ralph Marvell (*The Custom of the Country*) also goes under:

Ralph sometimes called his mother and grandfather the Aborigines, and likened them to those vanishing denizens of the American continent doomed to rapid extinction with the advance of the
invading race. He was fond of describing Washington Square as the
'Reservation'. ...

The vulgarians with whom Lily and Ralph grapple unsuccessfully are accurately and acidly observed.

But Edith Wharton, like Dreiser, rarely does more than
harrow the reader, and then sometimes less thoroughly.
There is nothing tragic in Lily's downfall; nor in that of
Ralph – with whom the author seems impatient, as she is
with Lawrence Selden, the ineffectual friend of Lily Bart.
There is no great *clash* in Edith Wharton: the newer society
ousts the old with contemptuous ease, and the individual is
vanquished as much through his own weakness as from the
power of society. The absence of a fully realized conflict is
especially noticeable in her later novels. In *Hudson River Bracketed* it is as if she gropes for a non-existent norm. The hero,
Vance Weston, is a young writer out of Euphoria, Illinois.
Euphoria is crudely drawn, as though the author had borrowed her material from Sinclair Lewis (Vance's father, like
Babbitt, is in real estate).[1] Where then is the norm, if not in
the caricatured Euphoria? At first, it would seem to reside
in an old house on the Hudson: 'this absurd house' was for
Vance 'his embodiment of the Past': it 'was to him the very
emblem of man's long effort, was Chartres, the Parthenon,
the Pyramids'. But then the house ceases to affect Vance,
who buries himself in the teeming life of New York – is defeated by it – would like to return to his first love, poetry
(Edith Wharton published two volumes of verse), but does
not know where he stands – and at the end of the book has
nothing left save a sense of vocation. Everything else, Edith
Wharton implies, has gone for one of her generation: even
the literary world of New York is singularly unappetizing.
By 1928 the *parvenus* themselves have gone, almost, and
Washington Square with its 'Aborigines' is not even a

1. It is interesting to remember that Lewis dedicated *Babbitt* (1922)
to her.

memory: for in *Hudson River Bracketed* a guide conducting a
tour of the city shouts through his megaphone:

We are now approaching the only remaining private residence on
Fifth Avenue, belonging to one of the old original society leaders
known throughout the world as the Four Hundred.

Like Henry James, Edith Wharton also uses the international theme, but with less effect. The drama that might
lie in the marriage of the mid-Western Undine Spragg to a
French aristocrat (in *The Custom of the Country*) is weakened by
the fact that Undine is an odious character, incapable of a full
relationship with anybody. Her husband's code therefore has
little significance for the reader. One might say that Edith
Wharton is most people's Henry James: similar preconceptions and similar themes, manoeuvred more briskly and superficially. To compare her stories and novels with those of
James helps to define the scope of both: her not inconsider-
able talent is dwarfed by his. It also helps to throw into relief
their common search for a literary kingdom. *Kingdom* indeed: as their standards of conduct were lofty, so their vocabulary, like that of Emily Dickinson, acquired regal overtones. James's Milly Theale is a 'princess', Edith Wharton
talks of 'thrones'. But the motive behind such words is
austere rather than snobbish; perhaps the words for what
they sought to convey did not exist, in uncontaminated
clarity.

Henry Adams was another American with lofty expectations that his own time and country could not, or did not,
fulfil. The Adams Family even outshone the James Family.
Henry Adams's grandfather and great-grandfather had been
Presidents of the United States, while his father was minister
to England during the Civil War. There was every reason to
suppose that Henry would imitate them.

In fact, he found it impossible to participate in American
public life. Instead, he became the most private of citizens,
insisting on the enormity of his own failure, generalizing from
the fate of the Adamses to the fate of the American nation,
and – more widely still – to that of the entire globe. Henry's

modesty has seemed to hostile critics a form of conceit on a gigantic scale, and there has been much argument as to whether he was merely sulking, or whether his diagnosis was not more profound than that of his contemporaries. Certainly there was in him a touch of '*roi ne puis, duc ne daigne*'. But like his friend Henry James, he was a man of the rarest temper, who loved his country in his fashion. In middle age, when he was working as a historian in Washington, Henry Adams told his English crony Charles Milnes Gaskell that America was 'the only country now worth working for, or pleasant to work in.' He had been furious at what he thought British duplicity during the Civil War, and he continually criticized England for its crass materialism. As a young man he disliked France, and in later life, while he drew close to some aspects of French life, the general corruption of France provoked him to disgusted comment. Europe as a whole, he felt, was rotten; revolution was only a matter of time.

Nevertheless, Adams was not at ease in America. For the last thirty years of his life he travelled incessantly, as if to escape the spectacle of a Washington full of dishonest barbarian representatives. 'West of the Alleghenies,' he wrote of America as it was in 1892, 'the whole country might have been swept clean, and could have been replaced in better form within one or two years.' He was not much more polite to the country east of the Alleghenies; and if he found Europe no better in many respects, the Old World did provide him with a solace of a kind he could not get at home.

But before he turned to Europe, Henry Adams did what he could with America. Like other Bostonians, he had the critical rather than the creative temperament. Summoning up truly Bostonian reserves of industry, he applied himself to American history. His labours culminated in the nine-volume *History of the United States during the Administrations of Jefferson and Madison* (1889-91), a work as fluent and as amply buttressed with research as the volumes of Francis Parkman. He had chosen the period for various reasons. It lay between the administrations of his ancestors, which he could not with propriety discuss. Moreover, it was the formative period in American history, and he hoped to explain to himself the pattern – if any – of human events. Like Mark Twain, who may have had similar reasons for delving into the past, he concluded that there was no pattern. Jefferson, Madison, and Monroe were 'mere grasshoppers kicking and gesticulating on the middle of the Mississippi river', history was 'simply social development along the lines of weakest resistance'.

However, in his nine volumes he displayed the liveliest interest in human vagaries, together with the wide view that makes the work a classic. But he afterwards arrived at a theory of history grandly pessimistic enough to suit himself. He lit upon the law of entropy, and fitted it to history to prove that human energy was being constantly and irrecoverably dissipated. Society, like any other organism, would run down, until a stage of stagnation was reached. This stage, Adams maintained, was not remote, but imminent; for the modern scene was marked by tremendously rapid and ever-accelerating change. Adapting the Rule of Phase of the American scientist Willard Gibbs, he argued that human energy was being wasted at a rate subject to mathematical calculation. World history might thus be divided into three phases, of which the third or Electric phase, ushered in by the dynamos he saw installed at the Chicago and Paris Expositions, would run from 1900 to 1917. There might be a fourth, Ethereal phase, that would 'bring Thought to the limit of its possibilities in the year 1921'.

One's immediate reaction is that Adams was wasting his own energy: the hypothesis is untrue, and there was no reason to take it seriously when he propounded it. But Adams loved analogies. As a poetic version of a disintegrating world, this one pleased him; and, tired of the current talk about history as a science, he thought it worth while to put the matter to a test. In this, he acted somewhat as Canute at the water's edge. Who knows whether Canute did not, in his inmost heart, think the waves *might* pause? And if they advanced, as was probable, he would have the pleasure of scolding his courtiers. So Adams with his fellow-historians. 'History,' he said in a letter, 'will die if not irritated. The only service I can do to my profession is to serve as a flea.'

Happily, his theories stimulated Adams to produce two first-rate books. History was a movement from unity to multiplicity; and in terms of human happiness, unity offered everything that multiplicity snatched away. Holidaying in northern France, in 1895, he found its atmosphere strangely attractive. Its village churches and great cathedrals filled him with delight. He plunged into the music, the poetry, and the philosophy of the twelfth and thirteenth centuries, and found peace: a peace which he identified with Unity, in the figure of the Virgin Mary, and also Energy, in the shape of the temples men had raised to Her. Women had long exerted a powerful influence on Adams. The heroines of his two novels, *Democracy* (1880) and *Esther* (1884), count for much more than the heroes. In the company of women, which he came to prefer to that of most men, one could cling to the illusion that life was graceful and ordered: an illusion that vanished as soon as one met their harassed husbands.

This feeling, and his reverence for the great shrines of northern France, Adams voiced in *Mont-Saint-Michel and Chartres* (1904). From the eleventh-century masculinity of Mont-St-Michel, mankind passed to the twelfth century, growing gentler and more feminine, expressing itself in romances and in Gothic architecture, above all in Chartres. This period was for Adams the finest in all history. He loved to speak of his ancestors as rooted in Normandy, an infinitely more congenial starting-place than Boston. In it, he could pay tribute to Woman (as, he noted, very few Americans except Whitman had done), and find relief from Law, from a Puritan deity and a mechanistic universe. *Mont-St-Michel* is a work of pure affection, and to call it Adams's form of expatriation is only to stress how passionately Americans of his calibre have sought the great, good place – not expecting it to come to them.

At the other extreme is *The Education of Henry Adams*, with which the public first became acquainted in 1918, though it had been privately printed in 1907. *The Education* is intended as a study of twentieth-century multiplicity. An auto-biography couched in the third person, it attempts to exhibit in Adams's own life the chaos of the Electric Phase, after the relative tranquillity of the Mechanical. Instead of the Virgin, man stands before the comfortless Dynamo. All is a delirium of change. If the *Education* were merely a lament for the past, it would be tedious; and the final chapters, in which Adams explains his theories without reference to his own life, are necessarily uninteresting to the average reader. But the book as a whole is a brilliant document, extravagantly humble, beautifully written, full of ideas and personalities. Is Henry Adams posturing? The question should not detain us. His general picture is true as a work of art is true. It is a memorable portrait of an era.

Hardly less enjoyment and insight are to be got from Adams's correspondence. He is one of the best letter-writers in the language, and whether he is describing the South Seas or the Arctic Circle, a book just read or an idea just conceived, he brings to them all an idiosyncratic and witty alertness that makes one more than ready to forgive him his pose of despair. He is the liveliest of Jeremiahs, the most accomplished of failures. If his work is not entirely typical of his time, in America, nobody else's is either. Adams is as much a part of the story as Howells or Dreiser or Henry James; we must bring him into it, ignoring his protests that he wishes to be left out.

France was as useful to Gertrude Stein as to Henry Adams, though in a vastly different context. He came to it as a survivor (he said): she came as a forerunner, settling herself in Paris in 1902 and living there (or thereabouts) for over forty years. In 1902 she was a quick-witted, well-to-do young woman who had studied psychology (she had been a pupil of William James, the great brother of the great Henry). She was not an established writer, though some of her early themes showed a certain originality. Among them was a piece about a young man dragging his father by the hair through an orchard. 'Stop,' said the old man; 'I only dragged my father as far as this tree.' Henry Adams felt that there was no link between one generation and the next; Gertrude Stein felt that each new generation must inevitably war with the old. This knowledge gratified her, however, for, unlike Adams, she believed the future to be full of promise. With the aid of psychology she was to uncover truth. Previous American writers had had the same ambition. Yet though she sometimes used the vocabulary of, say, Howells – 'I am trying to be as commonplace as I can be' – she differed from the early realists as much as cubism from impressionism.

The comparison with painting is important. For her interest in psychology was in large part an interest in *language*. William James, who coined the expression 'stream of thought' (which was altered subsequently to 'stream of consciousness'), was struck by the way in which, in certain states of mind, words appeared to exert a supremacy over rational meaning. Under the influence of nitrous oxide, he found himself inventing such impressively nonsensical propositions as: 'There are no differences but differences of degree between different degrees of difference and no difference'. This is the philosopher's mind off the leash. Gertrude Stein was determined to cast her own mind off the leash. In Paris, through her brother Leo, she became intimate with then-obscure young artists who were to become the foremost painters of this century. They – Picasso, Braque, Matisse – were doing in paint exactly what she was trying to do with words: to break away from convention, to let the medium triumph over the subject, to attain simplicity. The same thing was happening in contemporary music. In Paris all the arts evolved together, in a way completely unfamiliar to Adams's Boston, or Miss Stein's native Pittsburgh.

The revolt from the spirit of the Beaux Arts, for her as for Picasso, meant two things, as far as simplicity was concerned. First, art was to aim at the ultimate in economy. It was to be uncluttered, beautifully bare, as unemotional as the prose of Defoe (which Gertrude greatly admired) but far more abstract. (Impatience with extrinsic subject-matter has been characteristic of the modern movement: it has, for example, recently led the American poet William Carlos Williams to argue that the novel is inferior as an art-form to the poem, since it cannot by its nature reach 'the underlying nudity'.) Second, came a distrust of smoothness, a cult of crudity. In part this was inherent in the newness of what was being attempted:

Sure, she said, as Pablo [Picasso] once remarked, when you make a thing, it is so complicated making it that it is bound to be ugly, but those that do it after you they don't have to worry about making it and they can make it pretty, and so everybody can like it when the others make it.

Partly, too, crudity was a self-imposed condition, a result of refusing to take anything for granted:

So then I said I would begin again. I would not know what I knew about everything what I knew about anything.

Such was the background of Gertrude Stein's work. She set out to create a new literature that was to show 'the inside of things'. In some of her writing she tried to divorce words from their usual meanings, and to arrange them like objects in a cubist composition, simply for pleasure's sake:

I saw representative mistakes and glass cups, I saw a whole appearance of respectable refugees, I did not ask actors I asked pearls, I did not choose to ask trains, I was satisfied with celebrated ransoms.

In other work she described people and situations in a language that was full of repetitions and banalities, like an abstraction of the common speech of uneducated people. She hoped thereby to convey the 'immediacy' of existence. Indeed, in *The Making of Americans* (written 1906–8, though not published until 1925), an enormously long and clumsy book, she thought she covered every facet of human nature. She first aroused interest beyond her circle of friends with *Three Lives* (1909), a volume suggested to her by a reading of Flaubert's *Trois Contes*. Two of her three tales – all of which are set in America – deal with elderly German servants, the third with a Negro girl, Melanctha. *Three Lives* is one of her most readable books, and as an experiment in methods of narration it is on the whole very successful. The complexities of Melanctha's life, her vague cravings and her unhappiness, are evoked largely in dialogue, and without condescension. Gertrude Stein's other well-known book, a highly entertaining one and a valuable record of her friendships, is *The Autobiography of Alice B. Toklas* (1933), an account of herself purportedly through the eyes of her companion-secretary Miss Toklas.

Much of her other work, however, is difficult, not so much from obscurity – it is usually possible to see what Gertrude Stein is getting at, and her automatic writing is pleasing, in small quantities – as from repetition. Never was a creative writer so free with definitions and explanations, some of them shrewd, many whimsical and arbitrary. Her emphasis is upon concentration, penetration. Nouns are only 'names' and are to be omitted where possible; the verb is what counts in a sentence. Punctuation is likewise a hindrance: out go the question-mark, the colon, the semi-colon. Yet the result is not clarity but diffuseness and impenetrability. In limiting her vocabulary she achieves an occasional charming crispness in short statements (though often they are paraphrased from other people, including her brother Leo, who said of the absentminded Miss Toklas that 'if I were a general I would never lose a battle, I would only mislay it'). But when she embarks on a lengthy exposition she flounders. In supposing that narration proceeds by a series of imperceptibly varied stages, like movement recorded by the frames in a strip of film, she ignores the vital question of pace: for though a film consists of a great number of images, it would be insupportable if these were to be examined one at a time: they have to be taken at the gallop to make any total effect. Gertrude Stein is in fact obsessed with the process at the expense of the product. She is a writer's writer in several senses, and it is this that constitutes her importance in American literature.

For American literature has suffered from an under-dose of confidence and professional knowledge. Emerson sighed in vain for 'the friendly institution of the *Café*' in Boston, where writers could meet; fifty years later, Dreiser had no idea that other authors shared his interests, and could have helped him with *Sister Carrie*. To this under-dose Gertrude Stein added her over-dose. Massively confident, she was sure that *The Making of Americans* was 'the beginning, really the beginning of modern writing'. Many treated her as a joke, but for some young writers she was a person to believe in, if only as a technician. After the Armistice they found her embedded in the cultural life of Paris, benign, omniscient, and pleasantly American. She had been unashamedly sentimental over the doughboys, as she was to be about their G.I. sons; she read the Paris *Herald-Tribune* in preference to French newspapers (and gave the young Picasso a taste for the Katzenjammer Kids); General Grant was one of her heroes; she liked to play 'The Trail of the Lonesome Pine' on her gramophone: she *understood*. She talked to them professionally about the writer's problems. She conferred status upon the native idiom, serenely sure that the provincial gaucheries of America were close to the new mood of cosmopolitan literature, having in some ways anticipated it. To Eugene O'Neill, to Sherwood Anderson, to Ernest Hemingway (who proofread for her, and wrote in 1923 that 'she has a wonderful head'); [1] to these and other Americans in their apprentice days she imparted the valuable assurance that the unaffected prose of Mark Twain and the American newspaper-column was, with modifications, the ideal vehicle of the *avant-garde*. She is entitled to rank with Twain as one of the major formative influences upon modern American prose. One might say facetiously that he is its father, and she its mother. It is a curious reflection upon American writing that Hannibal, Missouri and Paris, France have both been necessary factors, and that the least self-conscious of styles should require the most self-conscious of corroborations. But then, as Gertrude Stein acutely observed, in comparing her own people with the Spanish, Americans

1. He said this to Edmund Wilson, who has reprinted some perceptive early comments on Hemingway in *The Shores of Light* (London, 1952), 115–24.

have no close contact with the earth such as most europeans have. Their materialism is not the materialism of existence, of possession, it is the materialism of action and abstraction.

Action and abstraction: *Huckleberry Finn* and *The Making of Americans*: the need to stay at home and the need to get away from home in order to understand it. Or, 'America is my country' (as Miss Stein explains her own compromise) 'and Paris is my home town'. This dual tug is apparent in the whole movement of expatriation, making it impossible for most American writers to remain long absent without incurring a guilty conscience, or to retain intact personalities in the face of European influence. Earlier writers, even before the Civil War, flounder and contradict themselves when discussing the problem. 'If I were in your position,' Hawthorne writes to Longfellow in 1854, from Liverpool, 'I think that I should make my home on this side of the water, – though always with an indefinite and never-to-be-executed intention to go back and die in my native land.' Yet elsewhere, particularly in his more public utterances, Hawthorne speaks very differently. These wistful asides are only part of the story, for him and others. The apparent paradox was that only as America became more American could it afford to be more European. Viewed one way, the solution of Henry James or Gertrude Stein was a betrayal of American wholeness. Viewed another way, it was a mark of American confidence. The uneasy murmur of Hawthorne (or Irving, or Longfellow) becomes in these later figures a (relatively) calm assumption that Americans can have the best of both worlds – or at any rate should try to.

THE NEW POETRY

—————

EDWIN ARLINGTON ROBINSON (1869–1935)

CARL SANDBURG (1878–   )

NICHOLAS VACHEL LINDSAY (1879–1931)

EDGAR LEE MASTERS (1869–1950)

ROBERT FROST (1875–1963)

WILLIAM CARLOS WILLIAMS (1883–1963)

EZRA POUND (1885–   )

WALLACE STEVENS (1879–1955)

THE NEW POETRY

—

By 1910 or so, the realist movement in prose that Howells had helped to inaugurate forty years previously had lost much of its impetus. Crane, Norris, and other promising authors were dead; Dreiser had apparently disappeared into hack journalism (though he reappeared with *Jennie Gerhardt*, in 1911); and Howells knew that to most young writers he was himself 'comparatively a dead cult'. A good deal of energy had been diverted into 'muckraking' literature like Gustavus Myers' *History of the Great American Fortunes* and Jane Addams' *Twenty Years at Hull House* (an account of settlement work in Chicago), which were both published in 1910.

Yet if there was a temporary lull in the development of American fiction, there was plenty of life in other art-forms during these years when O. Henry was pouring out his slick and nimble stories of 'Bagdad-on-the-Subway'. In this same New York the photographer Alfred Stieglitz established his famous salon at 291 Fifth Avenue, and as early as 1908 was introducing to America some of the painters whom Gertrude Stein and her brother had discovered in Paris. Also in 1908, the 'Ash Can' school of American painters[1] held a New York exhibition meant to show the public that realism need not be confined to the medium of the printed word. The critic James G. Huneker helped to inform the public of the revolutionary achievements of Diaghilev and the Ballet Russe, of Stravinsky and Debussy. Rumours of the London 'Imagistes' came across the Atlantic. In 1913, New York had its chance, at the Armory Show of post-impressionist art, to see the work of the same artists that Roger Fry had introduced to London three years previously, at the Grafton Galleries. Nor were

---

1. So called because of their alleged fondness for painting city backyards. See Oliver Larkin, *Art and Life in America* (New York, 1949), 336.

these excitements confined to New York: the Armory Show, for example, was also sent to Chicago and Boston. The redoubtable American woman played her part. Though Gertrude Stein remained oversea, Mabel Dodge Luhan settled in New York in 1912, after a ten-year sojourn in Italy, determined to bring enlightenment to the United States. Amy Lowell was hardly less active in Boston, while in Chicago Harriet Monroe and Margaret Anderson were eager to do battle for the sake of culture. Isadora Duncan, the dancer from San Francisco, gloried in an enlightenment which others thought scandalous. Magazines came into being to voice the new sentiments in the air. In 1912 Harriet Monroe founded *Poetry: A Magazine of Verse* (a title whose seeming tautology made it clear that she was primarily interested in poetry, not in pieces *about* poetry). 1914 saw the beginning of Margaret Anderson's *Little Review* (like *Poetry*, a Chicago venture) and of the *New Republic*. In that year, too, H. L. Mencken and George Jean Nathan became joint editors of *The Smart Set*. The fiddles, as J. B. Yeats observed, were tuning up. More than most dates, 1912 defines the effective start of a rich era in American poetry, an era not interrupted by the European war that broke out in 1914. Though America herself joined the war in April 1917, her poets were able to continue what they had begun in the vital pre-war years (though the prose writers had to some extent to learn over again when the war was over).

One could say of 1912, in the words of the Negro song,

> There's a good time coming, and it's not far off –
> Been long, long, long on the way. ...

In that year several of the poets who were about to make their name had had to wait a long time for the moment. Edgar Lee Masters was forty-three, Robert Frost was thirty-seven, Carl Sandburg thirty-four, and Vachel Lindsay and Wallace Stevens both thirty-three. The 'new poetry', which came so much later than the comparable movement in prose, had thus had a lengthy gestation: it was no firework display of precocious talent. Nearly all its practitioners had cast about uncertainly, before finding the appropriate words and form.

Some poets never did quite fit together all the necessary ingredients. Sidney Lanier has been instanced as one poet who hung between two worlds; another and more famous was Edwin Arlington Robinson. Robinson, a poet of New England and the exact contemporary of Edgar Lee Masters, came near to first-rateness but just missed it, perhaps because of too-great isolation and obscurity in his formative years, perhaps also from a deficiency of temperament, something hesitant and fastidious in his reaction to his time. Interested in Zola and in Hardy, he tried to write prose, moving away from it gradually by trial and error into his own poetic style. It was a painful, hangdog progress for him; though his first volume of poems was published (privately) in 1896, it was not until the 1920s that the public rewarded him. When it did, his success was considerable; he was three times a Pulitzer prize-winner. This very fact is indicative, perhaps, of the extent to which he fell short of true mastery; he had not altered greatly in these twenty-odd years: public taste moved forward just far enough to accept him where it would not accept other 'modern' poets. His dour, questing, pessimistic poetry was sufficiently linked to conventional verse to pass for that, though it was a great deal better. Many of his early poems were portraits of lonely, wayward, confused, insecure men. They were subtle portraits, sometimes catching exactly the dry New England idiom. Such poems as 'Isaac and Archibald', 'Miniver Cheevy', 'Eros Turannos', and 'Mr Flood's Party' – to choose four deservedly fastened on by anthologists – have a wit and point underlaid by a deep perception of futility. He shows the human situation, however glossy its superficial look, to be complex and comfortless. Even in 'Miniver Cheevy', a comic poem in some ways –

> Miniver loved the Medici,
> Albeit he had never seen one;
> He would have sinned incessantly
> Could he have been one –

even here, the final note is one of failure:

> Miniver Cheevy, born too late,
> Scratched his head and kept on thinking;
> Miniver coughed, and called it fate,
> And kept on drinking.

Emily Dickinson (like Gerard Manley Hopkins) gives the sense of having come before her time; but Robinson, like Miniver Cheevy, suggests a man born too late – or supposing that he has been born too late. Something, we gather, is wrong; but neither his complaint nor his remedy is entirely satisfying. The New England dryness that is one of his strengths, preserving him from too literary a formulation, is also, it may be, one of his defects; as in Frost, one sometimes suspects that the reticence is not courage but drabness, concealing not deep despair but a hollowness. There is a lack in Robinson of the contemporary awareness – not the ephemerally up-to-date quality of the best-selling novelist, but the profound one of the poet. He seems not quite able to match theme and thought. His poems, despite their dignity and felicity, have an air of charade; and (especially in the popular Arthurian trilogy) of an unduly prolonged charade, whose answer one has guessed after the first scene. Not sure – not wholly, possessedly sure – of what he is about, not finding the way through, he becomes diffuse and, with consummate verbal dexterity, repeats his points again and again. A similar uneasiness may be detected in other poets of the time: in the English Georgians, and in such Americans as William Vaughn Moody and Trumbull Stickney, both of whom occasionally capture the modern manner, only to lose it again in a plethora of words.

It was Chicago that led the movement when it came. The Chicago of Dreiser's *Sister Carrie*, or Norris's *The Pit*, or Henry B. Fuller's *The Cliff-Dwellers* (1893), or Robert Herrick's *Memoirs of an American Citizen* (1905), or Upton Sinclair's *The Jungle* (1906) – all of them portraying a crass and brutal city – was also a place of growing civic pride. The second city in the United States, it saw no reason why it should not overhaul New York culturally as well as in population. In 1892 it had acquired a university; the following year it had housed the huge Columbian Exposition; and in 1912 it had Harriet's Monroe's *Poetry*. Gratifyingly, its hinterland began to produce writers. The three Illinois poets, Carl Sandburg, Vachel Lindsay, and Edgar Lee Masters, were all destined to contribute to what can be called the American, as distinct from the cosmopolitan, movement in modern poetry. Brought up a thousand miles from the Atlantic, all three considered themselves the more American on that account. All three were strongly drawn to Abraham Lincoln, also of Illinois: Lincoln the apotheosis of the plain man, the martyr, the man of sorrows – the epitome of America. Sandburg wrote a six-volume biography of his hero; Lindsay was born in Springfield, the town that Lincoln knew best; and Masters's father had been the law-partner of William Herndon, Lincoln's former partner in the same profession.

'In infancy I never heard of New England': so wrote Lindsay, and in essence the same was true of Masters and of Sandburg (the son of a Swedish immigrant). The Mississippi Valley was their heartland, in an emotional as well as in a geopolitical sense. Chicago was their metropolis, and their poetry aimed at catching the atmosphere of the central region of which it was the capital. Sandburg and Lindsay in particular tried to answer the great American *public-people* conundrum – that of making the ordinary extraordinary, of plucking significance out of common events.

The dangers were great, when the effort was made. It was fatally easy for the poet to slip into the rhetoric of the platform, to become excessively concerned with manliness, to surrender to a glib evocation of Western, pioneering America, to lose the individual in the crowd: in a word, to substitute for his private vision a public tableau. Nor was the language of the streets a simple thing to apply to poetry. Slang and dialect become quickly dated, or are unintelligible, or merely a hindrance to understanding; or can seem falsely 'folksy'. Sandburg and Lindsay began by identifying themselves as far as possible with the people; in fact, Sandburg

grew out of them, for he worked as a casual labourer before
he started to write.

They were assisted in their efforts to create a poetry of and
for the masses, first, by the sympathetic attitude of the modern movement towards 'anti-poetic' themes and vocabulary; second, by the genuine vitality of American popular
speech; and third, by the special contribution of the Negro,
with his exuberant-sad philosophy of the underling and his
exceptional gift for rhythmic expression. These were wonderfully formulated in jazz, the unique, untrained musical form
which, as one Negro said, emerged not from the world of wine,
women, and song, but out of 'booze, brothels, and blues'.

With such aids, the poetry of Carl Sandburg came into
being. His first poems, published in 1904, were ignored. Ten
years later, however, the poetry-reading world was ready
for his verse. His poem 'Chicago' won a prize; possibly the
award was influenced by the fact that his poem appeared in
Harriet Monroe's magazine, and praised the city. But when
his *Chicago Poems* came out a couple of years later, the response to Sandburg was unmistakably enthusiastic. It was evident that he had learned from Whitman but he was not a
mere echo of Whitman despite the similarity of outlook. His
poems, though some ran into long, prose-like statements,
were usually short and laconic and colloquial. They celebrated the clangour of Chicago, the sunlit prairie, the simple
man:

> I speak of new cities and new people.
> I tell you the past is a bucket of ashes.
> I tell you yesterday is a wind gone down,
> 　　　a sun dropped in the west.
> I tell you there is nothing in the world
> 　　　only an ocean of to-morrows,
> 　　　a sky of to-morrows.

Like Whitman, Sandburg concedes in these poems that the
world has much ugliness and unhappiness. But he writes of
injustice like an old-time radical; it makes him angry but not
despondent. Basically, he is content, for he is in love with his
world, and finds poetry in its commonest incidents – the base-

ball game, the 'wop' or 'bohunk' workmen at their toil, the prairie farm-life, the city prostitutes, the jazz ecstasy of Negroes.

After forty years, not all of these poems have worn well. But on the whole they are still alive and immediate in a way that the poems of Robinson are not. They are warm-hearted yet not sentimental; their slang is a genuine idiom that fuses with Sandburg's tenderness to humanity:

> Take any streetful of people buying clothes and groceries, cheering
>   a hero or throwing confetti and blowing tin horns ... tell me
>   if the lovers are losers ... tell me if any get any more than the
>   lovers ... in the dust ... in the cool tombs.

Sandburg seemed to prove that one could make taut verse out of the most unpoetic of settings, and apply slang to serious themes to deepen, not to travesty them. Thus 'Ossawatomie', a poem from Sandburg's third volume (*Smoke and Steel*, 1920), that deals with John Brown, gains from its informality, as may be judged from the final stanza:

> They laid hands on him
> And the fool killers had a laugh
> And the necktie party was a go, by God.
> They laid hands on him and he was a goner.
>   They hammered him to pieces and he stood up.
> They buried him and he walked out of the grave, by God,
>   Asking again: Where did that blood come from?

Vachel Lindsay, in the few fine poems among a collection of weakly whimsical or declamatory verse, has a comparable impact. As a young man, a bad artist and bad poet, he dreamed largely, determined 'to be the great singer of the Y.M.C.A. Army; to reconcile culture and manliness; to be by 1905 the biggest man in Chicago'. But Chicago knew nothing of him until 1913, when Harriet Monroe's magazine printed his 'General William Booth Enters Heaven' – a poem that proved he had accomplished the first and second of his three naïve ambitions. In the intervening years he had tramped America, 'trading rhymes for bread', likening himself to other wandering men: to 'Johnny Appleseed', who had roamed the Middle West, sowing the seeds of future orchards; to Daniel Boone, pioneering across the Appalachians into Kentucky; to the Barnum-like circus men; to travelling temperance reformers; to the gypsies; to the revivalist preachers, particularly the Campbellites who 'breathed fire, but they thought in granite'. These went to the making of his American hagiography, to which he added (besides Lincoln) John Brown, Andrew Jackson, Governor Altgeld of Illinois, the Democratic leader William Jennings Bryan and others. It was a strange album of enthusiasms, that found room also for motion-picture stars and Keats, for Poe, Whitman, Twain, O. Henry. Out of them he evolved a form of heavily accented, dramatic verse that he later called the Higher Vaudeville. It was meant to be read aloud, with the participation of an audience, as an evangelist at a camp-meeting would draw upon his congregation. 'General William Booth' was the first of these poems to reach a sophisticated public:

> Booth led boldly with his big bass drum –
> (Are you washed in the blood of the Lamb?)
> The Saints smiled gravely and they said: 'He's come.'
> (Are you washed in the blood of the Lamb?)

If these poems had been meant as a joke – if there had been the least hint of condescension – they would have been intolerable. However, they were meant seriously, and therefore Lindsay was able to encompass a delightful jocularity:

> His sweetheart and his mother were Christian and meek.
> They washed and ironed for Darius every week.
> One Thursday he met them at the door: –
> Paid them as usual, but acted sore.
>
> He said: – 'Your Daniel is a dead little pigeon.
> He's a good hard worker but he talks religion. ...'

Like Sandburg, he had learned from the Negroes. His father had read *Uncle Remus* aloud to him, there were Negro servants in their Springfield home, and he always considered himself part-Southerner: 'the inexplicable Mason and Dixon's line, deep-dyed and awful, ran straight through our hearts'. In his best poetry he dealt with the occasions when ordinary people are powerfully moved, by the glitter of cos-tumed actors, the beat of a hymn-tune, the histrionics of preacher or politician. Out of their brass-band garishness, their swing near to fraudulence and hysteria, he made a unique poetry:

> All the funny circus silks
> Of politics unfurled,
> Bartlett pears of romance that were honey at the cores,
> And torchlights down the street, to the end of the world.
>
> There were truths eternal in the gab and tittle-tattle.
> There were real heads broken in the fustian and the rattle. ...

The West – the world of 'tomorrows', of American myth – entered Lindsay's vision in a fantasy that was the fantasy of everyman in America. His vision was, when clear, endowed with an innocence that enabled him to produce a few en-chanting poems for children ('The Moon's the North Wind's Cooky', 'Yet Gentle Will the Griffin Be') and that recalls the paintings of the Douanier Rousseau, in which gross mat-ter-of-fact and world of dream so effortlessly merge.

Sandburg and Lindsay walked the tight-rope; if the tension of their verse slackened, they were precipitated into extremes of prosiness or sentimentality.

> I am the gutter dream,
> I am the golden dream

sang Lindsay's circus calliope. In much of his verse the mira-culous combination collapsed. The same thing happened by degrees to Carl Sandburg, though he had a robuster talent and a more sustained career. Always stirred by the spectacle of the common man, by his sayings and his songs, Sandburg was able to voice these in his moving and monumental life of Lincoln (2 vols. 1926; 4 more, 1939), and his *American Songbag* (1927) was a useful collection of popular ballads. In *The People, Yes* (1936) he tried with some success to state his faith in everyman by weaving together a miscellany of pro-verbs and wisecracks. But gradually, by a process of dilu-tion, by the conquest of ordinariness over the poetic moment,

Sandburg's writing became less memorable. The good tough concentration of his early verse yielded to incantatory repetitions, and even (in *Remembrance Rock*, 1948) to a dropsical prose chronicling of the American epic. Yet he was the honestest of men, and failed latterly only in trying to do the hardest of things.

There was a loss of touch, too, in the case of Edgar Lee Masters, the third local poet of the 'Chicago Renaissance' (*Renaissance* is the wrong word, since it was Chicago's first birth of culture). All through his younger years Masters laboured at poetry of a conventional sort. Then, suddenly, he found a new voice. His inspiration came from the Greek Anthology, with its brief epigrams and epitaphs; from a poignant sense of the incomplete lives led by people in the little towns of Illinois; and from the efforts of others – especially Carl Sandburg – at free verse. In 1914 he began to write the poems that form his *Spoon River Anthology*. They represent the self-spoken epitaphs of the citizens buried in an Illinois cemetery. The tone varies between an elegiac sadness, an occasional lyrical affirmation of life, and – the overwhelming impression of the book – a gaunt, rueful exposure of shame and disappointment. Husbands and wives, parents and their children tell 'what happened' from their own point of view. The epitaphs thus overlap, to build up a composite picture of a community in which the individual is isolated, yet involved with his fellows in the common guilt, which somehow none could help:

> Oh many times did Ernest Hyde and I
> Argue about the freedom of the will.
> My favourite metaphor was Prickett's cow
> Roped out to grass, and free you know as far
> As the length of the rope.

But one day Prickett's cow breaks loose – and gores the speaker to death. As poetry, the *Spoon River Anthology* now seems as undistinguished as this extract suggests. As a comment on human nature, it is not, on the whole, profound. But in its time it was the most widely-read document of the 'new poetry', and it has retained enough strength and sincerity for us to see why. Though his subsequent writing was marred by an unpleasantly denigratory outlook (e.g., in his 'debunking' biography of *Lincoln, the Man*, 1931), Masters contrived in *Spoon River* to do what Hamlin Garland and others had tried to do in prose. In his way Masters, like Sandburg and Lindsay, assisted in widening the scope of poetry to a degree that would have seemed unthinkable to an earlier generation.

Another poet who won recognition at the same moment was Robert Frost, who, though born in California, regarded New England as his home, and has made it the background of almost all his poetry. He was thirty-eight when, in 1913, he at last interested a publisher in his work. This was in England, where he had moved the previous year, to 'write and be poor without further scandal in the family'. With his first published volume, however (*A Boy's Will*), he established himself at once; his second (*North of Boston*, 1914) was still more successful; and on his return to America in 1915 he settled on a New Hampshire farm, where he continued to write and to win an ever-growing reputation.

Frost, whom many describe as America's finest poet of the century, was less obviously a product of the modern movement than the others mentioned above. Though his metres are varied, they are at first glance quite orthodox. He uses the speech of New England, but not as a vernacular intended to jolt the reader. The city – that intoxicating theme for the writer of his time – has no place in his work. He is the countryman, with the countryman's apparent conservatism; for rural life, with its heavy seasonal rhythm of growth and decay, imposes its own continuity on those who live amongst it. Yet Frost's tone was 'modern': he could never be confused with Whittier – to name another poet of rural New England. He struck no attitudes; he made it clear that he was determined not to be poetical. The poetic element must come out of the scene as some extra and unbidden reward. Sandburg and Lindsay, while insisting on their share in everyday experience, thought of themselves (like Whitman) as *bards*, or at any rate minstrels. Frost, on the other hand, was a farmer: the poetry was, so to speak, a dividend. The farm was a large part of himself, his anchor to reality, not local colour or a week-end gesture.

His poetry cropped out of this farmer's world, every part of which he knew, and knew how to render in words with a brilliant, offhand ease. His reticent, poor, dignified New Englanders are evoked in monologues a little like those of E. A. Robinson, or of Robert Browning, but with a difference. His people speak cautiously amid intervals of silence, making each word count. Volubility would be alien to them. They do not go on and on, as in Robinson, or explode, as in Browning. Their lonely farms, the cold winters and all-too-brief summers; the imminence of failure, of the wilderness, of death – all give one the sense of people living tensely. The tension comes out in the poetry, and the moments of relaxation have by contrast an almost extravagant gaiety. The hardihood, to repeat, is that of life in New Hampshire as such, not that imposed by the poet, though of course Frost describes it with a professional mastery.

But there is a distinction here, and in making it one may find a reason why Frost, though a beautiful writer, is not a poet of the highest rank. A poem, in his own words, 'begins in delight, it inclines to the impulse, it assumes direction with the first line laid down, it runs a course of lucky events, and ends in a clarification of life – not necessarily a great clarification ... but in a momentary stay against confusion. ... It finds its own name as it goes and discovers the best waiting for it in some final phrase at once wise and sad. ...' The final phrase is not a moral but, rather, the crust of the loaf: the reader must cut his own sandwiches if he wants them. Another, indirect statement (or an attitude that Frost admires) lies in the final lines of his 'Oven Bird':

> The bird would cease and be as other birds
> But that he knows in singing not to sing.
> The question that he frames in all but words
> Is what to make of a diminished thing.

Once again we are at the conundrum; in his aversion to poeticising, the poet denies much of what was hitherto regarded as his material and his function. With Frost, the course of events is incomparably expressed: he cannot be beaten on his home ground. But the clarification – the moment in which the poet must reveal himself, however unobtrusively, as poet – is sometimes inadequate: too faint, too evasive, too much a mere shrug of the shoulders. One's doubts are not allayed by Frost's more deliberate attempts at clarification, which seem to indicate that the stay is momentary: that he has come to set more store by the matter-of-fact than by the deeper kinds of truth. Nonetheless, Robert Frost was an important poet, who has written some perfect poems – which is a rare enough commendation.

Frost and the Midwesterners, though it would be misleading to stress their remoteness from world movements, were somewhat separated from the Eastern poets of the era whose development was urban and cosmopolitan. These had links with London and Paris (Frost when in England had lived in the country, not in London). New York, in its Greenwich Village section, offered them a more satisfying Bohemia than that of Chicago, as well as the opportunity to become acquainted with parallel advances in art, music, and the drama. However, they had a certain amount in common with the Chicagoans; if their solutions were different, their problems were much the same, and Harriet Monroe's *Poetry* found room for all of them. The verse of William Carlos Williams reveals some of these similarities and differences.

Williams, born in New Jersey, became a doctor and continued to practise his profession while also maintaining his existence as a poet. He made his poetry out of the stuff of life in Rutherford, New Jersey, but however coarse and prosaic his material, he transformed it with his poet's vision. Another poet, Wallace Stevens, has said of Williams that 'his passion for the anti-poetic is a blood passion', and that yet one finds in his work 'the conjunction of the unreal and the real, the sentimental and the anti-poetic, the constant interaction of two opposites'. Here Williams differs from Frost, in his life and in his poetry; he recognized the cleavage between inner and outer experience (or between interpretation and experience), where Frost tended, in putting first things first, to put last things (eschatology) nowhere. Yet again the American conundrum. Williams has not always known the answer. One of his most-praised short poems reads:

> so much depends
> upon
> a red wheel
> barrow
> glazed with rain
> water
> beside the white
> chickens

This has a glistening, child's-eye immediacy, and its structure is artfully artless. But if the poet confined himself to such impressions one would soon tire of the demonstration. However, unlike Frost, Williams continued to improve because he brought to his themes the fierce concern of the poet as poet. He insisted upon the need for interpretation, and though for years condemned to the inbred obscurity of the little magazines (the ones that, in the famous phrase, died to make verse free), he retained the fresh sense of the scene about him while refusing to simplify his response. He developed a close, affectionate knowledge of his fellows yet was not mawkish about them. They never became The People for him; and so as a statement of reality

> The beauty of
> the terrible faces
> of our nonentities

goes deeper than much of Sandburg, or than some of Frost. So do his lines on a baseball game:

> It is summer, it is the solstice
> the crowd is
> cheering, the crowd is laughing
> in detail
> permanently, seriously
> without thought

'No ideas,' Williams has said, 'but in things': but he did not allow the *thing*, despite the pre-1917 delight in emancipating itself from didactic and decorative shackles, to pass itself off as the ultimate of poetry. So, in recent years he began to make an astonishingly effective answer to the conundrum in the first instalments of his long poem 'Paterson', which is the name he gives his New Jersey home town. Later instalments have not altogether sustained the early promise of 'Paterson'. Williams is sometimes an ungainly poet, snatching hastily at ideas, a little at the mercy of free-verse mannerisms of a kind that never seduced Frost. His choppy lines and muttered diction are hard for non-Americans to understand. But he is a good poet, with a wide vision.

As a medical student at the University of Pennsylvania, Williams became friendly with two other young people who shared his interest in poetry. One was Ezra Pound, late of Moscow, Idaho; the other, the daughter of an astronomy professor, was Hilda Doolittle. Their friendship lasted, with valuable results for Williams. Pound was a formidably precocious, irritating youth, utterly devoted to words and ideas. His devotion led him, and likewise Hilda Doolittle, to London, where they made common cause with a small group led by the philosopher T. E. Hulme and calling themselves the Imagist(e)s. The group announced a new style of poetry which, in Hulme's well-known phrase, was to be 'cheerful, dry, and sophisticated'. Poetry was 'no more nor less than a mosaic of words, so great exactness is required for each one'. *Mosaic* well describes the quality aimed at in Imagist verse; for the laying of a mosaic calls for great care and technical skill, and yet produces an effect of impressionist boldness – or, more exactly, of *pointillist* boldness, as in the painting of Seurat. Or, as Pound expressed the matter, 'the point of Imagisme is that it does not use images *as ornaments*. The image is itself the speech.' What had been trimming was now to be integrated in the poem, out of an extreme regard for economy and concentration; formal metrical devices were to give place to 'the sequence of the musical phrase'. At this stage Pound and the others (Pound, as always the disinterested

bully, was soon dominating the group) were mainly influenced not by symbolism but by the poetry of the Orient.
In Chinese and Japanese verse (as they knew it through the
translations of Judith Gautier and from the work of the Boston Orientalist Ernest Fenollosa) they found the perfect reticence: words distilled. Tremendously excited – at this
crucial period, in London as in Chicago, everything seemed
'new' – they set out to achieve the quintessential in their
own verse. Pound had written a thirty-line poem, only to destroy it as a work of 'second intensity'. Six months later he
used the same theme – a moment of sudden emotion at seeing beautiful faces in a station of the Paris métro – in a poem
of fifteen lines. After another year (the time-factor seems significant here, as though the process were akin to the aging of a
liqueur) he had reduced the poem to its final, two-line form:

> The apparition of these faces in the crowd;
> Petals on a wet, black bough.

Pound wrote a few other poems of similar 'intensity', and
Hilda Doolittle (who signed her work H.D. – compressing
the very *name* of the poet) also produced some solid, pleasing
little Imagist pieces.

The movement soon attracted another American poet, the
Bostonian lady Amy Lowell, who arrived in London in the
summer of 1914, with her mulberry-coloured car and two
chauffeurs in matching livery. Before long she was the leader of what Pound, now off on other scents, described as
'Amygism'. For a while she was faithful to the cause. Then
she, too, deserted it, in favour of polyphonic prose. Too ebul-
lient to confine herself to a formula as restrictive as Imagism,
she eventually wrote a life of Keats that ran on for 1160
pages.

Imagism was only a way-stage. Its limitations can be seen
in the poem by Pound quoted above, which is pared down
beyond the point of maximum intensity, until it has become
a semi-private allusion. The image in itself offers only frugal
possibilities for poetry; in all but the most skilful hands it is
hardly more than the decorative flourish it came into being

to destroy. Still, it was an important way-stage, if not quite as novel as its founders supposed, or as revolutionary as they hoped. Both a symptom of change and a force for change in the world of poetry, the movement had a passion and an exhilaration characteristic of the time. Its insistence on economy and its advocacy of the free-verse line continued to be valuable after the Imagists had scattered in their various directions. While the movement was active, it reached back into America, where Pound preached through the medium of Miss Monroe's *Poetry*.

A little after his Imagist phase, Pound also took advantage of Margaret Anderson's *Little Review*, to make it too a stronghold of modernism. This he did from Europe, where he was firmly settled. Omnivorous as perhaps only an American can be, he sampled everything that could be of use to the New Poetry, helping to ensure that it should pass through its first joyful iconoclasms and experimental excesses, to attain maturity. French symbolism, the elegies of Sextus Propertius, Provençal balladry, Oriental verse-techniques, Middle English: all these and other forms Pound incorporated in his poetry. His erudition exasperated the average reader, and was sometimes queried by the expert. His arrogance, after World War I, led him into a Poundian type of fascism. Yet his personal eccentricities, unhandsome though they are, do not detract from his vast exploratory significance. What he has meant to American poets, not to mention British ones, is clearly shown in such books as the autobiography of his friend William Carlos Williams. Pound rendered invaluable service to such contemporaries, not by his wild denunciations of America, but by demonstrating that the professional poet, if he had the courage to renounce popular favour, could come out of Moscow, Idaho, and yet take the whole world for his province.

The poetry of Wallace Stevens has, even more than that of Williams, the kind of technical excellence that Pound set as a goal. Wallace Stevens worked for an insurance company, and became one of its senior officials; but the job bore only an antithetical relation to his writing. He has spoken of

himself as a romantic poet, using the epithet to define his innocently implicated relationship to the world about him: one
who (in his own words) 'still dwells in an ivory tower, but
who insists that life there would be intolerable except for the
fact that one has, from the top, such an exceptional view of
the public dump and the advertising signs. ... He is the her-
mit who dwells alone with the sun and the moon, and insists
on taking a rotten newspaper.' He did not like his own time,
but he was not concerned to indict it (except indirectly), still
less to propose a new order of society. His criticisms are of a
special, exquisite order; but as his first published poems (in
Poetry, 1914) showed, there was never anything sickly about
him: he belonged to the modern movement, and was not a
survivor from the Mauve Decade (as Thomas Beer christened the 1890s). Here is his 'Disillusionment of Ten O'Clock':

> The houses are haunted
> By white night-gowns.
> None are green,
> Or purple with green rings,
> Or green with yellow rings,
> None of them are strange,
> With socks of lace
> And beaded ceintures.
> People are not going
> To dream of baboons and periwinkles.
> Only, here and there, an old sailor,
> Drunk and asleep in his boots,
> Catches tigers
> In red weather.

A critic of the early 1920s,[1] who quoted this poem, read Stevens a stern lecture for playing with words as though they
were trinkets. One may agree with him that it consorts oddly
with Sandburg, Lindsay, Masters, or even Williams. One
sees that Stevens is fond of colours; that they connote vitality and imagination, by contrast with the dull respectability
of a white night-gown; that the imagery might be called artificial and far-fetched; that the scene described is not 'real',

1. Louis Untermeyer, *American Poetry Since 1900* (London, 1924).

neither is the sailor a real sailor, though one would accept
him in a ballet.

In subsequent poems Stevens sometimes led the reader a
longer dance, down stranger avenues, approaching nonsense (as in his choice of titles – 'Le Monocle de Mon Oncle',
'The Paltry Nude Starts on a Spring Voyage' – that bear
no apparent relation to the poem): approaching indeed the
inconsequentialities of Dada and Surrealism. Meret Oppen-
heim, one of the Surrealists, made a cup (complete with sau-
cer and spoon) out of fur. Some of Wallace Stevens' poems,
it might be argued, have a comparable effect; fur-teacup
verse, they are bizarrely imaginative, and they are 'useless'
in that they offer the reader no advice or consolation, nothing but delight of a sophisticated order. Or, like certain
eighteenth-century verse, or some of the poetry of the Sit-
wells, they present experience through the diffractive medium – so to speak – of a highly civilized sensibility.

Yet these remarks miss the import of Stevens. The view of
the public dump matters to him; it represents poetry's 'fundamental and endless struggle with fact'. His 'fact' is usually not everybody's fact:

> Crow is realist. But, then,
> Oriole, also, may be realist.

Reality and imagination, and their interplay, are one of his
main themes. He is not impressed by Surrealism, because 'it
invents without discovering. To make a clam play an accor-
dion is to invent, not to discover.' Poetry, he thinks, can (and
perhaps must) reach reality by the unlikeliest routes, but
not by jumping into the dark. All kinds of fragrance or scin-
tillation are desirable, provided that the poet knows of the
public dump of anti-poetic ordinariness. In these terms, it is
clear that 'Disillusionment of Ten O'Clock' is not a mere
exercise in colour-values, as Stevens' early critic grumbled.
It will bear close investigation; it is entire; it comes out effortlessly, not with the squeezed gymnastic grunt of some Imagist verse of the same length. Though it has the flat bright
air of a stage-set, it is much more than a *décor*. It makes sense;

it is an excellent parable of dullness and poetic reality. In some of his later volumes (e.g., *Auroras of Autumn*, 1950) his debate is a little too explicit – 'G. E. Moore at the spinet', Randall Jarrell has said. It is still the American conundrum, in which the poet seeks 'the gibberish of the vulgate', and tries 'by a peculiar speech to speak'

> The peculiar potency of the general,
> To compound the imagination's Latin with
> The *lingua franca et jocundissima*.

But the conundrum has rarely been so fastidiously treated. Wallace Stevens is one of the most accomplished poets of our century. Like Marianne Moore, whose work begins after World War I, he ceased to be worried by crude equations of *people* and *public*. Taking for granted a craftsman's isolation that filled Melville with guilt and despair, he pursued his subtle goals with an adult tranquillity. Along with his more boisterous colleagues, he indicated that American poetry had come of age. There was no longer a cultural lag where Europe was concerned. Indeed, such Americans as Pound and Gertrude Stein were foremost in the European *avant-garde*, and beckoned on others. Though the main body of the American public followed far in rear (even farther behind than the public in Britain or France), this hardly perturbed the poets of the miraculous era. They could speak to one another in the little magazines. And they revelled in the old American game of deriding authority. Amy Lowell, a collateral descendant of J. R. Lowell, who 'had had that elderly gentleman held in front of [her] as a model ... all [her] life', was overjoyed at being told by someone that she was the better poet. While few others could have had so oppressive a connexion with a previous generation, all shared her conviction that there was a revolution in progress.

FICTION SINCE WORLD WAR I

SHERWOOD ANDERSON (1876–1941)

SINCLAIR LEWIS (1885–1951)

ERNEST HEMINGWAY (1898–1961)

F. SCOTT FITZGERALD (1896–1940)

JOHN DOS PASSOS (1896–   )

JAMES T. FARRELL (1904–   )

JOHN STEINBECK (1902–   )

WILLIAM FAULKNER (1897–1962)

THOMAS WOLFE (1900–38)

CHAPTER TWELVE

FICTION SINCE WORLD WAR I

—

WITH the Armistice of 1918, and the peacemaking of 1919
(and the 18th Amendment of the same year, that in theory
made America a 'dry' nation), the American prose-writer
entered a new period of revolt. In some ways this was a continuation of earlier movements. But the writers themselves
did not think so; they acknowledged no kinship with pre-
war writers, except perhaps Theodore Dreiser. Henry Adams
had said that the generations in American history were dis-
continuous: the younger did not learn from the older one,
nor could it. Few of Adams's contemporaries would have
agreed with him. However, his *Education*, when published in
a popular edition in 1918, made an immediate appeal to
young people convinced that if they knew none of the answers, at any rate they had clues of which their parents had
no inkling. Since they learned from Adams, who was old
enough to be their collective grandfather, it might seem that
he disproved his own theory. Such an objection, though,
would have been met with the argument that Adams could
make contact with them because he was out of touch with his
own era. The post-war generation, the 'Lost Generation' –
when had any age-group been so self-consciously aware of
itself? – laid eager claim to lost souls from the past. In reviv-
ing such figures as Melville it apologized for the stupidity of
its ancestors.

It is hard to estimate how much of this belief in the uniqueness of its generation, and of its problems, was due to the
war. Undoubtedly the war was an enormous event. The puzzling factor, to Europeans, is the disproportionate nature of
its effect upon Americans. In duration, or cost (in lives,
money, spiritual exhaustion) it meant comparatively little;
the doughboys on the Western Front saw action for a mere
four or five months. Yet the disgust at the war, and the re-
vulsion from it, were almost universal in America: one reason

why Edith Wharton fell out of favour as a novelist was
that, in *The Marne* (1918) and *A Son at the Front* (1923), she
actually spoke of the war as though it were a meaningful
struggle. It was not only wealthy Republicans who opposed
Wilson's Treaty of Versailles; he had no fiercer opponents
than the intellectuals of the *New Republic*. Americans had entered the fight under the assurance that it was a crusade
('Lafayette, we are here') – or at any rate in the expectation of fun and heroics in the Old World at the Government's
expense. They left the scene sure that they had been duped:
that it was not, after all, their war. Many Europeans experienced, and wrote of, a similar disillusionment. But the American recoil was sharper. It was as though the sensitive dough-
boy passed overnight from the emotions of Rupert Brooke to
those of Wilfred Owen – with the difference that instead of
the tragic resignation of Owen he felt an almost personal
affront and indignation. One of two things seemed to have
happened in the Great War to the American writer of the
1920s. Either he enlisted before the arrival of the main
American forces (Faulkner in the R.A.F.; Hemingway, John
Dos Passos, E. E. Cummings in ambulance units) – in which
case he tended to conclude that the war was a nightmare
which ought not to involve him. Or, like Scott Fitzgerald (or
'Studs Lonigan', or the young cadet in Faulkner's *Soldier's
Pay*) he failed to get overseas – in which case he felt doubly
cheated, having known only the backwash of disillusionment. In Dos Passos' *Three Soldiers* (1921), in Cummings's
The Enormous Room (1922), and in some of Hemingway's
work, the hero is an American, looking on at a war fought by
other people, for slogans which he, as a detached observer,
sees to be sham.

Things commonly believed in are false; the 'artist' is isolated from the rest of society: these were, in general, adopted
as axioms by the writers of the Lost Generation. That they
were negative statements was typical of an era of negations.
They were, however, cheerful negations. The writer was not
so hopelessly alienated as he chose to pretend. Or at least
the novelist was not. For, quite apart from the comforting

communion of the little magazines (which always seemed to find new backers), he received a surprising amount of support from the public he denounced. In fact, in broad issues the writer of fiction was not seriously at variance with his public. Plenty of Americans agreed with him that the war had been futile and horrible, that Prohibition was a mistake, that sex was important, that life in Paris or on the Riviera was more stimulating than life back home. They liked to have such topics described to them in the crisp, unpretentious prose which the writer strove to perfect. They recognized in the style of Sinclair Lewis or Ernest Hemingway something not too far removed from their own conversation, or from the newspaper column of their favourite sports-writer. (Many of the authors of the 1920s began as journalists; Ring Lardner in fact started as a sports-writer.)

Still, the writer insisted that there was an essential division between the genuine and the false, the sophisticated and what Mencken called the 'booboisie'. The cry of the writer in the post-war years was for liberty: liberty for the individual to express himself. Freud contributed much more than Marx to the ideology of the period, though the Marxian gospel did not seem incompatible. Freud (as popularly interpreted) gave scientific sanction to what the novelist and playwright wished to say. More, he assisted the biographer to pull authority down from its pedestal: the vogue of debunking biography set in. The imposing figures of past and present were exposed as sorry, thwarted wretches. The free soul must seek liberty: this was the categorical imperative of the 1920s as it had been for Thoreau – though with altered emphases. One must have sexual liberty; the 'Puritans' (the convenient term for one's unloved ancestors) had led warped lives because they refused the call of the flesh. So had the 'Victorians': the 1920s could not forgive a writer like Howells his lack of sexuality (for him, *intercourse* implied the prefix *social*: for them, *sexual*). One must walk out of marriages that ceased to be satisfying, sexually or socially. The individual must go barefoot, metaphorically and even literally: the writings of the time are full of people who take off their shoes, and perhaps their clothes as well, to walk in the grass, to lie close to the soil. Civilization was oppressive: by contrast, one exalted the primitive. The Negro, with his 'dark laughter', was greatly envied, since he held the clue to the art of living that the white world had forgotten. Mabel Dodge Luhan, a member of a rich and socially prominent family, who had lived in Italy before the war and in New York during it, went afterwards to New Mexico, where her fourth husband was a Taos Indian named Antonio.[1] Indeed, American women (who like their British cousins now had the vote) added powerfully to the emancipation of the decade. The richer they were, the more emphatic their gestures tended to be, since wealth enabled them to follow impulse wherever it led.

Yet the years after Armageddon were productive ones for the American novelist. His prose medium was admirably adapted to what he had to say. His principal theme – that of secession from society – was one that had long engaged the American writer. Hitherto a somewhat native theme, it was now a formula that fitted the European scene, and one that European writers imitated. Like jazz and cocktails, it represented an American demeanour. It was youthful, frank, uncommitted, and quick. Its extremes of high-spiritedness and glum disappointment expanded the horizons of a battered and jaded Europe. This was a remarkable time for the American writer.

Among these writers, Sherwood Anderson was the seceder *par excellence*. An Ohio business-man, married, he suffered a nervous breakdown and walked out on both his family and his job. Establishing himself in Chicago, he began to write, and at the age of forty – with the encouragement of Carl Sandburg and the Chicago author Floyd Dell – produced *Windy McPherson's Son* (1916), a novel about a man not unlike himself, who also abandons his business in order to 'find truth'. In one way or another, this was to be Anderson's pattern for the rest of his career. As his novels and short stories

1. D. H. Lawrence lived for a while in the Taos colony: his widow still does.

were imagined variations on the theme of his own life, so in writing of his own life (*A Story-Teller's Story*, 1924; *Tar, a Midwest Childhood*, 1926) he made himself over in the desired image of the artist in revolt. Carl Sandburg and Gertrude Stein met in his work. With the one can be associated his eagerness to write of the Midwesterners from whom he came, whose speech was in his ears and whose dilemmas he thought he deeply understood. From the other he derived great technical benefit. He learned from her *Three Lives* and *Tender Buttons* (1914) the necessity for craftsmanship that made it a complicated process to tell the truth. This respect for technique, characteristic of the time, often saved him from the incoherence which lay near the heart of his subject. Yet, while liking Gertrude Stein, with whom he became firm friends when he visited Paris in 1921, he was shrewd enough to see that her own writing failed to communicate. She was important, he wrote in 1922, 'not for the public but for the artist who happens to work with words as his material'.

How much he managed to learn of his craft was shown by his first widely successful book, *Winesburg, Ohio* (1919). This is a collection of stories, or sketches (it was always being denied that Anderson's stories were stories), about a small town of the kind Anderson knew from his boyhood. Some of the characters are old, crabbed, and eccentric, or borne down by failure. Others are restless adolescents. But all – young, old and in-between – are puzzled people. They have been misunderstood, they seek to understand, they long for love and recognition; or else, wrapped in their obsessive fancies, they voice ideas though certain no one will listen to them. Winesburg holds them all, as Spoon River cemetery holds its inhabitants. Their dreams burgeon when its streets have gone dark. The stories are given unity by their common setting, for most people in Winesburg know something of one another. Yet the closeness of acquaintance underlines the degree to which its citizens are remote from one another. A young reporter named George Willard enters the stories, in some as an actor, in others merely a confidant. His presence also helps to correct the centrifugal tendency of Anderson's plots; and his departure from Winesburg at the end of the book, bound for the City on the morning train, gathers all the sketches together in a young man's vision of escape.

The stories in *Winesburg* are uneven in merit. The young, and their awkward love affairs, are beautifully rendered, for the Andersonian yearning has exactly the quality of adolescence. Some of the elders, too, are sensitively defined – as in 'The Philosopher', where the half-mad Dr Percival declares that 'everyone in the world is Christ and they are all crucified'. The effect of the story lies in the fact that, while this assertion is almost ludicrously untrue of the doctor's immediate situation, it nevertheless contains a general truth.

Though Winesburg is a credible place, it is not Anderson's explanation of small-town life. He wrote the book in a Chicago lodging-house, and said that 'the hint for almost every character was taken from my fellow-lodgers..., many of whom had never lived in a village'. To him, Americans are the same wherever they officially reside. All are foot-loose, homeless seekers; few find what they are looking for. He explored the search for 'truth' through a succession of novels and stories. On the whole, the stories are better, for Anderson seems to think in episodes, and his novels therefore are apt to consist of moments of perception set in long tracts of questioning. At his best, as in 'The Egg' and 'I Want to Know Why' (from the collection called *The Triumph of the Egg*, 1921) he gives memorable glimpses of impotence or grief, and yet manages to suggest some of the sensuous joy of living. The weakness in Anderson has been his inability to develop sufficiently his main theme of aspiration toward liberty. One wearies of the perpetual questing of his characters, their reiterated insistence on the confusion of life and of their thoughts. Too often the confusion seems to have been in Anderson's own mind. Floyd Dell, reviewing *Windy Mc-Pherson's Son*, said that it was 'all through, an asking of the question which American literature has hardly as yet begun to ask: "What for?" ' His generation believed in asking the questions and letting the answers take care of themselves;

and what he wrote therefore meant a great deal to the younger men who followed him.

Sherwood Anderson, as Alfred Kazin has said, made the novel something of a substitute for poetry and religion, whereas Sinclair Lewis made it a branch of superior journalism. Where Anderson stressed the mystery and bafflement of life, Lewis recorded its details with the cynical expertise of a star reporter. In 1920, with the publication of his *Main Street*, it seemed that he had struck a mortal blow at the 'booboisie'. Another blow, of no less weight, was delivered two years later in *Babbitt*. The first had dealt with small-town life, exposing the utterly intolerable drabness, narrowness, and complacency of Gopher Prairie, Minnesota. The second performed a similar office for the American city ('Zenith') and for the business-men who were so proud of their place in it. Only Mencken was able to assault stupidity and banality with so much verve; the novels of Lewis were wonderfully readable sermons to the kind of texts that Mencken gleefully printed in the 'Americana' column of the *American Mercury* – a magazine that he founded, with Nathan, in 1924. Somewhere – in Iowa or Nebraska or Alabama – somewhere outside the one or two great cities where the enlightened few contrived to endure, there were follies of a gorgeous nature, that cried out for a satirist. This was Mencken's refrain: and Lewis provided the satire. In *Arrowsmith* (1925) he portrayed the wanderings of an honest man through the idiocies and corruptions of America. In *Elmer Gantry* (1927) he focused upon the national appetite for fake religious movements. In *Dodsworth* (1929), which described the sufferings of an automobile manufacturer on his first trip to Europe, Lewis shifted his ground somewhat, to compare America with Europe (one of the stock obligations of the American novelist). Novels continued to flow from him; in 1930 he won the Nobel prize for literature (the first American to do so). But with successive books, his touch became less sure, his criticism of America more perfunctory, until, near the end of his life, he startled a European audience by telling them, 'I wrote *Babbitt* not out of hatred for him but out of love.'

When one re-examines *Main Street* and *Babbitt* at this distance from their first appearance, it becomes clear that Lewis belonged in many ways to the people he castigated, that when he wrote of George Folansbee Babbitt, the 'realtor' of Zenith, he did not know whether he loved or hated him. Having subjected Gopher Prairie and Zenith to a merciless accounting; having laboured to convince the reader of the appalling silliness of their citizens; having shown the cruelty with which they treat the outsider: having done all this, Lewis still lingers over his material, taking back half of what he has said. Thus in *Main Street* Carol Kennicott leaves her tiresome husband. So might Sherwood Anderson have ended a novel. But Lewis brings her back to Dr Kennicott – a solution he can make plausible only by suggesting that, after all, her husband is a sturdy, honest person, while Carol has been weak and self-centred. We see that, in comparison with Mencken or Ring Lardner, Lewis is basically much fonder of his America. It is raw, as he was raw when he found himself an undergraduate among smooth Eastern boys at Yale. But it is what he knows; and familiarity breeds affection as well as contempt. Perry Miller has noted that Lewis adored Dickens, and had nothing to do with Gertrude Stein or other prophets of the age. But perhaps the America of the 1920s held fewer resources for social satire than Dickens's England. At any rate, though Dickens had his faults, he never tried to pass Mr Podsnap off as Mr Pickwick. This is what Sinclair Lewis tends to do; his aim is divided, and his total effect therefore blurred, though each part may have the exactitude of a Sears, Roebuck catalogue. The *New Yorker*, when it started in 1925, frankly addressed itself to the 'caviar sophisticates' and 'not [to] the old lady in Dubuque'. Lewis was less certain about either his audience or his target; the impossible creature from Dubuque might turn out to be a relative, and he liked his relatives.

Ernest Hemingway's answer to the problem was to avoid the orthodoxies of the American scene, and to set his characters – even where they were Americans – in other contexts. The answer fitted his own experiences, as an ambulance-driver and then – after the Armistice – as a correspondent covering the Graeco-Turkish imbroglio for a Canadian newspaper. As we have said of Stephen Crane, the warcorrespondent is free from all ties except the requirement to cable his story punctually to some far-off agency that pays him. A craftsman in words but not a city-intellectual, he is a member of a secular order with its own special rules and immunities. Hemingway's early choice of career developed by stages toward the craft of fiction. When he arrived in Paris in 1922, bearing a letter of introduction from Sherwood Anderson to Gertrude Stein, he was still a humble novice in the world of letters, grateful when she and Ezra Pound bluepencilled his first efforts (some of them poems). It was she, according to Miss Stein, who first told him about bull-fighting. As late as 1926, when he parodied Sherwood Anderson's *Dark Laughter* in his hilarious *Torrents of Spring*, Hemingway still had a good deal of 'literature' to get out of his system. Dedicated to Mencken and interlarded with quotations from Fielding, his book was full of skittish references to Henry James, the *American Mercury*, Sinclair Lewis, and so on. He also still had the American scene – especially the woods of northern Michigan, where he had hunted and fished as a boy. These are the setting of several of his first stories. The war, which haunted him, was not yet a subject he could handle at length. His first important novel, *Fiesta*[1] (1926), treated the war as the recent disaster which nobody cared to talk about, though it had maimed his hero sexually and had blighted the other characters in less evident ways.

The narrator-hero, Jake Barnes, is an American newspaperman working in Paris. He is in love with Lady Brett Ashley, a beautiful and promiscuous woman who returns his love, as far as this is possible. The other main characters are Brett's bankrupt fiancé Mike (a Scotsman), an American writer-friend of Jake's named Bill – and another American, Robert Cohn. Jake, Bill, Mike, and Brett form a circle of understanding from which Cohn is excluded by an inability to share their code. This code of behaviour, though rarely

1. Published in America with the title of *The Sun Also Rises*.

made articulate, is extremely important to Hemingway; as Lady Brett says, 'It's sort of what we have instead of God.' Obedience to the code, and departures from it, give shape to most of Hemingway's writing. There is a resemblance here to Rudyard Kipling, another novelist whose characters often find in action an outlet for an almost mystical sense of commitment. On the surface, the 'commitment' of Jake and his associates does not amount to much. Their behaviour could be called foolish and irresponsible; for example, they drink too much. Yet those who are 'all right' can spot one another at once. They are usually expert in certain subjects, but must never attitudinize. Understatement is the rule; and Hemingway likes some Englishmen – Harris in *Fiesta*, the big-game hunter in 'The Short Happy Life of Francis Macomber' – for being inarticulate as well as competent. His favoured ones form a freemasonry, with a private, joking conversation-slang of their own. A key-word is *aficionado*, applied here to those who know a great deal about bull-fighting. Jake and his friends meet at Pamplona for the bull-fights; Jake has *aficion*, and 'those who were aficionados could always get rooms even when the hotel was full'.

Outside the charmed circle stands Cohn. He is too voluble; he discusses his emotions. After a brief affair with Brett, he refuses to face with dignity the fact that she no longer cares for him. He administers a thrashing to a young matador Brett has attracted, only to discover that the other man has somehow worsted him spiritually. Indeed, for Hemingway defeat is a more interesting condition than victory. Men all, sooner or later, go down to defeat: it is how they face the ordeal that determines their status. This is not to say that life holds no pleasures for Hemingway. He, and his characters, set great store by food and wine, sex, trout-fishing, skiing, shooting, and so on. But these are all tests of manhood, of *aficion*; in the autobiographical *Green Hills of Africa* (1935) Hemingway naïvely confesses just how much his sense of his own integrity depends upon the result of each day's pursuit of game. The ultimate test, for him as for Stephen Crane, is death. In war, badly wounded, Hemingway had felt its presence so close that nothing else afterwards could ever seem as real. He must push nearer and nearer to whatever truth its proximity held. For this reason the bull-fight, in which the skirmish with death is ritualized, holds a particular prominence in his imagination. He writes admirably of its dangers and beauties: in fact he has consecrated a whole book (*Death in the Afternoon*, 1933) to the subject.

It has often been said against Hemingway that he gravely handicaps himself by dealing with violent action rather than the act of intelligence: that he has falsely equated expression with insincerity. It is true that he seems most at home with characters who say little. His code does at times appear absurd; in his poorer writing (as in *Across the River and Into the Trees*, 1950), knowledge degenerates into knowingness – on the level of what to tip a waiter – and courage is confused with the assertion of maleness. The nihilism of *Fiesta* and of its successor, *Farewell to Arms* (1929) seems a convincing statement of the mood of war and of the post-war years. The stunned nerves of the 1920s arouse our sympathy. But the mere numbness of a Harry Morgan (*To Have and Have Not*, 1937), does not, in a later decade. Nor is the famous prose, with its purposely flat simplicity, altogether free from monotony. And Hemingway's dialogue has a little too much stylized repartee:

> 'They got a cure for that.'
> 'No, they haven't got a cure for anything.'
> ('A Pursuit Race')

Yet Hemingway is a writer of remarkable gifts. His initial contribution, in the novel and in the short stories of *In Our Time* (1924), *Men Without Women* (1927), and *Winner Take Nothing* (1933), has had an extraordinary influence upon others: so much so that the innumerable imitations of Hemingway have almost spoiled one's palate for the genuine article. But on re-reading, his first novels and his best stories are still powerful and fresh. Rigorously confining himself to the matter in hand, refusing the aid of literary artifices, Hemingway extracts an amazing richness from his rare excursions below the surface of the narrative. In *A Farewell to Arms*, for example, the rhythm of the seasons is unobtrusively matched to the course of the campaign, with no editorializing from the author. Victory comes in the spring. In the autumn it is otherwise:

There was fighting for that mountain too, but it was not successful, and in the fall when the rains came the leaves all fell from the chestnut trees and the branches were bare and the trunks black with rain.

Equally effective is this brief mention of the blood dripping on to the hero from a dying soldier who lies on the stretcher above him in an ambulance:

The drops fell very slowly, as they fall from an icicle after the sun has gone.

Hemingway was a careful writer who never hurried into print. Revealing (in *The Green Hills of Africa*) a curious embarrassment at the thought that he might be mistaken for an *artist*, he has justified his occupation to himself as a *craft*, requiring the same slow, hard apprenticeship as fishing or any other skill. (Though he does reveal in his choice of titles that he was aware of literature – a man who might be a subscriber, as he was in fact, to *Partisan Review*.) If he was liable to exalt form to the detriment of content, he followed his craft faithfully. Within his own framework of motive and event, he was a virtuoso. For instance, when he reproduces the speech of people who are not English (notably in *For Whom the Bell Tolls*, 1940, where he is among Spanish peasantry), he renders their words in an ingenious 'translated' English which reminds the reader that they are actually speaking in Spanish. Again, in *For Whom the Bell Tolls* he shows himself perfectly able to handle educated people whose emotions and ideas are complex. This book, though it contains some excellent writing, is not, however, his best. One never fully accepts the juxtaposition of the Hemingway-person in his writing with the simple man. Is the waiter really a friend? Does the peasant really respect the foreigner? Or is there something inadequate in this figure of the

American-foreigner? What is he doing away from his own country, his own job? The journalist/correspondent cannot reach to the heart of experience in a strange land. Nor can the soldier, whose life is divided between the destruction at the front and the counterfeit gaiety of furlough. It is proxy living, in pidgin-language.

Whether or not Hemingway pondered such problems, his short novel, *The Old Man and the Sea* (1952), avoids the insincerities that surround the concept of the *aficionado*. He tells of a Cuban fisherman who is a simple man but not a simpleton. The Cuban's fight with a great fish is in a way an illustration of the Hemingway code, but in its purest form. There is hardly a trace in it of the braggart sportsman, or of the sham lyricism that overcomes most writers when they discuss the lives of the Latin poor. After *Across the River and Into the Trees*, Hemingway told an interviewer that

In writing I have moved through arithmetic, through plane geometry and algebra, and now I am in calculus.

At the time this sounded like the arrogance of a man who had become hopelessly entangled in his own legend. Indeed, it had an odd echo of Gertrude Stein. There was the same fatal obsession with technique, as if that could transfigure the banality of what was being conveyed. The *Old Man*, however, seemed to justify Hemingway's pride. Beginning, like Sherwood Anderson, with the notion of man shut off from his fellows, he passed somewhat unconvincingly (in *To Have and Have Not* and *For Whom the Bell Tolls*) to the theme of human solidarity. In *The Old Man* he managed to tell a story of a man on his own that is a parable of all humanity. Yet it was not the large novel Hemingway was rumoured to be producing. The only published works of his final years – years of depression, culminating in suicide – were some distressingly slack and mannered pieces on Spanish bullfighters, which might almost have been concocted by a parodist. One slim posthumous volume has appeared: *A Moveable Feast* (1964), a memoir of Paris in the early 1920s. It is a real achievement: alive, precise, firmly shaped. The character sketches are tight with the sense of affection or antipathy, alliance or combat. He is nice about Ezra Pound and a few others, and amusing yet rather malicious on Gertrude Stein and Scott Fitzgerald. But this is a sad small book for Hemingway to have ended on. It is as if he were an old champion, turning over his scrapbook to comfort and hurt himself. The prose is 'in condition', the demeanour of an old man who manages to hold himself like a young one.

Like Anderson, Lewis, and Hemingway, the writer Scott Fitzgerald grew up in the Middle West. Like Lewis, he came East to college, though instead of Yale he chose Princeton. The Middle West was the place of origins: the destination, for Fitzgerald, was somewhere splendid, improvident, aristocratic, where everyone was (like himself and his wife) young, handsome, witty, and free. His writing parallels his own experience to a poignant degree; both are the record of youth searching wildly for a perfection that does not exist. Fitzgerald longed for some central certainty, from which he could look out upon the world, safe from hurt. So, he attended a university for the sons of well-to-do Easterners, and strove to be a success among his classmates. In the army he envied those who had been in action, and had thus entered the inner sanctum of danger. He wrote in a short story ('The Offshore Pirate'), of men coming out of the trenches, watched by the hero, that 'the sweat and mud they wore seemed only one of those ineffable symbols of aristocracy that were forever eluding him'.

Since Fitzgerald had been unable to adopt these symbols, he concentrated upon others: in particular, upon the aristocracy of wealth. The very rich, as he told Hemingway and as he said in 'The Rich Boy', 'are different from you and me. They possess and enjoy early, and it does something to them.' What it did to them was not necessarily good, nor likely to endear them to the rest of the population. Fitzgerald knew this; and that the idea of American aristocracy was in large measure spurious, partly because the continuity essential to the aristocratic ideal was lacking in American life, where 'there was no norm, it was doubtful if there ever had been a norm'. Nevertheless, like Edith Wharton he clung to a conception of a specially privileged group, while realizing with her that the actual group was worth little. But whereas her group served as a theoretical standard, a repository of good manners and fairly good behaviour against which to judge the shoddy conduct of the rest of society, Fitzgerald had no idea of contrasting one group against another. He was merely fascinated by the magic properties of wealth, and by the immunity it could purchase – immunity from everybody else who was an outsider. With wealth – and also youth, looks, and success, which were part of aristocracy – one was an *aficionado* on the grand scale. All doors opened; all headwaiters were deferential; all boat-trains, liners, limousines, suites, and mansions were available. One could follow the sun. Poverty was mean, grey, narrow; with money one could be generous, expansive, original. The minor disasters of life – the lost ticket, the wet holiday, the cramped quarters – could all be remedied. Largesse was a word that meant both a tip and a way of life.

It was an adolescent way of life, and perhaps Fitzgerald never entirely got away from it. Certainly his first books, the collections of stories (*Flappers and Philosophers*, 1920; *Tales of the Jazz Age*, 1922) and the novels (*This Side of Paradise*, 1920; *The Beautiful and Damned*, 1922), are callow by comparison with his later work. His characters are too evidently projections of himself, dreaming extravagantly and extravagantly disappointed. The hero of *This Side of Paradise*, looking back gloomily over his twenty-four years, reflects 'I know myself but that is all'. *All!* This hero, and the other young men and women, are almost wilfully immature. Fresh from their fashionable schools and colleges, they have no desire to develop; development means growing old, and they clutch at their small score of years as though it were unthinkable to be over thirty. Their love affairs are febrile, yet passionless; while the idea of parenthood is repellent to them – how could any generation be younger than their own?

However, even at its most juvenile, Fitzgerald's work was fluent and carefully constructed. From the first, he meant to be a writer. If his characters seemed frivolous, and his own life equally so, Fitzgerald still regarded himself as a professional. He was, so to speak, seriously frivolous, as serious as Hemingway was behind the camouflage of stiff drinks and sporting gear. 'I know myself' was not altogether a brash claim. He had an astonishing knack of observing sensation while he indulged in it.

The only way I can describe young Anson Hunter is to approach him as if he were a foreigner and cling stubbornly to my point of view. If I accept his for a moment I am lost – I have nothing to show but a preposterous movie.

That is how he approaches the theme of great wealth, in 'The Rich Boy'. He is tempted by it, and he struggles to maintain a detachment rendered difficult by the fact that he has nothing positive to offer in place of the chilly aplomb of 'the very rich'. Or rather, what he has to offer is confused in his mind with wealth. It is: joy, beauty, tenderness: all of which fade with age, for they are all aspects of youth.

In *The Great Gatsby* (1925), Fitzgerald shows wealth and youth at variance. Jay Gatsby, despite his huge house, his lavish parties, and his mysteriously dishonourable sources of income, is primarily a spokesman for youth. His life, for all its grotesque external clutter, is dedicated to the recovery and renewal of an early love affair with Daisy. It is for this pure end that he has amassed his fortune. But Daisy is married to Tom Buchanan; and they are 'the very rich'. Though Tom has a mistress, and Daisy has never forgotten Gatsby, their wealth has made them peculiarly invulnerable. In the end, the Buchanans are still living together and Gatsby is dead – killed by a demented creature who does not realize that the Buchanans are to blame for his misfortunes. So the deluded faces the corrupt, and goes down to defeat. The situation is slightly reminiscent of that in Henry James's *The American*, in which the trusting Christopher Newman discovers that his wealth is powerless against the intrenched assurance of the Bellegarde family. The clash of wills is more

impressive in James's novel because the two sides are sharply
differentiated, and neither can be called shoddy, as we may
call the standards of Daisy, or even of Gatsby. Nevertheless,
The Great Gatsby is a brilliant little novel. Fitzgerald really
knows his world of wealth; and whether the characters are
rich or not, the appearance, gestures, and conversation of
each are rendered with an exact and witty ease. The narrator, in the scene but like Fitzgerald not wholly of it, gives the
story an extra dimension of detachment. And, above all, the
book has a moving elegiac quality. Never completely sup-
pressed even in the most brazen scenes, this quality wells up
when the narrator remembers his Midwestern childhood,
and again, finely, at the end, where Gatsby's effort to recapture the past and carry it into the future with him is related
to the old American dream of a new world, when, three centuries earlier,

for a transitory enchanted moment man must have held his
breath in the presence of this continent, ... face to face for the last
time in history with something commensurate to his capacity for
wonder.

After *The Great Gatsby*, Fitzgerald produced acceptable
short stories, but did not finish another novel until *Tender is
the Night* (1934). The reviewers, in the socially-conscious
1930s, dismissed it as a hangover from a vanished era. Most
of the expatriates were home again. The money had run out,
Europe had turned sour. But Fitzgerald wrote of an American expatriate, Dick Diver, disintegrating from too much
money and domestic problems, coming back to America at
last not in repentance, but to hide from abject failure. The
reviewers were too hard on *Tender is the Night*, though recent critics have more than redressed the balance. In some
respects it is a better book than *Gatsby*; it is more ambitious
and reveals an even more sensuously alert intelligence. But
the intelligence is of a professional order. Fitzgerald has
learned more fully how to construct a novel; he incorporates
a wider range of characters; his prose is a constant pleasure.
Yet the early limitations have remained, and the elegiac
note that sustains *Gatsby* is here flawed. There is a nobility

in the error of Gatsby; there is a tinge of self-pity in those of Diver which seems to have been passed on unwittingly by the author. Nevertheless, *Tender is the Night* is abundantly talented. One never feels that its author has dried up, as critics alleged at the time. That Fitzgerald continued to hold on to his technical gift is demonstrated by his unfinished novel of Hollywood, *The Last Tycoon* (1941), as well as by the documents in the posthumous volume called *The Crack-up* (1945). Many American novelists have written themselves out, being wedded to insubstantial themes, and insufficiently devoted to their craft. Hemingway and Fitzgerald both had the devotion, and if Fitzgerald had lived he might perhaps have joined Hemingway in proving that professional intelligence can lead the writer toward a deeper knowledge.

If Fitzgerald is, rightly or wrongly, associated with 'the Jazz Age' of the 1920s, the name of John Dos Passos is linked with the next decade, when he became one of America's most prominent novelists. Yet he had already made his name. Born in the same year as *Fitzgerald*, he displayed an equal precocity: his first novel, *One Man's Initiation – 1917*, was published in 1920, the same year as *This Side of Paradise*. And with his second book, *Three Soldiers* (1921), Dos Passos took his place among the young writers (including the middle-aged young man, Sherwood Anderson) who were defining the character of their time. His hero in *Three Soldiers*, John Andrews, is a composer who enlists because he is tired of freedom and hopes 'to start rebuilding the fabric of his life, out of real things this time, out of work and comradeship and scorn'. But instead, military life (in America and then in France) arouses a wild repugnance in him. At the end, a deserter writing a piece of music inspired by Flaubert's *Tentation de St Antoine*, he is arrested by the military police and marched off, leaving his unfinished score to blow away in the wind (instead of taking it with him like a sensible fellow). So, Dos Passos seems to imply, must all sensitive men suffer at the hands of the machine: the final chapter is called 'Under the Wheels'. The only gesture left to the Artist is

secession – if the world will let him secede. This will be recognized as one of the typical situations of the early 1920s –
the period when there was actually a little magazine called
Secession. The Artist (including Dos Passos himself, a product
of Harvard) is right, the world is wrong. John Andrews
among the uniformed ranks is, in the words of the old joke,
the only one in step.

How, then, was Dos Passos able to write the trilogy *U.S.A.*,
which has been described as an example of 'the collectivist
novel'? The answer is a commentary on the evolution of the
American intellectual in his 'journeys between wars' (a
phrase that Dos Passos used as a title for a collection of his
travel-writings). Briefly, social protest supplanted aesthetic
protest. The anger of the Artist at the materialism of American life modulated into the anger of the Radical at social in-
justices. Dos Passos did not become a 'proletarian' novelist;
there had always been an element of radicalism in his work.
From the beginning, he tried to represent both the lonely
individual and the sensations of the crowd. In *Three Soldiers*
he introduces three very dissimilar men, as if to embrace the
whole of American society. But two drop out, leaving the
stage to Andrews, who in his turn abandons his former interest in 'comradeship', to voice aesthetic protest.

However, in *Manhattan Transfer* (1925) the collectivist principle is more confidently tackled. Dos Passos now attempts
to crowd all of New York into one book, by methods that
foreshadow *U.S.A.* There is a multitude of characters,
whose lives interweave, on various social levels; they are
traced through twenty years or so, growing up, growing old,
rising and falling in the success scale. The general narrative
is doggedly prosaic, the dialogue painstakingly accurate.
But there are passages of impressionist description. And there
is still a central character, Jimmy Herf, who is clearly a descendant of John Andrews. In some respects Herf is worse off.
He is no longer the Artist, merely the Would-Be Artist, intelligent but ineffectual. Still, at the end he secedes. In his
case the act is not convincing; it is a reprieve-happy-ending
tacked on to a tale of trial and conviction. Others have been

eaten up by the voracious city; Herf, walking out of it, away
from his unimportant job and his broken marriage with only
a few cents in his pocket, is a figure out of Sherwood Anderson mixed up in a metropolis from Dreiser.

With the *U.S.A.* trilogy (*42nd Parallel*, *1919*, and *The Big
Money*, published in 1930, 1932, and 1936), Dos Passos has
no longer even his faith in secession. He covers the same
ground, but with a larger sweep, taking all America into
account. The narrative swings matter-of-factly from one to
another of his many characters: the handsome, fraudulent
public men; the successful and frustrated women; those who
drink themselves to disaster; the radicals with their 'comradeship and scorn'; those who betray the workers; the
aesthetic poseurs: these and others are handled by Dos Passos with a circumstantial unloving competence. The narrative is accompanied by three famous devices, of which two –
the Newsreels and the Biographies – emphasize the documentary nature of the trilogy, the concern of the 1930s to
write of real gardens with real toads in them. The Newsreels
are a medley of newspaper headlines, fragments of popular
songs, etc.; the Biographies are brief, vivid sketches of
important men and women who typify the periods covered
by the work. The other device – that of the Camera Eye – is
a survival from the aesthetic Dos Passos. Keeping pace chronologically (more or less) with the other parts, the Camera
Eye sections, written in a prose-poetry with hints of E. E.
Cummings and Gertrude Stein, look out on the crass scene
from the viewpoint of a person one assumes to be the author.

As in *Manhattan Transfer*, but now with an added anger
and despair, *U.S.A.* covers the defeat of the individual on all
fronts. The rich are all corrupt; even if (like some of Upton
Sinclair's heroes) they give away all they have and join the
poor, they do not find salvation. For though the poor may
be decent people, they will accomplish nothing. Sacco and
Vanzetti go to their death in spite of years of radical effort.
The unjust triumph, only to sicken of their success. There are
few happy people in this trilogy, whose tone grows progres-
sively darker. In sum, it is a massive indictment of America.

It might be unreadable to-day if Dos Passos had merely ask-his riddle, damned his capitalists, and then ended with a vision of the workers' paradise. But he comforts himself with no such easy hope. He concludes, instead, with a sketch of a nameless vagrant, not an Andrews or a Herf but an average citizen, trying to thumb a lift along a highway that leads nowhere.

Yet though this is a less superficial view than that of Marxist novels of the time, it does not seem quite adequate. *U.S.A.* is still a unique achievement in breadth, and as an attempt to incorporate within the framework of the novel everything from tabloid news to esoteric verse. But it is already slightly antiquated. A century hence it may appeal as a kind of academy-piece of the 1930s, large and workman-like – a Frith's *Derby Day* done without joviality. It is readable; one likes the endless, crammed sensation, and one appreciates the effort to diversify the structure. But the cracks show; the less ambitious experiments of *Manhattan Transfer* are almost preferable. The Camera Eye, for example, is brilliant in parts, and its intention – presumably to leaven the mass with some evidence of sensibility – is laudable. But why call it by such an objective, 'documentary' name when it is such a subjective device? And if it is a subjective device, why disconcert the reader by allowing it occasionally to cover the same situation as the narrative? Again, the handling of the characters is open to criticism. Some disappear when they are just beginning to arouse one's interest; others linger on like guests after a party whose host is unable to get rid of them. And the Joycean habit of running words together – *rumbottle*, *fruit-steamer*, *icegrey* – is pointless, once the novelty has worn off. In short, the honesty and the experimentations of *U.S.A.* are not enough to make it a great book. It is, though, a good book, better than some subsequent novels by Dos Passos which exude a mellowly patriotic odour like those American tobaccos that are heavily flavoured with maple syrup.

There are similar inadequacies in the work of James T. Farrell and John Steinbeck, writers with considerable gifts whose best work belongs to the Depression decade. Neither was a Marxist, though like Dos Passos they responded to the radical politics of the period. Farrell wrote of Chicago, and of the Catholic Irish among whom he had grown up. These, though poor, are not slum-dwellers. Their ruin is moral rather than economic. Like Dos Passos' U.S.A., Farrell's Chicago is a place where life is poisoned at the source. Studs Lonigan, the central character of Farrell's trilogy of that name, can find no fulfilment. With his friends, he can express himself only in violence, with now and then a lurch into sentiment or false piety. Farrell, however, has another character, Danny O'Neill, who rises out of this meaninglessly destructive environment, via a tetralogy. (An era that complained of the *longueurs* of Henry James was ready to absorb enormous novels, on the popular level of *Anthony Adverse* and *Gone With the Wind* as well as on the rather more demanding plane of Dos Passos and Farrell. On their plane, it seemed that they too must tell all: as though by mere multiplication of detail one might arrive at truth, much as the urban ecologists accumulated data to support a thesis that somehow disappeared among its own corroborations.) O'Neill would in an earlier generation have served as an instance of success, since after all he overcomes the dangers that have dragged down Lonigan. But Farrell, and Don Passos, find difficulty in reconciling the successful individual (as exemplified in their own careers) with their feeling that nothing good can come out of a corrupt America. They seem happiest in opposition. Perhaps the 'scorn' Dos Passos speaks of is a necessary ingredient to most American novelists of this century. With Farrell, the sincerity of this scorn is not in question; nor is the skill of his novels' surface texture. But underneath are confusions that weaken his work. The same can be said of John Steinbeck, who (in *Of Mice and Men*, 1937, and *The Grapes of Wrath*, 1939) records certain surface elements of the Depression years with amazing fidelity, but whose efforts at deeper understanding alternate awkwardly between a *mystique* of the Land, an unfocused radicalism, and a sort of biological contempt for humankind.

One aspect of the Depression mirrored in Steinbeck, who

writes admirably of his own California, is the interest in regionalism. Against the stereotyped sprawl of America was contrasted the place, the region, the person who by standing still had retained his individuality. Perhaps there was no genuine region in America except the South, which though a vast and various area was united by historical ties of a special permanence. At any rate, this period saw the emergence of several Southern regionalisms. There was the sociological group at Chapel Hill, North Carolina; the literary group of Sewanee, Tennessee; – and there was William Faulkner's Yoknapatawpha County, Mississippi (with its county seat at Jefferson). Faulkner lived in Mississippi, though Yoknapatawpha – the scene of most of his writing since *Sartoris* (1929) – does not exist on a map; indeed, some Southerners maintain that his version of the South bears no resemblance to reality. The vital point, however, is that Faulkner has been able to use the South as a basis for literature. One might reverse this and say that the South has used *him*, since his vision of it is obsessive and ambivalent. At one moment he is the Southern aristocrat, proud and courtly, watching his plantation fall a prey to the avarice of an upstart. At another moment he is proving that the aristocrat is no better than the interloper, and that the fine Southern tradition is a falsehood. At still another moment he is the champion of the illiterate poor white; and then, of the Negro – or of the Indians who owned the land before white and black ever came to the country.

In fact, Faulkner's vision of the South is not merely complex: at times it is incoherent, and turns back upon itself. But in any one story or novel he is usually engrossed with one particular facet of the vision; and it is possible to state his position in broad terms. A clue is provided by these words:

There are people who have an appetite for grief, pleasure is not strong enough and they crave pain, mithridatic stomachs which must be fed on poisoned bread, natures so doomed that no prosperity can soothe their ragged and dishevelled desolation.

The quotation might well be from Faulkner, though actually it is from Emerson's essay on 'The Tragic' (1844). One of the key-words in this chapter has been *defeat*. Hemingway's people are defeated; so are Fitzgerald's, Dos Passos', Farrell's. Another key-word has been *secession*. Faulkner's people also experience defeat, but they do not secede. Their ancestors attempted secession from the North, only to be beaten. The Civil War, the shattered economy, the emphasis on family, the affection and hatred engendered by the Negro: all these have bound the South in a communion of defeat that involves the individual beyond any possibility of escape. For Faulkner, the key-word is *doom*. One should qualify this statement by admitting that some of his writing is wildly funny – for example, the short story 'A Courtship', or the horse-trading episode in *The Hamlet* (1940). But the statement still holds good if we substitute for *doom* a somewhat lighter word – say *fatality*. (Both words occur frequently in Faulkner.)

His characters' involvement with one another is taken for granted by all of them, and Faulkner offers no explanation to the reader. There is a Faulknerian 'code' which like Hemingway's has to do with courage, honour, duty. But if Hemingway is tongue-tied about his code, Faulkner in some of his books is still less explicit. We perceive gradually, in tracking through his most important clusters of novels – *The Sound and the Fury* (1929), *As I Lay Dying* (1930), *Sanctuary* (1931), *Light in August* (1932) – that the code operates as a compulsion. Its servants could not act other than as they do, and Faulkner takes it for granted that although certain acts will arouse intense opposition, all parties to the quarrel grasp its general principles. Though many of his characters behave stupidly, obscurely, evilly, they have no hesitation. Their gestures are willed, positive, firm, even when they are negative gestures – as when hunted men (in the story 'Red Leaves', or at the end of *Light in August*) cease to offer resistance. There is indeed a curious combination of violence and passivity in Faulkner. At their most heated moments his characters are apt to behave mechanically, as though agents rather than actors in the drama. This frozen passion is well conveyed in a typical piece of the author's prose (from *Light in August*):

He turned into the road at that slow and ponderous gallop, the two of them, man and beast, leaning a little stiffly forward as though in some juggernautish simulation of terrific speed though the actual speed itself was absent, as if in that cold and implacable and un-deviating conviction of both omnipotence and clairvoyance of which they both partook known destination and speed were not necessary.

The reader is in the position of an inexperienced judge, hear-ing a case of some intricate tribal wrong, in which the evi-dence is thrown at him haphazard, in which some of the witnesses refuse to speak at all, and in which he feels un-easily that no verdict is feasible, since the litigants have a different set of moral scruples from his own. The suit has been arranged by an outside agency; for the litigants, the court is only a place in which to vent their grievances. The law, if any, lies in the complex of experience in Faulkner's imagined county of Yoknapatawpha. Its furthest basis in time is the land, the wilderness so beautifully evoked in his long story 'The Bear'. Closest to the land are the Indians, of the period just before the white man drove them out. But they are degenerate at this stage, with their slaves and their ill-run plantations. Man has begun to destroy the wilderness, and has implanted upon it the curse of slavery. All else fol-lows, as Faulkner would say, 'implacably': the inordinate pride, the distorted chivalry, the lost war, the mean com-mercial aftermath, the inescapable Negro presences, the re-bellious sexuality of adolescent girls, the inbred anger of their brothers.

Out pours the whole tormented history of the South, some-times with astonishing lucidity, more often in the rank, over-grown, ornate style that Clifton Fadiman has called Dixie Gongorism. In *The Sound and the Fury*, we are introduced to the Compson family through the mind of the idiot Benjy; and though Faulkner is never more 'difficult' than this, it is a part of his method to plunge the reader into the scene and leave him to find out what everybody is talking about. It is not always easy, where people go by nicknames and ances-tral names are handed on, to discover *who* is being talked about, in which generation: the stories go rooting back into the past, where their plots germinated. Even when the main lines of the story are established, the significant detail is embedded in a mass of information, allusion, and conjecture. The effort of detecting it imposes a considerable and not always justifiable strain upon the reader.

Why, then, do we consent to lose ourselves in the destructive, fantastic chaos of Yoknapatawpha? Partly because in his best books, such as *The Sound and the Fury* and *Light in August*, Faulkner opposes to the idea of doom that of endurance: the latter with the double connotation of suffering and survival. It is the proud who are doomed – the Sartorises, Sutpens, and Compsons – and the humble Negro or poor white who endure. One is not fully persuaded by this pardon for humanity; at times Faulkner appears to be arguing that only a mindless and animal indifference will enable man to preserve himself. But he rises above this level in the rich comedy of Lena Grove's pilgrimage. She is more than a shiftless poor-white girl with an illegitimate baby: she is the huge warm trap of womanhood that awaits all men, no matter what their stratagems of escape. And in the figure of Dilsey, the Negro woman who has tended the doomed Compsons and has 'seed de first en de last', Faulkner makes us believe that the Negroes who have brought the curse to the South are not themselves accursed. Again, in his later work (*Intruder in the Dust*, 1948; *Requiem for a Nun*, 1952; *A Fable*, 1954, which deals with a mutiny in the French army in 1917, on the Western Front; *The Town*, 1957; *The Mansion*, 1959) Faulkner seems to be admitting the contentions of his Nobel Prize speech (1950): namely that the writer must believe in man's future. Hitherto his present-day South had little to recommend it. The novels of his last years show a warmer interest in characters like the lawyer Gavin Stevens who are decent and articulate. The chronicle of the mean, ubiquitous Snopeses has mainly a dimension of length, and lacks the giant quality of a true saga. Yet even here the Faulkner anecdote (as finally illustrated in *The Reivers*, 1962) is amazingly vivid. In his imperious, offhand way, he manages to force the reader into a fascinated acceptance of his Mississippi realm even when it seems most inwardly odd, most contortedly and anachronistically hateful. Few American writers have had such large assurance.

In Thomas Wolfe, also a Southerner, we find rhetorical preoccupations of another order. He combines a kind of Southern romanticism; the Artist-isolation of the 1920s; an earlier, Byronic or Shelleyan personality (like a good Romantic he died young – at the age of thirty-eight); and the documentary fullness of the 1930s. One can assemble some such list and still think of more elements: of Whitman, of Rabelais, even of Swinburne, whose parody of himself ('Nephelidia') could apply also to the 'message' of Wolfe:

Life is the lust of the lamp for the light that is dark till the dawn of the day when we die.

But when the list has been compiled, one still has to say that Thomas Wolfe is nobody else but himself. His novels are a serial outpouring of his own experiences, as a boy in North Carolina, at college, then as a struggling writer (first a playwright), wandering in Europe and returning to live in New York and Brooklyn; and the hero of these adventures, whether called Eugene Gant or George Webber, is unmistakably Wolfe himself, writing a saga that might have been literally almost endless. It is true that in his last years he modified a little his wild determination to absorb the whole of life, to read all the books in all the libraries. But even his diminished scale is bigger than anyone else's. No one but he could have said (in 'The Story of a Novel', 1936) with such deprecating innocence, that

it is a great deal more important to have known one hundred living men and women in New York, to have understood their lives, to have got, somehow, at the root and source from which their natures came than to have seen or passed or talked with 7,000,000 people upon the city streets.

Only one hundred! No one but Wolfe, in the same piece, could have referred to the million-word manuscript of a novel as 'the skeleton of a book'. He knew of course that this was prodigiously long – twice as long as *War and Peace* – but despite all the cutting that his devoted editor Maxwell Perkins nerved him to accomplish, he could not feel that a single word was really redundant. All should go in because all was potentially significant. In four novels, two of them posthumous and all of them mere excerpts from his torrent of manuscript, he had by no means exhausted his material: it was as inexhaustible as life itself – for, as he told Scott Fitzgerald, 'a great writer is not only a leaver-outer but also a putter-inner'. The meaning of life – the demand for reassurances – is his theme. Man – Wolfe – seeks 'a stone, a leaf, an unfound door'; he is lost, as all Americans are lost, because their home is a place from which they have grown away, and which has not yet been replaced by any other permanent or satisfying allegiance:

The deepest search in life ... was man's search to find a father, ... the image of a strength and wisdom external to his need and superior to his hunger ...

This search is pursued by Wolfe through extremes of exuberance and disgust. He embraces life, only to shun it because it horrifies him, and because as a writer his most precious asset is freedom. Lonely and homesick, in America and still more in Europe, he cherishes his comfortless exile, somewhat as Henry Miller did. It gives him the sharpest sense of his own identity, as well as the conditions of efficient work. There are to be friendships but – as in the traditional foreign policy of America – no entangling alliances. Paradoxically, his isolation brings him closest to his own country: 'I discovered America during these years abroad out of my very need of her'.

The faults in Wolfe are those of Hemingway in reverse. Where Hemingway restricts his vocabulary almost to the point of penury, Wolfe errs toward prolixity; he succumbs to high-flown words like *forever* and *nevermore*. Where Hemingway suppresses emotion, Wolfe engulfs the reader in feeling. He sometimes fails to digest his autobiographical material;

we find Gant or Webber dwelling on their physique, their talent, 'successful' people, the malignity of critics, more than is justified by his presentation of them: a neurotic Wolfe glowers visibly out at us, talking a little like Robert Cohn. But though he lapses into errors of which Hemingway is guiltless, and though he is not to be compared with Hemingway as an innovator and an influence on other writers, Thomas Wolfe is not a mediocrity. When he forgets his role of harried, persecuted Artist, and invests his energy and sympathy in the rest of the world, he is a wonderfully pleasing author. Sinclair Lewis realized as much when in his Nobel prize speech he magnanimously praised Wolfe's first, recent book, *Look Homeward Angel* (1929). Sensuous, acute, a natural mimic, Wolfe seizes upon people and places with avidity; his notorious love of food (with its smells, colours, preparations, tastes) is typical of his general appetite for experience. Even where he records hateful or drab experiences, they are not dreary. If he is naïve, he has the writer's essential naïveté: namely, he is sure that what he says matters, and that the subject under his hand, even if it has been done a thousand times already, is as new with possibility as tomorrow morning.

Anderson, Lewis, Hemingway, Fitzgerald, Dos Passos, Farrel, Steinbeck, Faulkner, Wolfe: these are only a few of the novelists and short-story writers to emerge in America after the Armistice. Several of them are dead, and other names are now circulating in their stead. The newer climate is discussed in the final chapter of this book. The older one has passed into history, into acceptance, and almost into staleness, so rapid and ruthless is the sequence of literary generations. Yet these men shared an intellectual climate that in retrospect seems fresher than ours. There was a buoyancy in their atmosphere. In the 1920s they enjoyed a decade of revolt, unfettered by any 'official' view. If their society was in decay, literature itself showed every sign of life. Any fire, it appeared, might contain a phoenix; the important thing was to make a bonfire and set light to it. Though the 1930s brought a grimmer mood, there were still compensations. The re-discovery of America, for the returned expatriates and for those who had never been away, was one. The esteem of Europe was another. Between 1930 and 1938 no less than three Americans (Sinclair Lewis, Eugene O'Neill, and Pearl Buck) won Nobel prizes for literature, two others (Faulkner and Hemingway) were to join them in the 1950s and John Steinbeck in 1962. Continental critics paid the most respectful attention to Faulkner and Steinbeck, and also to Erskine Caldwell, Dashiell Hammett, and others into whose violent chronicles they read profound meanings. (Sometimes, indeed, they mistook for Americans such European imitators of transatlantic toughness as James Hadley Chase and Peter Cheyney.) Many an English writer, depressed by the starched effect of his own prose, envied the relaxed and 'modern' idiom of the Americans even if he did not like what they were saying. Was it the era of the common man, long foretold by Tocqueville? Then the American writer knew how to sound like a common man. Was it the era of exile? The American writer was an old hand at exile: he could show his European colleagues around the place, for he had been there before. What was wrong with the era shows up in his philosophy, which now seems thinner and less coherent than it did at the time. But we should also recognize that he was peculiarly at home in his time, and peculiarly qualified to lead conducted tours around it.

THE AMERICAN THEATRE

EUGENE O'NEILL (1888–1953)

SIDNEY HOWARD (1891–1939)

S. N. BEHRMAN (1893–   )

PHILIP BARRY (1896–1949)

MOSS HART (1904–1961)

GEORGE S. KAUFMAN (1889–1961)

ROBERT SHERWOOD (1896–1955)

ELMER RICE (1892–   )

JOHN HOWARD LAWSON (1895–   )

THORNTON WILDER (1897–   )

MARC CONNELLY (1890–   )

CLIFFORD ODETS (1906–1963)

TENNESSEE WILLIAMS (1914–   )

ARTHUR MILLER (1915–   )

THE AMERICAN THEATRE

—

To an even greater extent than that of England, the American drama of the nineteenth century was a bastard art-form. Its popular manifestations – as in England – had a good deal of vitality. The Negro minstrel show, for example, had developed by 1850 into a formalized three-part amusement that retained its verve for a generation or so. The burlesque (or 'burleycue') performance that emerged a little later was likewise loosely organized in three parts, each with its characteristic routines and vulgarities. Vaudeville – the American equivalent of the Victorian music-hall – managed to be robust without the bumps-and-grinds coarseness that accompanied burlesque. The legitimate theatre, however, produced very few plays of permanent interest. It was an age when the actor and the producer counted for more than the playwright. The big names were those of men like Edwin Forrest, or the Anglo-American Booths, Jeffersons, Boucicaults, Sotherns, and Barrymores, or the actor-manager 'play-doctor' David Belasco. But the play itself was not the thing. Often it was imported from Europe. It seems typical that *Our American Cousin*, the play at which Abraham Lincoln was assassinated in 1865, had been written by an Englishman, Tom Taylor. Often a successful play was an adaptation of a novel – *Uncle Tom's Cabin* and *The Gilded Age* are instances – and so not written in terms of the stage. Where an author like W.D. Howells wrote directly for the theatre, he brought no startling novelty to the medium. The public – as Henry James discovered painfully in London – demanded melodrama lavishly staged. It liked large casts, romantic plots, and spectacular effects. Though it applauded patriotic sentiments, it did not insist on seeing American plays. The absence before 1891 of an adequate international copyright put native playwrights at an added disadvantage, and the growth of syndicates and circuits made it still more

difficult for the young author to gain a hearing. Thus in
1881, the year of Ibsen's *Ghosts*, the American theatre was
represented by *La Belle Russe*, a play concocted by Belasco
out of two written by other authors. It was a melodrama set
in England and first advertised, for reasons of prestige, as
'from the French'. In 1888, the year of Strindberg's *Miss
Julie*, Belasco collaborated with Daniel Frohman to write
and stage a piece entitled *Lord Chumley*. Belasco had a genuine theatrical talent – shortly afterwards he directed a striking production of Sophocles' *Electra* – but there was a vast
gulf between his long span of achievements and those of Ibsen and Strindberg, Hauptmann and Sudermann, or of
George Bernard Shaw (whose first play, *Widowers' Houses*,
was put on in 1892).

The American theatre, then, lagged behind that of the
Continent, or even of England. In 1900 or thereabouts there
was little indication that the United States would make important contributions to world theatre. There were, it is
true, some signs of life in the early years of this century. The
opening of the New Theatre at Chicago in 1906, and of a
similarly named venture three years later in New York,
marked a welcome though abortive attempt to encourage
experimental drama. In 1905 George Pierce Baker was able
to start the course in play-writing that later grew into the
famous 47 Workshop at Harvard. The poet-dramatist William Vaughn Moody was beginning, in *The Great Divide*
(1906) and *The Faith Healer* (1909), to feel his way toward
adult theatre. Though he died in 1910, something of his
sensitive and intelligent approach was evident in two plays
of that year. One, by his former pupil Josephine Peabody,
was *The Piper*, a verse drama on the theme of the Pied Piper
of Hamelin that was chosen from a large field for production
at the new Stratford Memorial Theatre. The other, by
Moody's friend Percy MacKaye, was *The Scarecrow*, a dra-
matization of Hawthorne's fantastic story 'Feathertop'.

But the awakening of the American theatre was not accomplished through poetic drama or through adaptations
like MacKaye's. It was not enough merely to emphasize the

role of the playwright: there had to be a decisive break with
the theatrical conventions of the commercial theatre. By
the start of World War I the necessary conditions for such a
break were present. The Little Theatre movement had got
under way; throughout America small groups of amateurs
were eager to try out new plays, the shorter and simpler the
better. In 1915, a number of artists and writers who made
up a summer colony at Provincetown, Massachusetts, band-
ed together to amuse themselves under the name of the
Provincetown Players. Their first stage was the porch of a
building. Next summer, the young playwright Eugene
O'Neill came to Provincetown and was soon one of the
leaders of the group. The son of a successful actor of the old
school, he knew the theatre from early childhood on. But
he did not make it his livelihood until he had explored the
world outside. He abandoned Princeton for a spell of pros-
pecting with a mining expedition in Honduras. Later, an
enthusiasm for Conrad and Jack London whetted his appetite for adventure at sea. He shipped as a seaman to Buenos
Aires; to South Africa and back to the Argentine; to New
York, and from there on several voyages to England. There
were intermittent illnesses, and periods of beachcombing,
followed by experience as a newspaper reporter. In the win-
ter of 1913–14 he wrote several plays, among them the one-
act *Bound East for Cardiff*. Next, he joined G. P. Baker's 47
Workshop; and thence, via Greenwich Village, he reached
Provincetown, where *Bound East* was performed in 1916, the
first of a long run of his work staged by the Players.

This was the beginning of a remarkable era in the American theatre. New York was the centre of activity, though
there was plenty of life in other places. The Provincetown
Players maintained a little theatre in Greenwich Village,
and were able to keep in existence during 1917–18, when
America was at war. By 1920 they were sufficiently developed to stage some full-length plays in addition to the
one-act pieces of the modest early days. Though their audiences were far smaller than those of commercial theatres,
they were enthusiastic ones. Free from box-office obligations,

the Players could be as experimental as they liked. With them, the playwright came into his own; for by 1925, they had produced no less than ninety-three plays, by forty-seven different authors. Their authors, nearly all American, included Edna Ferber and Edna St Vincent Millay.

Moreover, there were other theatre-groups in New York. The Washington Square Players had been formed in 1914, with similar experimental aims. Their run of one-act plays was interrupted by the war, but they reappeared in 1919 as the Theatre Guild. By 1925 they had prospered enough to build their own Guild Theatre; and here, before the Guild gradually became too conservative, there were many distinguished productions of American and European plays. It was they who performed Eugene O'Neill's *Marco Millions* (1928), *Mourning Becomes Electra* (1931), and *Ah, Wilderness!* (1933); and he had been one of the Guild's founding members. Some of his plays were also presented by the Neighborhood Playhouse, which was built and endowed for an amateur company in 1915, though after the war it was taken over by professionals.

Other large cities had kindred groups. None of these, of course, ousted the commercial theatre. Easily the most popular American play of the 1920s was *Abie's Irish Rose* (1924), which ran in New York for over 2,500 performances. No play by O'Neill came anywhere near to such commercial success. However, the small experimental theatres indirectly influenced Broadway, and their playwrights became known to a wide public. Very few people troubled to remember that *Abie's Irish Rose* was the work of one Anne Nicholls: but a great many had heard of O'Neill.

As America's foremost playwright, he did a great deal to establish the modes of the modern theatre in the United States. His work illustrates, therefore, some of the main trends in modern American drama. One of its most striking features is the combination of deliberately drab prose realism and of boldly inventive expressionist technique. It is as though Henrik Ibsen and Berthold Brecht had come together in the same person. In a sense, they had. When

O'Neill began to write, American drama still had to make for itself the discoveries that Ibsen had indicated a whole generation previously. Yet by the end of the war European drama was branching out into expressionist fantasies like Georg Kaiser's *Gas* and Karel Čapek's *R.U.R.* Eugene O'Neill and his colleagues telescoped the whole process into a few years; American drama caught up with Europe almost overnight.

The first necessity was to establish an Ibsen-like realism, in place of the theatrical conventions that dominated the American theatre. Instead of elaborate drawing-room or scenic sets, O'Neill substituted (in such plays as *Bound East for Cardiff* and *The Moon of the Caribbees*) the deck or fo'c'sle of a tramp steamer. Instead of complicated plots, full of coincidence and high-minded stubbornness, O'Neill offered a seaman dying unheroically in his bunk, or an unromantic debauch with native women and native liquor. Instead of stilted dialogue and melodramatic 'asides', O'Neill's rough characters spoke in the authentic idiom of their situation. It was 'the gibberish of the vulgate' adapted to the theatre; and although O'Neill has moved a long way since *Bound East*, a late play like *The Iceman Cometh* (1946), set in a Bowery saloon, shows that his sense of common speech has been one of his more permanent assets. His feeling for politer speech has never been so sure; as he said in a letter about his *Mourning Becomes Electra*,

It needed great language ... I haven't got that. And, by way of self-consolation, I don't think, from the evidence of all that is being written today, that great language is possible for anyone living in the discordant, broken, faithless rhythm of our time. The best one can do is to be pathetically eloquent by one's moving, dramatic inarticulations![1]

In consequence, most of his plays are disappointing to read. They seem flat on the printed page, and at a casual glance their detailed stage directions – when they call for realistic

1. Quoted in Arthur H. Quinn, *A History of the American Drama from the Civil War to the Present Day* (2v. in 1, New York, revised edn., 1936), ii, 258.

settings – might not seem very different from the directions
for the kind of play O'Neill's father had acted in.

But there are all kinds of differences. O'Neill considered himself a serious playwright. His realism, though it
may occasionally appear stale, began as a fresh attitude to
the possibilities of drama. So did his expressionist tendencies, which began to reveal themselves quite early in his
writing. *The Moon of the Caribbees* (1918), for example, was
gruffly matter-of-fact; yet the offstage native chanting foreshadowed more ambitious efforts on his part at expressionism. *Beyond the Horizon* (1920) was a realistic, or naturalistic,
play; but *The Emperor Jones*, produced in the same year,
brought Brecht into the picture along with Ibsen – and this
although when he wrote it, O'Neill says that he had never
heard of expressionism. Tomtoms beat in the background,
almost throughout the play; there are several sets intended
not to be lifelike but to create a mood, and at the end of one
scene 'the walls of the forest fold in'; the cast includes a
group of 'Little Formless Fears' (each looking like a black
'grubworm about the size of a creeping child'), as well as a
number of shadowy Negro figures, among whom Brutus
Jones in his delirium of fear passes backward in time to his
primeval Congo origins. Several subsequent plays employed
expressionist devices. In *All God's Chillun Got Wings* (1924),
O'Neill introduces the theme of negro-white relationships
with a contrasted street-scene:

People pass, black and white, the Negroes frankly participants in
the spirit of Spring, the whites laughing constrainedly, awkward in
natural emotion ... From the street of the whites a high-pitched,
nasal tenor sings the chorus of 'Only a Bird in a Gilded Cage'. On
the street of the blacks a Negro strikes up the chorus of: 'I Guess
I'll Have to Telegraph My Baby'. As this singing ends, there is
laughter, distinctive in quality, from both streets.

A Congo mask on the wall of a room has a special relevance,
and the walls keep closing in, as in Poe's 'Pit and the Pendulum', to heighten the oppressive emotions of the couple who
live within them. In *The Great God Brown* (1926) the principal characters wear masks, which are removed from time

to time and even transferred from one person. (Dion Anthony: Dionysus and St Anthony warring in the same man) to another (Brown: a 'visionless demi-god of our new materialistic myth').[1] In *Lazarus Laughed* (1927) there are choruses, masked to represent seven stages of life and seven different types of person, each type clad in a distinctive colour, so that there are forty-nine combinations of 'period and type'. This play was beyond the scope of most little theatres. So was *Strange Interlude* (1928), a drama of Wagnerian length which, while it did not rely upon expressionist techniques, was novel in that the inner thoughts of the characters (often at variance with their conversation) are continually exposed by means of asides. And in the trilogy *Mourning Becomes Electra*, another ambitious venture, O'Neill seeks an extra dimension of significance by retelling the Greek legend in American circumstances. The end of the Civil War is equated with the downfall of Troy; Agamemnon is recognizable as Brigadier Ezra Mannon, Clytemnestra as Mannon's wife Christine, their son Orin as Orestes, their daughter Lavinia as Electra, and so on. Their porticoed New England house is an appropriately classical setting, and the local townsfolk serve as a chorus.

The plays mentioned are only a part of O'Neill's output. For twenty years he wrote with seemingly inexhaustible energy. There were naturalistic plays like *Anna Christie* (1921) and *Desire under the Elms* (1924), and experimental efforts like *The Hairy Ape* (1922), *Marco Millions* (1928), and *Dynamo* (1929). Several failed to please the public, and the success of others may have depended largely on the brilliant stagings that were a feature of the expressionist drama of the 1920s. After 1934 O'Neill retired to his study, and though he continued to write, no new play of his was performed until *The Iceman Cometh*, twelve years later. A year afterwards he wrote *A Moon for the Misbegotten*. But then O'Neill was faced by serious illness, culminating in his death in 1953, and his final work did not reach the stage during his lifetime.

1. Quoted in Quinn, ii. 193.

7 The Literature of the United States

Taken as a whole, his plays show a constant attempt to suggest deeper meanings that underlie 'the discordant, broken, faithless rhythm of our time'. O'Neill said that he was not interested in the relation between man and man – the superficial material of the majority of plays – but only 'in the relation between man and God'. By 'God' he appears to have meant various things. In general, he has been concerned with humanity's craving for fulfilment – the Sherwood Anderson query of 'What *for*?' – and with humanity's frustrations. His technical experiments show him trying to overcome not only the limitations of prose-language but also the limitations of his outlook. His plays are therefore sometimes more earnest than profound, more complicated than subtle. The early pieces have a rough, grave, memorable dignity. He was still capable of achieving this wonderful greyness and graininess, reminiscent of the texture of an enlarged photograph, in subsequent work, especially when he resorted to autobiography. *Long Day's Journey into Night*, written in 1940 and produced in 1956, is a play of real strength. But most of the later ones, while often remarkably effective examples of stagecraft, tend to lack nobility. In *Lazarus Laughed* he spoke of men as 'those haunted heroes'. But the majority of his characters are not heroic enough; and they are haunted by Freudian and biological ghosts. The effect is somehow to debunk them. They are caught in a universal grubbiness. There is no grandeur, for instance, in the characters of *The Great God Brown*, or in those of *Strange Interlude*. The *Mourning Becomes Electra* trilogy, one of his best works, acquires a certain loftiness from its Greek overtones. But even here, as O'Neill himself felt, there was a deficiency. It is fine melodrama: it is not quite tragedy. Since his characters lack stature, their affirmations are not fully convincing. The laughter of Lazarus, or of the Negroes in *All God's Chillun*, rings a little false. Love, Life, and O'Neill's other synonyms for God seem not to be omnipresent, at any rate in their pure form, but to be perpetually out of reach, impossible aspirations on which to ring down the curtain.

Nevertheless, there are qualities of greatness in O'Neill. He did more than any other man to transform the American theatre, and his influence has spread throughout Europe. He has, unquestionably, been America's foremost dramatist, as one may see by listing the achievements of the others. He has more weight, for instance, than such relatively orthodox (and skilful) playwrights as Sidney Howard, S. N. Behrman, and Philip Barry (all products of the 47 Workshop); or than Robert Sherwood, Moss Hart, and George S. Kaufman. Howard's *They Knew What They Wanted* (1924) and *The Silver Cord* (1926) deal tenderly and accurately with the problems of a young woman married by a trick to an old man, and of excessive maternalism. Behrman's *Biography* (1932) is a witty, polished comedy of the repercussions that arise when a highly popular and unconventional woman is persuaded to write her memoirs. Philip Barry, besides writing admirably smooth pieces for the commercial theatre, tried his hand at more difficult themes. His *Hotel Universe* (1930), a play about American expatriates and their involved affairs, has an elderly mystic whose importance for the other characters is akin to that of the psychoanalyst Harcourt O'Rcilly in T. S. Eliot's *The Cocktail Party*. Barry's *Here Come the Clowns* (1938) is an ingenious allegory of right and wrong. As for Robert Sherwood, his *The Road to Rome* (1927) is a brittle comedy of Hannibal's invasion; *The Petrified Forest* (1935) is a well-contrived, eventful play that is also equipped with sundry messages; and *Idiot's Delight* (1936) pictures the scene in a European resort hotel after a war has broken out – the cast includes a pacifist and a wicked manufacturer of munitions. Hart and Kaufman have collaborated successfully to write such fast-moving comedies as *You Can't Take It With You* (1936) and *The Man Who Came to Dinner* (1939).

All of these plays have their virtues. Several are better written than O'Neill's work, in that the dialogue is neater and more felicitous. Yet none has his intensity. A similar conclusion can be reached about other American expressionist performances of the 1920s, however exciting they seemed at the time. There was Elmer Rice's *The Adding Machine* (1923). As a mere youngster, Rice had attracted attention nine years before with *On Trial*, a murder play that borrowed the motion-picture device of the 'flashback' to tell its story. Subsequent plays, some of them performed by a New York group called the Morningside Players, were not particularly unusual. *The Adding Machine*, however, was stridently experimental. Its principal character is a dull little accountant known as Mr Zero; some other characters are known by numbers only. Executed for the murder of his employer, he finds himself working an adding-machine in the Elysian Fields, only to be returned to earth again at the end of the play, to undergo another miserable cycle of existence, and then another and another, until he will eventually become the completely soulless slave of his machine.

Or there was John Howard Lawson's *Roger Bloomer*, produced in the same year as *The Adding Machine*, with a symbolic ballet and abstract settings. In 1925 Lawson presented in *Processional* what he called 'a jazz symphony of American life'. Gilbert Seldes' *The Seven Lively Arts* (1924) had given a vivacious, sympathetic account of the movies, the comic strip, vaudeville, and other popular art-forms. Other intellectuals – E. E. Cummings and Edmund Wilson among them – shared Seldes' enthusiasm for these indigenous amusements. So did Lawson, whose *Processional* was a bright though somewhat self-conscious piece of expressionism modelled upon the patterns of vaudeville. Gifted stage designers like Robert Edmond Jones and Norman Bel Geddes did much to assist the impact of the modern drama.

Expressionist techniques did not altogether die out with the 1920s, but like other aspects of the theatre they were modified by the altered mood of the Depression years. Even more than the novel, American drama changed with the times. As in the novel, Freud yielded place to Marx. For the spiritual liberty of the individual, authors substituted the theme of economic injustice. Perhaps the American drama of the 1930s accomplished less than the previous decade. Some American critics, in a penitentially anti-Communist frame of mind, apparently feel impelled to reject plays they formerly applauded, as 'tendentious', 'propagandist', and so on. So they are; yet it would be a pity to overlook their effectiveness, or to under-estimate the liveliness of American drama in the Roosevelt era. It did the orthodox theatre no harm to concern itself a little more closely with economic realities. Thus, Sidney Kingsley's *Dead End* (1935) owed its success in part to a spectacular setting that included a tank of water, representing New York's East River, into which urchins dived and re-emerged dripping wet. But this lavishness was given a point; Kingsley's intention is indicated by his epigraph from Tom Paine: 'The contrast of affluence and wretchedness is like dead and living bodies chained together'.

Such contrasts offered excellent opportunities for satire. The theatre responded with such delightful productions as the musical play *Of Thee I Sing* (1931), by George and Ira Gershwin, and the revue *Pins and Needles* (1937), staged by the International Ladies Garment Workers Union and then sent on a nation-wide tour, to enable all America to enjoy sharp and sprightly numbers like 'Sing Me a Song of Social Significance'.

Another consequence of the Depression was an increased interest in *American* dramatic material. This was evident in several ways. There was a general turning homeward; the novelist-playwright Thornton Wilder, for instance, had written during the 1920s of other places and epochs. Where he had then examined *The Bridge of San Luis Rey* (1927), he now looked at *Our Town* (1938), a charmingly relaxed though 'experimental' play about 'Grover's Corners, New Hampshire' in the early years of this century. It begins without curtain or scenery; when the audience is all seated, the Stage Manager enters, arranges bits of furniture, and finally introduces the play. There are interjections from actors planted in the auditorium; one asks, 'Is there no one in town aware of social injustice and industrial inequality?' – but it is clear that Thornton Wilder is not bothered by such questions. His small town is, unlike Spoon River or Winesburg, a homely community, bathed in the warm light of retrospection. (*The Skin of Our Teeth*, 1942, has some similar merits, but suffers from a certain cosmic cuteness.)

Affection for America's regional corners was not entirely a new feature. 'Folk drama' had grown up in the 1920s, and had had forerunners—Frank Murdoch's *Davy Crockett* (1872), to mention only one. The movement for folk drama, which centred in college and little theatres, was apt to be a trifle artificial. Yeats or J. M. Synge could draw upon an ancient folk-heritage: America's, however, was a patchy affair of yesterday. The Red Indians might be considered as the American *folk*; but they had been belatedly co-opted for the role, and could not properly fill it. When Frederick H. Koch founded the Dakota Playmakers at the University of North Dakota, in 1910, he did his best to extract material from that bare region. He found the task easier among the uplands of North Carolina, to whose university he transferred in 1918. His Carolina Playmakers consisted of students who performed plays specially written for them and produced by Professor Koch. As an undergraduate at North Carolina, Thomas Wolfe had first become interested in drama. The Playmakers' most successful author was Paul Green, a colleague of Koch who has written many plays about Negroes, planters, and poor whites. The most famous of them, *In Abraham's Bosom* (1926), ends in a lynching: this regional movement was more avowedly liberal than that of the Tennessee Agrarians.

Though the South had a richer folk-past than other areas, it had no monopoly of folk-drama. At Cornell University, Alexander Drummond accumulated a repertory of plays based on the history of New York State; while Lynn Riggs dealt with the white and Indian folkways of his native Oklahoma. His *Green Grow the Lilacs* (1931) formed the basis of the sensationally popular musical comedy *Oklahoma!* (1943). Riggs hoped 'to recapture in a kind of nostalgic glow' the atmosphere of 'the old folk songs and ballads'. But this atmosphere was undoubtedly strongest and most genuinely alive among the Negroes, whether in the South or in New York's Harlem. In New York during the 1920s there was a succession of Negro plays (some under the auspices of the Ethiopian Art Players, formed in 1923) and of swift-paced, high-spirited Negro musicals like *Chocolate Dandies* and *From Dixie to Broadway* (both 1924). The climax of Negro entertainment was reached, however, in the 1930s. Marc Connelly's *The Green Pastures* (1930) has been criticized as a folksy, white man's concoction of Negro religious sentiment. Even so, its all-Negro cast, its version of Negro colloquial speech, and its Negro spirituals brought it close to a poeticized folk drama as Synge or García Lorca might have understood the term. Du Bose and Dorothy Heyward's novel *Porgy* (1925) was also a white view of Negro life; but as dramatized by the Heywards it too made excellent theatre; and as a folk opera done by the Gershwin brothers, *Porgy and Bess* (1935) has been deservedly famous.

Negro productions were a notable feature of the notable though short-lived Federal Theatre, which, like the Federal Writers' Project, was an offshoot of the New Deal W.P.A., organized in 1935 to allay the effects of severe unemployment. While writers were engaged in compiling quantities of guide-books and folklore narratives, actors and producers and stage-hands and dramatists were rescued by the Federal Theatre. Under its auspices the brilliantly gifted young producer Orson Welles staged his Negro *Macbeth* (1936), in a tropical Haitian setting, before leaving the project to found his own Mercury Theatre. The Chicago Theatre Project's Negro *Swing Mikado* (1939) was such a hit that in the same year the commercial stage imitated the idea in the *Hot Mikado*. The efforts of the Federal Theatre were usually on a more modest scale. Its companies put on performances in every part of the United States, ranging from puppet shows and vaudeville to Shakespeare and Euripides. Sometimes they played to audiences who had never hitherto seen a theatre show.

They staged miracle and morality plays; and they invented a technique – the 'Living Newspaper' – that combined the methods of radio features and documentary cinema into what could be regarded as modern morality plays. *Triple-A Plowed Under* tackled the woes of the farmer who could not find a market for his crops; *One-Third of a Nation* commented harshly on America's housing conditions. Other samples of the Living Newspaper were equally effective. But they were frankly hostile to American capitalism, and the Federal Theatre as a whole fell under suspicion as a collectivist enterprise wasting the tax-payer's money. After prolonged argument, its Congressional appropriation was ended in the summer of 1939, and this astonishing movement came to an abrupt end less than four years after it had been initiated.

The modern morality play, with God and the Devil supplanted by class warfare, flourished in the unmistakably Marxist productions of New York's Theatre Union, and in the Group Theatre that grew out of the Theatre Guild at the end of the 1920s. The Group Theatre discovered Clifford Odets, probably the most forceful American playwright since O'Neill. His *Waiting for Lefty* and *Awake and Sing* (both produced in 1935, though the latter was an earlier work) established him as a passionately sincere author fully in sympathy with the Group Theatre's ideas of ensemble acting as they had learned these from Stanislavsky and the Moscow Art Theatre. Though it is only a longish one-act piece, *Waiting for Lefty* is an almost perfect example of a proletarian morality play. The stage is the platform of a union meeting; there are violent speeches and noisy interjections; half a dozen simple little episodes are interspersed to show the lives of the committee members, and how each came to be present. At this distance the propaganda seems crude, the notes for production doubly so: 'Do not hesitate to use music wherever possible. It is very valuable in emotionally stirring an audience.' But the play, in common with Odets' other best work, is still curiously moving. The stage can stand more didacticism than the novel, provided that the handling is not stagey. Odets avoids stageyness. And his principal weapon has nothing to do with propaganda. It is his perfect command of the American spoken language. His dialogue crackles with life. His villainous capitalists now sound a little absurd; his working men do not : their words are – as Emerson said of their predecessors' speech – 'vascular and alive'. This mastery of the common idiom has been one of the main assets of the American theatre.

By contrast, experiments at verse drama have looked anaemic. Perhaps that is not the word to define Wallace Stevens' early *Carlos among the Candles* and *Three Travellers Watch a Sunrise* (produced in 1917 and 1920 respectively). But they could never be popular with a wide audience; they are poetry, but they are not drama. The word could be applied to the poetic dramas of Maxwell Anderson. They are worthy efforts, yet even *Winterset* (1935), the most powerful, does not gain much from its verse. Archibald MacLeish's verse plays, some of them for radio, are competent in construction and ambitious in intent. But the older ones sound a shade tinny; while the more recent *JB* (1958) – based on the Biblical story of Job, and performed on Broadway with great acclaim – is oddly hollow despite the author's technical mastery. It has the ingredients of greatness, yet they are too self-consciously assembled.

In the 1920s American drama tended to seek its effects in 'theatre poetry' – that is, in stage effects – rather than in the written word. In the 1930s the Depression and its attendant ideologies impregnated the theatre, making the American vernacular seem more impressive than any poetic rendering of speech. Since then, the patriotic war years and the confused aftermath have shown no strong impulse in any particular direction. The commercial theatre has seen a series of exuberant musicals which make their British counterparts look limp and sticky. But commercialism has on the whole deadened invention. The exorbitant cost of Broadway productions has discouraged experiment. The little theatres, which in the 1930s began to rechristen themselves 'community' theatres, have continued, and so has summer stock; but not even praiseworthy ventures like the Pasadena Theatre have been able to emulate the verve of the Provincetown Players. One hopeful sign has been the growth of 'off-Broadway' productions, staged in small improvised theatres. Among their achievements have been a dramatized version of Dos Passos' *U.S.A.*, and Jack Gelber's *The Connection*, a fiercely intent play about drug-addicts. Television has failed to lead to the much-touted renaissance in dramatic writing, except for the witty, impish work of Gore Vidal and the brilliantly observed awkwardness of Paddy Chayevsky's *Marty* and *The Bachelor Party*.

Otherwise, O'Neill is dead. Clifford Odets retired for a while to Hollywood and was unable to repeat his pre-war form, though his *Flowering Peach* (1955) suggested that he still might have had much to say. John Steinbeck has tried, so far without success, to apply his talents to the theatre. Dos Passos, who wrote *Airways, Inc.* (1929) and other interesting plays at the start of the Depression, has not since returned to the theatre; the adaptation of *U.S.A.* was done by other hands. The irrepressible William Saroyan seemed about to capture the field with *My Heart's in the Highlands* and *The Time of Your Life* (1939); but in subsequent plays he surrendered too readily to his flair for improvisation, writing pieces that were neither real enough nor fantastic enough. Thornton Wilder, an author of exceptional intelligence and resilience, may still be heard from again, perhaps for his new cycle of one-act plays on the Seven Ages of Man.

America's most widely discussed playwrights since the war have been Tennessee Williams and Arthur Miller. Williams shot to fame with *The Glass Menagerie* (1944) and *A Streetcar Named Desire* (1947). He has had other and more equivocal successes with such plays as *Cat on a Hot Tin Roof* (1954). Arthur Miller established his reputation with *Death of a Salesman* (1949) and took it further, among the critics, with *The Crucible* (1953) and two one-act plays composing *A View from the Bridge* (1955). These plays have wrenched the hearts of American audiences, perhaps because in some instances the characters portrayed come so close to being commonplace, or to revealing in sombre form the current American 'problems' and maladies. Identification with them is as hard to resist as it is uncomfortable. *The Crucible* indeed wears very well. Based upon the Salem witch-hunts of the late seventeenth century, it was interpreted by audiences of the 1950s as a comment on McCarthyism. It proves to have more permanent value. Williams showed Southern romanticism drained to the pathetic dregs of a shabby gentility in which the Southern belle, traditionally renowned for purity, slips into promiscuity, or in middle age vainly tries to find a suitor – any suitor – for her unloved daughter. But these were sad rather than tragic plays; and in subsequent work the pathos has yielded to a sort of modern-Gothic *mélange*, in which Williams' no doubt genuine preoccupations have been stylized into fashionable nightmares of castration, incest and homosexuality. Miller is a playwright of more solid perception. But he too has run into difficulties. The more recent plays of both men, while not negligible, resemble the unproduced work of Saroyan, though much more performable, in that they lie in a limbo between poetry and prose, ordinariness and symbolism. One might say of these two writers that, like many of their contemporaries, they *know* almost too much for their own good. In *The Confidential Clerk* (1954) and *The Elder Statesman* (1958) of T. S. Eliot it would seem that the author strives for ordinariness, and in achieving it has weakened significance. With playwrights like Williams and Miller, it would seem that they try to move in the opposite direction, out of the prosaic toward the poetic. It is as if these two, with their ambitiously 'experimental' sets and their intermittently 'fine' utterances, *hope* that their characters mean more than their speeches *say*, and are intellectually aware of a host of hidden meanings. The dilemma is one that the contemporary theatre has not solved. Broadway's recent seasons have been dominated by indifferent plays and mediocre musicals, and the experimental theatre has been enlivened by only two contributions – or three if we include the 'theatre of assault' of the Negro author LeRoi Jones. The two other contributions are by a novelist and a poet. Saul Bellow's *The Last Analysis* (1964) both mocks and builds upon psychoanalysis. Its hero is an old comedian who seeks to rescue himself from nonentity by re-enacting his own psychic history. Robert Lowell's *The Old Glory* (1964) is a trilogy of verse plays based on Nathaniel Hawthorne's 'Endecott and the Red Cross' and 'My Kinsman, Major Molineux' and on Melville's 'Benito Cereno'. The verse is low-keyed but dramatically effective; 'Benito Cereno' is topical yet timeless. These experiments suggest the native possibilities of the American theatre; Beckett, Ionesco, Genet and Artaud in Europe may have important lessons too for the United States.

Indeed Europe is again responding to the work of an American playwright – Edward Albee, whose first two plays, *The Zoo Story* (1958) and *The Death of Bessie Smith* (1959), had their premières in Berlin. New York audiences were jolted by the articulate, matter-of-fact fantasy of *The American Dream* (1961), which Albee describes as 'a stand against the fiction that everything in this slipping land of ours is peachy-keen'. He goes on: 'Is the play offensive? I certainly hope so; it was my intention to offend – as well as amuse and entertain.' His talent for incriminatory-recriminatory dialogue is even more strikingly apparent in the recent play *Who's Afraid of Virgina Woolf?*

POETRY AND CRITICISM SINCE WORLD WAR I

———

E. E. CUMMINGS (1894–1962)

MARIANNE MOORE (1887–   )

HART CRANE (1899–1932)

STEPHEN VINCENT BENÉT (1898–1943)

ARCHIBALD MACLEISH (1892–   )

ROBINSON JEFFERS (1887–1962)

EZRA POUND (1885–   )

T. S. ELIOT (1888–1965)

IRVING BABBITT (1865–1933)

PAUL ELMER MORE (1864–1937)

JOHN CROWE RANSOM (1888–   )

ALLEN TATE (1899–   )

ROBERT PENN WARREN (1905–   )

CLEANTH BROOKS (1906–   )

VAN WYCK BROOKS (1886–   )

POETRY AND CRITICISM SINCE
WORLD WAR I

—

In Chapter Eleven, which described the beginnings of modern poetry in the United States, it was suggested that these were in part 'native' and in part cosmopolitan. The American poet was interested in what John Ciardi calls 'the capture of the American voice-box';[1] like the earlier, prose realists, he found it exciting to express himself in a novel vocabulary and to play with new technical devices. Certain poets, notably Carl Sandburg, continued after the war to stress the Americanness of what they were doing. Others were able to take it for granted.

This question has now almost if not entirely ceased to engage American poets. However, in 1920, William Carlos Williams attacked his friend Ezra Pound as 'the best enemy United States verse has'. With Pound he associated the young American poet T. S. Eliot, who for the past six years had been living in England, and who in 1927 was to become a British citizen. Williams' charge was that Pound and Eliot had harmed the cause of American poetry by slipping off to Europe, there to absorb an alien (and mainly French) inspiration, 'content with the connotations of their masters'. By contrast, Williams, Sandburg, and others had remained faithfully at home and striven to create (in what Williams named 'the western dialect') a native poetry. As late as 1951 Williams was still a little bothered by this apparent defection; the native effort, he contends in his *Autobiography*, was impeded by Eliot's *The Waste Land* (1922), 'which gave the poem back to the academics'.

Williams is a better poet than polemicist. His antithesis of America – Europe was no longer of serious interest to many poets even in 1920; by 1951 it had become oddly anachronistic.

1. John Ciardi (ed.), *Mid-Century American Poets* (New York, 1950), xii.

It does not fit the facts. For one thing, the native poets who have been too exclusively concerned with native themes have not stayed the course. There was some truth in Pound's assertion to Williams, in 1917, that the *echt* American qualities were 'fizz, swish, gabble of verbiage': in other words, a fatal tendency to rhetoric, and a fatal suspicion of the intellect – shortcomings which have weakened Sandburg's work, and have sometimes vitiated that of Williams himself, as far as intellect is concerned. Since the Imagist movement, American poetry has been to a striking extent an international (or non-national) affair, its leaders also among the leaders of European poetry. To attempt to isolate their 'American' traits is to misunderstand their achievement. However, Williams' criticisms are not altogether without significance. They remind us once more of the American preoccupation with the sometimes irreconcilable claims of yesterday and to-morrow. Modern American poetry has succeeded to a remarkable degree in bringing the two together. For this reason it may perhaps have been America's greatest literary contribution to the period – greater than her contributions to the medium of fiction, some of which are now only of historical value. Europe also in our time has had to consider the divided paths of tradition and revolt; the American answer in verse has therefore had a particular force and relevance. American seriousness, in criticism as in poetry, has helped to counter Britain's excessive fondness for the amateur spirit in letters; the American willingness to experiment, with vocabulary as with verse-forms, has been as valuable for the rest of modern poetry as the acute American desire to find a firm base.

In fact, the antithesis in modern American poetry has not been between America and Europe, but between innovation and conservatism – a related but by no means identical polarity. The 'capture of the American voice-box' was an early victory, long absorbed into the pattern, though an important victory. Its results can be seen in all sorts of verse; the idiom has been accepted, and can be handled with little of the early self-consciousness. Here, for example, is a small poem by Louise Bogan, *Several Voices out of a Cloud*:

Come, drunks and drug-takers; come, perverts unnerved!
Receive the laurel, given, though late, on merit; to whom and
  wherever deserved.

Parochial punks, trimmers, nice people, joiners true-blue,
Get the hell out of the way of the laurel. It is deathless. And it isn't
  for you.

The colloquialism of this poem is exaggerated in order to startle the reader, but there are innumerable other instances of poems that employ the vernacular with unobtrusive assurance. Miss Bogan's poem was published in 1938; by then, the conversational verse of W. H. Auden showed that at least one British poet had also captured a voice-box. Perhaps his subsequent removal to the United States, and adoption of American citizenship, indicated that he felt especially at home with the American compound of polite speech and *lingua franca*.

Other and more ambitious innovations have been introduced by American poets. Those of E. E. Cummings have probably been the most spectacular. Some of the experiments he was to make, and his general viewpoint, were suggested in his first book, the piece of autobiographical prose entitled *The Enormous Room* (1922). In this he made plain his contempt for authority and his reverence for the individual, which he conveyed in a highly personal style, full of unusual epithets, strong verbs, and grammatical transpositions:

To the left and right through lean oblongs of stained glass burst dirty burglars of moonlight.

I will get upon the soonness of the train and ride into the now of Paris.

His first book of poems, *Tulips and Chimneys* (1923), seemed a dazzlingly fresh and vigorous expression of romantic anarchism. He celebrated love and the other joys of individuality as exuberantly as he castigated the boredoms and degradations of those he was later to dismiss as 'mostpeople':

Mostpeople have less in common with ourselves than the square-rootofminusone. You and I are human beings; mostpeople are snobs

He began too to invent typographical devices, as methods of measuring time:

```
                            pho
           nographisrunn
           ingd o    w,    n      phonograph
                                  stopS.
```

'Mr Lowercase Highbrow' – as an imaginary interlocutor addressed him – became 'e.e.cummings', and in further volumes of verse (including *XLI Poems*, 1925; *Vi Va*, 1931; *No Thanks*, 1935; *1 × 1*, 1944) continued to conjure with syntax and typography. Love is still the supreme gift, 'wonderful one times one'; and 'soonness' is the prelude still to the highest moments which are 'now'. Life, Cummings insists, is a series of unfolding discoveries: 'Always the beautiful answer who asks a more beautiful question.' The series, he says, is 'growth'. Recent critics have queried whether there is much growth or development in Cummings' poetry, despite its technical ingenuities. After quarter of a century it still offers a simple message of unfettered individualism in superficially complex terms. Yet, if it seems more amusing than profound, much credit is due to E. E. Cummings for being as amusing as he is. No one has been better able to convey the light, lilting gaiety, wittily abstracted, of the world as he has kept recommending it to us:

> anyone lived in a pretty how town
> (with up so floating many bells down)
> spring summer autumn winter
> he sang his didn't he danced his did.

If this is a mannerism, it is a very charming and agreeable one; if Cummings' attitudes have remained stuck in the 1920s, he has been able to carry over all the confident, carefree tones of that decade at its most light-hearted. He is to modern poetry what the American artist Alexander Calder has been to modern sculpture. Neither has attempted to be portentous; both have been accused of being facetious and immature. But both have at their best – Cummings in his verse and Calder with his mobiles – made art a delightful merry-go-round, brightly rotating and rising and falling, in a Bank Holiday sunshine.

Marianne Moore is another extremely original poet. But her work, though individual and feminine, is careful: she goes her own way with none of the haste, heat, errors, and eccentricities that are liable to accompany 'originality'. Her *Collected Poems* (1951) number only seventy or so, most of them short, though there are other poems that she has not cared to include in the volume. Most of them are in even stanzas whose lines are regulated by syllabic counting. Rhymes are pulled gently but firmly out of the poem; end-rhymes are sometimes supplied by breaking a word in the middle:

> Priorities were cradled in this region not
> noted for humility; spot
> that has high-singing frogs, cotton-mouth snakes and cot-
> ton-fields. . . .

The sense runs on across the formal pattern like a design painted over tiles. Her subjects are an anthology of rare and unexpected things, a poet's scrapbook of clocks and jewels and living creatures, taken from such sources as the *Illustrated London News*. She has spoken of her own 'exaggerated tendency to visualize'; certainly her observation is as deliciously exact as that of eighteenth-century engravings of botany or zoology. Here is a stanza from 'The Jerboa':

> By fifths and sevenths,
> in leaps of two lengths,
>   like the uneven notes
>   of the Bedouin flute, it stops its gleaning
>   on little wheel castors, and makes fern-seed
>   foot-prints with kangaroo speed.

She can describe an ostrich or an elephant with equal felicity. Her notes are a help to understanding, since her meaning is condensed, and since Miss Moore often follows a 'hybrid method of composition' in quoting directly from her sources. It might be argued that such a method shows that she has not fully assimilated her material. Yet this is not so; rather, she begins where the conventional lyric leaves off,

rejecting an easy 'meaning' in favour of definitions that are
at once more precise and more subtle. Marianne Moore's
world is full of delicate, exotic objects; her affection for them
is akin to Whitman's rejoicing in 'the pismire ..., and a grain
of sand, and the egg of the wren' – except that her admiration emerges indirectly out of her meticulous commentary.
Like Wallace Stevens, whose verse has often been compared
to hers, she is a difficult yet rewarding poet, who selects her
unusual details with complete assurance, and uses them to
develop a deeply-considered theme, not as embroidery: indeed, in a poem like 'Those Various Scalpels' she seems to
catalogue details in order to query their ultimate value (in a
manner faintly reminiscent of the Puritan poet Edward
Taylor). The careful reader can extract a great deal from
Miss Moore's work; and for such other poets as T. S. Eliot,
William Carlos Williams, Cummings, and Stevens, it is (in
W. H. Auden's words) 'a treasure which all future English
poets will be able to plunder'.

    Hart Crane, in a brief life ended by suicide, aimed higher
– in some ways – than Marianne Moore. Her first little book
of verse was published in 1921 (in London) when she was
thirty-four. Crane had had a poem accepted by Margaret
Anderson's *Little Review* in 1916, when he was only half that
age, and by 1921 he was an experienced poet. In the following year, 1922, Eliot's *The Waste Land* appeared. Crane
was already familiar with Eliot's work, and with that of Ezra
Pound; *The Waste Land* affected him as deeply as it did other
poets of the period. Yet it made him, like W. C. Williams, a
little uneasy. He knew it for a great work, endowed with an
authoritative air that only a major poet could command.
But he regretted its assumption that there was little hope
for the twentieth century – and, therefore, for that most contemporary of lands, America. He would, himself, move 'towards a more positive, or (if I must put it so in a skeptical
age) ecstatic goal'. The poems in *White Buildings* (1926) revealed how seriously and ambitiously he was seeking the
goal, which he tried to reach conclusively in the long symposium of his faith called *The Bridge* (1930). Its main symbol

was Brooklyn Bridge, the fine structure over New York's
East River built by the Roeblings. Whitman before him –
and before the bridge was completed – had written magnificently of 'Crossing Brooklyn Ferry', as a joy to be shared
by others, fifty or a hundred years hence. And Whitman,
Crane wrote in 1929, 'better than any other, was able to
coördinate those forces in America which seem most intractable, fusing them into a universal vision. ...' Whitman
is the principal hero of *The Bridge*; it is to him that Crane
speaks in the splendid section, 'Cape Hatteras'. Like his predecessor, Crane is fascinated by the ocean across which the
early voyagers came to the new continent. But his America
is not the same as Whitman's; the Machine Age has arrived,
and 'unless poetry can absorb the machine, i.e. *acclimatize* it
as naturally and casually as trees, cattle, galleons, castles,
and all other human associations of the past, then poetry has
failed of its full contemporary function'. Crane's 'ecstasy',
then, is sought by blending the old America with the new
one, in which

> spouting pillars spoor the evening sky,
> Under the looming stacks of the gigantic power house
> Stars prick the eyes with sharp ammoniac proverbs,

and in which the Wright Brothers have conquered space.
Dynamos and aircraft have to be synthesized with other
elements of America from which he can draw comfort. Some
of these elements were possibly suggested to him [1] by William
Carlos Williams' prose experiment, *In the American Grain*
(1925). Crane's list includes Columbus, Cortés, Pocahontas,
Rip Van Winkle, Poe, and Melville. They are introduced
not so much as an ironic counterpart to the present, as items
in an American heritage, significant fragments of what was
to be called the 'usable past'.

    The Bridge is a remarkable achievement, with some superb

1. Though in a letter of 21 November 1926 Crane, after highly praising
Williams's book, says: 'I put off reading it, you know, until I felt my own
way cleared beyond chance of confusions incident to reading a book so
intimate to my theme' (*The Letters of Hart Crane, 1916–1932*: New York,
1952, 277–8).

passages. However, it is not a unified achievement. It frequently spills over into a handsome but unconvincing rhetoric. The American elements are a disparate collection; stubborn symbols, they resist transposition: they belong somehow in different leagues. Crane's exultant brilliance jars against his other moods of despair and disconsolate loneliness. He can write boldly, in the 'Cutty Sark' section, of

> Pennants, parabolas –
> clipper dreams indelible and ranging,
> baronial white on lucky blue!

But in 'The Tunnel', a horrible subway plunge under the city makes him ask Poe

> why do I often meet your visage here,
> Your eyes like agate lanterns – on and on
> Below the toothpaste and the dandruff ads?

Though he invokes Whitman, it is the haunted and homeless figure of Poe that characterizes much of the work. The rhythm of the dynamos is the pulse of nightmare. The proud airman crashes – and even wills his crash, like that strange expatriate figure, Harry Crosby, whom Crane addresses in one of his last poems, 'To the Cloud Juggler':

> Expose vaunted validities that yawn
> Past pleasantries ...

Some of these last poems, from the Caribbean, are as good as the best parts of *The Bridge*. But soon after writing them, Crane jumped to his death from a New-York-bound ship: an act which was taken as proof that his endeavour, like that of Icarus, was foredoomed.

On the whole, other American poets preferred to stress the dissonances of modern life, rather than cast about for a conciliatory formula. Of those who, like Crane, tried to make use of the American past, the most popular was Stephen Vincent Benét, whose *John Brown's Body* (1928), a long narrative poem of the Civil War, found favour with the general public. Though it has much to recommend it, *John Brown's Body* shows how easily the idea of the American heritage could become standardized and sentimentalized – a set of all-too accessible figures and situations. In the Depression years 'social protest' was superadded to the American scene as an attitude. Thus, Archibald MacLeish, who had spent most of the 1920s in Europe, returned to the American continent with *Conquistador* (1932), a verse narrative of Cortés' war against the Aztecs; he wrote some verse dramas powerfully redolent of the decade; and by 1939, his *America Was Promises* marked a decline from his early excellence into hollow, declamatory, 'public' verse. It seemed a natural, though unfortunate, step from this to *The Irresponsibles* (1940), in which he wagged a disapproving finger at his literary brethren and exhorted them to stand up for democracy. By contrast, the chilly Californian nihilism of Robinson Jeffers was a refreshing tonic. Loving the ocean and wild animals as much as he disliked humanity, Jeffers wrote grimly and memorably from his western perch, looking forward to a future with

> The cities gone down, the people fewer and the hawks more numerous,
> The rivers mouth to source pure; when the two-footed
> Mammal, being someways one of the nobler animals, regains
> The dignity of room, the value of rareness.

Jeffers has often based his verse upon themes from antiquity, deriving from them 'a more ideal and also more normal beauty, because the myths of our own race were never developed, and have been alienated from us'.

Much of this interest of American poets in conservative, non-American standards owes its impetus to Ezra Pound and T.S. Eliot. They were the wandering scholars of modernism in poetry, the young men from civilization's periphery in search of worthy schools; free from Europe's insularities, they were subjects of the holy empire of letters. Pound had arrived on the European scene several years before Eliot, and for temperamental as well as chronological reasons passed through a somewhat different apprenticeship. The movements in which he involved himself – Imagism, Vorticism – had an element of iconoclasm which he has never

altogether outgrown. The sources from which he first drew –
Browning, the early Yeats, Villon, and so on – were of a
slightly antecedent order to those of Eliot. For Eliot, as
Pound admiringly noted, managed to educate himself in
such a way as to be, while deeply read in the literature of the
past, a complete modern. It is true that when he and Pound
became acquainted, in the opening stages of World War I,
his education was not finished. He had much to learn from
his compatriot; his dedication of *The Waste Land* to Pound
was no empty courtesy: he owed much to Pound's preliminary explorations, and to Pound's scrutiny of the poem while
it was in composition.

By the end of the war these two, as Pound later wrote, had
decided

that the dilution of *vers libre*, Amygism, Lee Masterism, general
floppiness, had gone too far and that some counter-current must
be set going. ... Results: poems in Mr Eliot's *second* volume, also
'H.S.Mauberley'. Divergence later.

Or, as Eliot said in his 'Reflections on "Vers Libre"' (1917),

freedom is only truly freedom when it appears against the background of an artificial limitation.

The poems by Eliot that Pound referred to were published in
1920, as was his own *Hugh Selwyn Mauberley*. These poems,
and *The Waste Land*, have an importance that can hardly be
over-emphasized. A world away from Edgar Lee Masters
and 'general floppiness', their tone varies from light irony
to intense seriousness. They sense the tragedy of the war far
more fully than most of their 'native' contemporaries, for
whom – as we have noted – it seems to have been almost an
affront rather than a tragedy. In oblique, marvellously compressed lines Pound and Eliot contrast to the strident, frag-
mented overtones of 1920 the far different undertones of
Europe's past. They do this partly by means of quotation
from other writers, sometimes in other languages. The result
has been criticized as unnecessarily allusive and obscure. It
does indicate a wider knowledge of European literature than
most readers can lay claim to. But it is not a form of pedantry.

Rather, the modernity of Pound and Eliot has included a vivid awareness of the past, this (as Eliot wrote in 1917) composing 'a simultaneous order' with the present. Hence the extraordinary rightness of Eliot's – and to a hardly lesser extent Pound's – borrowings from other poets, eras, tongues.

However, as Pound remarked, he and Eliot diverged. In 1920, Eliot published a volume of essays entitled *The Sacred Wood*, which included the famous piece on 'Tradition and the Individual Talent'. The same year saw the publication of some essays by Pound under the name *Instigations*. The difference in titles is characteristic. For Pound, nothing was quite sacred. In his earlier years he instructed his books to

> Greet the grave and stodgy,
> Salute them with your thumbs at your noses.

And while he has shared with Eliot a readiness to explore the past, both for useful literary material and for principles of conduct, his search has been somewhat derisive and irritable. He has been, so to speak, an anti-clerical lover of cathedrals, or an iconoclast in pursuit of an iconography. In Eliot's historical scheme the timeless and the temporal go together; the mind of Europe changes generation by generation, but 'abandons nothing *en route*'. In Pound's scheme (which also includes Asia) certain periods are so exciting that he relives them in his work. In common with Browning, he is very much a poet of *monologue* – someone, either himself or a character, is usually *talking* – and often his aim is to speak familiarly out of some bygone era as though it were to-day. His fine poem 'Provincia Deserta' ends:

> I have walked over these roads;
> I have thought of them living.

His sense of the past is less continuous than Eliot's. Thus, his enthusiasm tends to be reserved, among the poets, for those who can be identified as innovators (e.g. Chaucer), not for those (like Milton) who represent the maturity of a tradition. Both he and Eliot have an enormous respect for Dante. But where Eliot is impressed by the mental unity of Dante's Christendom, Pound seems more interested in the freshness of Dante's world. The *Divine Comedy*, he says, was written 'to MAKE PEOPLE THINK' – as though it might have had *Instigations* as a sub-title. Pound's *Cantos*, as their name declares, have their source in Dante. Like the *Divine Comedy*, they will (when complete) consist of 100 cantos. Some of Dante's persons – Arnaut Daniel, Brunetto Latini, Bertrand de Born, Ulysses – figure in them. But they are not in any parallel sense a record of spiritual progress. The redemption offered is primarily economic: redemption, that is, from the sin of usury, the medieval sin that Pound applies as his measure and explanation for much of man's history. Anger replaces humility; Pound's hell, Eliot has well said, is for other people. The Christian tradition, indeed, means little to Pound; he relies upon the wisdom of Confucius, or of the early leaders of his own country, Jefferson and John Adams. In both his prose and his poetry, his learning seems to consist of innumerable gobbets that form a Poundian anthology or *Summa* of human experience. The shape of his *Summa* may elude the casual reader who does not realize that Pound's apparent levity masks a profound seriousness, or that his seemingly scrappy and random statements are the product of long study and thought, presented in the briefest possible way, as 'ideograms'. The more careful student of Pound may, however, conclude that while Pound's system makes sense, and contains a great deal of value, it is ultimately incoherent. And this despite Pound's almost unrivalled poetic talent, which makes the *Cantos* so rich an experience. The trouble is not that Pound has created a private vision. Other men – W.B. Yeats, for example – have done the same; and one does not demand of them an itemized catalogue, as though their work were a property up for auction. A certain idiosyncrasy appears to be a necessary prerequisite for most of the major imaginative *œuvres* of our time; at any rate, its 'public' visions have lacked intensity. Nor can it be said that Pound has been flighty; his convictions have been developed and sustained through half a century of unremitting effort. For other writers he is a tremendously important writer, and there is no doubt that he is a major poet. There is no rule as to how private an author may be. Yet Pound's privacy has, in part, a hostile and aberrant quality. On some days the estate is open to the public; on others, trespassers will be prosecuted.

The poetry and criticism of T. S. Eliot has, by contrast (despite its revolutionary impact), always had an air of consummate maturity. His academic beginnings took in Harvard, the Sorbonne, Germany, and Oxford; his poetic study included a close examination of the French symbolists (particularly Jules Laforgue) and of the English metaphysical authors. He learned from Dante, Blake, Ben Jonson, Baudelaire. His exceptionally fine intellect was matched by a miraculously subtle poetic talent; and consequently, whatever he wrote, from the first poems like 'The Love Song of J. Alfred Prufrock' (1915), at once took its place in modern literature, becoming a classic while it was still new. For a generation, Eliot was almost universally regarded as the foremost living poet of the English language. His emphasis on tradition has therefore had a considerable effect upon his contemporaries. Even in his early and lightly ironic work, his criticism was restrained; it had nothing of hysteria or manifesto about it. As 'Gerontion', or as Tiresias in *The Waste Land*, he speaks as an old man – while yet a young one. By 1927, he described himself in the preface to the essays *For Lancelot Andrewes* as 'classicist in literature, royalist in politics, and Anglo-Catholic in religion'. In an article written a couple of years later, Edmund Wilson objected that Eliot had 'evolved for himself an aristocratic myth' that had no more plausibility than other private systems: than that, for example, of Ezra Pound.

The difference, however, as T. S. Eliot's subsequent writing made clear, is that his own system is firmly defined, and eminently reasonable to those who also adhere to the Christian religion. Those who do not, or who in any case have found his gravity a little oppressive, are forced to reckon with the fact that his poetic genius continued to evolve. His dryness did not become aridity, but rather the quality ascribed to certain champagnes. Though he exasperated Americans like William Carlos Williams by seeming to reject his background, he made amends in recent years. Thus, he has written of *Huckleberry Finn* with generous insight, acknowledging that he, too, born in St Louis not far down-river from Mark Twain's Hannibal, has retained a memory of the Mississippi. Moreover, his lifelong interest in the possibilities of poetic drama does not square with the accusation that he is a disdainful would-be aristocrat. His experiments in this medium, starting with *Sweeney Agonistes, an Aristophanic Melodrama* (printed in *The Criterion*, 1926–7), have shown a steady progress, through *The Rock* (1934), *Murder in the Cathedral* (1935), *The Family Reunion* (1939), and *The Cocktail Party* (1950), toward an ideal of 'that collaboration of the audience with the artist which is necessary in all art and most obviously in dramatic art'. These words come from an essay that he wrote on 'Marie Lloyd', as far back as 1923. He was well aware that he had not yet attained the ideal, and that a fastidious dogmatism made some of his work sound more sanctified than he would like. But at the heart of his effort – as the great *Four Quartets* once more demonstrated – there lay an essential modesty. If his writing occasionally seemed bloodless, or a shade pontifical, it was never contentious and ill-tempered. And his critical evaluations were balanced by a lively and sympathetic appreciation of the nature of creative effort.

One cannot say as much for those extremely able American critics Irving Babbitt and Paul Elmer More, under the former of whom T. S. Eliot studied at Harvard. Middle-aged men by the end of World War I, both had by then made their principles clear. But the follies of the 1920s provoked them to heightened activity. Asserting the values of humanism, they and a few followers accepted the word – sometimes with 'new' as a prefix – as their battle-standard. The Humanists spoke of taste, discipline, standards, the beauties of Hellenism, the necessary moral content of art. They wrote excellently of the literatures they admired. They attacked the modern heresies of science, romanticism, and naturalism – by which they meant in general the opposite of their own canons. According to Babbitt, who argued the matter with great force in *Rousseau and Romanticism* (1919) and *Democracy and Leadership* (1924), the modern age had carried the revolt against authority – a rebellion instigated by Rousseau, Babbitt's arch-enemy – to the point of chaos. The romantic stress on personality had led to a denial of all absolutes and positive values; self-expression had become the norm – the only norm. What was needed, in life before in literature, was a return to ethical imperatives; and perhaps creative literature, in this respect, attended upon criticism.

There was a good deal of wisdom in what the Humanists said, especially as a diagnosis of the ills of modern society. As Babbitt stated, with reference to the much-abused Puritans, the withering away of Christian virtues like 'awe and reverence and humility' had left an empty space, in the individual as well as in society. 'What has tended to disappear is the inner life with the special type of control it imposes.' In its stead, 'there has been an increasing resort to outer control'.[1] T. S. Eliot agreed with some of their strictures. And the other critics, who derided them, often received as much derision by way of reply. H. L. Mencken, for instance, seems at this distance to have lost the argument with the Humanists. But if Mencken and his allies were too close to their time, the Humanists were too far away from it. Disliking its assumptions, they detested its literature, and said so shrilly, pronouncing anathemas like a priesthood that redoubles its severity in an attempt to fill its empty churches. The absolutes that the New Humanists posited, or Babbitt's famous 'inner check', seemed theoretical and cold; the 1920s preferred the warm confusion of modernism. Their symposium *Humanism and America* (1930) was at once answered by another, the *Critique of Humanism*, and in 1931 by George Santayana's *The Genteel Tradition at Bay*. Santayana, a onetime Harvard colleague of Babbitt, maintained that the Humanists' Platonic and Christian postulates were evidence that New England culture had reached a tired and donnish

---

1. This type of diagnosis has recently been more fully developed by David Riesman in his sociological study, *The Lonely Crowd* (1950).

decadence. The Puritan and Transcendental heritage had produced – as Santayana went on to imply in his novel, *The Last Puritan* (1936), and as Eliot said – minds 'refined beyond the point of civilization'.

Santayana was by no means the only writer to couple the New Humanism unfavourably with New England. The introduction to *I'll Take My Stand*, another symposium published in 1930, declared that

The 'Humanists' are too abstract. Humanism, properly speaking, is not an abstract system, but a culture, the whole way in which we live, act, think, and feel. It is a kind of imaginatively balanced life lived out in a definite social tradition. And, in the concrete, we believe that this, the genuine humanism, was rooted in the agrarian life of the older South and of other parts of the country that shared in such a tradition. It was not an abstract moral 'check' derived from the classics. ... We cannot recover our native humanism by adopting some standard of taste that is critical enough to question the contemporary arts but not critical enough to question the social and economic life which is their ground.

Allen Tate, one of the contributors to the book, said in his article that

New England was one of those abstract-minded, sharp-witted trading societies that must be parasites in two ways: They must live economically on some agrarian class or country, and they must live spiritually likewise. New England lived economically on the South, culturally on England.

The sub-title of *I'll Take My Stand* was *The South and the Agrarian Tradition*. The other contributors, who described themselves as 'Twelve Southerners', included John Crowe Ransom, Robert Penn Warren, John Gould Fletcher, and Donald Davidson. They took their stand for 'a Southern way of life against what may be called the American or prevailing way', and agreed 'that the best terms in which to represent the distinction are contained in the phrase, Agrarian *versus* Industrial'. The Agrarians, with their headquarters at Vanderbilt University in Nashville, Tennessee, had previously been known as the Fugitives, from the name of a periodical that they edited from 1922 to 1925. In a way, they were

merely voicing the ancient Southern grievance against the
North: New England had long been identified as the South's
chief foe, and for the best part of a century Southerners had
been insisting on the superiority of their own static agrarian
economy over the demented, urbanized materialism of the
North. But now their protests had a fresh point. Northerners
also began to deplore the consequences of the Machine
Age; Allen Tate was not alone in supposing that the suicide
of his friend Hart Crane had something to do with the impossible pressures of modern city life. Northerners also, as we
have seen, were ready to condemn New England. Much of
what was written by T. S. Eliot, or by the influential New
York critic Lewis Mumford, could be regarded as grist for
the Agrarian mill. Regionalism, in the Agrarian formulation,
had ceased to be parochial, though it continued to employ
some of the old sectional arguments. If New England leaned
culturally upon England, the South did not, according to
Allen Tate and his associates. It, he insisted, had gone
quietly on its own path, not because it was backward and
slothful but because it was mature; 'the South could be ignorant of Europe because it *was* Europe; that is to say, the
South had taken root in a native soil'. Other Agrarians took
up the theme. In his article, John Crowe Ransom stated that
the South 'is unique on this continent for having founded
and defended a culture which was according to the European principles of culture'; and Donald Davidson said 'the
specious theory that an "independent" country ought to
originate an independent art, worthy of its national greatness, did not originate in the South'. Or, as Allen Tate wrote
in 1939, for a *Partisan Review* symposium, only the 'regional'
writer (like himself) could draw upon the whole literary past
of Europe-*and*-America. The 'nationalist' writer, on the
other hand, 'either naïvely assumes the "nationalism" of
mere observation (Sandburg), or tries to pour myths into
"America" from the top of his mind (Crane)'.

Wallace Stevens, participating in the same discussion,
more or less agreed with Tate, in dismissing 'factitious
Americanism'. The Southerners, then, had arrived via

occasionally dubious means at a quite mature non-American position. They were unfair in their remarks on New England, whose European-ness had always had some genuine elements. And they tended to romanticize the South, arguing that its planters had constituted a 'squirearchy' rather than an aristocracy, and that the values they had handed down would be destroyed if the South accepted industrialism (as it had already done in several places). Their South, indeed, like W. B. Yeats's Ireland, was somewhat unreal, yet also – in literary terms – a valuable domain. It did have traditions, and its writers did feel sure enough of themselves – especially as poets – to merge their regional pride in the general world of letters.

Perhaps it is misleading to speak of Agrarianism before speaking of individuals, as though the movement explains its members. The Agrarians were a motley group, who though they may yet die in Dixie, do not now all live there; we are concerned here with only three of them: Ransom, Tate, and Warren. Of these, Allen Tate was never wholly committed to Agrarianism, and for a while sought another allegiance by becoming a Catholic. Nevertheless, the Southern background is helpful to remember in a consideration of their work. Moreover, a consciousness of this background does seem to have helped these men to clarify their writing. John Crowe Ransom, the eldest, began in 1919 with an awkward little volume, *Poems About God* – none of which he has included in later collections. These particularized about the South with not enough precision, and generalized a little too rhetorically. But in the later volumes *Chills and Fever* (1924) and *Two Gentlemen in Bonds* (1927), which form the bulk of his careful *œuvre*, Ransom showed the nicest balance between what he afterwards distinguished as structure and texture. 'A poem,' he said in 1941, 'is a *logical structure* having a *local texture*'; and in the essay where this definition occurs one can see that Southern regionalism has provided him with a deeply significant metaphor. By 'ontological insight', he suggests, the critic is to notice how particulars are a matter of texture, and universals of structure – and how both must be present in a poem, as in a furnished house, in which 'the paint, the paper, the tapestry are texture'. Ransom is not a gaudy poet; but the word *tapestry* is characteristic: we realize that the kind of establishment Ransom has in mind is a survival from a former age. His poetry often deals with antiquity: old men, old buildings, lineage, children confronted with the ancient mystery of death. His vocabulary is appropriately decorous ('Roger Prim' was an early pseudonym), its richnesses are frequently – and deliberately – archaic. The effect is of a beautifully poised intelligence: an effect equally apparent in his critical writing. The South, he knows, is a crumbling place, in some ways resembling Robert Frost's New England. Amused and sad, he says of it (in 'Antique Harvesters', one of his best poems):

> Declension looks from our land, it is old.

Yet behind the fatigue and the slight absurdity of the Southern vision he perceives a love and loyalty that are very important to him. 'Antique Harvesters' ends:

> True, it is said of our Lady, she ageth.
> But see, if you peep shrewdly, she hath not stooped;
> Take no thought of her servitors that have drooped,
> For we are nothing; and if one talk of death –
> Why, the ribs of the earth subsist frail as a breath
> If but God wearieth.

Allen Tate, a no less accomplished poet, has likewise contemplated the South, and the world, with a discriminating and witty detachment. The biographer of Stonewall Jackson and Jefferson Davis, he regrets his ruined region, and the spoiled nation in which (he wrote in 1927, in the 'Epistle' to Edmund Wilson, 'a Syracusan domiciled at Rome'):

> Once we had marvelled country-wise,
> My friend. You know that light was brief.
> Mile after mile the cities rise
> Where brisk Adonis tied the sheaf.

But his regret is for the most part light and classical. The harm is done, the dissonances multiply. Though he invokes

the Confederate dead in his handsome *Ode*, there are no
words to speak at the desolate autumn scene:

> We shall say only the leaves
> Flying, plunge and expire.

At times there is an edge of asperity or despair, as in 'Aeneas
at Washington' (published in *The Mediterranean and Other
Poems*, 1936):

> Stuck in the wet mire
> Four thousand leagues from the ninth buried city
> I thought of Troy, what we had built her for.

However, his classical urbanity comes to his relief – if one
can attribute urbanity to a former Agrarian. Tate's volumes
of criticism, from *Reactionary Essays* (1936) to *The Forlorn
Demon* (1953), prove that, like Ransom, he is an exceptionally sensitive, thoughtful student of literature. 'The kind of
criticism that dominates our intellectual life' (he complains
in *Reactionary Essays*) 'is that of the French mathematician
who, after reading a tragedy by Racine, asked: "*Qu'est-ce
que cela prouve?*" It proves nothing; it creates the totality of
experience in its quality; and it has no useful relation to the
ordinary forms of action.' He and Ransom describe themselves as Aristotelian in their critical thought, and dislike
what they call Platonic forms of literature, which fail to
make the necessary fusion that Tate admires in Donne, or
in Emily Dickinson, who '*perceives abstraction* and *thinks sensation*'. Thus, though they based themselves originally upon a
regional pride, their thought had led not into 'folksiness',
but scrupulously away from it. Their standards, it has been
observed, 'are aesthetic and metaphysical rather than sociological, economic, historical, psychological, or moral'.

A similar spirit can be seen in the writing of the Kentucky
poet-critic-novelist Robert Penn Warren, though in his case
there is a colloquial energy and a fascinated absorption in
ambiguities of good and evil that set him a little apart. His
novel *All the King's Men* (1946) is the story of the rise and fall
of a Southern politician not unlike Huey Long. But it is a
complicated exercise in morality, in which villainy and

virtue are mixed together and inseparable. So are they in Warren's well-known 'Ballad of Billie Potts', which has a plot resembling that of Albert Camus' play *Le Malentendu* (and also mentioned by Camus in his novel *L'Étranger*. It would be most interesting to compare the existentialist implications of Camus with Warren's sense of the Southern wanderer coming back to his home, to evoke the love of his parents only after they have killed him).

As a critic, however, Warren is as precise as one could wish. Even more exacting is the criticism of his friend and colleague Cleanth Brooks, another Southerner who though not himself a poet has devoted most of his career to the exegesis of poetry. In *Modern Poetry and the Tradition* (1939) and *The Well Wrought Urn* (1947) he is largely concerned with the ways in which a great poem succeeds. It does so, he says (quoting Coleridge)

in the balance or reconcilement of opposite or discordant qualities: of sameness, with difference; of the general, with the concrete; the idea, with the image; the individual, with the representative; the sense of novelty and freshness, with old and familiar objects; a more than usual state of emotion, with more than usual order. ...

This, as Brooks comments, is a series of paradoxes; and poetry at its best (as in the metaphysical writers, whom Brooks – like Ransom, or of course like Eliot – much admires) unites apparent paradoxes by way of metaphor. Poetry itself, in this sense, might be taken as a metaphor of the American intellectual in relation to his country. The extremities of his isolation have encouraged him to place the highest value upon art. Cleanth Brooks's *Well Wrought Urn* is reminiscent of Wallace Stevens' 'Anecdote of the Jar', which begins:

> I placed a jar in Tennessee,[1]
> And round it was, upon a hill.
> It made the slovenly wilderness
> Surround that hill.

The work of art, Brooks and the others who have evolved the 'New Criticism' contend, exists *apart* from everydayness.

1. Perhaps near Vanderbilt University?

Here, one may sometimes infer, are supposed to be the absolutes, the timeless essences, that modern man is seeking.

If 'we boldly pre-empt the poem for our own purposes' (to use Brooks's words) the result may, however, be an investigation that is at once too thorough and too narrow. This has been the objection of some other critics to the New Criticism. Perhaps criticism as practised by such subtle authors as Yvor Winters, R. P. Blackmur, Kenneth Burke, or Stanley Edgar Hyman is apt to be excessively 'formalist' or unsympathetic to the non-literary factors that in some way or other influence literature. But these are men of great sensibility as well as analytical ability; it is only in the hands of the mediocre practitioners that this so-called New Criticism seems ponderous or arid. Nor has it been the only mature critical work in America; in their different lines F. O. Matthiessen, Perry Miller, Edmund Wilson, and Lionel Trilling have all made brilliant contributions. Indeed, the mass of ambitious critical writing has grown so large that some Americans feel it is crushing creative effort. Its mass is a little alarming. But it has not of itself harmed the creative writer. In poetry, certainly, the older figures have continued to produce distinguished work. Richard Eberhart and half a dozen others are examples of this truth. A few dazzling early reputations have not been sustained. But poets appear to have better staying power than novelists; and current American poetry, which is discussed in the concluding chapter, has many excellences.

This hurried account has left out a good deal of critical writing that has emphasized the fact of *America*. There is, for instance, the prominent contribution of Van Wyck Brooks. Like the Humanists or the Agrarians, he has always thought tradition important. But in his early work – *Wine of the Puritans* (1908), *America's Coming-of-Age* (1915), *Letters and Leadership* (1918) – while urging Americans to take literature seriously, he was at pains to show how sterile American letters had been. Attempting to apply psycho-analytical methods in *The Ordeal of Mark Twain* (1920) and *The Pilgrimage of Henry James* (1925), he argued that these writers had lost their way through inhibition and evasion of their native possibilities. More recently he has revised his opinions. In the five graceful volumes to which he has given the collective title of *Makers and Finders: a History of the Writer in America, 1800–1915* (1936–52) he has presented the United States not as a cultural wasteland but as a country teeming with talent, idiosyncrasy, and aspiration. Van Wyck Brooks is most successful in the first volumes, before the scene has grown too cluttered with makers and finders. All of the five books have something of the anecdotal charm of, say, Isaac D'Israeli's *Curiosities of Literature*. The final one, though, stops at 1915, with an acerbity that helps us to understand why James T. Farrell associated Brooks with Archibald MacLeish in what he called 'the League of Frightened Philistines'.

Taken in sum, the American achievement in poetry and criticism, as well as in historical and other forms of scholarship, has been extraordinarily impressive. Lewis Mumford, Harry Levin, Alfred Kazin, Richard Hofstadter: these and a score of other names spring to mind. We tend to discuss modern American literature too exclusively in terms of fiction, and often generalize from the novel or short story, as if all American writing were equally violent, active, and unintellectual. Anyone who glances at the work of the many gifted Americans in other fields will soon perceive that a large body of American literature is, on the contrary, subtle, sophisticated, and mature.

CHAPTER FIFTEEN

AMERICA AND THE WRITER
SINCE 1945

THE last few years have not been tranquil in the United States. The peace seemingly restored in 1945 proved not to have been restored at all. Far from being able to relax and enjoy the fruits of victory, America faced more serious and more intractable problems than ever before in her history. True, she was also richer and more powerful than ever before. But the prosperity was accompanied by acute tensions and divisions; and world leadership did not come easily to a nation that had so long prided itself on being exempt from the conflicts and alliances of the Old World. Intelligent Americans urged their fellow-countrymen to accept their new responsibilities. Less intelligent and more bigoted Americans, finding a spokesman in the late Senator Mc-Carthy, sought a simple explanation for their problems. With him, they believed that they were the victims of a con-spiracy – the conspiracy of world Communism, acting inside the very centres of American life: the federal government, the schools, Hollywood, even within the churches. Witch-hunts and spy-manias swept the country. Caution and con-formity became epidemic. It was difficult for writers and other intellectuals, while the mood lasted, to maintain their dignity. Some claimed, a little exaggeratedly, that they were being persecuted: it became almost a point of pride, for some, to insist that their telephones were being tapped. Others hastened to apologize in public for past errors in their thinking. Others again, insensibly, abandoned their inter-est in political ideas in favour of a kind of apolitical con-servatism. The national mood was nervous, aggressive–defensive, lost. Americans looked back nostalgically to the supposed certainties of the early Republic, or to the highly coloured drama of the Civil War (the subject of score upon score of books), or to the informalities of the 1920s and the dedications of the 1930s. In retrospect, each of these eras seemed to be enviably self-possessed and extraordinarily remote. Americans felt cut off from their own past.

Shock upon shock continued to buffet the America of the 1960s. No sooner did one crisis die away than another claimed the headlines. The courage and growing militancy of the civil rights movement, the disciplined intransigence of the Black Muslims and the killing of their chief spokesman, Malcolm X; the reluctant discovery that the nation's affluence was accompanied by widespread and perhaps growing poverty; the murder of President Kennedy, in circumstances of weird confusion; the involvement in Vietnam: all these outran conjecture so swiftly that it began to seem that the old division of history into generations of twenty or thirty years would have to be replaced by some shorter unit – say, a lustrum of five years. One consequence was an intense desire to know exactly what was going on. More than ever Americans discussed their 'identity', personal and national.

How were they to define their own era? Sociology has supplied some of the answers. Two works in particular have been extremely influential. One of these is *The Lonely Crowd* (1951) by David Riesman, Nathan Glazer, and Reuel Denney. The other is William H. Whyte Jr's *The Organization Man* (1956). From Riesman's book – significantly subtitled *A Study of the Changing American Character* – Americans conclude that they are becoming a nation of conformists, 'other-directed' where their ancestors were 'inner-directed'; a nation of people with no fixed standards or beliefs, striving to resemble their next-door neighbours. From William H. Whyte, Jr, it appears that the average American, however sentimentally he regards the frontiersman, the pioneer, the 'rugged individual' of the national past, is now likely to work for a large, paternalistic business corporation, which exercises an insidious though not deliberately tyrannical influence over his own behaviour and that of his family. Not all sociologists have been as relatively dispassionate as Riesman and Whyte. In *The Power Elite* (1956), C. Wright Mills angrily contends that the United States is governed by a quite small interlocking directorate of corporation heads and military chieftains. In *Growing Up Absurd* (1960), Paul Goodman argues that there is a simple though serious reason for the spread of juvenile delinquency in the United States: the goals of American society are shoddy, and so the American adolescent declines to fit himself for full membership in it. Michael Harrington's *The Accidental Century* (1965) offers a comprehensively radical criticism of the 'decadence' of the modern industrial order, which controls where it should allow freedom of action and leaves alone where it should control. Whatever their viewpoint, such books attest the uneasiness and self-consciousness of contemporary America, and the readiness of Americans to accept the idea that they are isolated from their own past.

With the desire for enlightenment came a new respect for the factual, the documentary, the authentic, the analytical. Norman Podhoretz argues that much of the best work of 'creative' writers in recent years has taken the form of high-level journalism. He is not the only one to prefer the Norman Mailer of *The Presidential Papers* to the Mailer of *An American Dream*, or to be more moved by the essays of James Baldwin than by his novels. Others have found the critical essays of Mary McCarthy brilliant and incisive where her novel *The Group* struck them as sprawling gossip. Not everyone would agree with Podhoretz – himself a magazine editor. The late Randall Jarrell said in *A Sad Heart at the Supermarket*:

Our age is the age of articles: we buy articles in stores, read articles in magazines, exist among the interstices of articles: of columns, interviews, photographic essays, documentaries; of facts condensed into headlines or expanded into non-fiction best-sellers; of real facts about real people.

Jarrell might have added that we read books made up, like his own, from articles previously printed in magazines. Or we might add on his behalf that Jarrell, a fine poet, was perhaps an even finer critic. He was certainly correct in noticing, with Podhoretz, the quantity of sub-genres. Magazine journalism is nothing new. What is relatively new is the interview as a literary form. It provides, to use a favourite word of the 1960s, 'instant' literature. Neither editors nor readers would be so indulgent to its loose, self-regarding, public–private quality if they did not obscurely feel that it fills a need — for actuality, for being in the know.

As for 'documentaries', these too are not altogether new. James Agee's *Let Us Now Praise Famous Men* was a great though neglected imaginative record of Southern sharecroppers as they lived in 1936. Reprinted in the 1960s, it stands beside Oscar Lewis's *Children of Sánchez* (1961), the 'autobiography' of a family in Mexico City, as a masterpiece of honest and sympathetic social observation. Truman Capote's *In Cold Blood* (1965) probably deserves equal recognition, though some critics have been exasperated by the circumstances of its publication. Capote's account of two criminals and the four people they murdered in Kansas was extravagantly publicized before it ever came out. Certain reviewers seemed to feel that there was something too shrewdly calculated in a devotion that made him a millionaire. They were on surer ground in resisting the claim that Capote had invented the 'non-fiction novel'. A similar theme was explored by Thomas De Quincey ('On Murder Considered as One of the Fine Arts') well over a century ago. However, Capote's feat of reconstruction is genuine and important. He withholds sympathy from neither killers nor victims. He has had a deserved luck in discovering a story whose details would strain credulity if presented as fiction, and which is yet convincing.

When we shift to avowed novels, the turnover of the generations is an astonishing feature. Since 1945 a dozen reputations and movements have come and gone. There is for example the former vogue for conservatism catered to by Herman Wouk in his two best-selling novels *The Caine Mutiny* (1951) and *Marjorie Morningstar* (1955). They represent with an almost sociological exactness the condition of mind of middlebrow America in the early 1950s. They affronted American intellectuals, however, by reversing standard situations in American fiction. In *The Caine Mutiny*, after seeming to portray a regular naval officer as neurotic and incompetent, Wouk nevertheless thumps home the moral that the 'service' has its own wisdom, which includes the principle of rigid loyalty to superior officers – a conclusion which not even a middlebrow American novel would have been likely to reach in an earlier era. In *Marjorie Morningstar*, Wouk argues a double lesson: first, that the heroine is wrong to repudiate her religious heritage (in this case Jewish), and second, that she is right to repudiate the world of Bohemians and intellectuals in favour of a comfortable and appropriate marriage to a businessman. A comparable plot to that of Sinclair Lewis's *Main Street*, but with the important difference that Wouk is far more assertive in his defence of bourgeois standards.

The position of James Gould Cozzens is more complex. He is an able writer whose first novel was published as far back as 1924. He achieved widespread recognition with *Guard of Honour* (1948), an account of life on an American air force base. He achieved sensational success with *By Love Possessed* (1957), a long, involuted novel with a number of highly articulate characters. Sober critics acclaimed *By Love Possessed* as a masterpiece. One or two asserted that it was, at last, that chimera, the definitive Great American Novel. Counter-critics demolished these claims, pointing out that the book is pretentious, wordy, and fatigued rather than mature in its assessment of human conduct. One feels that the counter-critics were right, though possibly a little hard on Mr Cozzens. Why, then, the initial acclaim? In part, it would seem, because Americans still *do* hanker after the Great American Novel. Some of them had been predicting that Cozzens would produce it. They willed themselves into believing that his novel was great because it appeared to fit the specification: the specification, that is, of the 1950s. It was lengthy, it was ambitious, it was jaded in tone, it was concerned with polite society and educated people (though some of their behaviour was violent enough to suit lower tastes). Could Cozzens be seen, therefore, as an American equivalent to Thomas Mann or Marcel Proust? Was this the final proof that an American novelist could go beyond the stark patterns of Hemingway, the depravities of Faulkner? Have American critics grown embarrassed by the tough-guy formulae of their fiction? Whatever their reasons, some critics continue to demand contemporary greatness; and some other novelists apparently endeavour to rise to the demanded heights, with a curious excess of intent. William Styron is one of these. His *Lie Down in Darkness* (1951) is a well-constructed, well-written novel that goes on too long and tries too hard. The same can be said of his *Set This House on Fire* (1960). One could mention the work of other novelists – enormous, confident, nuanced, Jamesian–Wolfeian, and oddly overblown.

For some years *the* voice of the post-war generation seemed to be that of Jerome D. Salinger, the author of *The Catcher in the Rye* (1951) and of a quite small number of short stories. The majority of these first appeared in the *New Yorker*; a much-discussed pair were reprinted as *Franny and Zooey* (1961). Salinger speaks for the young urban American of middle-class parentage. In his world no one is starving, or much concerned with what might be called public issues. The code of his characters, though as sharp as that of Hemingway's, has little to do with heroism. As in Hemingway, the people he admires are above all sincere – a word they would probably not use except in mockery. His anger is reserved for sham. Salinger's ideal people are children; he is as nice about them as any Victorian lady novelist. Next best are adolescents. Few of his adults emerge intact from the corruption of growing up. Indeed they do not grow *up* but *down*. In *The Catcher in the Rye* Salinger surveys the American scene through the eyes of a confused and incoherent yet peculiarly likeable adolescent, Holden Caulfield, whose only certainty is that he can detect a phoney but who has a passionate devotion toward the few genuine people in his life. In the cluster of stories that deal with a family named Glass – the Glass Menagerie as facetiously labelled – the situation is more intricate. The brothers and sisters in the family are highly intelligent, but their dilem-

mas are of the same order as Holden Caulfield's. They are
disgusted by the frauds of everyday life and by the consola-
tory catchwords that are supposed to constitute a framework
of belief. They are capable of poetic insight and of a quasi-
religious exaltation in which Christian mysticism and Zen
Buddhism are eclectically mingled. Salinger exactly catches
– and has helped to define as a mode – one level of modern
American society, with its irreverence, its desire for wholeness, its self-indulgence. But his despairs, like those of the
Glass family, begin to seem whimsical, narcissistic, and
even old-fashioned. To the very latest sub-generation of
readers and critics, Salinger's achievement is, perhaps
harshly, put in the past tense. The verdict is that he produced a modern version of *Huckleberry Finn* in *Catcher in the
Rye*, then pyrotechnically fizzled out.

Another type of literature associated mainly with the
1950s was produced by the 'Beat' writers. They obviously
had some features in common with Salinger – a distaste for
'square' (i.e., conventional, insensitive) behaviour, a deep
restlessness, an indifference to the past (especially, perhaps,
the recent past), a dislike for whatever is 'square' about the
United States itself, a search for truth, life, love, experience,
and so on, a readiness to believe that there is something to be
learned from Zen philosophy with its casual, rather wayward doctrine of no-doctrine. The Beatnik movement has
received so much publicity that we can now hardly separate
its genuine from its factitious aspects: or indeed, its American from its international ramifications. In origin it is a
phenomenon of the West Coast, more especially of the San
Francisco region. The Beat style in dress and talk spread to
New York and to other large cities; the Beat style in literature has likewise been widely adopted.

In fiction the best-known practitioner is Jack Kerouac.
His first popular novel, *On the Road* (1957), has been followed by a batch of others with the same characteristics. All
are markedly autobiographical, and written in a loose incantatory prose. These books recount the adventures of a
group of young people who refuse to be tied down to steady

jobs and do their best to avoid other entanglements, such as matrimony. Kerouac characters live as simply as possible, and on the spur of the moment. They drive great distances: travel is both a liberation and a narcotic for them, for it is the mere travel, at speed and with a motiveless determination, that really matters. They also sit still and talk a great deal, quoting tags of Zen at one another and enthusing over what is good in the world.

There is something attractive about the Beatnik fashion. To the extent that contemporary America is, in Alfred Kazin's phrase, a 'prig's paradise', a prosperous and lifeless civilization, Kerouac and his associates are making a genuine gesture of protest. They can be seen as the latest protesters in a long and worthy American tradition that reaches at least as far back as Thoreau and that certainly includes Walt Whitman. Some of the more senior authors who have been linked with the Beat movement, notably the poet Kenneth Rexroth, are capable craftsmen. The Beat mode of writing, too, has the justification of tradition. Like Whitman, Kerouac and others celebrate the First Person Singular: *myself* as the proper subject of literature, *my own* spontaneous impressions as things possessing a unique value. Kerouac does manage now and then to convey a Whitman-esque ecstasy.

But most of the time he states rather than conveys, and gossips rather than writes. He has published far too much, and revised far too little. The collective narcissism of the Kerouac circle is ultimately boring and trivial. Like others before them who have led the *vie de Bohème*, their creative effort is dispersed in the effort to simulate creativity. As with cookery, the product is consumed daily, leaving behind only a faint aroma. Moreover, the emphasis on spontaneity, which came near to spoiling much of Whitman's poetry, militates against serious literary achievement. The Beat style seems likely to contribute more to American slang than to American letters. It is both garrulous and inarticulate – private, rambling, cynical–sentimental. If Kerouac is repetitious and imprecise, the fault is no less apparent in the Beat poetry of Allen Ginsberg or Gregory Corso. There is a great deal of ferocity in it. Surrealist effects are aimed at. But there is more bad temper than indignation. It is a hit-and-miss poetry, a display of personality – and so a dangerously attractive kind of poetry for the legion of young Americans who want to be great writers but have no talent except the talent (temporary, alas) for being young.

To go on scolding Beat writing for more than a few lines is to exaggerate its importance. No doubt its importance will always be exaggerated: it will figure in the literary histories because it looks like a 'movement', because it is easily describable, and because, after all, it does represent an aspect of America in the 1950s. So this may become known to posterity as the Beat Decade. If so, the description will be as misleading as to call the 1920s the Jazz Age. Zen was not the only doctrine quoted by writers in the 1950s, any more than dancing the Charleston was the only pastime of young people thirty years before.

Some writers go their own way, competently and unmodishly, and so tend to be left out of literary team-lists. Wright Morris, for example, is a figure who cannot be neatly categorized. Nor can the admirably professional Edwin O'Connor. John O'Hara is often said to have been at his best in the 1930s with such novels as *Appointment in Samarra* and *Butterfield 8*. This is probably true of his novels. But his short stories of the 1960s are miracles of condensed observation. And though the South is no longer in the forefront of American fiction, the names of Flannery O'Connor, Peter Taylor and several other Southern writers command respect. Flannery O'Connor died young. So did Edward Lewis Wallant, who was only thirty-six when he died in 1962, leaving behind four novels either in print or ready for posthumous publication; *The Human Season, The Pawnbroker, The Children at the Gate, The Tenants of Moonbloom*. They are excellent novels about the clumsy and alien poor living squalidly in Northern cities. The moments of joy – epiphanies – are a little contrived, but grow out of an authentic tenderness which has nothing to do with sentimentality.

Another highly individual writer who has become well known for his semi-sociological work is Paul Goodman. His *Empire City* (1959), on which he worked intermittently for twenty years, is a rich, chaotic fantasia, devoid of formal plot and peopled by brilliant, anarchic monsters. It is written in a queer medley of styles, ranging from the formality of Edith Wharton through the clichés of Horatio Alger to the quick slang of metropolitan America. It is about New York City, about all cities, about the horrors of modern life, about intellectuals and their dreams and nightmares. *The Empire City* is not easy to read, but is a book of rare quality.

Ralph Ellison has been variously analysed as a Negro writer and as a 'one-book' novelist. His *Invisible Man* was published in 1952. In the next fourteen years he was represented only by a volume of essays, *Shadow and Act* (1964). But *The Invisible Man* was cited in 1965 by a panel of two hundred authors and critics as the work of American fiction most likely to endure of all those published since 1945. F. W. Dupee has pointed out that it may owe some of its imaginative power to its having been written before the explosion of Negro protest. 'What romancer or straight novelist,' Dupee asks, 'could improve on the looks and speech of Sheriff Jim of Selma, Alabama, or contrive an imbroglio more outrageous than that evolving from the triple murders in Philadelphia, Mississippi?' A more recent novel would almost inevitably have taken on something of the nature of a tract. By temperament Ellison is less of a sermonizer than James Baldwin. His essays show that he has tried to resist the inverted stereotypes of the civil rights movement with their absolute indictment of 'Whitey', 'The Man' – namely, the white man. However there is nothing placatory about *The Invisible Man*. It is a furious fantasy, as savage in its concluding account of a Harlem riot as the apocalyptic novels of Ignatius Donnelly and Jack London, or as Richard Wright's passionately angry *Native Son* (1940), whose main character, Bigger Thomas, is a defiant *Untermensch*. But *The Invisible Man* is more mythical, more ambitious, more subtle than these. Most prophecies soon smell of their own time: this one has come true.

Another writer who stands apart is Vladimir Nabokov, the Russian-born author of *Lolita* (1955). A scholar, a stylist and a wit, Nabokov is in some senses caricatured by being described as an 'American' author. But it is enough for us that he writes in English, that he resided for twenty years in the United States, and that some of his best work is set in America. *Lolita* has achieved notoriety for wrong reasons, and is widely regarded by the public as a 'dirty' book, a mere essay on the perverted sexual appeal that a 'nymphet' or young girl may hold for a middle-aged man. *Lolita* has contributed, in a way no doubt unintended by Nabokov, to a 'revolution' in public taste; Henry Miller is no longer banned in the United States, and to an audience fed on William Burroughs' *Naked Lunch*, Terry Southern's *Candy*, or Hubert Selby Jr's *Exit to Brooklyn*, it may already seem quaintly old-fashioned. *Lolita* is a somewhat obsessive book; the theme is pursued with an absorbed subtlety that the reader may find distasteful. But it is also, as Lionel Trilling says, a book about love which achieves a beautiful statement of that emotion when the hero finally encounters his lost Lolita and recognizes that despite her cheapness she is still deeply dear to him. It is moreover a book of astonishing wit and verve. No one has written better than Nabokov of the vulgarities of the American scene – for example of the squalors and absurdities of American motels, a rich subject which at last found its poet-sociologist in Nabokov. The same ruthless hilarity, the same outsider's fastidious insight, are evident in another novel by Nabokov, *Pnin* (1957), the story of an ageing Russian emigré who teaches at an American college. America, exile, the academic background, scholarship, pedantry, private obsession are all brought together in *Pale Fire* (1962), with a virtuosity that makes most contemporary novelists seem almost empty-handed by comparison. Nabokov has every gift except clumsiness.

Three other American novelists with a distinctly superior

range and resilience are Bernard Malamud, Saul Bellow, and Norman Mailer. All three are Jewish, as are a high proportion of America's best novelists, artists, and critics. Being a Jew is, like being a Negro, a much-discussed situation in the United States. Minorities may be disabled by their problems. Until lately this has been the plight of the Negro intellectual. Less brutally excluded, the Jews in America have managed to retain their particular identity, as a plus not a minus quantity, and to become spokesmen for society as a whole. Their view was ready-made for a newly alarmed and urbanized civilization. They have been able to contribute erudition, alertness, detachment, cosmopolitanism, survivors' wisdom. Once Americans were ready to realize that Jews were not aliens, it was possible for them to define the majority by means of the minority. 'All men are Jews', says Malamud.

He can write with equal assurance and felicity about Jews and about Gentiles, though the interaction fascinates him. He can contrive as a 'magic realist' to discuss with wonderment the skills of baseball (*The Natural*, 1952). He can extract painful comedy from the errors and misgivings of a Jewish teacher in a rural academic environment (*A New Life*, 1961). His surest writing, in *The Assistant* (1957) and the stories in *The Magic Barrel* (1958), is about poor people, city Jews, salesmen and shopkeepers who have not broken out of the first immigrant mould into the higher banalities of the suburbs and the professions. They are worried, dyspeptic, non-violent, entangled people, like those in Wallant's novels. It might sound ironic to call them a chosen race – except that they feel themselves to have been chosen, even if it is only for calamity. Their ill luck endows them with a moving, inelegant humaneness. They are sustained by hints of salvation, or rather of remission if not of reprieve: some slight remission of sins, some partial remission of sentence for decent behaviour.

This world of shabby streets and lonely men forms the setting of the early work of America's finest living novelist, Saul Bellow. *Dangling Man* (1944) is the chronicle of a young man who is waiting to be called up for military service. He has left his civilian job, and month after month goes by before the army summons him. He is in limbo, a city drifter, a frequenter of afternoon movies, whose liberty becomes increasingly burdensome. *The Victim* (1947) is a subtle account of a good-natured, rather fussy Jew persecuted by an obnoxious, half-mad yet peculiarly pathetic Gentile who battens upon him and insists that he is to blame for the wreck of the Gentile's career. The question of which of the two is the real victim is left open. Bellow's third novel, *The Adventures of Augie March* (1953), is longer, bigger, looser, and written in the Bellovian style which he has since perfected: personal, anecdotal, witty, colloquial and also elaborate. 'I kicked over the traces,' Bellow explains of this novel, 'wrote catch-as-catch can, picaresque.' *Augie March* is indeed a picaresque novel, to the extent that its hero, a young man from Chicago, has no particular moral scruples and a wide curiosity about human nature. He is a fairly passive charac- ter: things happen *to* him, and his response, at first cheerfully acquiescent, is to pull out from each adventure, leaving himself free for the next. At times the invention sags and we seem merely to accumulate detail. The conclusion is somewhat frenetic. But Augie lives acutely, perceptively, and on the whole generously. Though the style is a little too uniformly high-pitched to escape monotony, it per- mits Bellow to pass easily from rough slum talk to poetic utterance. It imparts a hectic, swaggering quality to the book.

The same style and spirit animate *Henderson the Rain King* (1959). Henderson is, if this can be imagined, an upper-class version of Twain's Connecticut Yankee, with the vital dif- ference that he makes a mess of things throughout and yet grows in the process. Augie, like his author, is a Jew, born among the immigrant poor. Henderson is a rich, privileged Gentile. He is also a wanderer, and like Augie a person of neutral convictions who nevertheless looks for a meaning in life. Henderson goes to Africa, roaming among strange tribes and learning tranquillity among them before he sets off home again. He is spoilt but not ruined, and this is what Bellow seems to be saying about modern society too. The search for individual freedom is part of a search for a social order. The person who is nothing but the product of his society is a mere integer. The person who tries to be totally private is doomed to even worse failure. The novelist (or critic or moralist) who harps upon modern man's 'alienation' is in Bellow's wise and vigorous view a cliché-monger, an encourager of self-pity. This is not a matter of pretending that modern life is idyllic. Much of it is horrible. But it *is* life; and the only sensible recourse is to live it to the full, as Henderson does. This attitude is splendidly affirmed in Bellow's *Herzog* (1961). Some critics have complained that *Herzog*, the odyssey of a scholarly American Jew, is too loose and too much in the nature of a semi-autobiographical fantasia interspersed with intellectual digressions. *Herzog* is a portrait of a contemporary intellectual, and the central character Moses Herzog is given the benefit of the doubt – of his own many doubts. But he is the most diverting and endearing of modern heroes. Some years ago Philip Rahv observed that American novelists were incapable of portraying intellect and the intellectual. There was a good deal of truth in this when he wrote. *Herzog* is a triumphant exception. One of the most learned, articulate and genuinely intelligent characters in the whole of modern fiction, he is not merely an abstraction but a believable and richly interesting man, awkward and wilful and bruised but yet alive, indomitable, oscillating between fury and delight. He lives in his mind and in his memory. Less perfect in definition than Bellow's brilliant novella *Seize the Day* (1956), *Herzog* is a truly large conception.

The third novelist whose work has been much discussed ever since his first novel, *The Naked and the Dead* (1948), is Norman Mailer. This is still the best American fictional account of the 1939–45 war, though James Jones's *The Thin Red Line* (1963) achieves some of the same intensity of horror. The success of *The Naked and the Dead* posed special problems for Mailer. It established him immediately as an 'important' novelist, and this seemingly obliged him to act as a figure whose creative struggles had to be performed in public. His next novels, *Barbary Shore* (1951) and *The Deer Park* (1955), were serious endeavours on very different themes. *The Deer Park* is good on the Hollywood milieu, though it suffers from Mailer's inability to decide whether the sexual styles of southern California are a proof of decadence or of pioneering efforts along the last frontier – the frontier of the orgasm. *Advertisements for Myself* (1959) contains miscellaneous pieces, including his essay on 'The White Negro' and a remarkable frontiersman's fragment of a projected novel. A subsequent collection, *Presidential Papers*, assembles some likeably boastful and perceptive essays on the America of the Kennedy years. *An American Dream* (1964) is a bad novel which like some other inferior work of Mailer's is bad without being negligible. Flamboyant, sexually blatant, frequently preposterous, it is redeemed in part by Mailer's energy and curiosity.

In extreme form, Mailer's career illustrates a fascinating duality in the outlook of present-day America. This is often expressed as a conflict between 'high' and 'mass' culture, and usually with the implication that the latter weakens the former. Some analysts have seen that the distinction between the two is not always very sharp. Dwight Macdonald has argued that, with the popularization of 'culture' in the United States, there has been a spread of middlebrow taste – 'Midcult' is his term. It involves undiscriminating approval of a variety of products, including even so-called 'avant-garde' work, and leads to a general debasement. The fairly good is the enemy of the truly good.

This formulation rightly draws attention to the market-place aspects of contemporary culture. But it does not offer a convincing picture of 'high' culture. The duality illustrated in Mailer's work is rather different. 'Modern' art has been in existence so long that there is, in the words of the critic Harold Rosenberg, a 'tradition of the new'. Both the artist and an increasingly high proportion of the general public attach high value to innovation. The widely approved idea of being a 'pioneer' has merged with the formerly unappreciated and defiant idea of belonging to the 'avant-garde'. Though he is out in front, he is so in the sense in which a runner leads the field. If he slows up he will be overhauled and left behind. So an element of competitiveness enters into the notion of being an innovator. If an artist slackens the pace, he will be beaten by his rivals. They engage in a contest, often highly publicized, in which critical esteem and financial success are almost synonymous. Hence the tendency, so noticeable since 1945, for art-styles to be swiftly imitated by commercial art – in advertising, window-display, and clothing fashions. Hence too the tendency for art-styles to change almost as rapidly as fashions in dress, and for each style to be as dominant, while it is in full swing, as it is temporary. 'Action painting' or abstract expressionism held the galleries in total subjection, only to yield to 'pop' art, which in turn was replaced by 'op' art. The works of art produced in this rapidly changing climate are by serious men, intensely involved in the idiom of the moment. They have not 'sold out' or 'gone commercial'. Yet their art as an economic fact bears a close resemblance to other aspects of a consumer economy which lives by novelty, and so by planned or at any rate effective mechanisms of obsolescence.

The apparent connexion between built-in obsolescence and changes in art-styles has struck several commentators. Does the same connexion exist for certain forms of literature? In fiction at least the parallels seem close. Though writers like Mailer complain that the public ruins them, and though they sometimes use a 'traditional' vocabulary to express this complaint, they can hardly pretend that they perish of neglect. Starving in a garret is not a feature of the American author of the 1960s, if he writes novels with any claim to being 'advanced'. Agents and publishers are tireless in their search for unknown talent. One successful book is enough to convince the aspiring young novelist that he has found his profession. True, most novels do not make money. But novelists are taught to expect them to do so. They begin

to expect critical *and* financial recognition. They are egged
on by publishers and reviewers. They are invited to lecture
at universities and to pass on their secrets to other would-be
writers at summer schools and conferences. They are in
demand as television panelists. Columnists seek quotable
and if possible outrageous remarks from them for gossip
columns. *Esquire* and *Playboy* will pay them handsomely for
'far-out' stories and articles. They may be summoned to the
White House – and may gain additional *éclat* by refusing the
invitation. They may even think of running for political
office, as Norman Mailer and Gore Vidal have done. In
short, their personalities as well as their printed words are
taken into account. They become celebrities, as if they were
actors or pop singers.

In order to become famous they must hit upon a distinctive 'signature'. To maintain their standing they must
however write novels which possess novelty – which are
'new' and 'news'. Small wonder that some writers, while
revelling in the limelight, find the strain intolerable. Mailer
at the age of twenty-five was typed as a war novelist, and has
made heroic efforts to define fresh and different themes in
subsequent novels. He has taken himself seriously, as a
writer should. But like Hemingway before him he has made
the drama too personal and too public. He has seen his own
struggles as Promethean, and like Hemingway has spoken
of himself as if he were a prize athlete or boxing champion,
constantly challenged for first place. One critic, perhaps
unfairly, has maintained that Mailer's *An American Dream*,
which deals with crime and punishment (or more accurately,
crime without punishment), was written in deliberate emu-
lation of a one-time and all-time champ, Dostoyevsky, even
to the point of being produced serially for a magazine.

Mailer, in common with other ambitious novelists, no
doubt aims at work of permanent value. But the conditions
in which he works are those of built-in obsolescence. What is
new rapidly becomes old – in the slang term, 'old-hat'.
Styles, in writing as in fashion, are easily imitated. The
number of ways of being new is limited. Insult, diabolism,

sexual extravagance are among the ways. Each has its limits. As Mary McCarthy has said, in 'The Tyranny of the Orgasm', explicit sexual encounters are not rewarding material for the novelist. The sex act in itself is brief and impersonal. Mailer's excellent story, 'The Time of Her Time', in *Advertisements for Myself*, gains its effect from the fact that the couple who make love in it dislike one another. Their coupling is mere combat.

Talent and prowess, the writer and what he writes, are apt to become fatally interwoven. The rewards are considerable. At the peak of his fame the successful novelist is rich, courted, photographed, interviewed. His celebrity is international; for as with other products of a consumer economy, his work leaps across national boundaries, swiftly translated. He helps to set styles in other countries. The shops in large airports may carry his latest book in two or three different languages. Paperback editions prolong its life and increase his income. But his worries are also considerable. Though he may become neurotic about competition, the competition is real enough. He may round on his critics, or accuse his publishers of spending too little on advertisements. He may – with an engaging candour, in the case of Mailer – do his own advertising. But he is growing older; and the young are the arbiters whom he must please. He tends to become obsessed by youthfulness. Unless he has kept his head, or has exceptional talent, he tends to drop away, outmoded along with his brand of fiction, discarded like the painters and the pop singers who have also lost favour.

It is a cruel process. The public is fickle, and treats yesterday's idols with malice and animus, waiting to hear that they have hit bottom, taken to drink, killed themselves. *Whatever became of ...?* – these dethronements are epitomized in the callous query, to which no answer is expected, of gossip columnists. It is doubly cruel in the case of a number of able American artists and writers. For the pop singers fall silent when no one wishes to employ them. The extinction of a painter or a novelist is often protracted. He continues to produce his work. It is still shown or published. But hardly anyone looks or listens. There are consolations of a sort. One is that he may be guaranteed a minor, permanent fame as a museum piece while he is yet alive and even quite young. The writer may be enshrined in anthologies. Diligent students may fasten on him as a subject for a dissertation. These gestures may soothe his *amour-propre*. They cannot disguise the truth that he belongs to yesterday: he and his writings are obsolete.

It is not all loss. Writing which is in vogue often has an electric immediacy. Young writers, surf-riders upon nowness, sometimes glitter with talent. If their fall is sometimes swift, so is their movement to maturity. They catch assurance from their contact with the public. They learn quickly from one another. American fiction is alive with the sense of the present moment. The general level has never been so high. The styles of the 1960s – pop art, black comedy, high camp, sexual phantasmagoria – are strikingly various and exuberant. Joseph Heller's *Catch-22*, until it falls away in the final chapters, is a brilliantly sustained satire on modern warfare. John Barth's *The Sot-Weed Factor* and William Pynchon's *V* are as plumply mock-erudite as Burt Blechman's *How Much?* is terse and pungent. Terry Southern's *Flash and Filigree* is surrealist and deadpan (several of these authors may have benefited from Nabokov and from the caustic little novels of Nathanael West, who died the sudden death of urban man in a California car crash in 1940). Kurt Vonnegut Jr is one of the few who have demonstrated the immense possibilities of science fiction by going beyond the conventions of the craft. His *Cat's Cradle* is dazzlingly imaginative, and contains more worthwhile ideas than half a dozen novels which try to be heavily portentous. Perhaps he and certain other present-day surf-riders have come to terms with the conditions of their art in the 1960s. Certainly there is no lack of quality. John Updike (*The Poorhouse Fair*, 1959; *Rabbit, Run*, 1960; *The Centaur*, 1963), a novelist with a poet's sensibility, writes as if from an inexhaustible intelligence.

These remarks barely apply to poetry of the 1960s. Being

less in the public domain, the poets may in the long run prove less subject to obsolescence. They are nearly all private people, who might justly complain that America disregards them. There is no dominant poetic style or movement, though there are coteries with their little magazines and their sharp assertions of dogma and heresy. A great deal of poetry is written and though much of it, as in all times and places, is rubbish, a surprising amount is of a very high order. The most promising figure of the immediate post-war years, Robert Lowell, has extended his reputation and is now considered to be America's best living poet. A member of a well-known Boston family, Lowell repudiated a large part of his heritage. He backed away from Harvard; he became a Catholic; he went to jail during the war as a pacifist. But the Puritan past, and the rather pathetic recent history of his family, absorbed him, and he wrote magnificent, apocalyptic poems about the stormbound New England coast and its seedy hinterland. More recently he seems to have left the Catholic Church and to have reached a tentative truce with his Boston environment. The fragment of prose autobiography and the poems gathered in *Life Studies* (1959) are deeply personal and yet detached and meditative. Here are Boston and its neighbourhood, sad, horrible, and touching; the poet's singular yet universal history, from nervous childhood to precarious maturity. Here are the deepest despairs of modern America, told with a gentle authority that is a world away from the loose attitudinizing of the more notorious examples of Beat versification. His verse translations of Racine and others are beautifully Lowellized. The poems in *For the Union Dead* (1964) sustain the perfect confessional note. They do not tell all: they tell just enough.

Several other American poets have a comparable mastery: the late Theodore Roethke, for instance, and Elizabeth Bishop and John Berryman, whose 77 *Dream Songs*, like his earlier *Homage to Mistress Bradstreet*, demand and repay the closest attention. A score of other poets have said memorable things: Richard Wilbur, John Frederick Nims, Maurice

English, W. D. Snodgrass, Howard Nemerov, Louis Simpson, William Stafford, Sylvia Plath, Anne Sexton, W. S. Merwin, Donald Hall, Howard Moss, Carolyn Kizer, George Starbuck, David Wagoner, Robert Creeley, Adrienne Rich, Robert Bly, Lawrence Ferlinghetti, Charles Olson. The list could be quarrelled with. It could also be doubled.

If America's good contemporary poets are self-possessed the same could be said in a somewhat different sense of certain superior works in current literary criticism. Consider for instance, the theme and manner of Charles S. Feidelson's *Symbolism and American Literature* (1953), R. W. B. Lewis's *The American Adam* (1955), Richard Chase's *The American Novel and its Tradition* (1957), Harry Levin's *The Power of Blackness* (1958), and Leslie A. Fiedler's *Love and Death in the American Novel* (1960). All make quite large claims for American literature, and are concerned with its uniqueness: with the features that set it apart from European literature. This, a perennial effort in the history of American literary criticism, forms indeed a part of the history of American nationalism. As they must in the very nature of the situation, the latest expounders of the problem maintain that there is more to American experience than outsiders have commonly realized. But they make the assertion with more sophistication than their predecessors. They do not necessarily say that American literature is magnificent: they are sure, however, that it is complex and even mysterious. For Charles Feidelson it is deeply symbolic. For Mr Lewis it involves a dialectical debate, high-minded if not always profound, between innocence and tragedy. Nor is this the whole story. Between the optimism of the belief that America is 'Adamic' and promises a new start for mankind, and the contrary pessimistic conviction that Adam fell as bitterly in America as elsewhere, and that there are no new starts in man's long ordeal, Mr Lewis discerns a third force. He calls it the party of 'irony', which refused to accept these rigid extremes and which wrote with altogether admirable maturity about the true condition of human (and American) existence.

For Harry Levin the special, subtle characteristic of American literature has been its dwelling upon darkness. He takes his title from a comment by Melville upon Hawthorne, and examines the work of Poe and others to sustain his argument. For Richard Chase, too, there is something special about the American novel. Its most interesting achievements, which he is careful not to overpraise, lie for him not in realism but in the idea of the novel as a 'romance'. He is not impressed by the imaginative level of the realistic novel as produced, say, by W. D. Howells or Theodore Dreiser or Sinclair Lewis. He is, rather, fascinated by the oddity, the symbolic nature, of the dominant tradition in American fiction – a tradition stretching from Charles Brockden Brown and James Fenimore Cooper down to Hemingway and Faulkner.

Finally, Leslie Fiedler also thinks that the American novel is a queer business. It has, he believes, borrowed and kept alive the hectic, morbid, grotesque (and, in Europe, short-lived) romanticism of the Gothic novel. It is obsessed by necrophilic fantasies. It is deeply though covertly homosexual: the famous friendships in American fiction – those of Deerslayer and Chingachgook in Cooper, Ishmael and Queequeg in Melville, Huck Finn and Nigger Jim in Mark Twain – are masculine (and, moreover, between men of different races). There are, he suggests, no adult man-woman relationships in American fiction, though there are feverish sagas of rape, incest, and miscegenation. The nearest equivalent to Flaubert's *Madame Bovary* is Sinclair Lewis's genteelly evasive *Main Street*. American fiction has its glories, according to Fiedler; but they are bizarre glories in a literature of duplicity, where nearly everything means more than it says.

Some objections can be raised. If myth and symbol and archetype are hunted with sufficient diligence they can always be found. Hidden meanings can be wrung out of the most recalcitrant material; one can 'prove' almost anything. In the process, the literary merit of the work, as it might be apparent to the general reader, is in danger of being dismissed as irrelevant, so that more is lost than is discovered. One notices already the tendency of critics like Fiedler not only to pass rather cavalierly over authors who do not conform to the desired formulae but also to concentrate upon the minor and flawed writings of those whom they do favour. There is, too, a risk of a sort of inverse chauvinism: that is, of claiming for the American flag horrors and deficiencies that are actually international. Thus, Protestant countries in Europe have not on the whole contributed a rich literature of heterosexual passion; and English literature in particular reveals certain of the aspects that Fiedler would cite as symptoms of the *American* psychic heritage.

Two counter-arguments may be offered, in conclusion. One is that, after all, American literature (especially fiction: American modern poetry is not so easily defined) does exhibit curious features. These features were first made explicit in D. H. Lawrence's *Studies in Classic American Literature* (1923), but they had been hinted at beforehand. They rest upon observable elements of actual American society as well as upon what might otherwise be questioned as modish theorizing. They continue to shape contemporary American literature, though it becomes increasingly hard to distinguish between unconscious influences and deliberate manufacture of suitable myths, in a situation in which every budding writer may have taken a college course that instructs him in such arcana. There *is*, though, truly more than meets the eye in American literature; and the European is wise to cultivate an excess of sympathy for these hidden intimations, rather than decide that American literature is a literature of mere surfaces. It is better to be 'taken in' than to be left out.

The second comment is that, whatever we may pretend, literature does not exist in some timeless absolute, as if it were the standard metre or the standard kilogramme reposing in a vault. The writings of the past serve the purposes of the present. In present-day America the literature of the American past is called upon to provide fundamental testimony as to the quality of American experience. The endeavour is risky; the results may at times seem too obviously distorted. Nevertheless, with a good deal of seriousness, ingenuity, and even profundity, contemporary America is demonstrating that it knows there are no straight answers or perfect solutions to human predicaments. America may still believe its own predicaments are *sui generis*; but there is no longer any pretence that it alone among nations is exempt from the common fate of humankind.

NOTES ON FURTHER READING

<hr/>

(*Abbreviations*: N.Y. is New York; U.P. is University Press; repr. is reprinted; ed. is edited or editor; *Cambridge* is Cambridge Massachusetts; *P* is a paperback edition.)

GENERAL WORKS

(a) *Reference*. Clarence Gohdes, *Bibliographical Guide to the Study of the Literature of the U.S.A.* (Durham, N.C., Duke U.P., 2nd edn., 1963) is admirably arranged. James D. Hart (ed.), *The Oxford Companion to American Literature* (N.Y., Oxford U.P., 4th edn, 1966) is accurate and sensible. The *Cambridge History of American Literature* (4 v., 1917–21) is still useful though much of it has been superseded by the *Literary History of the United States* (3 v., N.Y., Macmillan, 1948), ed. by Robert E. Spiller, Willard Thorp, and others. The third volume of this is a valuable bibliography. There is a new revised volume of bibliography ed. by Richard M. Ludwig (1959). Other bibliographical guides include Lewis Leary, *Articles on American Literature, 1900–1950* (Durham, Duke U.P., 1954); Otis W. Coan and Richard G. Lillard, *America in Fiction: An Annotated List of Novels that Interpret Aspects of Life in the United States* (Stanford, U.P., 1956); and *Eight Modern Authors: A Review of Research and Criticism* (N.Y., Modern Language Association, 1956), on Poe, Emerson, Hawthorne, Thoreau, Melville, Twain, and Henry James. A fourth volume of Frank L. Mott's monumental *History of American Magazines* (*Cambridge*, Harvard U.P.) appeared in 1957, covering the period 1885–1905, and the three previous volumes (*1741–1850*; *1850–1865*; *1865–1885*) have been repr.

(b) *Anthologies*. For poetry see F. O. Matthiessen (ed.), *The Oxford Book of American Verse* (N.Y., 1950) and Geoffrey Moore (ed.), *Modern American Verse* (Penguin, *P*, 1954). Edmund Wilson's excellent compilation, *The Shock of Recognition* (repr. N.Y., Farrar, Straus, 1955; London, W. H. Allen, 1956), contains several books in one, including D. H. Lawrence's brilliantly opinionated *Studies in Classic American Literature* (1924). Good anthologies of literary criticism are Philip Rahv (ed.), *Literature in America* (N.Y., Meridian, *P*, 1957); Charles Feidelson Jr and Paul Brodtkorb Jr (eds.), *Interpretations of American Literature* (N.Y., Oxford U.P., *P*, 1959); and Morton D. Zabel (ed.), *Literary Opinion in America* (2 v., N.Y., Harper, *P*, 3rd edn., 1962).

(c) *Paperback Literary Series.*

Several paperback ventures are devoted wholly or in part to American literature. The 'Writers and Critics' series (Edinburgh, Oliver & Boyd) includes, e.g., useful introductions to *William Faulkner*, by Michael Millgate; *Mark Twain*, by Douglas Grant; and *Arthur Miller*, by Dennis Welland. Similar in compass are the 'American Authors and Critics Series' (NY, Barnes & Noble), and 'Twayne's United States Authors Series' (NY, Twayne). Prentice-Hall (Spectrum Books, Englewood Cliffs, N.J.) publish a set of volumes of 'Twentieth Century Views' on particular authors. *Emerson: A Collection of Critical Essays*, ed. by Milton R. Konvitz & Stephen E. Whicher (1962), is a good representative example. Briefer guides are provided by the 'University of Minnesota Pamphlets on American Writers' (O.U.P.).

(d) *General Histories and Interpretations.* The following are only a sample of a mass of able work:

Bewley, Marius. *The Eccentric Design: Form in the Classic American Novel.* London (Chatto & Windus), 1959.

Brooks, Van Wyck. *Makers and Finders: A History of the Writer in America, 1800–1915.* London (Dent), 1945–52. Five volumes containing information not readily available elsewhere.

Chase, Richard. *The American Novel and Its Tradition.* N.Y. (Doubleday), *P*, 1957.

Donoghue, Denis. *Connoisseurs of Chaos: Ideas of Order in Modern American Poetry.* London (Faber), 1966.

Feidelson, Charles S., Jr. *Symbolism and American Literature.* Chicago (U.P.), 1953.

Fiedler, Leslie A. *Love and Death in the American Novel.* N.Y. (Criterion), 1960; London (Secker & Warburg), 1961.

Green, Martin. *Re-appraisals: Some Commonsense Readings in American Literature.* London (Hugh Evelyn), 1963. Vigorously idiosyncratic.

Hoffman, Daniel G. *Form and Fable in American Fiction.* N.Y. and London (O.U.P.), 1961.

Hubbell, Jay B. *The South in American Literature, 1607–1900.* Durham (Duke U.P.), 1954. Compendious.

Jones, Howard M. *The Theory of American Literature.* Ithaca (Cornell U.P.), 1948; reissued 1965. An account of literary histories.

Kazin, Alfred. *On Native Grounds.* N.Y. (Reynal & Hitchcock), 1942, also *P.* A brilliant discussion of twentieth-century American prose literature.

Levin, Harry. *The Power of Blackness: Hawthorne, Poe, Melville.* N.Y. (Knopf), 1958, also *P.*

Lewis, R. W. B. *The American Adam: Innocence, Tragedy, and Tradition in the Nineteenth Century.* Chicago (U.P.), 1955.

Marx, Leo. *The Machine in the Garden: Technology and the Pastoral Ideal in America.* N.Y. (O.U.P.), 1964.

Millgate, Michael. *American Social Fiction: James to Cozzens.* Edinburgh (Oliver & Boyd), 1964.

Parrington, Vernon L. *Main Currents in American Thought* (3 v.). N.Y. (Harcourt, Brace), 1927–30, also *P.*

Pearce, Roy H. *The Continuity of American Poetry.* Princeton (U.P.), 1961.

Smith, Henry N. *Virgin Land: The American West as Symbol and Myth.* Cambridge (Harvard U.P.), 1950, also *P.*

Tanner, Tony. *The Reign of Wonder: Naïvety and Reality in American Literature.* Cambridge (U.P.), 1965.

Taylor, William R. *Cavalier and Yankee: The Old South and American National Character.* N.Y. (Braziller), 1961, also *P.*

Wilson, Edmund. *Patriotic Gore: Studies in the Literature of the American Civil War.* N.Y. and London (O.U.P.), 1962.

Winters, Yvor. *In Defense of Reason.* Denver (U.P.), 1947. Essays repr. from *Primitivism and Decadence,* 1937; *Maule's Curse,* 1938; and *The Anatomy of Nonsense,* 1943.

(e) *Ties With Other Countries.*

Brooks, Van Wyck. *The Dream of Arcadia: American Writers and Artists in Italy, 1760–1915.* N.Y. (Dutton); London (Dent), 1958.

Brown, Deming. *Soviet Attitudes Towards American Writing.* Princeton (U.P.), 1962.

Denny, Margaret, and Gilman, William H. (eds.). *The American Writer and the European Tradition.* Minneapolis (U. of Minnesota P.), 1950.

Gohdes, Clarence. *American Literature in Nineteeth-Century England.* N.Y. (Columbia U.P.), 1944; repr. Carbondale (U. of S. Illinois P.), 1963.

Pochmann, Henry A. *German Culture in America: Philosophical and Literary Influences, 1600–1900.* Madison (U. of Wisconsin P.), 1956.

Williams, Stanley T. *The Spanish Background of American Literature* (2 v.). New Haven (Yale U.P.), 1955.

CHAPTER 1: COLONIAL AMERICA

Boorstin, Daniel J. *The Americans: The Colonial Experience*. N.Y. (Random House), 1958.

The Works of Anne Bradstreet in Prose and Verse. N.Y. (Peter Smith), repr. 1932.

Franklin, Benjamin. *Papers*, a new multi-volume edn, ed. by Leonard W. Labaree and Whitfield J. Bell, Jr. New Haven (Yale U.P.), 1959–.

Jefferson, Thomas. *Notes on the State of Virginia*, ed. by William Peden. Chapel Hill (U. of N. Carolina P.), 1955.

Miller, Perry. *The New England Mind: The Seventeenth Century*. Cambridge (Harvard U.P.), 1939, repr. 1954.

Miller, Perry. *The New England Mind: From Colony to Province*. Harvard, 1953.

Miller, Perry (ed.). *The American Puritans: Their Prose and Poetry*. N.Y. (Doubleday), P, 1956.

Murdock, Kenneth B. *Literature and Theology in Colonial New England*. Cambridge (Harvard U.P.), 1949.

The Poems of Edward Taylor, ed. D. E. Stanford. New Haven (Yale U.P.), 1960.

Tyler, Moses C. *A History of American Literature, 1607–1765* (2 v. in 1). Ithaca (Cornell U.P.), 1949.

Wright, Louis B. *Cultural Life of the American Colonies, 1607–1763*. N.Y. (Harper); London (H. Hamilton), 1957.

CHAPTER 2: AMERICA AND EUROPE – THE PROBLEMS OF INDEPENDENCE

Beloff, Max (ed.). *The Debate on the American Revolution, 1761–1783*. London (Kaye), 1949; and (ed.) *The Federalist*, Oxford (Blackwell), 1948.

Cady, E. H. (ed.). *Literature of the Early Republic*. N.Y. (Rinehart), P, 1950.

Howard, Leon. *The Connecticut Wits*. Chicago (U.P.), 1943.

Spencer, Benjamin T. *The Quest for Nationality: An American Literary Campaign*. Syracuse (U.P.), 1957.

Tyler, Moses C. *The Literary History of the American Revolution, 1763–1783* (2 v.). N.Y. (Putnam), 1897.

Doren, Carl Van. *Benjamin Franklin*. N.Y. (Viking), 1938.

CHAPTER 3: INDEPENDENCE – THE FIRST FRUITS (IRVING, COOPER, POE)

Beard, James F. (ed.). *Letters and Journals of James Fenimore Cooper* (4 v.). Cambridge (Harvard U.P.), 1960–5.

Brooks, Van Wyck. *The World of Washington Irving.* London (Dent), 1945.

Davidson, Edward H. *Poe: A Critical Study.* Cambridge (Harvard U.P.), 1957.

Grossman, James. *James Fenimore Cooper.* London (Methuen), 1950.

Miller, Perry. *The Raven and the Whale: The War of Words and Wits in the Era of Poe and Melville.* N.Y. (Harcourt Brace), 1956.

Ostrom, John W. (ed.). *The Letters of Edgar Allan Poe* (2 v.). Cambridge (Harvard U.P.), 1948.

Quinn, Patrick F. *The French Face of Edgar Poe.* Carbondale (S. Illinois U.P.), 1957.

Reichart, Walter A. *Washington Irving and Germany.* Ann Arbor (U. of Michigan P.), 1957.

Williams, Stanley T. *The Life of Washington Irving* (2 v.). N.Y. (Oxford U.P.), 1935.

CHAPTER 4: NEW ENGLAND'S DAY (EMERSON, THOREAU, HAWTHORNE)

Brooks, Van Wyck. *The Flowering of New England, 1815–1865.* London (Dent), revised edn 1946.

Gilman, William H., and others (eds.). *The Journals and Miscellaneous Notebooks of Ralph Waldo Emerson.* Cambridge (Harvard U.P.), 1960, a new multi-volume edn.

Harding, Walter (ed.). *Thoreau: A Century of Criticism.* Dallas (S. Methodist U.P.), 1954.

Krutch, Joseph W. *Henry David Thoreau.* London (Methuen), 1949.

Matthiessen, F. O. *American Renaissance.* N.Y. (Oxford U.P.), 1941.

Miller, Perry. *Consciousness in Concord.* Boston (Houghton Mifflin), 1958.

Miller, Perry (ed.). *The Transcendentalists: Their Prose and Poetry.* N.Y. (Doubleday), *P*, 1957.

Pearce, Roy H. (ed.). *Hawthorne Centenary Essays,* Columbus (Ohio State U.P.), 1964.

Van Doren, Mark. *Nathaniel Hawthorne.* London (Methuen), 1949.

Waggoner, Hyatt H. *Hawthorne: A Critical Study.* Cambridge (Harvard U.P.), 1955.

Whicher, Stephen F. *Freedom and Fate: An Inner Life of Ralph Waldo Emerson.* Philadelphia (U. of Pennsylvania P.), 1953; *P* (Perpetua), 1961.

CHAPTER 5: MELVILLE AND WHITMAN

Allen, Gay W. *The Solitary Singer: A Critical Biography of Walt Whitman.* N.Y. (Macmillan), 1955.

Arvin, Newton. *Herman Melville.* N.Y. (Sloane); London (Methuen), 1950.

Arvin, Newton. *Longfellow: His Life and Work.* Boston (Little Brown), 1963.

Asselineau, Roger. *L'Évolution de Whitman.* Paris (Didier), 1954.

Brooks, Van Wyck. *The Times of Melville and Whitman.* London (Dent), 1948.

Chase, Richard. *Walt Whitman Reconsidered.* N.Y. (Sloane); London (Gollancz), 1955.

Davis, Merrell R., and Gilman, William H. (eds.). *The Letters of Herman Melville.* New Haven (Yale U.P.), 1960.

Doughty, Howard N. *Francis Parkman.* N.Y. (Macmillan), 1962.

Leyda, Jay. *The Melville Log, A Documentary Life of Herman Melville* (2 v.). N.Y. (Harcourt Brace), 1951.

Miller, James E., Jr. *A Critical Guide to 'Leaves of Grass'.* Chicago (U.P.), 1957.

Schyberg, Frederick. *Walt Whitman* (translated from the Danish by E. A. Allen). N.Y. (Columbia U.P.), 1951.

CHAPTER 6: MORE NEW ENGLANDERS (THE BRAHMIN POETS AND HISTORIANS)

Arms, George. *The Fields Were Green.* Stanford (U.P.), 1953.

Brooks, Van Wyck. *The Flowering of New England.* 1946.

Howard, Leon. *Victorian Knight-Errant: The Early Literary Career of James Russell Lowell.* Berkeley and Los Angeles (U. of California P.), 1952.

Levin, David. *History as Romantic Art: Bancroft, Prescott, Motley, Parkman.* Stanford (U.P.), 1959.

Tilton, Eleanor M. *Amiable Autocrat: A Biography of Doctor Oliver Wendell Holmes.* N.Y. (Schuman), 1947.

CHAPTER 7: AMERICAN HUMOUR AND THE RISE OF THE WEST

Bellamy, Gladys C. *Mark Twain as a Literary Artist.* Norman (U. of Oklahoma P.), 1950.

Blair, Walter. *Mark Twain and Huck Finn.* Berkeley (U. of California P.), 1960.

Bridgman, Richard. *The Colloquial Style in America.* N.Y. (O.U.P.), 1966.

DeVoto, Bernard. *Mark Twain's America*. Boston (Houghton Mifflin), repr. 1951.

DeVoto, Bernard. *Mark Twain at Work*. Cambridge (Harvard U.P.), 1942.

Lynn, Kenneth S. *Mark Twain and Southwestern Humor*. Boston (Little Brown), 1959.

Lynn, Kenneth S. (ed.). *The Comic Tradition in America*. London (Gollancz), 1958; also *P*.

Rourke, Constance. *American Humor: A Study of the National Character*. N.Y. (Harcourt Brace), repr. 1947 (also Doubleday, *P*, 1953).

Scott, Arthur L. (ed.). *Mark Twain: Selected Criticism*. Dallas (S. Methodist U.P.), 1955.

Smith, Henry N. *Mark Twain: The Development of a Writer*. Cambridge (Harvard U.P.), 1962.

Wecter, Dixon. *Sam Clemens of Hannibal*. Boston (Houghton Mifflin), 1952.

CHAPTER 8: MINOR KEY (EMILY DICKINSON AND OTHERS

Foster, Charles H. *The Rungless Ladder*. Durham (Duke U.P.), 1954. On Harriet Beecher Stowe and New England Puritanism.

Johnson, Thomas H. *Emily Dickinson: An Interpretive Biography*. Cambridge (Harvard U.P.), 1955.

Johnson, Thomas H. (ed.). *Complete Poems of Emily Dickinson*. Boston (Little Brown), 1960.

Leyda, Jay. *The Years and Hours of Emily Dickinson* (2 v.). New Haven (Yale U.P.), 1960.

Linscott, Robert N. (ed.). *Selected Poems and Letters of Emily Dickinson*. N.Y. (Doubleday), *P*, 1959.

Turner, Arlin. *George W. Cable: A Biography*. Durham (Duke U.P.), 1956.

CHAPTER 9: REALISM IN AMERICAN PROSE (FROM HOWELLS TO DREISER)

Berryman, John. *Stephen Crane*. London (Methuen), 1950.

Berthoff, Warner. *The Ferment of Realism: American Literature, 1884–1919*. N.Y. (Free Press), 1965.

Brooks, Van Wyck. *New England: Indian Summer, 1865–1915*. 1941.

Brooks, Van Wyck. *The Confident Years, 1885–1915*. 1952.

Cady, Edwin H. *The Road to Realism* and *The Realist at War* (2 v.). Syracuse (U.P.), 1956 and 1958. A biography of William Dean Howells.

Duffey, Bernard. *The Chicago Renaissance in American Letters*. E. Lansing (Michigan State U.P.), 1954.

Geismar, Maxwell. *Rebels and Ancestors, 1890–1915*. Boston (Houghton Mifflin), 1953.

Gelfant, Blanche H. *The American City Novel*. Norman (U. of Oklahoma P.), 1954.

Hoffman, Daniel G. *The Poetry of Stephen Crane*. N.Y. (Columbia U.P.), 1957.

Holloway, Jean. *Hamlin Garland: A Biography*. Austin (U. of Texas P.), 1960.

Kazin, Alfred, and Shapiro, Charles (eds.). *The Stature of Theodore Dreiser*. Bloomington (Indiana U.P.), 1955.

Langford, Gerald. *Alias O. Henry: A Biography of William Sidney Porter*. N.Y. (Macmillan), 1957.

Matthiessen, F. O. *Theodore Dreiser*. London (Methuen), 1951.

Rouse, Blair (ed.). *The Letters of Ellen Glasgow*. N.Y. (Harcourt Brace), 1958.

Schneider, Robert W. *Five Novelists of the Progressive Era*. N.Y. (Columbia U.P.), 1965.

Stallman, R. W., and Gilkes, Lillian (eds.). *The Letters of Stephen Crane*. London (Peter Owen), 1960.

Walcutt, Charles C. *American Literary Naturalism*. Minneapolis (U. of Minnesota P.), 1956.

CHAPTER 10: THE EXPATRIATES (HENRY JAMES, EDITH WHARTON, HENRY ADAMS, GERTRUDE STEIN)

Bewley, Marius. *The Complex Fate*. London (Chatto & Windus), 1952.

Brinnin, John M. *The Third Rose: Gertrude Stein and Her World*. Boston (Atlantic–Little Brown), 1959.

Edel, Leon. *Henry James, 1843–1894* (3 v.). London (Hart-Davis), 1954. In continuation.

Jefferson, D. W. *Henry James and the Modern Reader*. Edinburgh (Oliver & Boyd), 1964.

Jordy, William H. *Henry Adams, Scientific Historian*. New Haven (Yale U.P.), 1952.

Levenson, J. C. *The Mind and Art of Henry Adams*. Boston (Houghton Mifflin), 1957.

Matthiessen, F. O. (ed.). *The James Family*. N.Y. (Knopf), 1947.

Matthiessen, F. O., and Murdock, Kenneth B. (eds.). *The Note-books of Henry James.* N.Y. (Oxford U.P.), 1947.

Nevius, Blake. *Edith Wharton: A Study of Her Fiction.* Berkeley (U. of California P.), 1953.

Rahv, Philip (ed.). *The Discovery of Europe: The Story of American Experience in the Old World.* Boston (Houghton Mifflin), 1947, also P.

Samuels, Ernest. *The Young Henry Adams; Henry Adams: The Middle Years; The Major Phase.* Cambridge (Harvard U.P.), 1948, 1958, 1964.

CHAPTER 11: THE NEW POETRY (some of these titles are also of value for Chapter 14)

Brower, Reuben A. *The Poetry of Robert Frost.* N.Y. (Oxford U.P.), 1963.

Fussell, Edwin S. *Edwin Arlington Robinson: The Literary Back-ground of a Traditional Poet.* Berkeley (U. of California P.), 1954.

Hoffman, Frederick J., and others. *The Little Magazine: A History and Bibliography.* Princeton (U.P.), 1947.

Kermode, Frank. *Wallace Stevens,* Edinburgh (Oliver & Boyd), 1960.

Norman, Charles. *Ezra Pound.* N.Y. (Macmillan), 1960.

Ruggles, Eleanor. *The West-Going Heart: A Life of Vachel Lindsay.* N.Y. (Norton), 1959.

Sandburg, Carl. *Always the Young Strangers.* London (Cape), 1953. Autobiography.

Stevens, Wallace. *Collected Poems.* London (Faber), 1955.

Williams, William Carlos. *Autobiography.* N.Y. (Random House), 1951.

Williams, William Carlos. *Collected Poems* (2 v.). Norfolk, Conn. (New Directions), 1950–1.

CHAPTER 12: FICTION SINCE WORLD WAR I

Baker, Carlos, ed. *Hemingway and His Critics.* N.Y. (Hill & Wang, P), 1961.

Brooks, Cleanth. *William Faulkner: The Yoknapatawpha Country.* New Haven (Yale U.P.), 1964.

Casper, Leonard. *Robert Penn Warren.* Seattle (U. of Washington P.), 1960.

Frohock, Wilbur M. *The Novel of Violence in America.* Dallas (S. Methodist U.P.), revised edn 1957.

Geismar, Maxwell. *The Last of the Provincials ... 1915–1925.* London (Secker & Warburg), 1947.

Geismar, Maxwell. *Writers in Crisis ... 1925–1940.* 1947.

Hoffman, Frederick J. *The Twenties: American Writing in the Post war Decade.* N.Y. (Free Press), rev. edn. 1962. Also *P.*

Hoffman, Frederick J., and Vickery, O. W. (eds.). *William Faulkner: Three Decades of Criticism.* E. Lansing (Michigan State U.P.), 1961.

Howe, Irving. *Sherwood Anderson.* London (Methuen), 1951.

Magny, Claude-Edmonde. *L'Âge du roman américain.* Paris (Editions du Seuil), 1948.

Nowell, Elizabeth. *Thomas Wolfe.* N.Y. (Doubleday), 1960.

Schorer, Mark. *Sinclair Lewis: An American Life.* N.Y. (McGraw-Hill), 1961. London (Heinemann), 1963.

Tedlock, E. W., and Wicker, C. V. (eds.). *Steinbeck and His Critics.* Albuquerque (U. of N. Mexico P.), 1960.

Turnbull, Andrew W. *Scott Fitzgerald.* N.Y. (Scribner), 1962.

West, Ray B. *The Rise of Short Fiction in America, 1900–1950.* Chicago (Regnery), 1952.

CHAPTER 13: THE AMERICAN THEATRE

Downer, Alan S., ed. *American Drama and its Critics.* Chicago (U.P.), 1965. *P.*

Downer, Alan S. *Fifty Years of American Drama, 1900–1950.* Chicago (Regnery), 1951.

Engel, Edwin A. *The Haunted Heroes of Eugene O'Neill.* Stanford (U.P.), 1953.

Gelb, Arthur and Barbara. *O'Neill.* N.Y. (Harper), 1962.

Krutch, Joseph W. *The American Drama Since 1918.* N.Y. (Braziller), 1957.

Moody, Richard. *America Takes the Stage ... 1750–1900.* Bloomington (Indiana U.P.), 1955.

CHAPTER 14: POETRY AND CRITICISM SINCE WORLD WAR I (see also titles under Chapter 11)

Alvarez, A. *The Shaping Spirit.* London (Chatto & Windus), 1958.

Beaver, Harold (ed.). *American Critical Essays: Twentieth Century.* London (Oxford U.P.), 1959.

Bogan, Louise. *Achievement in American Poetry, 1900–1950.* Chicago (Regnery), 1951.

Eberhart, Richard. *Collected Poems, 1930–1960.* London (Chatto & Windus), 1960.

Elliott, George P. (ed.). *Fifteen Modern American Poets*. N.Y. (Rinehart), *P*, 1956.

Fenton, Charles A. *Stephen Vincent Benét*. New Haven (Yale U.P.), 1958.

Fiedler, Leslie A. *An End to Innocence*. Boston (Beacon), *P*, 1955.

Jarrell, Randall. *Poetry and the Age*. N.Y. (Knopf), *P*, 1955.

Kazin, Alfred. *The Inmost Leaf: A Selection of Essays*. N.Y. (Harcourt Brace), *P*, 1955.

Norman, Charles. *The Magic-Maker: E. E. Cummings*. N.Y. (Macmillan), 1958.

Ransom, John C. *Poems and Essays*. N.Y. (Knopf), *P*, 1955.

Rubin, Louis D., and Jacobs, Robert D. (eds.). *Southern Renascence: The Literature of the Modern South*. Baltimore (Johns Hopkins U.P.), 1953.

Squires, Radcliffe. *The Loyalties of Robinson Jeffers*. Ann Arbor (U. of Michigan P.), 1956.

Stewart, John L. *The Burden of Time: The Fugitives and Agrarians*. Princeton (U.P.), 1965.

Tate, Allen. *The Man of Letters in the Modern World: Selected Essays, 1928–1955*. N.Y. (Meridian), *P*, 1955.

Trilling, Lionel. *The Liberal Imagination*. London (Secker & Warburg), 1951. *Beyond Culture: Essays on Life and Literature*. London (Secker), 1966.

Warren, Robert Penn. *Selected Essays*. London (Eyre & Spottiswoode), 1964. *Selected Poems, 1923–1966*. N.Y. (Random House), 1966.

Wilson, Edmund. *The Shores of Light* and *Classics and Commercial*. London (W. H. Allen), 1952 and 1951. *The Bit Between My Teeth* (Allen), 1966.

CHAPTER 15: AMERICA AND THE WRITER SINCE 1945

Allen, Donald M. (ed.). *The American Poetry: 1945–1960*. N.Y. (Grove); London (Evergreen), *P*, 1960.

Baumbach, Jonathan. *The Landscape of Nightmare: Studies in the Contemporary American Novel*. N.Y. (N.Y.U.P.), 1965, *P*.

Baldwin, James. *The Fire Next Time*. London (Michael Joseph), 1963.

Bell, Daniel. *The End of Ideology: On the Exhaustion of Political Ideas in the Fifties*. Glencoe, Ill. (Free Press), *P*. 1960.

Bone, Robert A. *The Negro Novel in America*. New Haven (Yale U.P.), rev. edn, 1965. *P*.

Boorstin, Daniel J. *The Image: What Happened to the American Dream?* N.Y. (Atheneum), 1961; London (Weidenfeld & Nicolson), 1962; *P* (Penguin), 1962.

Eisinger, Chester E. *Fiction of the Forties.* Chicago (U.P.), 1963. *P.*

Fiedler, Leslie. *No! In Thunder: Essays on Myth and Literature.* London (Eyre & Spottiswoode), 1963.

Frohock, Wilbur M. *Strangers to this Ground: Cultural Diversity in Contemporary American Writing.* Dallas (S. Methodist U.P.), 1961.

Goodman, Paul. *Growing Up Absurd.* N.Y. (Random House), 1960; London (Gollancz), 1961.

Harrington, Michael. *The Other America: Poverty in the United States.* Harmondsworth (Penguin), *P*, 1963.

Hassan, Ihab H. *Radical Innocence: Studies in the Contemporary American Novel.* Princeton (U.P.), 1961.

Jarrell, Randall. *A Sad Heart at the Supermarket: Essays and Fables.* London (Eyre & Spottiswoode), 1965.

Lerner, Max. *America as a Civilization.* N.Y. (Simon & Schuster), 1957; London (Cape), 1958.

Macdonald, Dwight. *Against the American Grain: Essays on the Effects of Mass Culture.* London (Gollancz), 1963.

Malin, Irving. *New American Gothic.* Carbondale (S. Illinois U.P.), 1962. The fiction of Truman Capote, Carson McCullers, J. D. Salinger, Flannery O'Connor, John Hawkes and James Purdy.

Malin, Irving. *Jews and Americans.* Carbondale (S. Illinois U.P.), 1965. *P.*

Mills, C. Wright. *The Power Elite.* N.Y. (Oxford U.P.), 1956.

Podhoretz, Norman. *Doings and Undoings.* London (Hart-Davis), 1965.

Riesman, David, and others. *The Lonely Crowd: A Study of the Changing American Character.* N.Y. (Doubleday), *P*, 1953. *Abundance for What? And Other Essays.* N.Y. (Doubleday), 1964.

Rosenberg, Bernard, and White, D. M. (eds.). *Mass Culture: The Popular Arts in America.* Glencoe, Ill. (Free Press), 1957.

Sontag, Susan. *Against Interpretation.* N.Y. (Farrar, Straus & Giroux), 1966.

Trilling, Diana. *Claremont Essays.* London (Secker & Warburg), 1965.

Trilling, Lionel. *Beyond Culture: Essays on Life and Literature.* London (Secker & Warburg), 1966.

Whyte, William H., Jr. *The Organization Man.* N.Y. (Doubleday), *P*, 1957; Harmondsworth (Penguin), *P*, 1960.

SOME DATES IN AMERICAN HISTORY

1584	Founding of the unsuccessful colony of Roanoke [North Carolina].
1607	Founding of Jamestown, by the Virginia Company of London.
1619	Appearance of the first Negro slaves in North America (at Jamestown, brought by a Dutch ship).
1620	Founding of Plymouth Colony [Massachusetts] by the Pilgrims of the *Mayflower*.
1630	Founding of the Massachusetts Bay Colony.
1664	Capture of New Amsterdam (New York) from the Dutch.
1681	Grant of Pennsylvania to William Penn.
1732	Grant of charter for the colony of Georgia to General James Oglethorpe.
1754–60	French and Indian War, culminating in the defeat of the French in North America and cession of French territories (by the Treaty of Paris, 1763).
1775–83	American Revolutionary War; independence of the colonies formally recognized by the Treaty of Paris, 1783.
1787	Constitutional Convention held at Philadelphia.
1789–97	Presidency of George Washington.
1801–9	Presidency of Thomas Jefferson.
1803	Purchase from France of the Louisiana Territory (between the Mississippi and the Rocky Mountains), from which thirteen new states were eventually formed.
1808	Further importation of slaves into the United States prohibited.
1812–14	War of 1812 against Britain.
1818	Northern boundary (from the Great Lakes to the Rocky Mountains) fixed at the 49th parallel of latitude.
1819	Purchase of Florida from Spain.
1820–21	Missouri Compromises over slavery (involving the admission to the Union of Missouri as a slave state, simultaneously with that of Maine as a free state).

1823	Announcement of the Monroe Doctrine (no further European colonization accepted on the American continent).
1829–37	Presidency of Andrew Jackson.
1836	Declaration by Texas of independence from Mexico, and establishment of the 'Lone Star Republic'.
1845	Annexation of Texas to the United States.
1846	Acquisition of the Oregon Territory.
1846–8	Mexican War (acquisition from Mexico of territory between the Rocky Mountains and the Pacific, including the present states of California, Arizona, New Mexico, etc.).
1850	Further compromise over slavery, after prolonged and heated debates between north and south.
1856	Republican Party nationally organized (though a northern body, replacing the old Whig party in that section).
1859	John Brown's raid on Harper's Ferry, Virginia.
1861–5	Presidency of Abraham Lincoln (Republican; assassinated 1865); Civil War, ending in Southern defeat.
1867	Purchase of Alaska from Russia.
1869–77	Presidency of General Ulysses S. Grant (Republican).
1869	Completion of the first trans-continental railroad.
1890	Sherman Anti-Trust Act, designed to combat monopolistic practices in business.
1891	Formation of the Populist Party.
1896	Klondike gold-rush.
1898	Spanish–American War (invasion of Cuba; occupation of the Philippines; annexation of Hawaii).
1901–9	Presidency of Theodore Roosevelt (Republican).
1904	Panama Canal begun (opened 1914).
1909	Henry Ford's Model T first produced.
1912	Admission to statehood of New Mexico and Arizona, the 47th and 48th states of the Union.
1913–21	Presidency of Woodrow Wilson (Democrat).
1919	18th Amendment to the Constitution (prohibition; repealed by the 21st Amendment, 1933).
1920	19th Amendment (female suffrage).
1921–3	Presidency of Warren G. Harding (Republican).

1923–9	Presidency of Calvin Coolidge (Republican).
1927	Execution of Sacco and Vanzetti.
1929–33	Presidency of Herbert Hoover (Republican).
1929	Collapse of New York stock-market.
1933	Inauguration as president of Franklin D. Roosevelt (Democrat); beginning of New Deal legislation.
1940	U.S. population 132 million (*c.* 17 million in 1840).
1953	Inauguration as president of Dwight D. Eisenhower (Republican).
1953–5	Rise and fall of Senator Joseph McCarthy.
1954	Supreme Court directs end of racial segregation in public schools. Rapid spread in next decade of Negro protests – ranging from non-violent demonstrations to extremist Black Muslim movement – against continued racial discrimination.
1957	Inauguration for second and last term as president of Dwight D. Eisenhower (Republican).
1959	Admission to statehood of Alaska and Hawaii, the 49th and 50th states of the Union.
1960	U.S. population 180 million.
1961–3	Presidency of John F. Kennedy (Democrat; assassinated November 1963; succeeded by his Vice-President, Lyndon B. Johnson).

INDEX

INDEX

(*Note*: *biog.* indicates a biographical reference, *bibl.* a bibliographical one. Principal references are shown in italics)

MORE ABOUT PENGUINS
AND PELICANS

If you have enjoyed reading this book you may wish to know that *Penguin Book News* appears every month. It is an attractively illustrated magazine containing a complete list of books published by Penguins and still in print, together with details of the month's new books. A specimen copy will be sent free on request.

Penguin Book News is obtainable from most book-shops; but you may prefer to become a regular sub-scriber at 3s. for twelve issues. Just write to Dept EP, Penguin Books Ltd, Harmondsworth, Middle-sex, enclosing a cheque or postal order, and you will be put on the mailing list.

Some other books published by Penguins are described on the following pages.

Note: *Penguin Book News* is not available in the U.S.A., Canada or Australia

THE MODERN WRITER AND HIS WORLD

G. S. Fraser

Yeats, Eliot, Auden, Larkin; Wells, Lawrence, Greene, Murdoch; Shaw, Priestley, Osborne, Wesker; Grierson, Richards, Leavis – many people have read widely among the leading poets, novelists, dramatists and critics of the twentieth century, yet for the general reader very few books have tried to relate all the main movements and innovators since the 1880s to the changing English scene.

This edition of *The Modern Writer and His World* has largely been re-written and contains fresh chapters on developments in the 1950s – the new wave of novelists, 'anger' in the theatre, the Movement and the Group in poetry. It is, in effect, a new book and still the only one to offer the intelligent non-specialist reader both an analysis of the major writers (and most of the minor ones) and also an overall awareness of the total literary and social scene as something from which the great, apparently isolated, figures cannot be divorced.

After an introductory survey, 'The Background of Ideas', the author deals in turn with poetry, the novel, drama and criticism. Here, from the opening pages on the meaning of 'modernism' to the closing appreciation of Auden's 'The Dyer's Hand', is the world of the modern writer.

LITERATURE AND CRITICISM

H. Coombes

Literature and Criticism is concerned above all with the bricks and mortar of writing – words. There are chapters on Rhythm, Rhyme, Imagery, Poetic Thought, Feeling and Diction. Both poetry and prose are discussed, and there is an appendix of passages as exercises.

The bare contents, however, give little idea of the excellence of this introduction to literary appreciation. For here is a sound and unpretentious teacher who knows how little most of us know and who can help us, without scorn or pedantry, to tell sense from nonsense, sincerity from affectation, and beauty from dead decoration.

'Excellent chapters on Rhythm, Rhyme, and Imagery and a really splendid one on Feeling' – *Time and Tide*

'A very useful book for sixth forms, first-year undergraduates, and adult education classes. . . . A sensible and sensitive book' – *The Times Literary Supplement*

A SHORT HISTORY OF ENGLISH LITERATURE

Sir Ifor Evans

The first edition of Sir Ifor Evans's *Short History of English Literature* was acclaimed by Ivor Brown in the *Observer* as follows:

'Professor Evans writes to the classical model, as brief, as lucid. He relates the arts to society instead of penning them in the study. As a judge he is tolerant and undogmatic, but never slack in his standards. He is fair to all and gushes over none. . . . This justice of approach is coupled with a mastery of phrase which makes the writing lively without being exhaustingly exhibitionist in judgement or epigrammatic in style.'

Since its first appearance it has served countless readers as an invaluable map to the broad field of English literature. Now, revised throughout, and extended to include the major poets, dramatists, and novelists of the post-war period, it is with us again, as reliable and readable a guide as ever, but with wider range and a more recent perspective.

A HISTORY OF THE UNITED STATES: I
THE BIRTH OF THE U.S.A.

R. B. Nye and J. E. Morpurgo

This volume is the first of a two-volume *History of the U.S.A.* now revised and brought completely up to date, which represents a collaborative effort by an Englishman and an American to study American history from its beginnings to the present day. With each supplying to the other an understanding of naturally different points of view, the result is an interpretation of men, trends and events that often differs from that usually found in briefer histories of the United States.

The authors are convinced that the history of the United States cannot be divorced from that of the rest of the world and have paid especial attention to the place of the United States in the pattern of world events. But because they are equally certain that America is American and must be understood on its own terms they have given most attention to the development of its own distinctive way of life.

Aimed at providing readers on both sides of the Atlantic – and all over the world – with a fresh understanding of the American past, this history places more than usual emphasis on the growth of American ideas, in politics, the arts, religion and society.

Here, in relatively small compass, is a survey of the American spirit and mind as it has matured over three centuries of swift and complex development.

Also available:

A HISTORY OF THE UNITED STATES: 2
THE GROWTH OF THE U.S.A.